# SAINSBURY'S

## *Pocket*
# FOOD & WINE
## *Guide*

### BY KATHRYN McWHIRTER
### AND CHARLES METCALFE

Published in the UK exclusively for
J Sainsbury plc, Stamford House, Stamford Street,
London SE1 9LL
by Websters International Publishers Limited,
Axe and Bottle Court, 70 Newcomen Street,
London SE1 1YT

IBSN: 1 870604 17 2

Printed by Graphicom, Vicenza, Italy

Conceived, edited and designed by
Websters International Publishers

# CONTENTS

# HOW TO USE THIS BOOK

Over 28,000 mouthfuls with different combinations of food and wine have gone into the making of this book. We tasted everything. We hope you enjoy the results!

To use the book at its simplest and easiest, all you need to do is turn to the directory on page 261, look up your chosen dish, and read off the perfect wine partner. If you want a greater choice of wine, the main section (from page 6) details other excellent, good or fair matches, and points out any real clashes that are best avoided. Where one wine stands out as a brilliant match, it has been highlighted as a 'perfect partner' (look for the ★★ sign). Wines given one ★ are the closest we managed to find to a perfect match.

This comprehensive reference section is divided into 12 categories by food type: fish, meat, vegetables, herbs and so on. Within each section, listed alphabetically, you will find ingredients, such as aubergine, thyme and guinea fowl, as well as specific dishes such as chicken casserole, chocolate mousse and spinach soup.

Most classic and well-known dishes are here. But if your dish is out of the ordinary – say, smoked salmon with prawn mousse and asparagus – you may need to look up several food entries and reach a compromise to suit all the ingredients. Where a dish comes from a particular region and there is a local wine that traditionally partners it, this is also highlighted. Often, however, a wine from some far-away place goes better than the traditional local wine.

And that's it, if you are happy to trust our taste buds. But if you want to understand why certain combinations taste better than others, the later sections prepare you to do it yourself. They show you how to analyse the taste of a wine and work out which foods it might go well with, and how to choose from the shelves a wine with the right sort of taste for your menu.

Obviously it's not possible in a pocket-size book to list every appropriate wine. In listing the wines that match a particular dish, we often refer to wine styles and grape varieties; for example, if you need red Loire Cabernets, you could choose a Chinon, St-Nicolas-de-Bourgueil, Bourgueil, and so on. If you are unsure about which wine to buy, *Matching Food to Wine Styles* and *Grape Varieties* (from page 204) will give further guidance; otherwise you can always ask at your wine shop.

# MATCHING FOOD TO WINE

Try an experiment: take a good red wine, and taste a mouthful with each of the following – grilled steak, grilled steak with Dijon mustard, Cheddar cheese, Stilton and Brie. It will taste quite different each time – sometimes better, sometimes much worse, depending on which wine you choose. The food will taste different, too, alongside the wine. And if you serve a sauce with your grilled steak, it will taste different again.

Even after a year of marathon tasting sessions for this book, drawing on 250 opened wines at a session, we are still often surprised by the best matches. You can make educated guesses at what might taste best (see *Matching Food to Wine Styles* on page 204 to learn more about the basic principles of wine and food pairing) but the only sure way is to try it out.

Really awful wine and food pairings are mercifully fairly rare. But you need to choose carefully to find tastes that are really complementary. Disgusting clashes apart, it's perfectly enjoyable, of course, to drink a good wine that has nothing particular in common with the food you are eating. After all, we drink orange or apple juice, beer, milk, tea or even Coca Cola with our food without sparing a second's thought for how the flavours blend together.

But it does add a bonus of pleasure to a meal if the wine chimes in perfectly with the food, just as it does if a sauce really suits and enhances the flavour of a piece of meat or fish. For most dishes there are numerous wines that will go reasonably well. We have tried to sniff out the best.

## SYMBOLS AND TERMS

❢ *red wines* ❢ *rosé wines* ♀ *white wines*
★★ *the perfect wine partner for this food*
★ *a very good, but not quite perfect match*

**VdP**: *Vins de Pays*. 'French country wines' from a specified region.
**QbA**: *Qualitätswein bestimmter Anbaugebiete*. A simple, inexpensive German quality wine.

**The 10 Beaujolais Crus from the lightest to the fullest:**
Chiroubles, Regnié, Brouilly, Côte de Brouilly, Fleurie, St-Amour, Chénas, Juliénas, Morgon, Moulin-à-Vent.

# SOUPS

You may not want to drink wine with soups. If you do, you will probably need a fairly delicately flavoured wine, as the ingredients in the soup are often diluted by the liquid. If your particular choice of soup does not appear below, look up the individual flavours, and choose something on the lighter side. Be careful when serving red wines with very creamy soups, as the tannin in the wine will clash with the fat.

## ARTICHOKE (JERUSALEM) SOUP
♀ *unoaked, medium-acid, medium-dry whites*

The flavour of Chenin Blanc goes very well with this soup, effectively matching the mild sweetness in the artichoke. South African Chenin is ideal, but demi-sec Chenins from the Loire, such as Anjou Blanc, also match well. Alsace Tokay-Pinot Gris Reserve and Bianco di Verona are successful, and Rueda from Spain goes quite well. Basic German wines such as Liebfraumilch tend to be too sweet, but Rhine Riesling Kabinett is fine.
★★ *South African Chenin Blanc*

## ASPARAGUS SOUP ♀ *unoaked, dry whites, especially Sauvignon Blanc*

New Zealand Sauvignon Blanc is a real star with asparagus soup, just as it is with fresh asparagus and hollandaise. Sauvignon is a good flavour – Sancerre falls just short of perfection, as it is a touch too acid, yet otherwise perfect in flavour. There are good matches with Spanish Rueda and white Côtes du Rhône, and pleasant matches with Vernaccia, Frascati, Chablis, South African Colombard and unoaked Chardonnay VdP d'Oc.
★★ *New Zealand Sauvignon Blanc*

## BEETROOT SOUP (BORSCHT) ♀ *crisp, fresh, unoaked dry whites*

Simple Soave comes quite close to a perfect match. Pleasant alternatives are Italian Arneis or Frascati, Bulgarian or Bourgogne Aligoté, Hungarian Pinot Gris or Australian Riesling. ★ *Soave*

## BOUILLABAISSE 🍷 *light, dry rosés* 🍷 *unoaked, unaromatic, medium-acid whites*

TRADITIONAL PARTNER *Provençal white or rosé*

This lovely, rouille-enriched fish soup from southern France finds a lot of good partners. Following the star choice, Vernaccia, Italy succeeds too with Lugana and other Trebbiano wines. White La Mancha from Spain, white Châteauneuf-du-Pape, Côtes du Rhône, and Marsanne vins de pays and other gently flavoured southern French vins de pays make easy partners. (Avoid Sauvignon and Chardonnay, and aromatic grapes such as Gewürztraminer.) Bergerac and Bordeaux rosés are alternative perfect partners, and Spanish Tempranillo rosados from Valladolid or Valdepeñas go very well, too, although reds are quite simply horrid. ★★ *Vernaccia di San Gimignano* ★★ *Bergerac or Bordeaux rosé*

## CARROT AND ORANGE SOUP 🍷 *a variety of medium-acid, unoaked whites*

The lovely combination of carrot and orange goes brilliantly with Alsace Tokay-Pinot Gris Vendange Tardive, and very well with top-class Australian Semillon, medium-dry Australian Riesling and German Silvaner Spätlese (but not Trocken), Liebfraumilch, Niersteiner Gutes Domtal and other simple German Rhine wines, and Spanish Alella Clásico. Chilean Riesling, English medium white, Champagne, Vouvray Demi-sec, VdP des Côtes de Gascogne, South African Colombard, Saumur or Anjou Blanc Sec, or Penedés rosado will all serve well. ★★ *Alsace Tokay-Pinot Gris Vendange Tardive.*

VARIATIONS With **carrot and coriander** soup, Champagne, German Riesling Kabinett and Alsace Riesling are all contenders for the post of perfect partner, but none is absolutely ideal. Piesporter Michelsberg and other simple, inexpensive Mosel wines are adequate, as is medium-dry Australian Riesling, Silvaner Spätlese, VdP des Côtes de Gascogne and top-class Australian Semillon. ★ *Alsace Riesling*

## CELERY SOUP 🍷 *dry to medium-dry whites*

Frascati goes positively well, and a few other whites are all pleasant. Choose from Muscadet, Favorita, inexpensive Australian Rhine Riesling, Bianco di Verona or Liebfraumilch. ★ *Frascati*

## CHICKEN SOUP, CREAM OF ♀ *dry, medium- to highish-acid, unoaked whites*

Ingredients vary, but with the white, creamy chicken soup we tried, Alsace Pinot Blanc, white Corbières, Bordeaux Blanc and dry Vinho Verde turned out to be stars. Runners-up with our version were Chablis, simple, gentle, unoaked Chardonnays including simple white Burgundies, non-vintage Champagne, Cheverny, Muscadet, white Rioja and southern French Terret. ★★ *Alsace Pinot Blanc*

VARIATIONS With a clear soup cooked with **celery, carrot and onion**, the best bet is Bourgogne Aligoté. Also good are Bordeaux Blanc, southern French Terret vin de pays, dry Vinho Verde, Soave, and simple unoaked Chardonnay (but Australian and California ones are too strong). ★★ *Bourgogne Aligoté.* With a thick **chicken and mushroom** soup, try Bordeaux Blanc, Penedés whites from Spain or light, unoaked Chardonnay.

## CLAM CHOWDER ♀ *unoaked, light, bland, not-too-fruity whites*

It is the salt pork and tomato that flavour this milk-based American soup. The clams have very little influence. The soup's flavour is still gentle, however, and is better with Sancerre than with other Sauvignon Blancs, but you can equally well serve a VdP des Côtes de Gascogne, or a Soave. Pleasant combinations are with Pinot Grigio, unoaked white Rioja or a simple Sicilian white. ★ *Sancerre*

## COCK-A-LEEKIE ❢ *light, softly tannic reds* ♀ *off-dry, gently flavoured, unoaked whites*

This mild dish calls for gentle flavours in the wine. The sweetness of the leeks and prunes also suggests a medium-dry white. That's why off-dry South African Chenin (known there as Steen) is so good, and an inexpensive, not-too-flavourful Australian Riesling works well for the same reason. Though dry, Frascati is also quite good, as is simple Penedés white, while Rueda Superior really enhances the leek flavour. (Oak, and wines made from the Sauvignon Blanc grape, clash.)

Reds are mostly too strongly flavoured, but Loire reds, Valpolicella and light vins de pays all go acceptably well.
★★ *off-dry South African Chenin Blanc*

## CRAB BISQUE ♀ *unoaked, bland or aromatic dry whites*

Unoaked, not-too-acid Chardonnays are best, Australian ones work best of all (look for one that is labelled 'unoaked'). Pleasant matches among blander whites are Soave, Penedés whites, VdP des Côtes de Gascogne, Yecla or Valencia dry whites from Spain, or southern French Picpoul. Agreeable aromatic partners are Arneis, dry Muscat, Australian Semillon and Semillon-Chardonnay. Gewürztraminer and Sauvignon Blanc do not work.
★★ *unoaked Australian Chardonnay*

## CUCUMBER SOUP ♀ *a few gentle whites*

Most wines taste too acid, too bright or too strong with this delicate soup. A gentle white from Conca de Barberá or Penedés in Spain will come to the rescue.

## FISH SOUP ♟ *dry Grenache rosés ♀ soft, gentle whites*

If you're sitting under a parasol in Provence, try a glass or two of Provençal rosé with the classic rust-coloured 'soupe de poissons'. Of the whites, Rueda from north-west Spain is the star, but other good choices are white Rioja, white Penedés, and Conca de Barberá, Chablis (and other unoaked Chardonnays), or Lugana. If you've made the soup at home using a richly flavoured seafood stock, it can cope with more full-bodied wines, such as oaked white Rioja or white Châteauneuf-du-Pape. White La Mancha works well with tomato and onion in the soup. ★★ *Rueda*

## FRENCH ONION SOUP see ONION SOUP

## GAZPACHO ♀ *dry whites with medium to high acidity*

TRADITIONAL PARTNER *Spanish white*

This delicious cold soup from southern Spain goes well with the Airén whites of La Mancha, Valdepeñas and the deep south, and with Penedés or Conca de Barberá whites. The whites of Rioja and Navarra, on the other hand, are less good with the flavour of green pepper. The top white choice from Spain is Rueda, whether made from the traditional Verdejo or from Sauvignon Blanc. A really bright and fruity Penedés white, particularly one containing Sauvignon, also makes a lovely combination. Sauvignon Blanc chimes in well with the flavour of Gazpacho: Sancerre is especially delicious, and Bordeaux Blanc very good. Verdicchio and Muscadet both go pleasantly. But the real superstar is a simple, inexpensive Australian Semillon. ★★ *inexpensive Australian Semillon*

VARIATION With a **Seville-style Gazpacho**, made with red peppers, simple, inexpensive Australian Semillon is delicious, again. This brighter red version of Gazpacho is slightly sweeter because of the ripe-ness of the peppers. A ripe Sauvignon from Chile or Australia is better than cool-climate Sancerre. Aligoté and Alsace Pinot Blanc also go well. From Spain, Alella Clásico with its touch of sweetness is best; unoaked whites from Penedés, Conca de Barberá, Rioja or Navarra running close behind. ★★ *inexpensive Australian Semillon*

## LEEK AND POTATO SOUP ♀ *dry Syrah rosés* ♀ *unoaked whites*

Leek and potato soup made without cream goes well with Frascati and New Zealand Sauvignon, as well as Australian Semillon. It goes modestly with Bianco di Verona, Soave, Cortese, simple, unoaked Chardonnay, South African Sauvignon Blanc, white Côtes du Rhône or Rueda. Most reds are too tannic, but Dolcetto is a pleasant match despite its tannin, and Syrah rosés are quite good. ★ *inexpensive Australian Semillon*

VARIATION With **Vichysoisse**, Italy scores highly again: Frascati Superiore comes closest to a perfect match, and Bianco di Verona goes well. Or you can try Soave, or a Spanish white from Penedés or Conca de Barberá, or Chablis, which are all pleasant. ★ *Frascati Superiore*

## LENTIL SOUP ♀ *a few bland whites*

The earthy flavour of lentils is not very wine-friendly. Reds clash, and most whites taste too bright, too acid, too fruity, too honeyed or otherwise wrong. If you really want to serve wine with this soup, then Soave is the best bet.

## LOBSTER BISQUE (BISQUE D'HOMARD)
❦ *dry Cinsault rosés* ♀ *dry, medium-acid whites*
Recipes vary, but Arneis or a dry Cinsault rosé are the likely star choices, followed by a variety of whites, including Bordeaux Blanc, white Corbières, Soave, Frascati, or Valdadige Bianco from northern Italy, Penedés whites from Spain, and Austrian Grüner Veltliner. ★ *Cinsault rosé* ★ *Arneis*

## MINESTRONE SOUP ❦ *Dolcetto* ♀ *dry, not-too-fruity, not-too acid whites*
Recipes for minestrone vary, but Soave stands a good chance of matching most versions very well, or you can try Chilean Sauvignon Blanc. Dolcetto is a surprisingly pleasant match among red wines. Most others clash. ★ *Soave*

## MUSHROOM SOUP ❦ *soft, savoury, low-tannin reds* ♀ *dry, fairly neutral whites*
The gentle flavour of mushroom soup is easily blown away by fruity or aromatic whites. The successful whites are varied but pretty delicate in flavour. A modern Douro white is by far the best choice, with white Burgundy the next contender. Other decent whites are Chardonnay VdP d'Oc, Rueda from Spain, white Corbières, Bordeaux Blanc, Picpoul from the south of France, and German dry Riesling. Reds are mostly too tannic, but a few savoury ones do work: southern French Pinot Noir and southern Italian Cirò are good; also try California Pinot Noir, Austrian Blauer Zweigelt, mature Cahors, and Sangiovese from Umbria or Romagna. (For chicken and mushroom soup, see *Chicken Soup*.) ★★ *modern Douro white*

## ONION SOUP ♀ *unoaked, dry to medium-dry whites*
Soft, honeyed Pinot Blanc and Pinot Bianco are delicious star matches, and Alella Clásico from Spain, with its slight sweetness, is lovely too. (The natural sweetness in onions likes an echoing sweetness in the wine.) Other good matches are with Australian Verdelho and a simple, inexpensive Gewürztraminer, perhaps from Alsace. You can also try Viognier, Alsace Pinot Gris, Bordeaux Blanc, Chilean Sauvignon, German Silvaner Trocken and Alsace Sylvaner, and simple unoaked Chardonnays, including white Burgundy. ★★ *Alsace Pinot Blanc*

# FISH, SHELLFISH AND SEAFOOD

Fish – and indeed shellfish and seafood – can be slippery customers when you try to team them up with a perfect wine partner. For white fish served plain, that old adage 'don't drink red wine with fish' proves a fair one. Fruity, tannic red wines sweep aside their delicate flavours. But oilier fish, or white fish served with a sauce, will introduce fuller whites and light reds to the list of wine partners. Some seafoods and shellfish are so bland as to be virtually flavourless, but others have a very 'fishy' flavour which many white and red wines actually emphasize unpleasantly. As always, any accompanying sauce will probably dictate the final choice of wine partner. See also *Sauces*.

## Fish

The gentlest of wine flavours, soft fruit, and not too pronounced acidity, are the answer with the delicate flesh of white fish. These are best supplied by cool-climate European Chardonnay, light Italian whites or gentle Sauvignons. Fruity, tannic red wines are too strong, and a few fish – cod in particular – accentuate tannin or leave a slightly metallic aftertaste. Batter and frying raises the flavour intensity a notch, and widens the choice of wine to more flavourful whites or rosés. But the focus changes dramatically when you add a sauce to the fish. This is where those fuller California and Australian whites come into their own. Remember also that lemon juice squeezed over fish will call for a wine with enough tangy acidity to match it.

**ANCHOVY** Unsalted anchovies are served as tapas (nibbles) in bars across Spain, yet are rarely found elsewhere. More familiar outside Spain are tinned, salted anchovies. As a garnish, or added sparingly in a dish, their powerful flavours are fortunately muted by the other ingredients.

**Fresh Anchovy (Boquerones)** ♀ *light, gently flavoured, medium-acid whites*
Fresh anchovy's quite pronounced flavour is not easy to match to wine. Spanish whites tend to have too little flavour. Aligoté makes the grade; but choose a not-too-acid one from a ripe year in Burgundy, or a simple, inexpensive Bulgarian Aligoté. Trincadeira das Pratas from Portugal is a good alternative. ★ *Aligoté*

**Janssens Temptation** ♀ *bland whites*
This Swedish combination of potatoes, onions, cream and anchovies tastes delicious, yet is hard to match with anything but the most straightforward bland white wines. By far the best is ordinary Soave. The bright fruit of modern wine-making clashes. ★★ *inexpensive Soave*

**Salted Anchovies** ♥ *light Spanish reds* ♥ *dry rosés*
The star matches are low- to medium-acid rosés. Choose a Spanish rosado, made with the Tempranillo (Cencibel) grape, from La Mancha or around Valladolid. Syrah rosé is very good (but Grenache rosé works less well). Whites rarely clash, but they do not shine either. The tannin of red wine does clash, as does the herbaceous character of Cabernet-based wines. Should you want to drink red wine with salted anchovies, light, untannic Spanish reds, again made from Tempranillo, are a good choice. Choose a mature one for its softer fruit. ★★ *Spanish rosado*

**BASS** ♥ *dry rosés* ♀ *fresh, dry Pinot Blanc*
It's frustrating that with such a delicious fish a really great match can't be made. Acidity is always the obstacle. Tavel rosé – of the latest vintage – is the only star, though Pinot Blanc d'Alsace and dry German Weissburgunder go quite well. ★★ *young Tavel rosé*

**BREAM** Two quite different beasties swim under this name – fresh-water and sea bream.

**Fresh-water Bream** ♀ *unoaked, light whites*
This is the fish that avenges itself on anglers. Fresh-water bream hides loads of barbed bones in its flesh to spike your tongue. It has a good, very delicate flavour, which is easily overwhelmed by wine. The star is unoaked Chardonnay VdP d'Oc, with the right crisp, but gentle, undemanding flavours; lively, modern La Mancha whites are nearly as good. Spanish Rueda is quite good, and a fresh, modern Soave is fine. ★★ *Chardonnay VdP d'Oc*

### Sea Bream ♀ *young, medium-acid whites, especially gently flavoured Sauvignon Blanc*

Sea bream has a marvellously robust, meaty flavour and texture, ideal for grilling and barbecuing. Easily the best wines are Sauvignon Blancs: a gentle, well-made Sauvignon from Hungary is a star, and next best would be a Bordeaux Blanc. Avoid the really aromatic Sauvignons – New Zealand and the Upper Loire ones (Sancerre, Pouilly-Fumé, Reuilly, Menetou-Salon) are all too fruity. Chardonnays taste too fruity, oaked wines taste too oaky, and the gentle, less aromatic whites taste, well, boring. Lively whites, such as southern French Terret and Marsanne, are good, as are some Australian blended wines: Colombard-Chardonnay, for instance. ★★ *Hungarian Sauvignon Blanc*

### BRILL ♀ *bland Italian whites*

Brill isn't very 'brill', in fact. It has such a delicate flavour that almost any wine will overwhelm it. Of the very gentlest Italian whites, Lugana is easily the best, with Vernaccia di San Gimignano and Verdicchio following on behind. ★★ *Lugana*

### CARP ♀ *bland whites*

Carp is boring, heavy-fleshed, and often slightly muddy-flavoured. If you have to eat it plain, avoid bright, fruity and acidic wines. The gentle, earthy flavour of a German Silvaner Trocken is just perfect, and Alsace Sylvaner comes a close second. Verdicchio marries very well indeed. Traditional German and Polish recipes often include sweet stuffing ingredients, such as raisins, currants, sugar or spice cake. To match these, choose a sweeter Silvaner. ★★ *German Silvaner Trocken*

### CAVIAR ♀ *inexpensive, fairly bland, still or sparkling whites*

TRADITIONAL PARTNER *Vodka*

There are three main kinds of caviar: Beluga, the rarest and most expensive, large-grained-and creamy; Oscietra, smaller-grained, with a gentle, almost sweet flavour; and Sevruga, sharper, more intense in flavour. All are delicate, complex – and expensive. Pouring luxury on luxury, Champagne (especially Blanc de Blancs) goes *fairly* well with Beluga, but less so with the others. However, Crémant de Bourgogne, the sparkling wine of Burgundy, goes rather better with all the caviar styles. It's true for still wines, too: the wines that work best tend not to be the grandest. Maybe caviar's reputation for being so hard to match stems from gourmets rarely trying to partner it with anything but the tops.

With any caviar, the soft, creamy character of Italian Bianco di Custoza blends in beautifully. A fine Soave Classico is nearly as good. But Chardonnays are best, unoaked if possible. Try simple, well-made, unoaked ones from France, Italy and Hungary. In Burgundy, too, simple is best: inexpensive Mâcon-Villages is better than a Meursault. The flavours of *fine* Burgundy or Chablis, and of fine New World Chardonnays, are too strong and very often too oaky (though Sevruga comes nearest to coping).

The sharper tang of Sevruga partners Hungarian Furmint, white Crozes-Hermitage, fine dry Vinho Verde (though not one that names Alvarinho or Loureiro on the label), and even New Zealand Sauvignon Blanc. Other Sauvignons are too grassy for caviar. Following tradition, *expensive* vodka, super-chilled, will not let you down, but ordinary vodka and caviar make a horrible combination.
★★ *simple Chardonnay* ★★ *Bianco di Custoza*

CEVICHE ♀ *dry, lightly flavoured, hig- acid whites*
TRADITIONAL PARTNER *South American Sauvignon Blanc*
You have to like raw onion to enjoy a true ceviche (also spelled *cebiche*). Even if you don't eat the onion in the marinade, its flavour lingers in the fish. And finding a wine with a high enough acidity to match the lime or lemon juice is quite a challenge. Dry Vinho Verde certainly has the acidity, and the flavour works well, too. (Go for a mixed-grape one or a 100% Alvarinho). Next best is Sauvignon de Touraine (Sancerre is too strong). Dry English Seyval Blanc, Penedés and Conca de Barberá whites from Spain and very dry Champagne have nearly the right flavours and acidity, too. ★★ *dry Vinho Verde*

COD ♀ *dry rosés* ♀ *soft, unoaked, lightly flavoured whites*
Cod is a relatively 'unfishy' fish; and it's not too oily. But its very delicate flavour is easily overwhelmed by too much

fruit, oak or acidity in a wine. Cod also has the ability to winkle out large amounts of tannin from even quite untannic red wines like Beaujolais. This is not a fish to serve with, or cook in, red wine. Whether fried, grilled or baked, cod is best paired with soft, unoaked French, Italian or Australian Chardonnays, gently flavoured Sauvignon Blancs from Bordeaux, Chile and Spain, or a dry rosado from Spain or the Rhône. A bland, not-too-fruity Soave is also a good alternative.
★★ *gentle, unoaked Chardonnay*

## Salt Cod (Bacalhão de Gomes)
♟ *young, gently fruity reds* ♟ *dry rosés* ♀ *light, unoaked whites*

It's not just the salting that makes salt cod so much more flavourful than fresh cod. Left to dry on 'hurdles' in the sun, the salty fish takes on a fascinating high, gamy flavour. Roast salt cod is the national dish of Portugal, but Portuguese whites taste either flat or, in the case of Vinho Verde, too acid. Modern young red Bairrada, with its soft tannins, works well, and red Alentejo is not too bad. Best of all the reds, however, is Rioja Crianza, whose savoury flavour chimes beautifully in with the salt cod's gaminess, while its fruitiness balances the salt. Italian Bianco di Custoza makes a star white match, and German Silvaner Trocken, Austrian Grüner Veltliner, southern French Terret, South African Colombard, Spanish rosado and young red Rioja are all good. Oaked white Rioja, Touraine rosé and Oregon Pinot Noir are all quite good. The same wines match Bacalhão à Gomes de Sá (salt cod poached in water, then fried in olive oil with onions, garlic, potato and boiled egg). ★★ *Bianco di Custoza* ★★ *red Rioja Crianza*

## Smoked Cod ♀ *oaked whites*
This demands a relatively oaky wine, probably made by an Australian winemaker (whether in western Europe or Down Under). Oaked Chardonnays from Australia, New Zealand, California, southern France and Eastern Europe are excellent, with oaked Semillon-Chardonnay also good. The heavier the smoked flavour, the oakier

the wine must be. Oaked white Rioja stands up to a very smoky cod. ★★ *oaked Chardonnay*

**Taramasalata** ♀ *dry rosés* ♀ *highish-acid dry whites*
TRADITIONAL PARTNER *Retsina*
Whether home-made (from smoked cod's roe, breadcrumbs, milk, garlic and olive oil) or bought (usually tarter and less richly flavoured), taramasalata is tough to team up with wine, demanding high acidity. Despite its low acid, Retsina succeeds because of its resin. In the absence of real star matches, New Zealand Sauvignon is good (better than French and much better than California or Chilean ones) and Muscadet and Bordeaux Rosé are good. Vinho Verde might make a very good combination with bought taramasalata, but its acid tastes too hard with the home-made version. ★ *Retsina*

**DOVER SOLE** ♀ *lightly oaked, softly flavoured whites, especially Sauvignon Blanc*
Dover sole is one of the true aristocrats of the kitchen, with its firm white flesh and sweet, succulent flavour. Whether grilled, dusted in flour then fried in butter, or served with a sauce, Dover sole is a great fan of soft Sauvignon Blancs. As long as you avoid the most aromatic New Zealand and Upper Loire examples, you won't go far wrong with just about any other Sauvignon. Dover sole can cope with a light touch of oakiness, so as well as being delicious with unoaked Bordeaux Blanc or a good, modern VdP d'Oc Sauvignon Blanc, it can handle a lightly oaked white Graves. Sauvignons from places such as Australia, California or Chile are fine as well. If you don't like the flavour of Sauvignon Blanc, stick to a good Soave. ★★ *Bordeaux Blanc* ★★ *Sauvignon VdP d'Oc*

**ESCABECHE** (Italian: *escabecio* or *scavece*; Belgian: *escaveche*) ♀ *unoaked, crisp, lightly fruity whites*
There are two things to match in this dish: the fish (which may include shallow-fried sardines and/or mackerel, whiting, red mullet, eels, or, if you are preparing it at home, whatever fish you choose); and the sharply acidic marinade which then becomes the cooking liquid (containing onion, carrot, garlic, vinegar and water, thyme, coriander seed and cayenne). With white fish, the marinade will be dominant, but oily fish such as mackerel will make their own demands on the wine too. Whatever the fish, the wine

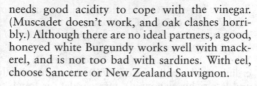

needs good acidity to cope with the vinegar. (Muscadet doesn't work, and oak clashes horribly.) Although there are no ideal partners, a good, honeyed white Burgundy works well with mackerel, and is not too bad with sardines. With eel, choose Sancerre or New Zealand Sauvignon.

### FISH AND CHIPS ♀ *dry rosés* ♀ *lightly fruity whites*

Better a refreshing glass of wine than a drenching in vinegar for your crisply battered fish. If it is cod, a good generic Bordeaux Blanc or one labelled AC Entre-Deux-Mers will do the job perfectly. Gentle Chardonnays and dry rosés are also good. If it's plaice, a gentle Chardonnay is excellent. A Muscadet or VdP des Côtes de Gascogne is pleasant, and the gentler Italian whites (Soave, Frascati and the like) go well, too. (Should you prefer another fish, just check its perfect partner and away you go.)

### FISH CAKES ♀ *light, unoaked whites*

The perfect partner depends upon the type of fish in the cakes. If you know, match the fish, otherwise plump for a Bordeaux Blanc – it blends in with lots of different fishes and also with onion. Gentle Italian whites, such as Frascati, are also good. Avoid anything too acidic.

VARIATIONS With **salmon fish cakes**, try a gentle Chardonnay such as inexpensive white Burgundy. A dry Muscat, or Pinot Blanc from Alsace might also be good.

### FISH PÂTÉ ♀ *dry, medium-acid whites*

For fish pâtés not mentioned, look up the individual fish entry; medium acidity is best.

VARIATIONS With **salmon pâté**, a dry Muscat or a soft white Burgundy is good. For **smoked salmon pâté** choose a Côtes de Gascogne or lightly oaked, gently flavoured Chardonnay; Cheverny or Champagne Blanc de Blancs are just as good. **Smoked mackerel pâté** is difficult to match, but dry Vinho Verde goes quite well, and Sauvignons don't clash. **Smoked trout pâté** is partnered well by Chablis.

**FISH PIE** ♀ *light, unoaked whites*
A mildly flavoured fish pie made with onion and white
sauce goes well with a soft, buttery, not-too-acid Chardonnay, a soft Sauvignon, for example from Bordeaux or
Chile, or gentle Italian whites such as Frascati. If the pie
also contains seafood, this may be the dominant flavour –
see *Shellfish and Seafood*.

**FISH SOUP** see *Soups*

**FRITTO MISTO DI MARE** ♀ *light, unoaked whites*
This mix of fish, deep-fried in a flour or batter coating,
may include small sole, anchovies, small octopus, squid,
small red mullet – or whatever fish happens to be available.
Fritto misto is normally served with lemon wedges, so the
major elements to match here are the fish and acidity. Bordeaux Blanc is, again, a reasonable catch-all wine, as are
Italian Soave, Frascati and Vernaccia di San Gimignano.

**GRAVADLAX** see **SALMON**

**GROUPER** ♀ *light, unoaked whites*
The look of this fish is a lot more exotic than its flavour.
Simply grilled, this copper-red beauty, with its silver-blue
spots, is a push-over for even the lightest of wines. The
gentle neutrality of Soave makes a perfect balance, and
bland white VdP des Pyrénées Orientales is not bad, but
Sauvignons are too aromatic, Chardonnays too rich, and
very few other wines match at all. An exception is Australian Semillon, on its own a bit too powerfully fruity, but
blended with a little Chardonnay it can make a reasonable
pairing. ★★ *Soave*

**HADDOCK** ♀ *light, crisp, unoaked whites*
Haddock's very mild taste can only take a limited amount
of flavour from a matching wine. Soft Sauvignon and
Semillon-based whites from Bordeaux and the surrounding regions are most successful. Other possibilities are the
crisp whites of Soave, in Italy, or of northern Portugal's
Dão region. ★★ *Bordeaux Blanc*
**Kedgeree** see *Rice and Grains*
**Smoked Haddock** ♀ *light, crisp, unoaked whites; dry
fino sherry*
When smoked, haddock is harder to match well to wine,

but the Bordeaux whites should still cope, and you can also try a modern-style white Rioja or even a glass of chilled manzanilla sherry. Finnan haddock, the smokiest of all haddocks, is extremely tricky to partner. Perhaps you should just eat smoked haddock for breakfast, then the difficult question of finding a good wine match really ought not to arise. ★ *Bordeaux Blanc*

## HAKE ♀ *unoaked or oaked, light whites*
Choose something not too bright, not too aromatic or too fruity for this slightly cod-like fish. Despite its quite positive flavour, gently flavoured wines work best. Of the Italian whites, Soave Classico is second only to the Vermentino, with Verdicchio following closely behind; basic Soave and Lugana make reasonable partners. A simple Bordeaux Blanc is also adequate, and Silvaner Trocken from Germany marries in quite well. Soft, simple Chardonnays, such as Chardonnay VdP d'Oc or an inexpensive Chilean Chardonnay, work quite well, both oaked or unoaked. And oaked white Rioja makes an unexpectedly good pairing. ★★ *Vermentino di Sardegna*

## HALIBUT ♀ *unoaked, light whites*
The crisp, honeyed flavour of Soave suits this delicate fish very well, as do Sauvignon Blancs from just about anywhere except New Zealand (which are too aromatic). Unoaked Chardonnays go well, too, and you won't go too far wrong with any light, dry white as long as it is not too acid – though nothing makes a truly stunning match. Try to steer clear of richly oaky Chardonnay as strong oak flavours will clash wildly with halibut. ★ *Soave*

### Smoked Halibut ❗ *Beaujolais ♀ aromatic, and oaked whites*
Smoked like salmon and thinly sliced as a starter, halibut clashes with oaked Chardonnay, but oaked white Rioja is a star. Dry Riesling and even Gewürztraminer are good, too. Unoaked Australian Chardonnays are fine, as are blends with Semillon and Colombard. Unexpectedly,

Beaujolais-Villages (or a lighter cru Beaujolais such as Fleurie or Chiroubles) makes an entirely satisfactory match. ★★ *oaked white Rioja*

## HERRING ♀ *unoaked, light whites*

Herring is a much underrated fish. It has heaps of interesting flavour and is full of those healthy natural fish-oils of which we're always told we should eat more. Its sweet flesh goes brilliantly with a good, honeyed Soave Classico, and with other creamy Italian whites such as Frascati. Another good match is the Terret grape of southern France. Oaked European Chardonnays (from France, Italy and Spain) make good mates for herring, although most Chardonnays from the New World are too intensely fruity. Sauvignon Blanc is too aromatic, unless muted by Semillon and oak in a gentle white Graves. ★★ *Soave Classico*

## Kipper see KIPPER

## Roll-mop Herring ♀ *medium-dry, acid whites*

Soused in vinegar, with a little sugar in the marinade, rollmops need to be matched by a correspondingly high-acid, slightly sweet wine. A medium-dry Vinho Verde (the flask-shaped bottle is usually a clue to medium-dryness) is probably the best bet, unless you can find a highish-acid, slightly sweetened French table wine. German whites taste too honeyed.

## Salt Herring ♀ *unoaked, light whites*

TRADITIONAL PARTNER Dutch gin

'Foul' and 'unpleasantly fishy' is our verdict on combinations of salt herrings with all red wines and many whites. (Salt herrings clash with very fruity or oaky whites.) However, Portuguese white Bairrada tastes positively good with salt herring. Soave, and other bland Italian whites, or Côtes du Tarn and other mildly flavoured southern French whites, make reasonable matches. Ideally, though, the answer lies with Dutch *oude Genever* (barrel-aged gin), which makes a sensational match and even straight vodka hits the spot. ★ *white Bairrada*

## Sprats ♀ *unoaked, light, fragrant whites*

Sprats are baby herring, milder and less oily than the grown-up version. Like herring, the star matches come from Italy, with soft Italian whites such as Soave Classico and Frascati. Gentle Sauvignons from Bordeaux, Eastern Europe, South Africa and Chile are all fine alternatives. ★★ *Soave Classico* ★★ *Frascati*

**JACK** ❢ *light, fruity Pinot Noir* ♀ *oaked, fragrant whites*

Jack is a meaty fish rather like a small tuna – but less oily – with firm, solid flesh. The best pairing by far is with oaked Australian Chardonnay, preferably one that has the butterscotchy flavours of malolactic fermentation (see page 226). White Burgundy and other oaked Chardonnays also work well. Jack is good with crisp Sauvignon Blancs, best with the fragrant gooseberry tang of an Upper Loire Sauvignon such as a Sancerre, but almost as good with Bordeaux or southern French Sauvignons. Spain has some successes too: oaked white Rioja echoes the success of Chardonnay, and Rueda follows the example of Sauvignon. A light, fruity Pinot Noir can be good if you want to make a change from white wines: try Oregon Pinot Noir, or Pinots from Victoria in Australia, or from New Zealand. ★★ *oaked Australian Chardonnay*

**JOHN DORY** ♀ *top Chardonnays; rich, fragrant whites*

John Dory (called St-Pierre in France, after the thumb-sized black mark on its side, which legend says is the thumb-print of St Peter the fisherman) is one of the real aristocrats of the fish menu. It has firm, meaty flesh, with a sweet, attractive flavour. Happily, it matches many of the world's best Chardonnays very well indeed. The rich, pineappley flavours of Australian, California, South African and New Zealand Chardonnays are almost as perfect as the subtle elegance of white Burgundy. Pouilly Fuissé is a particular success. The rich, soft whites of Rhône and the south of France (Châteauneuf-du-Pape, Hermitage, wines made from Marsanne, and their like) also partner John Dory well. The very gentlest Sauvignon Blancs such as Bordeaux Blanc are not too grassily competitive, and Rueda and unoaked white Rioja are happy, less costly, choices. ★★ *Pouilly-Fuissé*

**KEDGEREE** see *Rice and Grains*

## KIPPER ♀ *bland whites*

The intensely smoked flavour of kippers defeats any wine that is fairly fruity or aromatic. Chardonnay tastes wrong, and all Sauvignons are too aromatic. So it's back to the more neutral whites. Italy's Soave and Frascati are all acceptable, if not perfect, as are Terret and most Ugni Blanc-based whites from the south of France, and central Spanish whites such as La Mancha and white Valdepeñas. A light, fresh fino or manzanilla sherry also goes quite well. But the best match for the kipper is undoubtedly not wine at all but mature Dutch gin, straight from the freezer.

## LEMON SOLE ♥ *dry rosés* ♀ *crisp, unoaked whites*

Soft, easy, unoaked Chardonnays, rather than the most complex Burgundian or big New World Chardonnays are the perfect choice with these sweet-fleshed, smaller cousins of the noble Dover sole. Those from the state of Victoria, in Australia, are prime examples. The crisp, gently grassy white wines from Rueda, north-west Spain, also work very well, and modern white Rioja isn't bad. Most Sauvignons are too fruitily aromatic, though the Bordeaux blend with Semillon (and even a hint of oak) can perform well. Creamy dry rosados from Spain and the south of France are also satisfactory. ★★ *unoaked Victoria Chardonnay*

## MACKEREL ♀ *unoaked, light whites*

Oily mackerel is not an easy fish to partner with wine. Chardonnay is the best grape variety, the star a basic white Burgundy. Mâcon Blanc, Beaujolais Blanc or a simple Italian Chardonnay are also wise choices. Otherwise try a Soave or simple Muscadet. ★★ *inexpensive white Burgundy*

### Smoked Mackerel ♀ *light, highish-acid whites*

Smoked mackerel makes few really good matches either. Dry Vinho Verde is the only star, followed by Vernaccia di San Gimignano, southern French Terret and, surprisingly, Retsina. Try also Penedés or Conca de Barberá whites from Spain, Soave, Frascati, or Lugana from Italy, or an oaked Chardonnay. ★★ *dry Vinho Verde*

## MONKFISH (ANGLER FISH/LOTTE) ♀ *lightly oaked dry whites, especially Chardonnay*

Chardonnays are heaven-sent partners for this firm-fleshed, sweet-tasting fish. Known also as angler fish, monkfish lends itself wonderfully to poaching, sautéing and combining with sauces. And it's extremely wine-friendly. Chardonnay from California and from the Burgundian commune of St-Romain are especially good. Whites with too much oak, whether from Australia or Spain, overpower monkfish, as do too obviously modern and aromatic flavours, but all sorts of other wines, from German Silvaner and Austrian Grüner Veltliner to white Bordeaux, white Rueda and whites from the southern Rhône make very decent partners. You might even get away with a light red, if serving the monkfish in a red-wine sauce. ★★ *California Chardonnay* ★★ *white St-Romain*

**MULLET** Red mullet, the superior fish in flavour and texture, is not in fact a true member of the mullet family. (The lesser grey mullet is called just plain mullet in the US and Australia.)
**Grey Mullet** ♀ *dry rosés* ♀ *light, crisp, unoaked whites*
Chardonnay and most Sauvignon Blancs are too fruity for this firm-fleshed, fairly bland, sometimes slightly muddy-tasting fish. Even the gentle whites of Rueda in Spain are a shade too grassy for grey mullet, though a less aromatic South African Sauvignon might manage. Italian whites come into their own, the field led by Vernaccia di San Gimignano, and followed by Soave, Bianco di Custoza and Frascati. Terret and Tavel Rosé from the south of France are good. Another crisp, lemony match is a Spanish white from Penedés, and the lively, neutral flavour of the white Chasselas grape from Switzerland also works well. ★★ *Vernaccia di San Gimignano* ★★ *southern French Terret* ★★ *white Penedés*
**Red Mullet** ♀ *dry rosés* ♀ *crisp, dry, unoaked whites*
You could try Retsina, to evoke memories of sun-dappled Greek isles, but for a safe, reliable match, Soave is the best choice with this lovely, firm-fleshed fish, much sweeter and more aromatic than grey mullet. The crisp, gooseberry flavour of Touraine Sauvignon co-exists well with red mullet. It's not a true match, but you can taste both

without either spoiling the pleasure of the other. Otherwise, it's back to the Italian trio of Vernaccia di San Gimignano, Frascati and Soave Classico; dry Spanish and southern French rosés are pleasant. ★★ *Soave*

## PIKE ♀ *bland whites*

This is a strong contender for the title of dullest fish in the world; its heavily fluffy texture is really unattractive. Any wine is too bright for pike. White Dão comes nearest to a match – but this hardly makes for an exciting meal. In the Loire, pike is often served with beurre blanc – in which case the sauce is the main flavour to match.

## PLAICE ♀ *light, soft whites*

A lot of wines are too strong and bright for the fairly delicately fleshed plaice; acidity can be a problem, too. The lighter style of Chilean Chardonnay is a characterful match that doesn't overpower the dish. Italian Chardonnay and light Burgundy, even the simpler Australian Chardonnays, make satisfactory matches. Soave is fine, and Vernaccia, Bianco di Custoza, and Bordeaux Blanc are adequate, if unexciting, partners. For grilled or shallow-fried plaice the choice remains much the same. But when dipped in batter and deep-fried, plaice can take a touch more bright fruit and flavour in an accompanying wine – Portuguese Trincadeira das Pratas is a stunning partner. ★★ *Chilean Chardonnay* ★★ *Trincadeira das Pratas*

## SALMON ❗ *light, low-tannin reds* ♀ *soft, lightly flavoured, unoaked whites*

Poached salmon is not easy to match. Something in the fish reacts with acidity and tannin in most of the likely wine candidates to create an unpleasant bitterness. Of the obvious choices, very soft, gentle Chardonnays from the Mâconnais and Côte Chalonnaise come closest. And the very gentlest of Sauvignons will not interfere too much with the salmon flavour – but they are far from perfect. Much, much better is an unlikely pair from Alsace: the dry white Muscat and red Pinot Noir. The Muscat's floral perfume seems a mile away from the rich, soft salmon, but the result is delicious. The Pinot Noir is easier to understand – a light red with a meaty, pink-fleshed fish. Sancerre red would also be good, and a very light red Burgundy just about copes. ★★ *Alsace Muscat* ★★ *Alsace Pinot Noir*

VARIATIONS For salmon in a **cream sauce**, a soft white Burgundy such as Rully or Mâcon-Villages Blanc is good. If you cook the salmon in a **red wine sauce**, the possible range of red wines widens to take in Italian wines such as Chianti Rufina and Copertino, Rioja Crianzas and Reservas, southern French reds and reds from Bairrada in northern Portugal.

Gravadlax ♀ *medium-dry whites*
Vouvray Demi-sec and gravadlax make such a heaven-made marriage that it seems a pity to look further. The sweetness level is perfect and the high acidity level beautifully balances the salt, while the distinctive minerally, herby-spicy flavour of Vouvray is just right for the dill in the gravadlax. Demi-sec Montlouis from just across the Loire is also brilliant, and Anjou Blanc Demi-sec, Saumur Blanc Demi-sec or an off-dry South African Chenin Blanc (Steen) are quite good, though they cope less well with the sauce. ★★ *Vouvray Demi-sec* ★★ *Montlouis Demi-sec*

Salmon Fish Cakes see FISH CAKES

Smoked Salmon ♀ *oaked, dry whites*
Oaked California Chardonnay (the subtler the style the better) is a wonderful accompaniment to smoked salmon – the oak, the grape flavour and the buttery character of malolactic fermentation (see page 226) all blend in perfectly. Good, oaked white Burgundy can be just as good, but Australian Chardonnays tend to be too brightly fruity. Other good choices are Champagne Blanc de Blancs, oaked or unoaked Chablis Premier Cru, or good oaked Chardonnay vins de pays. Oaked or unoaked Bourgogne Aligoté is also delicious, and for a budget match, serve a Muscadet or Frascati. ★★ *oaked California Chardonnay*

## SALMON TROUT/SEA TROUT ❦ *light, fruity reds* ♀ *oaked, lightly fruity dry whites*
Salmon trout is more exciting and stronger in flavour than salmon. However, it will partner many of the same wines, including the light Pinot Noir d'Alsace, but is happy with a number of red wines – Sancerre Rouge, very light red Burgundy,

and light Tempranillo. Of the whites, the more character-ful Chablis Premier Cru is an ideal partner; Aligoté, dry Muscat, soft, unoaked Chardonnay and Australian Semillon-Chardonnay are all enjoyable, too. The grassy flavour of Sauvignon Blanc, however, is wrong for salmon trout. ★★ *Chablis Premier Cru*

### SARDINES ▌ *dry rosés* ♀ *lightly flavoured, unoaked dry whites*

There's something very fishy about many wines when they come into contact with oily sardines. And conversely, some wines, such as whites from Portugal's Dão and Spain's La Mancha regions, make the sardines taste even oilier. An absolutely delicious find for sardines is a modern white Trincadeira das Pratas from the Ribatejo region of Portugal. Tavel Rosé is an equally good and interesting alternative; Spanish rosado (made with Tempranillo) from Navarra or Rioja is also quite good. A soft Sauvignon – perhaps from Bordeaux or thereabouts, Aligoté, unoaked white Rioja, southern French Terret or Marsanne, Italian Verdicchio or Retsina, are all good partners. More aromatic Sauvignons taste disgustingly fishy; Chardonnays are too honeyed; and Muscadet is a real clash. ★★ *Trincadeira das Pratas* ★★ *Tavel Rosé*

### SKATE ♀ *gentle whites, especially Sauvignon Blanc*

Whether grilled, baked, fried, served 'au beurre noir' or 'beurre noisette', skate is set off to perfection by Jurançon Sec. Gentle Sauvignons from Rueda, Chile or South Africa are also successful; very aromatic ones are a bit domineering, though not bad. You could also serve it with a Rueda made from local Spanish grapes. Avoid Chardonnay, which the fish flattens – especially if the wine is oaked or buttery-flavoured from a malolactic fermentation (see page 226). Vinho Verde and Muscadet also clash. ★★ *Jurançon Sec*

### SNAPPER ▌ *light Spanish rosados* ♀ *soft, unoaked dry whites*

This delicate, reddish-coloured tropical fish is easily over-whelmed by any wine with bright, modern fruit, oak, medium to high acidity, or all but the gentlest of character. Chardonnays and Sauvignons are too much. The closest to a star match is Spanish rosado. Any not-too-powerful

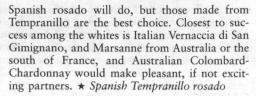

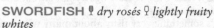

Spanish rosado will do, but those made from Tempranillo are the best choice. Closest to success among the whites is Italian Vernaccia di San Gimignano, and Marsanne from Australia or the south of France, and Australian Colombard-Chardonnay would make pleasant, if not exciting partners. ★ *Spanish Tempranillo rosado*

**SWORDFISH** *dry rosés* *lightly fruity whites*
A lot of wines are too strongly flavoured or too bright for this attractive, meaty, slightly oily fish. The star is Rioja rosado; other good matches are with Vernaccia di San Gimignano, gentle Bordeaux Blanc and white Châteauneuf-du-Pape, or other whites from the southern Rhône. White Rioja and Chardonnays have totally the wrong flavour. ★ *Rioja Rosado*

**TROUT** *dry rosés* *soft, lightly fruity whites*
Whether the trout is served 'Meunière' (fried) or 'au bleu' (poached) makes little difference to the wine match. The stars with this fish are Spanish and southern French Garnacha rosés. A number of white wines are also excellent: Frascati and Lugana are both delicious, and Vermentino, Spanish Rueda, white Crozes-Hermitage, southern French vin de pays Marsanne and unoaked white Rioja all make good complements to trout. Even Viognier and Condrieu, which rarely go with any foods, blend in nicely. Sauvignon Blanc has the right flavour: a soft Bordeaux Blanc hits the spot, but other Sauvignons are often too brightly fruity. Trout can't cope with too much acidity either: very light unoaked Chardonnays, basic Soave, or a not-too-sharply acid Bourgogne Aligoté will all be very pleasant. ★★ *Spanish or southern French Garnacha/Grenache rosés* ★ *Frascati* ★ *Lugana*

**Smoked Trout** *dry, bland whites*
Wine partners for hot-smoked trout must be low on aroma and absolutely dry. Apart from the star white, Bourgogne Aligoté, nothing really shines, but the following are passable: Bianco di Custoza,

white Dão, Hungarian Furmint, inexpensive white Burgundy or Chablis. ★★ *Bourgogne Aligoté*

VARIATIONS Though very like smoked salmon, **cold-smoked trout** is slightly harder to match to wine. Chablis Premier Cru complements it brilliantly, but straight Chablis and other Burgundian Chardonnays don't really match. Aligoté works again, however, whether from Burgundy or Bulgaria, and whether oaked or not. The other star is Champagne Blanc de Blancs (much better than other Champagnes, or sparkling Chardonnays from elsewhere). Oaked Chardonnays, especially from California, make a reasonable match. ★★ *Chablis Premier Cru* ★★ *Champagne Blanc de Blancs*

## Trout with Almonds (Truite aux Amandes)
♀ *light, unoaked whites*

With the exception of the excellent match with white Crozes-Hermitage, no wine that is gentle enough for the fish really reflects the deliciously toasty flavour of the almonds. Perhaps an inexpensive Australian Semillon-Chardonnay gets the nearest, but is a little too strong. Otherwise, you would probably be quite satisfied with the gentler whites of Italy – Frascati or Lugana, or Rueda or white Rioja from Spain, a southern French Marsanne, or a very gentle Bordeaux Blanc. ★★ *white Crozes-Hermitage*

## TUNA
### Tuna (fresh) ♀ *light, soft whites*

It is quite difficult to find a satisfactory partner for this quite dense, flavourful, meaty fish. Australian Semillon-Chardonnay goes pretty well, even when slightly oaked, though oak and bright fruit in most wines clash with tuna. A strong, buttery flavour of malolactic fermentation (see page 226) also clashes. This means matching tuna with good white Burgundy (which often has this flavour) is a bit of a mine-field, though some fine Burgundies and Chablis Premier Crus go reasonably well; other Chardonnays are not a success. Vernaccia di San Gimignano is an acceptable Italian white, and southern Rhône whites, including Châteauneuf-du-Pape Blanc, go reasonably well. ★★ *inexpensive Australian Semillon-Chardonnay*

### Tuna (tinned) ♀ *quite flavoursome whites, especially Chardonnay*

Tinning transforms tuna into a much more wine-friendly fish. It is delicious with gentle, not-too-aromatic Sauvignon Blancs from South Africa, Chile, the south of France, Bordeaux, Italy, or elsewhere, South African ones often making the best match. Basic Muscadet goes very well, and so does unoaked white Rioja. Inexpensive white Burgundies (including simple Chablis) and other basic Chardonnays are fine, as is Soave. Australian Semillon-Chardonnay, white Châteauneuf-du-Pape and Vernaccia are all acceptable. South African Colombard goes very well, and Côtes de Gascogne, with the right flavours but a little too much acidity, is excellent if served with a sharpish dressing. ★★ *South African Sauvignon Blanc*

**Salade Niçoise** see *Salads*
**Vitello Tonnato** see *Veal*

## TURBOT ♀ *lightly oaked or unoaked Chardonnay*

Turbot's nice firm flesh is not really very flavourful when served without an accompanying sauce. Chardonnay is the answer – except for rich, top-of-the-range white Burgundies which don't work (they have the buttery flavour of malolactic fermentation, see page 226) Chardonnays from Australia or New Zealand work, provided they are not too fruity or powerfully oaked, and similarly VdP d'Oc Chardonnay is good. Inexpensive to mid-range Chablis or white Burgundy are also fine. Many other wines are too bright. Rueda from northern Spain, though a bit grassy, comes nearest to an alternative match.
★★ *inexpensive Australian Chardonnay*

## WHITEBAIT ♀ *soft rosés* ♀ *light, crisp whites*

Spanish rosados, made either from Garnacha or Tempranillo, are delicious. Other top choices would be Lugana or Soave whites or a simple Bordeaux Blanc. You could also drink Verdicchio or Vernaccia from Italy, German Silvaner Trocken or Alsace Sylvaner, Penédes or Conca de Barberá whites from Spain, or southern French Terret. Sweetness is inappropriate and high acid clashes, but oak is no problem – oaked white Rioja makes a reasonable match. ★★ *Spanish rosado*

# Shellfish and Seafood

As any Breton will tell you, the local Muscadet is delicious when partnered with a wide variety of shellfish. The up-market Muscadet Sur Lie is especially good, and Sauvignon Blanc (including Sancerre and other Loire Sauvignons) is another star. So go for one of these two wine types if you want to partner a plateau de fruits de mer (mixed seafood platter). If you are poaching shellfish, use some white wine in the poaching liquid to assist the match. Mayonnaise has little effect on the choice of wine, unless you completely swamp the shellfish in it.

**BOUILLABAISSE** see *Soups*

**CLAMS** ♀ *gently flavoured, unoaked, not-too-fruity whites with medium to fairly high acidity, especially Sauvignon Blancs*
The sweet, flavoursome flesh of clams makes them easy to match with wines. Sauvignon Blanc has just the right flavour. Sancerre and South African Sauvignon are perfect served with plain clams, and Chilean and Bordeaux Sauvignon are also very good. Australian and New Zealand Sauvignons tend to have too much of a tropical fruit flavour; Touraine or St-Bris Sauvignons can be too acid. Other good matches are with Muscadet Sur Lie, simple Bordeaux Blanc, Pinot Grigio and Alsace Pinot Blanc.
★★ *Sancerre* ★★ *South African Sauvignon Blanc*
**Clam Chowder** see *Soups*

**COCKLES** ♀ *very bland whites*
You can wash these 'fishy' little shellfish down agreeably with Muscadet Sur Lie or southern French Terret, although even these are not ideal. Most whites emphasize the fish flavour unpleasantly, and some combine to give a metallic flavour. Reds simply don't work. See also *Pasta: Spaghetti alla Vongole*.

**CRAB** ❗ *very light, soft reds* ♀ *unoaked or lightly oaked, dry whites*
Crab has a strong taste, but it's one that doesn't pick too many quarrels with dry white wines. Strongly oaked wines do not work, however. Gentle Sauvignon Blancs are the star partners, closely followed by dry, unoaked Sauvignon-

Semillon blends, such as dry white Bordeaux. (More aromatic Sauvignons from New Zealand and the Loire are good accompaniments for a crab dish with ingredients such as tomato or onion that can cope with the wine's bright aroma.) English dry Seyval Blanc goes well, and dry Rieslings from Alsace, Germany and Austria, Spanish Rueda, white Crozes-Hermitage and Côtes du Rhône are all pleasant, as are Viognier wines and Italian Vernaccia and Arneis. Light reds, particularly those made from Gamay, are also agreeable, and gentle California Pinot Noir works surprisingly well, usually better than Pinot Noir from elsewhere. Serving mayonnaise with the crab slightly tones down the flavour, but in no way interferes with the choice of wine. ★★ *Chilean Sauvignon Blanc* ★★ *South African Sauvignon Blanc*

Crab Pâté ♀ *dry, bland whites*

Recipes vary, but a perfect wine match may prove elusive. However, English Seyval Blanc and Italian Frascati are star choices, and Arneis and Gravina both make good matches. You can also serve Verdicchio, Favorita, Austrian Pinot Blanc, Chardonnay (especially gentle ones), Yecla or Valencia dry whites from Spain, Bordeaux Blanc, Chilean or South African Sauvignon, South African Colombard or dry Muscat. ★★ *Frascati* ★★ *English dry Seyval Blanc*

## CRAYFISH, FRESHWATER (ÉCREVISSES) ♀ *bland to fairly bland, not-too-acid, not-too-fruity dry whites*

Any sauce is likely to dominate these delicately flavoured fresh-water shellfish. They do have a quite distinctive, slightly meaty, savoury character, and Spanish Albariño is alone among aromatic, flavourful wines in making a good match. A simple, inexpensive Alsace Pinot Blanc is the star choice with plain 'écrevisses à la nage', and Cinsault rosé a good alternative. Other pleasant choices are Frascati or a simple Sicilian white, Spanish Yecla, or Muscadet Sur Lie. ★★ *Alsace Pinot Blanc*

**LANGOUSTINE** ♀ *gentle, bland, low-acid, unoaked dry whites*

Frascati is by far the best choice to accompany these king-sized prawns, with or without mayonnaise. Austrian Grüner Veltliner, South African Sauvignon Blanc, Italian Lugana, white Châteauneuf-du-Pape or southern French Picpoul are also good. ★ *Frascati*

**Scampi** ♀ *bland whites or very gently flavoured Sauvignon Blanc*

Scampi, usually a combination of bits of langoustine and prawns, breaded and deep-fried, is fairly low on flavour. The best choice – white Châteauneuf-du-Pape – is dispro-portionately expensive, and even then it is not a perfect partner. Soave, South African Colombard, South African Sauvignon, Sancerre, Menetou-Salon, or Pouilly-Fumé and Reuilly from the Loire are all pleasant, and better value. If you like tartare sauce with scampi, choose a high-acid Loire Sauvignon, such as Sauvignon de Touraine or Haut-Poitou.

**LOBSTER** ♀ *oaked or unoaked, dry to medium-dry whites, especially Chardonnay or Riesling*

Chablis is the star with plain lobster: its honeyed flavour complements the lobster's sweet flesh to perfection. Euro-pean Chardonnay works pretty well all round – the lighter Côte d'Or Burgundies are very enjoyable, and less expen-sive white Burgundy and Italian Chardonnays are very pleasant. California Chardonnays may also be appropriate (those from Australia or Chile may be too fruity). The other successful grape variety is Riesling, particularly an off-dry, crisp German Riesling Kabinett. Austrian Grüner Veltliner goes well, and southern French Viognier, Crozes-Hermitage or Hermitage Blanc from the northern Rhône and Verdicchio all make pleasant partners. ★★ *Chablis*

**Lobster à l'Américaine** ♀ *dry whites*

The 'à l'Américaine' refers to a rich, delicious (and wicked) sauce, made with tomatoes, onion, garlic, white wine, fish stock, tarragon, brandy and lashings of butter. It is wonderful, but it does swamp the fairly delicate flavour of the lobster. Here, you are matching the sauce, not the lobster. Aromatic whites work wonders; the real stars are Arneis and Favorita, but Albariño, Sancerre and Chilean Sauvignon are all successful too, and Viognier goes pleas-antly. (New Zealand Sauvignon is too strongly flavoured,

and Muscat and Gewürztraminer are too power-fully aromatic.) White Châteauneuf-du-Pape, Rueda, Muscadet Sur Lie and VdP des Côtes de Gascogne are all good, straightforward matches.
★★ *Arneis* ★★ *Favorita*

**Lobster Pâté** ♀ *dry whites with low to medium acidity*
Recipes vary, but lobster pâté tends to be hard to match with wines. Viognier is often the best bet, but you can also try Italian Arneis or Valdadige Bianco, Spanish Penedés whites, Austrian Grüner Veltliner, Austrian or German dry Riesling, or white Corbières. ★ *Viognier*

**Lobster Thermidor** ♀ *fairly bland, dry whites*
Parmesan and bay leaf are much more dominant flavours than lobster in this dish and so these ingredients are the key to a successful match. Italian Vernaccia di San Gimignano is the closest to perfection; a gently oaked Australian Chardonnay is also good, as is Austrian Riesling Spätlese Trocken (other Rieslings are less success-ful). There are pleasant matches with Austrian Grüner Veltliner, white Châteauneuf-du-Pape, VdP des Côtes de Gascogne, Soave and Frascati.
★ *Vernaccia di San Gimignano*

**MUSSELS** ♀ *fairly bland, unoaked dry whites*
Mussels, simply steamed in a little wine, are eas-ily swamped by the wine in your glass. Muscadet Sur Lie has the most complementary flavour. Chilean Sauvignon, Seyval Blanc, or Spanish whites Yecla, Albariño and Rueda are good alter-natives. ★ *Muscadet Sur Lie*

**Moules Marinières** ♀ *dry whites with fairly high acidity*
The closest to a perfect match is with Muscadet Sur Lie; and there are plenty of good alternatives: Soave, Vernaccia, Vernaccia-Chardonnay blends from Tuscany, Bordeaux Blanc, and Picpoul from south-west France. Or try Loire Sauvignons, Sauvignon de St-Bris, Terret, Penedés whites, Bianco di Custoza or Gavi. ★ *Muscadet Sur Lie*
VARIATIONS The addition of cream and white sauce in **Moules à la crème** creates no brilliant wine

partners, but Muscadet Sur Lie and Rueda come closest. German dry Riesling is good, and Alsace Pinot Blanc, Sauvignon de St-Bris, Loire Sauvignons, unoaked white Rioja, Albariño, Hungarian Furmint, Italian Gavi and Vernaccia are all pleasant. ★ *Muscadet Sur Lie* ★ *Rueda*

## New Zealand Green-lipped Mussels ♀ *fruity, dry or dryish whites, especially Sauvignon Blanc*

TRADITIONAL PARTNER *New Zealand Sauvignon Blanc*

New Zealand Sauvignon Blanc is really a touch too powerful for these huge and wonderfully sweet-fleshed mussels. A South African or Chilean Sauvignon hits the spot more precisely, and other Sauvignons, including California, Australian and Sancerre, will go quite well unless their acidity is very high indeed. Alternative good partners are English dry Seyval Blanc or southern French Terret. ★★ *South African Sauvignon Blanc*

## OCTOPUS ♀ *a few off-dry whites, especially gentle Sauvignons*

Served plain, octopus finds few really good wine partners. Best are unoaked white Rioja and the least aromatic of Sauvignons, such as oaked Bordeaux Blanc. Provided they are not too aromatic, you can serve Sauvignon de St-Bris and Loire Sauvignons. Octopus is easily overwhelmed by other flavourings, so if the dish includes a sauce or herbs, concentrate on matching them.

## Octopus in Ink (en su Tinta) see SQUID IN INK

## OYSTERS ♀ *dry, highish- to high-acid, unoaked whites*

They have the right idea about oysters in Brittany. There's nothing like a bottle of crisp Muscadet to show them off at their best – except, perhaps, for a really dry Champagne Blanc de Blancs. Other Chardonnay and Chardonnay-Pinot Noir sparkling wines can also be very good – the drier the better. However, some New World sparkling wines taste too fruity. Best of the rest are simple (but not fine) Chablis, Sancerre, English Seyval Blanc, Rueda, Penedés and Conca de Barberá whites from Spain, and Frascati and Soave from Italy. Most New World whites are too ripely fruity, but a crisp Australian Semillon-Chardonnay can cope. Avoid all reds. Choose the most acid of the above if you are serving the oysters with lemon or vinegar. ★★ *Muscadet* ★★ *Champagne Blanc de Blancs*

VARIATIONS With **smoked** oysters, no wine is perfect, but a simple, not-too-fruity European oaked Chardonnay, especially from Hungary, blends in very well, as does the grassiness of Spanish Rueda. ★ *oaked Hungarian Chardonnay*.

**PAELLA** see *Rice and Grains*

**PRAWNS** ♀ *bland, dry whites*
Prawns have a far more delicate flavour than most wines; adding mayonnaise makes little difference. Dry Spanish whites from Valencia and Yecla are real stars. Nothing else comes close, but Spanish Albariño, Austrian Grüner Veltliner, Italian Lugana or Frascati, or Sancerre or VdP des Côtes de Gascogne are acceptable. ★★ *dry white Yecla* ★★ *dry white Valencia*

**Avocado with Prawns** see *Vegetables and Vegetable Dishes*
**Prawn Cocktail** ♀ *medium-weight, fairly high to high-acid, unoaked dry whites*
'Pink' cocktail sauce is not the wine-killer it is made out to be. You just need a white that will match its acidity, with a bit of body to stand up to its richness, and a fairly gentle flavour that won't swamp the prawns. The answer lies with high-acid Pinot Blanc from Austria, or English Seyval Blanc. Dry Pinot Blanc from Germany, and Austrian or German dry Riesling also go very well. Loire Sauvignons are very pleasant – Sancerre, Pouilly-Fumé, Reuilly, Menetou-Salon and Quincy – or try Italian Gavi, dry or nearly dry Vinho Verde, a simple Chablis or Aligoté. ★★ *Austrian Pinot Blanc* ★★ *English Seyval Blanc*

**SCALLOPS (COQUILLES ST-JACQUES)** ♀ *bland, not-too-fruity dry whites, especially Sauvignon Blanc*
Scallops vary a lot in flavour intensity and are not too easy to partner. Frozen ones often taste very bland, and so need very delicate wine partners. Fresh scallops cooked straight from the shell have a deliciously sweet yet still delicate flavour; for these, slightly more characterful wines are a good choice. However, Grüner Veltliner is a real star

with fresh scallops and pretty good with frozen ones too. Next best are Sauvignon Blancs, with soft Chilean Sauvignons leading the way, and followed by the sharper Sancerre, Pouilly-Fumé, Menetou-Salon or Sauvignon de St-Bris (New Zealand Sauvignon is much too strongly flavoured.) The flavour of Muscadet Sur Lie is just right, though it is a little too acid unless the dish contains some acidity, such as lemon juice. ★★ *Austrian Grüner Veltliner*

## Scallops Mornay ♀ *dry, fairly bland, unoaked or subtly oaked whites with medium acidity, especially Chardonnays*

The star wine is white Burgundy: simple or fine, it is a delicious match with scallops in a Gruyère-laced sauce. Unoaked, not-too-acid Chardonnays from Australia, or soft, unoaked Italian Chardonnays (such as Franciacorta Bianco) are especially good too. Seek out subtly oaked California, Australian or New Zealand Chardonnays, which are good. Chablis is too acid. Other very good matches are with Hungarian Furmint, southern French Terret, VdP des Côtes de Gascogne, and Yecla or Valencia dry whites from Spain. ★★ *white Burgundy*

## SCAMPI see LANGOUSTINE

## SEAFOOD SALAD (INSALATA DI FRUTTI DI MARE) ♀ *bland whites with good acidity*

Dressed with olive oil, lemon juice and lots of parsley, this wonderful medley of seafood is best served with Soave, if you want to drink the local wine, but a modern Spanish dry white from Valencia or Yecla is as good (modern, fresh ones have the acidity to cope). Also pleasant are Muscadet, southern French Terret or Picpoul, simple Viognier vin de pays, Austrian Grüner Veltliner, simple dry German Riesling, Pinot Grigio or English dry Seyval Blanc. ★ *Soave* ★ *Valencia dry white*

## SHRIMPS (PINK) ♀ *dry rosés* ♀ *bland, dry whites*

Aligoté is the best choice, Muscadet Sur Lie is good, and there are pleasant matches with Soave, Vernaccia, English Seyval Blanc, and Cinsault rosé. ★ *Aligoté*

VARIATIONS **Potted** pink shrimps are overwhelmed by most wines. Cinsault rosé is good again, or try a Chablis, Alsace Pinot Blanc or Crémant, Italian Lugana, Spanish Albariño or German dry Riesling. ★ *Cinsault rosé*

## SQUID ♀ *extremely bland dry whites*

Squid has a very delicate flavour; frozen squid can be practically tasteless. But even the best, freshest squid, plain grilled or fried in olive oil, finds few wine partners. Most wines are too flavourful, or the wrong flavour. Yecla or Valencia dry whites from Spain come nearest to a match.

VARIATIONS If you cook squid in **batter**, the batter and fat flavour overwhelms the squid. Try Bordeaux Blanc, Muscadet, VdP des Côtes de Gas-cogne, Soave or Frascati.

## Squid in Ink (en su Tinta) ! *medium-bodied, not-too-fruity or tannic, oaked reds* ♀ *dry, not-too-aromatic or fruity whites*

Red wines, especially oaked ones, are best with this famous Spanish dish of squid cooked in its own ink, with red wine, tomato, parsley, garlic and onion. The top Spanish red is a simple, oaked and not-too-brightly fruity Tempranillo. An oaked but not-too-mature Rioja or Ribera del Duero is also good. But the real stars come from Italy. The flavour of not-too-tannic Barolo and other Nebbi-olo wines from north-west Italy are brilliant matches; southern Italian Salice Salen-tino is also extremely good, as is Cirò. Or you could try a Sicilian red table wine, or a gentle California Pinot Noir. (The grassy flavours of Cabernet and Merlot don't work.) White wines are not very successful, but unoaked white Rioja or a bright, fruity Penedés white, Cava, unoaked, simple European Chardonnay, Chilean Sauvignon, or German dry Riesling are acceptable. (The same wines will work with octopus in ink.) ★★ *Barolo*

## WHELKS ♀ *dry, medium- to highish-acid whites*

Muscadet is the star; Aligoté and southern French Picpoul are both good. The flavour of Sauvignon Blanc works quite well, excepting those from New Zealand (and sometimes Australia), which are too tropically fruity. Other pleasant matches are with Soave, Vernaccia, Frascati, Gros Plant, Bordeaux Blanc, Austrian Grüner Veltliner, southern French Terret or Spanish Conca de Bar-berá white. ★★ *Muscadet Sur Lie*

# POULTRY AND GAME BIRDS

As poultry is usually fairly delicately flavoured, it is not surprising that white wines are more often the best choice of partner, but there are also plenty of star red matches. More flavourful birds such as duck and goose can cope with quite powerful but low-tannin reds. Even with these birds, however, other ingredients in the stuffing, sauce or marinade can easily take over as the dominant flavour.

## Chicken

Chicken's delicate flavour is easily obliterated by characterful wines. Modest, inexpensive wines are therefore likely to be the most appropriate: choose light- to medium-weight, dry or nearly dry whites; and lighter reds, equally without too much bright fruit or aromatic flavour. And oaky wines – red or white – really clash. There is little difference, when choosing a wine, between the different types of chicken, although the somewhat richer corn-fed and free-range chickens can stand up to wines with slightly more flavour.

### BARBECUED CHICKEN ❢ *not-too-tannic, gently fruity reds* ♀ *unoaked, lowish-acid dry whites*

Provided you don't singe the meat, the very gently smoky taste of barbecued chicken still calls for the same type of wines as roast or grilled chicken. (See *Roast Chicken* below). But the deciding factor for the choice of wine will probably be any accompanying sauce. See *Sauces*.
★★ *Jurançon Sec*

### CASSEROLES AND STEWS

Your wine choice depends on the ingredients, and on how reduced and concentrated you make the finished sauce.
VARIATIONS **White wine** used in a reduced sauce markedly increases the sauce's acidity, and this acidity is what you need to match. Very simple Chardonnay or Jurançon Sec are good if **cider** is the cooking liquid, but a medium cider or apples added in the sauce would call for corresponding sweetness *and* acidity in the wine: South African Chenin Blanc is a good match. For a **tomato-based sauce**, by far

the best choice is white wine, and one with good acidity: Italian Bianco di Custoza or an aromatic Sauvignon Blanc, such as Sancerre or Sauvignon de Touraine, are good. With **mushrooms** and perhaps a little **cream** in the sauce, the same wines work as for roast chicken – gentle whites and very soft, easy reds. For *Coq au Vin* and *Chicken Chasseur*, see separate entries below.

## CHICKEN CHASSEUR ❗ *fruity or savoury, not-too-tannic reds* ♀ *gently fragrant, oaked and unoaked, medium-acid whites*

With its flavourings of white wine, mushroom, shallot and (in most recipes) tomato, chicken chasseur is a dish that can take some acidity in a matching wine. A gentle Gewürztraminer is a wonderful match, and lightly oaked Chardonnays marry well, too. Chablis is good, as is the soft Spanish white from Rueda. An off-dry Pinot Gris matches the sweetness of the tomatoes. Red wine partners have to be ripe-fruited or lightly savoury to work: Australian Shiraz or Shiraz-Cabernet is good, as is Oregon Pinot Noir and Rioja Reserva. Côtes du Rhône-Villages works well, too. Or try mature red Bordeaux from a ripe vintage, a soft style of Barbaresco, or a ripe-fruited Alentejo red from Portugal. ★★ *Gewürztraminer*

## CHICKEN KIEV ♀ *unoaked, fragrant whites, especially Chardonnay*

Unoaked Chablis is the star with Chicken Kiev – anything from the basic to the grandest name works well. Unoaked Australian Chardonnay is also good, better than other white Burgundies, or California Chardonnay. Soave also suits this dish. ★★ *unoaked Chablis Premier Cru*

## CHICKEN LIVER ❗ *not-too-tannic, fairly fruity or savoury reds*

The strong flavour of chicken liver blends beautifully with the intense, savoury flavours of the Nebbiolo grape. Barolo and Barbaresco (both made with Nebbiolo) are good, though they can sometimes be a little strong when young, and a little too delicate when old. Beaujolais crus also make excellent matches, and red Châteauneuf-du-Pape is quite good. ★★ *Nebbiolo*

## Chicken Liver Pâté ❢ *not-too-tannic, fairly fruity or savoury reds* ♀ *simple, sweet whites*

At its purest, richest and simplest, with only butter, garlic and a dash of brandy added, pâté partners the same wines as plain liver. But in most shop-bought pâtés the liver flavour is diminished by other ingredients (particularly sugar!). With a pâté of this type, simple, sweet white Bordeaux wines (such as Premières Côtes de Bordeaux, Graves Supérieures, Cadillac, Ste-Croix-du-Mont and Loupiac), and Coteaux du Layon (sweet white Loire) are surprisingly delicious, but other sweet whites don't work. ★★ *sweet Graves Supérieures* ★★ *Beaujolais cru*

## CHICKEN PIE ❢ *vins de pays reds* ♀ *gentle whites*

Made with a mildly flavoured, creamy filling, chicken pie is best partnered by gentle wines such as Frascati, gentle Bordeaux Blanc, light, unoaked Chardonnays (including simple white Burgundies), Jurançon Sec and Aligoté. Inexpensive reds from Corbières, Minervois or VdP du Gard do very well. ★★ *inexpensive Italian Chardonnay*

VARIATIONS In **Chicken and ham pie**, the ham tends to be dominant and the flavour more substantial, so a Beaujolais-Villages, a light Beaujolais cru such as Fleurie, or Gamay vins de pays go well. Consult *Herbs and Spices* if the pie is heavily herbed. ★★ *Beaujolais-Villages*

## COQ AU VIN ❢ *fruity, unoaked or very subtly oaked, not-too-tannic, medium- to full-bodied reds*

TRADITIONAL PARTNER *Red Burgundy, Anjou Rouge*

Provided the oak flavour is subtle, you can safely match many Australian, California or other New World reds to this dish – Shiraz-Cabernet is brilliant, Australian Pinot Noir *very* good (far better, with its riper fruit, than the traditional red Burgundy), and ripe California, Chilean or Australian (if not too minty) Cabernet Sauvignon is also good. Red Bordeaux and grassy, herby Cabernets from cooler places work less well, and Zinfandel clashes. The flavour of simple Beaujolais or Gamay vins de pays works, and gutsier Beaujolais crus such as St-Amour and Moulin-à-Vent are a delight. Also good are red Côtes du Rhône, ripe Merlots and Provençal reds, and full, southern French vins de pays and red Burgundy make pleasant partners. With a really concentrated sauce, powerfully flavoured with bacon, glazed onion and mushroom, Beaujolais crus are a wonderful match. More savoury wines, such as Rioja Crianza, or from Italy, a Chianti or a not-too-tannic Barolo or Barbaresco, are also very good. ★★ *Australian Shiraz-Cabernet*

## CORONATION CHICKEN ♀ *off-dry rosés*
♀ *off-dry, gentle whites*

The gentle sweetness of the apricot and sugar in this dish are the main factors to take into consideration in finding a wine match. The curry flavour is very mild, and the mayonnaise and cream surprisingly unproblematic for accompanying wines. Only whites and rosés work, and the wine needs at least a touch of sweetness, but not too much acidity. South African Chenin Blanc and southern German rosé (Baden Weissherbst) are good, but the stars are fairly basic, sweetish hocks – somehow the sauce magically turns them into quite a good wine. Rheinhessen Kabinett and Spätlese are both very good (but avoid Riesling, as the acidity is too high). ★★ *inexpensive Rheinhessen Spätlese*

## DEVILLED CHICKEN ♀ *fruity Shiraz*
♀ *dry or medium-dry, lightly flavoured whites*

Devilled chicken is not as devilish as it sounds. Marinated in mustard, Worcestershire sauce and tomato ketchup, and then grilled, the chicken finds a perfect partner in South African Chenin Blanc: the touch of sweetness in the wine chimes in with the sweetish sauce. Australian Shiraz is the best of the reds. Otherwise, the same dry whites that partner plain roasted chicken (see *Roast Chicken* below) all work well: Jurançon Sec and very simple Chardonnay are both good. If the devilled sauce is quite sweet (with vinegar and more sugar added), demi-sec Vouvray and demi-sec Champagne have the right balance of acidity and sweetness to cope. ★★ *South African Chenin Blanc*

## FRICASSÉE ❦ *medium-bodied Cabernet* ♀ *light, low-acid whites*

The star choice with this gently flavoured dish is a light, unoaked southern French Chardonnay. Light Italian whites – Frascati, Soave, Vernaccia and Vermentino – are also good, and light Penedés or Conca de Barberá whites from Spain also blend in well with the white sauce. If you fancy drinking red wine, try a not-too-powerful Australian Cabernet. ★★ *unoaked southern French Chardonnay*

## FRIED (AND SOUTHERN FRIED) CHICKEN
❦ *not-too-tannic, gently fruity reds* ♀ *unoaked, lowish-acid dry whites*

You can serve slightly more flavourful wines of the same type as roast chicken (see below) with fried and southern fried chicken, although the very mildest whites, such as Frascati, fail to stand up to the dish. ★★ *Jurançon Sec*

## LEMON CHICKEN ♀ *highish-acid, bland whites*

Roasted with a cut-up lemon in the cavity, the juice of which is then squeezed into the gravy, lemon chicken is brilliant with Bourgogne Aligoté, or a good, bright, modern Hungarian Furmint. Other similarly styled whites go quite well, too: Muscadet, Cheverny, VdP des Côtes de Gascogne, Seyval Blanc and Champagne. Conca de Barberá and Penedés whites from Spain nicely emphasize the lemon zest flavour without overwhelming the chicken. If the amount of lemon juice used is kept fairly low, Italian Pinot Grigio and white Crozes-Hermitage have the right flavour. ★★ *Bourgogne Aligoté* ★★ *Hungarian Furmint*

## ROAST (OR GRILLED) CHICKEN ❦ *unoaked, low-tannin, light to medium-bodied, gently fruity reds* ♀ *unoaked, lowish-acid, light to medium-bodied, unaromatic dry whites*

Whether roasted (plainly) or grilled, chicken goes best with Jurançon Sec, followed by Frascati, simple dry white Bordeaux, or simple whites from the Penedés. Bland, low-acid whites work best, but simple white Burgundies, whether made from Chardonnay or Aligoté, are good; and light, unoaked Chardonnays are pleasant. Stronger flavoured or very fruity wines swamp the fairly delicate flavour of the meat. Some light or medium-weight reds are also successful, especially the lighter styles of Corbières,

Minervois and southern French vins de pays, or light, not-too-aromatic Shiraz, and simple, not-too-fruity Cabernet Sauvignon. Avoid oaked reds and savoury, too-brightly fruity or aromatic flavours, as these clash. ★★ *Jurançon Sec*

VARIATIONS Add other ingredients to the dish, and you can up the flavour level of the wine. Chicken roasted with lots of whole cloves of **garlic** can stand up to a more expensive (but not too oaky) New World Chardonnay or a good, traditional white Burgundy or Chablis up to premier cru level. It also copes with Australian or Bulgarian Cabernet Sauvignon. ★★ *Australian or California Chardonnay*. With **sage and onion stuffing**, the cedary character of a not-too-tannic Chianti Classico blends in wonderfully. Cabernet and red Bordeaux clash with the sage, but Shiraz is good, as is young red Côtes du Rhône. The sage also upsets many white wines, although Jurançon Sec still wins as a good match. ★★ *Chianti Classico*. **Tarragon** gives a fairly strong, aniseedy flavour to roast chicken that makes it a less acceptable match with red wines, but the same white wine guidelines apply as for plain roast chicken. Unoaked Chardonnay and South African Chenin Blanc are particularly good choices. ★★ *South African Chenin Blanc*. **Bread sauce** is hard to match, but red Minervois (which is also good with the chicken) is a real star. Simple white Bordeaux and Burgundy are passable partners, but Frascati clashes with the milkiness of the sauce. ★★ *red Minervois*

**SATAY** see *Thai Dishes*

## SMOKED CHICKEN ♀ *gently flavoured, oaked whites*

Simple, inexpensive oaked Chardonnay is the best choice, flattering the smoky flavour in the meat, but other oaked whites, particularly from Spain, are also good. Oaked Bourgogne Aligoté goes well, and Semillon-Chardonnay is a reasonable match. Reds, however, clash horribly. ★★ *not-too-expensive oaked Australian Chardonnay*

# Duck

The domestic breeds of duck have much more delicately flavoured meat than their wild cousins. But despite its delicate flavour, duck can take much fuller, more flavoursome white and red wines than chicken. But once again, the flavour of any sauces served with duck will dominate the dish; sweet sauces especially must be the focus of the wine choice. (For wild duck, see *Game Birds* below.)

## CONFIT DE CANARD ❗ *not-too-tannic, fruity or savoury reds* ♀ *dry, gently fragrant whites*

TRADITIONAL PARTNER *Jurançon Sec*

If you're visiting confit country in south-west France, choose a Jurançon Sec – the best of the local wines – or an up-market Bordeaux Blanc, Béarn Blanc, or a dry Pacherenc du Vic-Bilh to drink with this rich duck meat, heart-stoppingly preserved in its own fat. But the star white choice is Alsace Tokay-Pinot Gris – as the people of Alsace will agree. Confit de canard is also surprisingly good with Frascati. Other less perfect but still enjoyable white choices – all French – are white Châteauneuf-du-Pape, VdP des Côtes de Gascogne and southern French Terret. Sauvignons and Chardonnays have the wrong flavour. Confit de canard can also cope with slightly bigger reds than plain duck. Of the reds, not-too-tannic Barolo, Barbaresco or other Nebbiolos are real stars, and the flavour of Barbera blends in very well. Soft red Burgundy is also good, as is Spanish Tempranillo rosado. ★★ *Alsace Tokay-Pinot Gris* ★★ *not-too-tannic Barolo*

## DUCK BREASTS (MAGRETS DE CANARD) see ROAST DUCK

## DUCK PÂTÉ (PÂTÉ DE CANARD)

❗ *not-too-tannic, fruity reds* ♀ *medium-acid, dry and sweet whites*

Orange, port, other meats such as pork, and a touch of sweetness often find their way into duck pâtés. Whatever the other ingredients, for a pâté that *doesn't* contain foie gras, Chianti Classico is a successful choice. ★★ *Chianti Classico*

VARIATIONS If **orange** is an obvious ingredient, inexpensive Australian or Alsace Riesling or a Mosel Kabinett are good choices; Coteaux du Layon and other sweet whites from the Loire are brilliant. Other good reds include Rioja Crianza and oaked Tempranillo or Cencibel from Spain. ★★ *Coteaux du Layon.* As well as its perfect partners, a duck pâté sweetened with **port** goes quite well with Alsace or Washington State Late Harvest Riesling or Coteaux du Layon. ★★ *Graves Supérieures* ★★ *Mosel Kabinett.* Unsurprisingly, **pâté de foie gras** is superb with Sauternes, and with other wines that match foie gras (see below). ★★ *Sauternes*

## FOIE GRAS DE CANARD ♀ *sweet, medium-acid whites; fine, dry Australian Riesling and fine Chablis*
TRADITIONAL PARTNER *Sauternes*

Sauternes, as Bordeaux gastronomes have always known, is the unchallenged partner for this luxurious dish. There's something about the rich, sweet 'rotted' flavour of the botrytized (nobly rotted) grapes, and the creaminess and sweetness of the foie gras that makes a wonderful combination. Other sweet Bordeaux – such as Barsac, Premières Côtes de Bordeaux, Graves Supérieures, Cadillac, Ste-Croix-du-Mont or Loupiac, or those from the nearby Monbazillac region – are also good. (The California and Australian equivalent, botrytized Semillon, tends to be too sweet and overpowering.) Coteaux du Layon and sweet German wines are too high in acidity (as is sweet New Zealand Riesling), but California and Australian Late Harvest Riesling work well. The flavour of Riesling is good, and even dry Australian Rieslings, with their lower acidity, work well – but they must be the more expensive, *intensely* flavoured ones. Sweet Recioto di Soave is also a success, though it lacks the complexity of botrytis. Sweet Jurançon is good, though some are too strong in flavour, so too is unoaked Chablis Grand Cru, and a sweetish Alsace Pinot Gris Vendange Tardive is also delicious. However, foie gras clashes with Champagne, and with the tannin of red wines. ★★ *Sauternes*

**PEKING DUCK** see *Chinese Dishes*

**ROAST DUCK** ❢ *not-too-tannic, savoury reds* ♀ *crisp, medium-acid unoaked whites*

A soft, low-tannin red made from northern Italy's Nebbiolo grape blends in beautifully with the fairly delicate flavour of domestic duck. Barbera is also quite good, as is soft red Burgundy. But there are more whites than reds that make reasonable matches with roast duck: Alsace Tokay-Pinot Gris, VdP des Côtes de Gascogne, Jurançon Sec, Frascati, and Bordeaux Blanc are all good choices. (Oak, tannin and the flavour of Cabernet Sauvignon clash.) ★★ *modern, low-tannin Nebbiolo*

VARIATIONS With the classic **orange sauce**, the acidity and gentle sweetness of Vouvray Demi-sec from the Loire are just right. Sweet Bordeaux such as Premières Côtes de Bordeaux, Graves Supérieures or a modest Sauternes also go well, but you may baulk at drinking a fully sweet wine at this stage of the meal. ★★ *Vouvray Demi-sec*. With **cherry sauce**, German wines provide many of the best answers: a Riesling Spätlese from the Mosel is superb, and even soft, sweetish Kabinetts and QbAs from the Pfalz and Rheinhessen work quite well. A ripe Australian Verdelho is also a good foil for the sweetness of the cherry sauce. And that's just the whites – the cherry flavour widens the possible partners to a number of red wines as well. They have to be fruity. Beaujolais and the various Beaujolais crus are lovely, while Australian Shiraz and Cabernet Sauvignon wines are also very good. ★★ *Mosel Riesling Spätlese* ★ *Beaujolais cru*

**SMOKED DUCK** ♀ *oaked, crisp whites*

Oaked white Rioja is the answer to this tricky dish, but unlike plain roast duck, smoked duck does not find any good partners with Chardonnay – including white Burgundies. As an alternative, Muscadet is a pleasant choice. Red wines also clash. ★★ *oaked white Rioja*

# Goose

Goose is the richest of rich, fatty meats, even once you've pricked the skin and much of the fat has run out in the roasting. Once upon a time, it was the traditional Christmas meat, a sumptuously rich, celebratory meal. In our fat-conscious age, eating such a rich meat with all the trimmings seems almost sinful.

**CASSOULET** see *Pork*

**CHOUCROUTE** see *Pork*

**CONFIT D'OIE** see ROAST GOOSE

**FOIE GRAS** see *Duck*

**ROAST GOOSE** ❗ *not-too-tannic, fruity or savoury reds, especially Cabernet, and especially if mature* ♀ *off-dry, light whites*
Unadorned roast goose offers a perfect excuse to drink a really good bottle of mature, fine red Bordeaux, preferably from a ripe vintage. Clarets from the village of Margaux, with their sweet perfume, are particularly delicious. Also brilliant, especially if you enjoy the crisp, brown skin of the goose, is Australian Cabernet Sauvignon from Coonawarra or Barossa Valley. Other good reds include Australian Shiraz-Cabernet and Merlot, California Cabernet Sauvignon (as long as it isn't too tannic), Oregon Pinot Noir, Beaujolais or the Beaujolais crus (Fleurie, Moulin-à-Vent etc), red Châteauneuf-du-Pape, a mature Nebbiolo such as Barbaresco or Barolo, Rioja Reserva, and red wines from the Alentejo in Portugal. If you prefer whites, best choices are off-dry German Riesling Halbtrocken or Kabinett from the Pfalz and Rheingau, or Champagne (not Blanc de Blancs). Or, Aligoté, off-dry Vouvray, unoaked Chablis, off-dry Jurançon, basic wines from the Mosel, and Vinho Verde are all fine. ★★ *mature red Bordeaux* ★★ *Barossa Valley Cabernet Sauvignon* ★★ *Coonawarra Cabernet Sauvignon* ★ *German Riesling Kabinett* ★ *Champagne*

VARIATIONS When you start taking the fruity accompaniments into account, reds drop out of the picture. You need white wines with highish acidity and enough sweetness to balance the fruit. With **prune and apple stuffing**, sweetish Vouvray Demi-sec and German Riesling Kabinett come into their own, as well as even sweeter whites such as German Spätlese and Auslese Rieslings, other sweet white Chenins of the Loire (Coteaux du Layon, Coteaux de l'Aubance, Coteaux du Saumur) and perhaps a Pacherenc de Vic-Bilh from the south-west of France. ★★ *Vouvray Demi-sec*. For the traditional **sage and onion stuffing**, a red Côtes du Rhône or an Australian Merlot will go with both stuffing and goose, but avoid red Bordeaux, Cabernet Sauvignon and Shiraz as they clash with the sage. ★★ *red Côtes du Rhône*

# Guinea Fowl

It is much harder to find good partnering wines for Guinea fowl than for duck. The meat is only slightly more flavoursome than chicken, a little denser and darker, and very, very slightly gamy. It is also easily overwhelmed by other flavours, so once again it is important to take any accompanying sauce or casserole ingredients into account when choosing a wine.

**CASSEROLES AND STEWS** see *Chicken*

**ROAST GUINEA FOWL** ❢ ❢*light, low-tannin Pinot Noir* ♀ *medium-bodied, unoaked or lightly oaked, not-too-fruity, gently flavoured whites*
Guinea fowl demands quite particular flavours in the accompanying wine. A simple, buttery Chablis hits the spot, and a simple, unoaked southern French, Italian or Eastern European Chardonnay is next best. New World or 'New World style' Chardonnays are too fruity for this meat. Other reasonable white matches are with South African Chenin Blanc, white Côtes du Rhône, and Alsace Pinot Blanc. Practically all reds taste too tannic, but if you choose a very light, untannic Pinot Noir, such as Sancerre Rouge, the flavour of the grape variety works well. ★★ *unoaked, inexpensive Chablis*

# Quail

These tiny birds have such a diminutive flavour that they are easily overwhelmed by a wine, or indeed by a stuffing or sauce – and the latter will tend to be the focus of a wine match rather than the meat itself.

### ROAST QUAIL ♀ *bland whites*

The star choice is a gentle Spanish white from Rueda; very gentle Italian Chardonnay or German Silvaner Trocken also make good flavour combinations with plain roast quail, though even these are a touch *too* flavourful. Other reasonable matches are with Vernaccia di San Gimignano, Frascati, Bianco di Custoza, Soave and South African Chenin Blanc. When serving roast quail with a sauce or stuffing, your choice of wine will be affected by the latter's dominant flavours.
★★ *Rueda*

## Turkey

Turkey, with its slightly earthier, robustly flavoursome meat, can take wines with rounder, richer flavours than chicken. Red wines make better partners than white, as long as they are not too tannic. Whites must be dry and barely – if at all – touched by oak, and preferably not too marked by the buttery flavour of malolactic fermentation (see page 226).

### BLANQUETTE OF TURKEY ♥ *not-too-tannic, light, fruity reds* ♥ *Pinot Noir rosés* ♀ *gentle whites*

A number of white wines are very successful with this mild-flavoured dish. The southern French Terret, Chardonnay and Bianco di Custoza from Italy, and Conca de Barberá from Spain are all stars. Runners-up are Frascati, Soave Classico, Est! Est!! Est!!! and white Côtes du Rhône. White Burgundies do not really work, but inexpensive Chardonnays from California, Australia, Chile and elsewhere are possible, if a little strong in flavour. Whites are better than reds, but some light, fruity, low-tannin reds work adequately: try Beaujolais or Beaujolais-Villages or Teroldego Rotaliano. Australian Cabernet Sauvignon is a touch too tannic, but the fruit carries it through, and it nicely emphasizes the creaminess of the sauce. You could also try a Sancerre Rosé.
★★ *unoaked Chardonnay VdP d'Oc*

## CASSEROLES AND STEWS see *Chicken*

## CURRIED TURKEY ❢ *not-too-tannic, full-bodied, fruity reds* ♀ *fruity, medium-bodied whites*

Australia leads the way. Australian Verdelho, a ripe and intensely fruity white, is superb with this traditional, post-Christmas curry. Unoaked Australian Semillon or Marsanne are nearly as wonderful, and Australian Semillon-Chardonnay is an honourable runner-up. Pinot Gris from Hungary is also a star, and Italian Pinot Grigio goes quite well. A rich Alsace Pinot Blanc also makes an excellent match, and Champagne goes well if it has a touch of sweetness, as most 'dry' (*brut*) Champagnes do. Reds also need to be full and fruity, and not too tannic. The star red is modern red Portuguese Alentejo, with plenty of fruit, and the fruitiness of Australian Shiraz works well, too. You can also try a red Côtes du Ventoux, Australian Cabernets, or Spanish Tempranillos. ★★ *Australian Verdelho* ★★ *red Portuguese Alentejo*

## DEVILLED TURKEY see DEVILLED CHICKEN

## ROAST TURKEY ❢ *not-too-tannic, brightly fruity or rich reds* ♀ *dry, unoaked, gently flavoured whites*

There are several stunning choices of red wine to serve with roast turkey, but the star is Australian Shiraz; even those that overwhelm the turkey's flavour do so with great style and make a really lovely combination. The bright fruit of Australian Shiraz-Cabernet or Cabernet-Shiraz blends also suits turkey brilliantly. Not-too-tannic California, Australian or Chilean Cabernet Sauvignons are excellent. Red Bordeaux tends to be too tannic or grassy, and short on really ripe fruit. The very raspberryish flavour of northern Rhône reds is quite good, but not as good as a rich Shiraz. Zinfandel doesn't clash, but is too bright and fruity. Among whites, the gentle flavour of a simple Chablis works well, and Chablis Premier Cru is also good, though a little strongly flavoured. Other white Burgundies and Chardonnays are less successful. Spanish rosado made from the Garnacha grape is another possibility. Champagne (not Blanc de Blancs) makes a reasonable match, but a softer sparkling wine from California, New Zealand or Australia, made with the Champagne grapes, is a more appropriate flavour and character. ★★ *Australian Shiraz*

VARIATIONS The sauces and stuffings of Christmas make a big difference, and the variety makes matching quite hard. Consecutive mouthfuls might mix turkey with cranberry sauce, sausage-meat stuffing, chesnut stuffing, then bread sauce. Sharp and sweet **cranberry sauce** is perhaps best avoided altogether, especially if you wish to serve a fine wine: it tastes awful even with appropriately sweet, acid wines, and really dire with the reds and dry whites that otherwise go with turkey – and the wines taste disgusting, too. **Sausage-meats** have varying degrees of herbing. Add onion and *fresh* herbs (thyme, marjoram, parsley and a little bit of sage), and untannic California, Australian or Chilean Cabernet (very good with the turkey) are stars. Shiraz is quite good, but the flavour of the stuffing wipes out Chablis and clashes with Champagne. However, with sausage-meat strongly flavoured with *dried* herbs (often quite a lot of sage), Cabernet (especially from California) and Shiraz are much less successful, and Chablis and Champagne are again a failure. Recipes vary, but with (sausage-meat-free) **chestnut stuffing** a good red Côtes du Rhône or a soft fruity Merlot can be good (and both of these are adequate with turkey). With **apple and cashew nut stuffing**, Champagne is a good choice. Shiraz-Cabernet blends work brilliantly with **cranberry and orange stuffing**, Shiraz or Cabernet varietals do quite well, and Champagne and Chablis are adequate. **Sage and onion stuffing** is a difficult one to match. Too much dried sage clashes with Cabernet, Shiraz and Champagne. Red Côtes du Rhône is a star, and a ripe Merlot quite good, while Chablis just about copes. As for **bread sauce**, wines that flatter the turkey clash with the sauce, apart from Australian, California and Chilean Merlot, which go well, and red Côtes du Rhône, which is adequate. Oh dear. Will the food be crowded off your Christmas table by a multitude of glasses of different wines? Relax. Food purists who fancy all the trimmings will just have to compromise on the wine choice. Wine purists can choose the trimmings that suit their wine.

# GAME BIRDS

Most game birds have strong, dark meat that is usually well matched by big, flavourful reds. Even the delicate partridge is a red wine bird. Too much tannin, however, or too much bright fruit, is often out of place.

With surprisingly regularity, given the difference in flavour between the birds, the real star wines are Crozes-Hermitage, St-Joseph, Hermitage, Côte-Rôtie and Rhône vins de pays made with Syrah. These are also good solutions for pâtés, terrines or pies made from a mix of game meats. (Though Sangiovese di Toscana or Chianti may make a better match for pâtés or terrines in which the proportion of game is quite low.) If red wine is used in the sauce, the range of wines that are good accompaniments is greatly broadened, even with woodpigeon, which finds few matches when roasted plainly.

## Grouse

### ROAST GROUSE ❗ *not-too-tannic, medium- or full-bodied reds*
The strong, gamy, almost smoky flavour of grouse is set off brilliantly by the smoky character of Syrah, especially from the northern Rhône (St-Joseph, Hermitage and Côte-Rôtie, as well as Crozes). Syrah from further south in the Côtes du Rhône is quite good, but Australian Shiraz is too brashly fruity and overwhelms the meat. Nebbiolo from northern Italy is also a star, provided it is not too tannic – grouse dislikes tannin. (Very brightly fruity and oaky wines are also wrong.) Other fairly good matches are with Corbières reds, Rosso di Montalcino, and the powerful Amarone della Valpolicella, its rich, ripe fruit really complementing the very savoury, smoky character of the meat.
★★ *red Crozes-Hermitage*

## Partridge

One of the mildest-flavoured game birds, partridge tastes rather like very flavourful chicken, but with that added smoky tang of game.

### CASSEROLES AND STEWS see *Chicken: Casseroles and Stews*

## PARTRIDGE WITH CABBAGE (PERD-RIX AUX CHOUX) ❢ *not-too-tannic, fruity reds* ♀ *unoaked, gently fruity whites*

Wine pairings vary a little depending on whether white or red wine is used in this classic French dish made with cabbage, bacon and juniper. White Côtes du Rhône is good with either version. Hungarian unoaked Chardonnay is a wonderful match with a white wine version. Unoaked Chardonnays from elsewhere are reasonable, while Frascati is very good, and white Corbières quite pleasant. Cooked in red wine, the stew is as satisfying with an easy, light, savoury Rosso del Piemonte as with the white Côtes du Rhône. Nothing else is as good, but you could serve Hungarian Furmint, or southern French red vins de pays, Oregon Pinot Noir or Australian Shiraz. Tannin is best avoided. ★★ *white Côtes du Rhône*

## ROAST PARTRIDGE ❢ *fruity Shiraz or not-too-tannic, mature reds*

Reds are best, but partridge is easily overpowered by too much tannin, fruit or flavour, and it clashes with oak and grassy, herbaceous flavours. Fruity, flavourful Australian Shiraz is the delicious exception. The finer northern Rhônes are too strong, but Syrah vin de pays is good. Otherwise, try South African Merlot (less grassy than other Merlots) or a gentle, mature (but not grassy) red Bordeaux, ideally from St-Émilion or Pomerol. A light, savoury, untannic Côte de Beaune red also works, though a really fine, concentrated one drowns the partridge. You could also drink Bairrada if mature and/or not too tannic, or red Rioja. ★★ *Australian Shiraz*

# Pheasant

## CASSEROLES AND STEWS ❢ *elegant, not-too-tannic, fruity or savoury reds*

Casseroled in red wine, onion and garlic, pheasant is *perfectly* matched only by Crozes-Hermitage or other northern or southern Rhône reds. Beaujolais crus, such as Côte de Brouilly, and Oregon Pinot Noir are nearly as good, and the slightly earthy, savoury flavours of Chianti Classico and other Sangioveses, and of Barbaresco and other Nebbiolos, work well. For a not-too-high pheasant, red Rioja is good and Australian or Chilean Cabernet Sauvignon make a lovely match. ★★ *red Crozes-Hermitage*

## PHEASANT NORMANDE (FAISAN NORMANDE) ♀ *off-dry whites*

Reds don't really complement the apples and cream in this classic Normandy recipe, and many whites taste too dry. The apple also calls for a touch of sweetness in the wine. Hungarian Pinot Gris is excellent, vying for top match with an off-dry South African Colombard. Hock – German wine from the Rhine – works quite well. A light Australian Semillon is good, if a touch too fruity, or you can try soft, unaromatic Sauvignons from Bordeaux, Chile or South Africa, Vermentino di Sardegna, or a Spanish rosado. ★★ *Hungarian Pinot Gris*

## PHEASANT PÂTÉ (OR TERRINE) ❢ *young, vibrant or mature, savoury reds* ♀ *dry Chardonnay and/or Pinot Noir sparkling whites*

The pheasant flavour in the pâté (and terrines) tends to be muted by other ingredients, often pork. The star is a San-giovese di Toscana, which works well with a mix of game birds. Wines from the Gamay grape – Beaujolais-Villages, Beaujolais crus, or Touraine Gamay – are a good choice, as are Valpolicella or Rosso del Piemonte, or Portuguese Cabernet-Periquita blends. Of the whites, Champagne is good, but the richer, riper style of California, New Zealand and Australian sparkling wines (made with the Champagne grapes) is even better. ★★ *Sangiovese di Toscana*

## ROAST PHEASANT ❢ *lightly tannic, savoury reds*

Whether high or fresh, roast pheasant tastes stunningly wonderful with a light, savoury Oregon Pinot Noir. How-ever, light, very untannic red Burgundy is no more than acceptable. Crozes-Hermitage is another star, and untan-nic red Bordeaux, Beaujolais-Villages, Côtes du Rhône and soft Chianti/Sangiovese go quite well. The savoury fruit of a young red Rioja is just right for the gamey flavour, though it can't cope with a very high pheasant. ★★ *Oregon Pinot Noir* ★★ *red Crozes-Hermitage*

# Wild Duck

Wild breeds of duck have richer, darker meat, with far more flavour than the domestic duck (see *Poultry*), and can partner correspondingly more flavourful reds.

**MALLARD** ❢ *fruity, not-too-tannic, rich reds*
The Mallard differs from most other game birds in liking *fruity,* but not too tannic reds, while any savoury, gamy flavours in the wine are a bonus. Red Crozes-Hermitage or St-Joseph from the northern Rhône make really stunning matches, but Mallard can also cope with a fruitier Australian Shiraz or Shiraz-Cabernet. Southern Rhônes (Côtes du Rhône, Côtes du Rhône-Village, but not Châteauneuf-du-Pape) and Provençal reds go quite well. From Italy, Brunello di Montalcino, Chianti Classico and other rich Sangiovese wines and not-too-tannic Nebbiolo wines are successful. Rich Zinfandel is also excellent. ★★ *red Crozes-Hermitage*

# Woodcock

**ROAST WOODCOCK** ❢ *not-too-tannic, savoury or fruity, medium-bodied reds*
Flavourful reds, but nothing too fruity or tannic, are needed for this dark, savoury, gamy bird. Apart from the stunning match with Italian Cirò Riserva, a red from the Alentejo in Portugal makes a delicious combination, and so does a mature but still fruity fine red Bordeaux. The leathery character of Australian Shiraz or Shiraz-Cabernet marries well, and mature red Burgundy is fine. You could also serve Côtes du Rhône, or California Cabernet, Portuguese Ribatejo or Bairrada, Brunello di Montalcino or Oregon Pinot Noir. ★★ *Cirò Riserva*

# Wood Pigeon

The very dark, dense, almost smoky-tasting meat of pigeon is very hard to match when simply roasted. It has quite the wrong flavour for wines that have more than a minimum of tannin, fruit and oak, and it swamps gently flavoured wines – both whites and lighter reds. Mature wines are often the best choice, though sauces can change the story completely.

## CASSEROLE (MATELOTE) ❢ *rich, fruity reds*
Red wine, caramelized onions and bacon transform this wine-shy bird into a (red) wine-friendly pigeon casserole, very similar in flavour to coq au vin. Three super-star combinations with this classic French dish are Cirò Riserva from Italy, Oregon Pinot Noir and Portuguese Cabernet-Periquita blends. But other reds are nearly as delicious: Australian Shiraz-Cabernet, rich, red Minervois, Fleurie or other Beaujolais crus, Chianti Classico, Rosso Conero, red Alentejo, or Zinfandel. Or try Rioja Reserva, red Burgundy, Barberá, Rosso del Piemonte, Australian Shiraz, Côtes du Rhône, or Bairrada. ★★ *Oregon Pinot Noir* ★★ *Cirò Riserva* ★★ *Portuguese Cabernet-Periquita*

## ROAST PIGEON ❢ *not-too-tannic, savoury reds*
Mature reds with a minimum of tannin are the best option to complement this dark, slightly smoky, flavourful meat, but nothing makes a really *superb* match with plain roast pigeon. Whites are completely overwhelmed. Portuguese Periquita comes closest to a match, and Periquita-Cabernet blends from Ribatejo are pleasant alternatives. From Italy, a not-too-tannic Chianti Classico or a Cirò Riserva from southern Italy is quite good, and red Rioja goes quite well. ★ *Ribatejo red*

## WARM PIGEON BREASTS ON SALAD ❢ *fruity, medium-bodied, highish-acid reds* ⚲ *a few off-dry whites*
The fine-tuning depends on the type of salad dressing used. One made with (sweetish) balsamic vinegar and olive oil needs to be matched by a white wine with a touch of sweetness (or a brightly fruity red). The best red match, is with a good, fruity, but grassy vintage from Pomerol or St-Émilion in Bordeaux, and California and Australian Merlot or Bulgarian Merlot Reserve also go well. Zinfandel is another star, as is a fruity Alentejo or Cabernet-Periquita blend from Portugal. Valpolicella, Oregon Pinot Noir, Beaujolias crus, such as Fleurie, or Rioja Reserva are all acceptable alternatives. ★ *Pomerol*

# MEAT

The 'red wine, red meat' rule works. Almost. In the absence of a sauce, red wine does go better than whites with plain red meats. But you may need a much gentler red wine than you'd bargained for. Lamb and pork can both take fairly full reds, but unless it is cooked in red wine, beef needs light reds. Earthy venison and hare are difficult to match with anything without the aid of a sauce, and certainly no white could cope. And whatever the meat, anything more than a moderate level of tannin in a red wine is out of place. The 'white wine with white meat' rule stands up less well in practice. It's true for veal, which is quite overpowered by reds (unless, again, a sauce or other ingredient comes to the rescue). Pork goes better with reds but makes some good white matches too. But rabbit, definitely a white meat, calls for red wines. Boiled meats tend to need much lighter-bodied, more gently flavoured wines than roast or grilled meats, and fried meats may cope with something gutsier. But, as always, when you add other flavourings, the scope changes.

## Beef

Beef is not the great 'heavyweight' meat it's made out to be. Roast beef or steak, cooked plain, are best flattered by far lighter reds than you might expect. However beef is cooked, there's a good chance that the perfect partner will be wines made from the Gamay grape: Beaujolais, from the light, simple Beaujolais-Villages, up to the richer, finer Beaujolais crus (see page 5 for the full list), or Gamay de Touraine and Gamay vins de pays.

### BEEF BOURGUIGNONNE ❢ *low-tannin, ripe, really fruity, medium-acid reds* ♀ *dry or dryish whites*
TRADITIONAL PARTNER red Burgundy
A slight sweetness in this gently flavoursome dish succeeds with the ripe young fruit of soft, untannic red Burgundy. Ripe, inexpensive Cabernet

Sauvignons – perhaps from Chile, Australia or (most successful of all) California – make good matches, but they are all out-starred by Cabernet-Merlot blends. The super-ripe fruit of Australian Cabernet-Merlot hits the spot perfectly, and California and Chilean Cabernet-Merlots are also delicious. (Expensive ones may be too powerful.) Untannic red Bordeaux is also good, though Merlot-based St-Émilion and Pomerol is better than Cabernet-based Médoc. For white wine drinkers, a rich Pinot Gris from Hungary or Alsace makes a lovely partner (Italian Pinot Grigio is too light and tangy), and Alsace Pinot Blanc, Sauvignon de Touraine or other aromatic, high-acid Sauvignons, white Côtes du Rhône or Viognier are very pleasant. ★★ *Australian Cabernet-Merlot*

## BEEFBURGER see BURGERS

## BEEF STROGANOFF ❢ *medium-bodied, low-tannin reds ♀ gently aromatic, low-acid dry whites*

This is really a dish to serve with white wines, although Brunello di Montalcino, one of the few successful medium- to full-bodied reds, puts in a star performance as well. South African Colombard is top white, chiming in well with the creamy sauce, but the flavour of Riesling is also remarkably good. Alsace, New Zealand, dry Australian and German Riesling Trocken (dry) all work well. German Silvaner Trocken and Alsace Sylvaner are a little too acid, but complement the flavour of the sauce. ★★ *Brunello di Montalcino* ★★ *South African Colombard*

## BEEF WELLINGTON ❢ *gently tannic, fruity or savoury reds*

The paste of shallot and mushroom, Madeira and liver pâté sandwiched between the beef fillet and its pastry jacket has a strong character that rarely clashes, but equally rarely makes a positive match with wine. The successful partners are always red. They may be light- to medium-bodied like the excellently matched Beaujolais crus (such as Côte de Brouilly or Fleurie), very good northern Italian Dolcetto, or adequate Loire Cabernets (such as Bourgueil or Chinon). They can also be really full, like the perfect match with red Châteauneuf-du-Pape, or pleasant Rosso Conero from eastern Italy, or Australian Shiraz-Cabernet or Shiraz. ★★ *red Châteauneuf-du-Pape*

## BOILED BEEF AND CARROTS ❢ *light, low-tannin, fruity reds* ❢ *dry rosés*

The salty but gentle flavour of boiled beef requires lighter reds than roast, fried or grilled beef; intense or tannic reds are overpowering. And the natural sweetness of the carrots calls for fruitiness in the wine. Rosé also fits the bill – Spanish Tempranillo rosado is a star. Valpolicella Classico is by far the best red. Beaujolais-Villages goes quite well, and the Beaujolais crus (Fleurie, Juliénas and the like) have the right flavour although they are a little strong. ★★ *Tempranillo rosado* ★★ *Valpolicella Classico*

## BRESAOLA ❢ *soft reds* ❢ *northern Italian sparkling rosés* ♀ *unoaked, gentle Chardonnays*

TRADITIONAL PARTNER Valtellina Superiore
Served in the classic northern Italian way with olive oil, lemon juice and black pepper, these thin slices of cured and air-dried fillet have too delicate a flavour for most reds (even more so without the dressing). This includes the tannic red Valtellina traditionally drunk with this dish. Another Italian red, Valpolicella, however, is brilliant. Beaujolais-Villages is good, and the meat can just about stand up to a Beaujolais cru or southern French Gamay vins de pays. The Pinot-based sparkling rosés from northern Italy are a triumph. As for whites, unoaked Chardonnay del Piemonte works quite well, as do simple white Burgundy and other fairly gentle, unoaked Chardonnays from elsewhere. Southern Italian Vermentino works better than the local white grapes of the north. ★★ *northern Italian sparkling rosé* ★★ *Valpolicella Classico*

## BURGERS

**Beefburger** ❢ *unoaked, fruity, low-tannin reds* ♀ *unoaked, crisp whites*

The onions in a beefburger have a big influence on the wine match. Italian Dolcetto is the star choice, chiming in well with the onions, as does Italian Barbera (California Barbera is only adequate). Next best would be Fitou or other simple southern French reds, or a young red Rioja. Valpolicella, Italian reds such as Carmignano or Chianti, Australian Shiraz or Cabernet-Shiraz also go fairly well. Few whites have anything in common with beefburgers. A crisp, honeyed Chardonnay VdP d'Oc is best, followed by Vernaccia, Pinot Grigio or a not-too-aromatic Sauvignon. ★★ *Dolcetto* ★★ *Italian Barbera*

## Hamburger ¶ *unoaked, fruity, low-tannin reds*

Served plain, hamburgers are not overly wine-friendly. With their bright fruit, California or Oregon Pinot Noirs are stars, and Rosso di Montalcino, Chianti, and Dolcetto are pleasant alternatives. Red Burgundy from a ripe year also works well. Or you can try California Syrah, or California or Australian Cabernet. ★★ *California or Oregon Pinot Noir*

VARIATIONS Gherkins, cheese, raw onion, tomato ketchup, mayonnaise, salad, mustard: it all sounds like a wine-killer cocktail. In fact, though, the full-blown **cheeseburger** is really easy to match, easier than a plain hamburger. Mayonnaise (in small quantities) is not a problem, and Dijon mustard has a wonderful softening effect on tannic red wines. Medium- to full-bodied reds work. Brunello, Zinfandel or young red Rioja are really superb with cheeseburgers, though only acceptable with a simple hamburger. California or Oregon Pinot Noir are successful again – the bright fruit is a good foil for the cheese and relishes – and ripe, red Burgundy also works. The Portuguese Bairrada makes a good match; and Rosso di Montalcino, Chianti and Dolcetto are good. ★★ *Brunello* ★★ *Zinfandel* ★★ *young red Rioja*

## CARBONNADE À LA FLAMANDE ¶ *low-tannin, medium-bodied, gently flavoured reds ♀ bland whites*

It's a real challenge finding a wine to suit this gentle, beer-based stew. Most reds are too strongly flavoured or tannic, and most white wines are totally inappropriate. Valpolicella and Côtes du Roussillon come closest to a good red match, and a bright Côtes du Rhône red made by carbonic maceration (see *Tannin*, page 221) or a red Loire Cabernet such as St-Nicolas-de-Bourgueil, Saumur-Champigny or Chinon are all acceptable alternatives. Among whites, the bland character of Frascati or Hungarian Furmint are adequate. But since a creamy, faintly hoppy lager blends just perfectly, why bother? ★★ *lager*

## CASEROLES AND STEWS ❢ *low-tannin, light to medium-bodied, fruity reds*

The success of the match depends on the ingredients. The sweetness of onions, tomatoes, and root vegetables such as carrot or swede, calls for a fruity red – the Gamay grape is the likely answer. Gamay de l'Ardêche, and simple Beaujolais-Villages or a southern French Gamay vin de pays make good choices, as do simple, medium-bodied southern French reds such as Côtes du Roussillon, Minervois or Coteaux du Tricastin. For a really rich stew, move up to the Beaujolais crus (Fleurie and so on). If the sauce contains red wine, consult the entries for *Beef Bourguignonne* or *Daube of Beef*. See also *Goulash*.

## CHILLI CON CARNE ❢ *unoaked, medium- to full-bodied, fruity reds*

The chilli pepper does not affect the actual taste of the wine, but with that burning sensation in your mouth you may fail to appreciate a fine wine at its best, so stick to something fairly modest. Avoid sparkling or high-alcohol wines too – the bubbles and the alcohol are painful on a chillied tongue. Chilli con carne finds a lot of red wine partners: the stars are full Beaujolais crus, such as Côte de Brouilly or Moulin-à-Vent, and rich, single-vineyard Valpolicella or Coteaux du Tricastin. Portuguese Bairrada also goes well. Try also Crozes-Hermitage, red Bordeaux, unoaked or only lightly oaked Cabernet Sauvignon, Merlot, unoaked Zinfandel, Rosso di Montalcino, or Chianti Classico. ★ *Beaujolais crus* ★★ *single-vineyard Valpolicella* ★★ *Coteaux du Tricastin*

VARIATIONS **Cumin seeds** are an optional extra ingredient. The Beaujolais crus, or single-vineyard Valpolicella or Coteaux du Tricastin are still the best choices, Bairrada good, and a few off-dry whites complement the cumin flavour well. Try a simple white Burgundy or inexpensive, unoaked Chardonnay from elsewhere, Viognier, or South African Colombard. For a contrasting and amazing combination, try a New Zealand Riesling. ★★ *Beaujolais crus*

## CORNED BEEF HASH ▌ *Gamays or Cabernet Sauvignons* ♀ *unoaked Chardonnays*

The above three grape varieties rule here. The reds are more successful: the Beaujolais crus such as Juliénas are super-stars, but any other Gamay is also delicious. Bairrada and Valpolicella Classico are good, and Cabernets from California, Argentina, Chile, Australia or Bulgaria all work well, though some may be a touch too strong (few red Bordeaux are ripely fruity enough). Bordeaux or Bergerac rosé also make good, and interesting alternatives, and for a white, choose a simple Burgundy or other unoaked Chardonnay. ★★ *Beaujolais crus*

## COTTAGE PIE see SHEPHERD'S PIE

## DAUBE OF BEEF ♀ *lightly oaked, full, fruity or savoury reds*

There's probably a different daube – beef marinaded and casseroled with wine and vegetables – for every region of France. Here, the sauce dominates the choice of wine. For a really rich, thickly sauced recipe, the entry for *Beef Bourguignonne* (above) may be appropriate. Lighter sauces often have flavours similar to coq au vin: try red Bordeaux, Côtes du Roussillon, red Côtes du Rhône, Fitou, St-Chinian, Beaujolais crus such as Juliénas, red Burgundy, Chianti, young red Rioja or a modern Alentejo red from Portugal. ★★ *mature red Bordeaux*

## GOULASH ♀ *ripe, softly tannic reds* ♀ *ripe, full-bodied, fruity whites*

TRADITIONAL PARTNER Hungarian red

A good, ripe Chardonnay fits the bill here: try a good Burgundy from a ripe year – the star is Meursault – or a rich, ripe California, Australian or Chilean Reserve Chardonnay. Next in line are gentle, not-too-aromatic Sauvignons from warmer places such as Bordeaux, South Africa, California, Australia or Hungary. Hungarian Pinot Gris and Frascati stand up to goulash in a neutral way. A few odd-ball reds also go reasonably well: ripe red Côtes du Rhône, Chilean Merlot and California Barbera. ★★ *Meursault*

## HAMBURGER see BURGERS

## LASAGNE see *Pasta*

**MEATBALLS** ❢ *light to medium-bodied, gently tannic, fairly fruity reds* ♀ *dry, acid whites*

Call them faggots, polpettini, keftethdes (Greece), or koftah/kaftah (Middle East), meatballs are often very gently spiced, and tend to be dominated by onion. Reds are the answer: from Italy try Dolcetto or young Chianti, from southern France try Fitou, St-Chinian, Côtes du Roussillon or Corbières. An inexpensive Australian Shiraz or Shiraz-Cabernet is a good flavour but may be too strong. ★★ *Italian Dolcetto*

VARIATIONS **Cumin** flavour in Middle Eastern meatballs is beautifully complemented by Cabernet Sauvignon or Valpolicella. ★★ *Cabernet Sauvignon.* If **coriander** is a major flavour you might switch to white – Alsace Sylvaner or German Silvaner Trocken will really set off the herb flavour beautifully. ★★ *Alsace Sylvaner*

**MEATLOAF** see **MEATBALLS**

**OXTAIL** ❢ *rich, unoaked, mature reds* ♀ *ripely fruity, medium-bodied whites*

The sweetness of the root vegetables usually cooked with oxtail call for wines with really ripe fruit; more so if redcurrant jelly has been added. For such a sweetish version, ripely fruity whites score highest. Australian Marsanne is the perfect answer, or try Australian Reserve Chardonnay or Verdelho (Semillon doesn't work), Viognier, Condrieu or white Côtes du Rhône. Australian Shiraz is a star red. With a sauce that lacks this sweetness, reds go better than whites. Choose Vacqueyras, mature Brunello or Rosso di Montalcino, or Beaujolais crus such as Fleurie, a hot-climate Cabernet-Merlot or a California Mourvèdre. With sweet Marsala in the sauce, choose white Côtes du Rhône, or Dolcetto for a red. ★★ *Australian Shiraz* ★★ *Australian Marsanne*

**ROAST BEEF**

For wines to serve with plain roast beef, see the entry for *Steak* (below).

VARIATIONS Serving **horseradish** with beef is bad

news for wine. It strips the fruit out of many wines almost completely. The best answer is a very ripe Cabernet Sauvignon, perhaps from California – the horseradish takes the edge off its quality, but it still tastes good. Other possibilities are Dolcetto and Bairrada.

## SALT BEEF ❢ *Gamays ♀ light, bland whites*
The delicate flavour of cold, American-style thinly sliced salt beef is totally overwhelmed by almost all reds and inappropriate for almost all whites. Notable exceptions are Gamay de Touraine, winning for its complementary acidity and flavour, and the gently aromatic white Arneis from northern Italy. ★★ *Gamay de Touraine*

## SAUERBRATEN
TRADITIONAL PARTNER *lager*
The very vinegary marinade of this German dish leaves the meat super-tender but acidly hostile to wine. The sweetish-sour sauce and meat strip all the fruitiness out of red wines, and while some high-acid whites nearly cope, none is a pleasure to drink with Sauerbraten. Rheingau Riesling Halbtrocken comes the nearest. Lager doesn't make a positive match, but it co-exists pleasantly with the sour meat and sauce.

## SHEPHERD'S PIE ❢ *unoaked, soft, fruity reds*
If the perfect partner Côte de Brouilly and other Beaujolais crus seem too expensive to accompany this modest dish, go for a Gamay de l'Ardêche. Or soft, easy, unoaked southern French reds such as Minervois, Côtes du Roussillon, traditional Côtes du Rhône (not made using carbonic maceration – see *Tannin,* page 221), Coteaux du Tricastin or Fitou. As expensive, and almost good as a Beaujolais cru, is an untannic, mid-priced red Burgundy, or southern Italian Cirò Riserva. ★★ *Beaujolais crus*

## SPAGHETTI BOLOGNESE see *Pasta*

## STEAK (FRIED OR GRILLED) ❢ *low-tannin, softly fruity or mature reds*
The cut of meat, and the method and length of cooking, make little or no difference to the wine match. A perfect match is hard to find with plain steak. Whites and rosés taste too thin, acid and aromatic. Light reds fair better. The

lighter of the Beaujolais crus are the best bet – Regnié, Chénas, Chiroubles, Juliénas, St-Amour or Fleurie. The others are too strongly flavoured, unless mature. Fruity Dolcetto from northern Italy is delicious, and two savoury reds from southern Italy – Cirò Riserva from Calabria and Squinzano from Puglia – are as good as the Beaujolais crus. Inexpensive, low-tannin Cabernet Sauvignons from warm countries – California, Australia or Chile – have the right flavour if you don't mind their dominance over the steak. The same goes for Portuguese Bairrada and Italian Brunello – both are really *too* tannic and flavourful but have the *right* flavour to complement the steak. The best choice otherwise is an untannic Cabernet Franc from the Loire (Chinon, Bourgueil, St-Nicolas-de-Bourgueil, Saumur-Champigny, Anjou Rouge Cabernet), or Franciacorta from northern Italy. ★★ *light Beaujolais crus*

VARIATIONS A dollop of **Dijon mustard** solves all your problems. Magically, Dijon mustard neutralizes tannin and makes even quite a tough or basic red taste smooth and complex. California Cabernet is the star, and other rich, ripe, even tannic Cabernets are stars. Brunello, Barolo and Barbaresco work really well, and Bairrada makes a lovely, savoury blend. Beaujolais crus are still a good choice. Dijon mustard also tames Côtes du Rhône and red Châteauneuf-du-Pape. Cirò Riserva and Squinzano are still good, and Portuguese Alentejo shoots up the quality ladder. ★★ *California Cabernet.* **Maître d'hotel butter**, with its high lemon-juice content, calls for wines with highish acidity – and low tannin again. Beaujolais crus, even the fuller ones such as Côte de Brouilly or Moulin-à-Vent, are still stars. Scoring for highish acidity, Italian reds such as Chianti Rufina or Chianti Classico, Dolcetto, Barbaresco or Barbera, California Barbera and Loire Cabernet Franc are all good. ★★ *Beaujolais crus*

**Steak au Poivre** ❢ *medium-bodied, low-tannin reds*

Cooked with pepper, Cognac and cream, steak can take slightly more tannic reds, but intensely flavoured and very tannic wines will still overwhelm the meat. Just as perfect as Loire Cabernet Francs are Chianti Classico, and ripe, not-too-powerful Merlots from South Africa, California or New Zealand, the Pays d'Oc, or a good Bordeaux vintage. Next in line are Spanish Tempranillos, Rioja and Navarra reds, and light reds from Ribera del Duero, soft red Burgundies, California Barbera, Portuguese Bairrada, and Valpolicella. ★★ *St-Nicolas-de-Bourgueil* ★★ *Chinon* ★★ *Chianti Classico* ★★ *Merlots*

### Steak Tartare ♀ *dry, soft, bland, unoaked whites*

This is quite a challenging dish to match to wine. With the exception of Bourgogne Aligoté which works extremely well, high-acid wines do not work, and the raw egg yolk clashes horribly with the tannin of reds, oaked reds and whites (which contain wood tannins), and poorly made, cheap whites (which often contain tannins from the grape skins). Next best after the Aligoté are the bland Italian Pinot Grigio and Hungarian Furmint, with Austrian Grüner Veltliner, southern French Terret, Italian Est! Est!! Est!!! and simple, unoaked Chardonnay, including inexpensive white Burgundy, all acceptable alternatives. ★★ *Bourgogne Aligoté*

### Steak and Kidney Pie/Pudding ▮ *unoaked or gently oaked, savoury or softly fruity reds* ▮ *dry rosés*

Despite the distinctive suet flavour of the pudding, similar wines match both pudding and pie. The most delicious pairings are with reds that enhance the kidney flavour: Cabernets, and red Bordeaux, are good in general, but Australian Cabernets (especially from the Coonawarra district) bring an extra something to the mix, and mature red Bordeaux is also very good. The savoury character of red Burgundy chimes in with the kidney, as does Oregon or California Pinot Noir, though these are a touch too fruity. Bairrada and light red Côtes du Rhônes are both stars, as is Squinzano from Puglia in the heel of Italy. The Beaujolais crus and other wines from the Gamay grape are pretty good. Cirò Riserva, Barbaresco, Brunello, and California Mourvèdre, and Barbera, Alentejo red, Australian Shiraz and Carmignano are pleasant partners too. Spanish rosados, especially those made from Tempranillo, go deliciously well. No white is really good, but Alella (from Catalonia in Spain), or either California or Chilean Chardonnays are pleasant. ★★ *Australian Coonawarra Cabernet*

# Lamb

Lamb has a special affinity with a number of red wine styles – Rioja, red Bordeaux (claret), California Cabernet, Cahors, Bairrada – and goes especially well with a fine and mature version of any of these. The higher tannin and bright fruit of many young wines are too much for lamb. (Zinfandel is an odd exception; despite its bright fruit, even a young example is a fine complement to lamb.) Make sure you serve lamb *really* hot: lamb fat becomes curiously and unpleasantly mouthcoating as it cools, and wine finds it difficult to penetrate the greasy barrier and meet up with the taste buds. If you care about your wine, beware mint sauce and mint jelly, too, as they strip the fruitiness and much of the quality out of wine.

## CASSEROLES AND STEWS ♥ *medium- to full-bodied, lowish-tannin, ideally mature reds* ♀ *dry, not-too-fruity whites*

The wine choice really depends on the vegetables and sauce ingredients, but Cabernet Sauvignon, red Rioja, or – for a white option – Soave, stand a good chance of matching. If the sauce is not very rich, choose lighter styles of these wines. See also *Irish Stew* and *Lancashire Hotpot*.

VARIATIONS Casseroled with **flageolet beans**, lamb finds perfect matches with red Rioja Reserva and Italian Cirò Riserva. Bairrada, Chianti or Beaujolais-Villages among reds, and Vernaccia, Pinot Grigio, Soave Classico or Penedés or Conca de Barberá whites from Spain are all good alternatives. ★★ *red Rioja Reserva* ★★ *Cirò Riserva*

## COUS-COUS see *Rice and Grains*

## HAGGIS ♥ *full-bodied, low- to medium-tannin, not-too-intensely flavoured reds* ♀ *low- to medium-acid, not-too-fruity, dry whites*

Languedoc-Roussillon or red Côtes du Rhône with a lot of Grenache in the blend are the best bet with haggis; Spanish Garnacha or Rioja are nearly as good. Modern, not-too-tannic Bairrada

(or a mature traditional one) is good, as are lightish red Bordeaux and Loire reds made from Cabernet Franc such as Chinon and Bourgueil. Low-tannin red Burgundy, or gentle (not too expensive) Merlots also work well. For a white, try Soave Classico, Australian Semillon-Chardonnay, Champagne Blanc de Blancs, Chardonnay VdP du Jardin de la France, German Silvaner or Alsace Sylvaner.
★★ *full-bodied red Côtes du Roussillon*

## IRISH STEW ❗ *unoaked or lightly oaked, lowish-tannin, light to medium-bodied reds*
This gently flavoured stew is dominated by deliciously lamby potatoes. Cabernet is the right *flavour*, but many are too strongly flavoured, and the lighter Cabernets of the Loire are too acidic. Apart from southern French Cabernet vin de pays, a light, young Bulgarian or Romanian Cabernet or a light, inexpensive Chilean Cabernet are very good indeed. A light, fruity, modern Portuguese red from the Douro is delicious, and Fitou and Corbières go well.
★★ *southern French Cabernet vin de pays* ★★ *Douro red*

## KLEFTIKO see LAMB SHANKS WITH THYME

## LAMB CHOPS see ROAST LAMB

## LAMBS' KIDNEY ❗ *medium- to full-bodied reds with low to medium tannin*
Lambs' kidneys served with a soft, subtle, savoury, perfumed Barbaresco or Barolo is one of the world's best food and wine combinations (choose a soft modern-style wine, if possible at least five years old). Barbera is also superb, Cirò Riserva from southern Italy makes a lovely, savoury match, and Rioja Crianza and Gamay de Touraine are stars. Runners-up from Italy and still very good partners are Teroldego Rotaliano and Valpolicella Classico (either basic or single-vineyard). California, Australian or Oregon Pinot Noir are much more successful than red Burgundy, which tends to be a little too acid. ★★ *Barbaresco*

## LAMBS' LIVER ❗ *low- to medium-tannin, not-too-fruity reds*
Australian Shiraz, with its rich but not dominant fruit, takes the prize, with single-vineyard Valpolicella, young Rioja or Navarra Tempranillos and La Mancha reds vying

for second place. Beaujolais crus such as Côtes de Brouilly or Morgon are a touch too fruity but an appropriate flavour, and Zinfandel, California Barbera, Chianti Classico, red Burgundy or other Pinot Noirs all work well. ★★ *Australian Shiraz* VARIATIONS Despite the sweetness of the onions, very much the same styles of wines accompany **liver and onions**. The Australian Shiraz still shines, and California Sangiovese suddenly becomes a great success, while less expensive Valpolicella and Barbaresco are better partners here than with plain liver. Zinfandel seems too fruity. ★★ *Australian Shiraz*

## LAMB SHANKS BAKED WITH THYME (KLEFTIKO) ❗ *low- to medium-tannin, medium- to full-bodied reds*

This is a wonderful Greek dish: the lamb shanks are smothered in thyme, wrapped, and baked slowly for several hours. The meltingly tender lamb imbued with thyme makes for a really easy match with a wide range of red wines – there's something for everyone here. Even fairly tannic reds work, since thyme seems to tame the tannin as well as linking in with all sorts of different wine flavours. The Greek reds, Nemea and Goumenissa, both make wonderful accompaniments, red Rioja Crianza and Reserva are both brilliant, while Rioja Gran Reserva is quite good. The thyme chimes in deliciously with the slightly grassy flavour of (simple to fine) red Bordeaux and the minty flavour of Australian Cabernet Sauvignon. Other good matches are with mature Bairrada, Beaujolais-Villages, Chianti, Cahors, Brunello or Rosso di Montalcino, Zinfandel, Cali-fornia Cabernet, California, Oregon or Aus-tra-lian Pinot Noir, and Australian Shiraz. ★★ *Greek Nemea* ★★ *Greek Goumenissa*

## LANCASHIRE HOTPOT ❗ *light to medium-bodied, fairly fruity, low-tannin reds* ♀ *dry or nearly dry whites*

The sweetness of the onions, carrots and swedes all added in the pot goes well with fruity reds or whites with a touch of sweetness. Yet the best white matches are, surprisingly, a couple of bone-dry wines: Soave Classico and Bourgogne Aligoté. Super-fruity Australian Marsanne goes very well, as do not-quite-dry Alella from Spain, and Brut Champagnes. The best reds are Côtes du Rhône, Côtes du Roussillon or other southern French reds – the more traditionally made the better. Loire Cabernet reds (such as Bourgueil or Chinon) are a touch too grassy but still pleasant, as are light Cabernet Sauvignons from California and cool areas of Australia. Interesting red alternatives are Rioja Crianza, Valpolicella Classico, Sangiovese di Romagna. Of the whites, German Rheinhessen Kabinett and, unexpectedly, dry Muscat are good. ★★ *Soave Classico* ★★ *Bourgogne Aligoté*

## LIVER AND ONIONS see LAMBS' LIVER

## MOUSSAKA ¶ *unoaked or subtly oaked reds with medium tannin and acidity* ¶ *Tavel rosés*
TRADITIONAL PARTNER *Greek Naoussa*
Greek Naoussa is a brilliant accompaniment to this wine-friendly dish, and a young one is even better than a Grand Reserve. Greek Nemea is pleasant, Goumenissa or Limnio reasonable choices. Moving away from the native wines, go for a really lovely blend with the savoury fruit of an Australian, California or Oregon Pinot Noir (without too much obvious oak). A Spanish Tempranillo, French Cahors or Portuguese Bairrada, with their rather savoury flavours, are all very good matches. Tavel rosé is a very good choice, too. Pleasant alternatives are Chianti, southern French reds and vins de pays, basic South African red, or red Dão. ★★ *Greek Naoussa*

## ROAST LAMB ¶ *low- to medium-acid, low- to medium-tannin, not-too-fruity reds*
The Cabernet and Tempranillo grapes work wonders with roast lamb, roasted with or without herbs. Mature red Bordeaux (claret) is a classic, and wonderful, partner; mature California Cabernet is just as successful with plain roast lamb. Of the younger clarets, Pomerol or St-Émilion are more successful than the slightly too austere styles of the Graves or Médoc. Modern, inexpensive, not-too-tannic Cahors or any mature Cahors is a star. Red Rioja Gran Reserva is delicious, Rioja Crianza works very well, and

young or Reserva Riojas make pleasant matches. Mature Ribera del Duero and Navarra are notable successes too. Zinfandel is good despite its bright fruit, and a fine Greek Nemea is an easy, gentle choice. A word of warning – cooked, cold lamb fat disagreeably coats the mouth and blocks the wine flavours. ★★ *mature red Bordeaux*

VARIATIONS With **garlic and rosemary** red Rioja Gran Reserva becomes a real superstar, better than the still excellent mature claret. Rioja Reserva and Crianza are very good indeed, as is Zinfandel. Australian reds again make a reasonable match, but the California Cabernet is a bit too blackcurranty for the rosemary. Cahors clashes with the rosemary. ★★ *red Rioja Gran Reserva*. Roasting lamb with **thyme** changes the wine matches more radically, and creates new pairings. The thyme chimes in deliciously with the minty flavour of Australian Cabernet, especially from Coonawarra. See also *Lamb Shanks baked with Thyme*. ★★ *Australian Coonawarra Cabernet*. **Mint jelly** and **mint sauce** are both wine-killers, stripping out the fruit, and are best avoided if you want the wine to taste its best.

## SOUVLAKIA see ROAST LAMB

## SWEETBREADS ♀ *low- to medium-acid, not-too-fruity whites*
Simply sautéed in butter with a little stock, sweetbreads are very delicate indeed. Unoaked white Rioja would be best, or try Est! Est!! Est!!!, a light Italian Chardonnay, perhaps from Piemonte or Alto-Adige/Südtirol, Chablis Premier Cru, or Corbières Blanc. ★★ *unoaked white Rioja*

VARIATIONS Served with a **mushroom, butter and cream sauce**, sweetbreads are stunning with Corbières Blanc or unoaked Chardonnay VdP d'Oc. Italian and Chilean Chardonnay also work well; or try Chablis Premier Cru. Most reds are overpowering, but Spanish or other hot-country Merlots, red Rioja Reserva or Gran Reserva are a fairly good match with a rich sauce. ★★ *unoaked Chardonnay VdP d'Oc* ★★ *white Corbières*

# Pork

Pork is better suited to red wines, but don't ignore white wines – some partner this pale meat very well indeed. As fat emphasizes the tannin in red wines and makes them taste tougher than they really are, the red wines must be fairly low in tannin, especially when served with fatty joints and cuts, or with fatty sausages or charcuterie. Pork can take fairly strong wine flavours, but ideally nothing too intense. If you are buying free-range pork, or rare breeds such as Gloucester Old Spot, and wild boar, these have more flavour than mass-reared pork and can take slightly more intensely flavoured wines. A tasty joint of good pork, plainly roasted, makes an excellent background for showing off an appropriate fine red. But don't be tempted into serving apple sauce as it strips the fruit out of wine. Any sweetness in a sauce calls for a white with some sweetness, or a very fruity red.

## BACON see HAM AND BACON

## BLACK PUDDING see SAUSAGES

## CASSEROLES AND STEWS

Your choice of wine depends on the other ingredients rather than the pork. Any sweet ingredients (such as apple, prunes or sweet wine) will call for a corresponding sweetness in a white wine, or bright fruitiness in a red. See also *Cassoulet* and *Pork with Prunes and Cream*.

VARIATIONS Pork or wild boar, marinaded and cooked in **white wine, with onion, celery, garlic, oil, carrot, juniper and thyme**, is delicious with Rosso di Montalcino, southern Italian Cirò Riserva, Cahors, any red Rioja, Oregon Pinot Noir and Australian Shiraz-Cabernet. ★ *Rosso di Montalcino*. With **tomato, onion and white wine** try Alsace Pinot Gris or a lightly oaked Chardonnay, Australian Shiraz or Shiraz-Cabernet, Oregon Pinot Noir or Rioja Reserva. ★ *Alsace Pinot Gris*. With a **red wine sauce**, drink a fruity but not-too-tannic or oaky red: try an Australian, New Zealand or California Pinot Noir, Cabernet, or a Shiraz or Cabernet-Shiraz, or a Beaujolais cru or Rioja Crianza. ★ *New World Pinot Noir*. If **cider** is the cooking liquid, cider may be the best accompaniment, or you could try young Rioja, Valpolicella or Chianti

Classico. If the cider itself is sweet or slightly sweet, choose a South African Chenin, a Hungarian Pinot Gris or a Spanish Garnacha rosado.

## CASSOULET ❦ *unoaked, untannic reds*
❦ *Tavel rosés* ♀ *gently flavoured, unoaked whites*
There are a lot of elements to match in this dish: pork and sausage, confit d'oie (preserved goose) or confit de canard (duck), sometimes lamb, and the creamy, garlicky bean and breadcrumb mix that binds all the flavours together. Whites tend to be best. White Crozes-Hermitage, lively and full but very gently flavoured, is really superb, and Marsanne vin de pays is also very good indeed. Unoaked European Chardonnays marry well. So do not-too-aromatic or ripely fruity Sauvignon Blancs: try basic Bordeaux Blanc, or other softer Sauvignons from South Africa, Chile or California. Of the reds, Brunello di Montalcino makes a good, savoury, rich blend, and the easy, gentle, savoury flavour of young red Rioja Crianza is delicious. Tavel Rosé is also good. Lighter reds are fine: simple Beaujolais or Gamay de l'Ardêche go quite well. ★★ *white Crozes-Hermitage*

## CHOPS see ROAST PORK and
## CASSEROLES AND STEWS

## CHOUCROUTE ♀ *fairly high- to high-acid, quite fruity whites*
TRADITIONAL PARTNER *Alsace Riesling*
Much less acidic in character than German Sauerkraut, choucroute is remarkably easy to match with wines. Alsace Riesling makes an unbeatable combination (New Zealand Riesling is a touch too fruity, German Riesling Trocken a little too light and flowery, but both go reasonably well). Chablis, Chablis Premier Cru and Italian Pinot Grigio also blend in superbly. Other good matches are with Chardonnay VdP du Jardin de la France or northern Italian Chardonnays, Hungarian Furmint, or southern French Terret. An inexpensive Alsace Pinot Gris has the right flavour, but most are too rich and honeyed. ★★ *Alsace Riesling*

**HAM AND BACON** Despite their salt content, ham and bacon have quite a delicate flavour unless smoked. They are easily overwhelmed by strongly flavoured wines and the tannin of red wines, and prove quite difficult to match with either whites or reds.

**Boiled or Roast, Grilled or Fried Ham (unsmoked)** ❢ *light-bodied, unoaked, soft, fruity reds* ❢ *Tempranillo rosados* ♀ *light to medium-bodied, unoaked, bland or very slightly aromatic whites*

However the ham is prepared, grape variety is the key to success here – with red wines taking the prizes. The star wine is Beaujolais-Villages; not surprisingly, a light Beaujolais cru is very good, too, as is Gamay de Touraine. Syrah is the next grape to win favour – try a Syrah-based Côtes du Rhône, or its Australian counterpart, Shiraz, in blends with Cabernet Sauvignon. Spanish rosados made from Tempranillo go well. White choices are a simple Chablis, southern French Terret, a simple Spanish white from Penedés or Conca de Barberá, and South African Colombard. ★★ *Beaujolais-Villages*

VARIATIONS For ham (both smoked and unsmoked) served with **pineapple** the flavour and the slight sweetness of Alella Clásico from Spain is spot on. Liebfraumilch also matches very well. ★★ *Alella Clásico*

**Braised Ham with Lentils** ❢ *light, low-tannin reds* ♀ *gentle whites.*

Gamay de Touraine, which is a very good partner with the ham, is really delicious with the combination of ham and lentils. Côtes du Roussillon is another red star, while Dolcetto and Teroldego from northern Italy, and hot-country Merlots, marry well. Several whites are also successful – try Côtes de Duras or Bordeaux Blanc, Vernaccia, Pinot Grigio, Australian Colombard-Chardonnay or a medium English wine. ★★ *Gamay de Touraine*

VARIATIONS If you prefer **smoked** ham with lentils, choose a Gamay de Touraine or a hot-country Merlot. Whites don't really work. ★ *Gamay de Touraine*

**Honey-Roast Ham** ❢ *light to medium-bodied, low-tannin reds* ♀ *bland, light to medium-bodied, dry or nearly dry whites*

There's rarely a hint of the honey's sweetness on slices of bought, cold, honey-roast ham. Even if you make it yourself, the sweet glaze (and sometimes a gentle scent of cloves) only flavours the outside of quite a big joint of meat – and if you cut off the fat you will lose even that. So dry wines are perfectly appropriate partners. The very gentle flavour of northern Italian Pinot Grigio is best, and Arneis, though more aromatic, also works well. If you enjoy the fat and glaze, Spanish Alella or a Rheingau Riesling Halbtrocken have a touch of sweetness and a flavour that chimes in well. Otherwise, see *Boiled or Roast, Grilled or Fried Ham (unsmoked)* above. ★★ *northern Italian Pinot Grigio*

**Jambon Persillé** ❢ *lowish-tannin, medium-to full-bodied fruity reds with good acidity* ♀ *fairly high-acid whites, with a touch of sweetness*
TRADITIONAL PARTNER *Bourgogne Aligoté*
The lemon juice and white wine (traditionally the high-acid Bourgogne Aligoté) in the jelly call for good acidity in the wine; and a hint of sweetness is a good foil for the salty ham. In fact the local Aligoté tastes surprisingly flat with jambon persillé. Brut Champagne, with its good acidity and barely perceptible sweetness, is a brilliant match, while Kabinetts from Germany's Rheinhessen go well. From Spain, Alella is excellent; Sauvignon de Touraine and Italian Est! Est!! Est!!! make surprisingly good partners. Some reds work very well, too, particularly full reds from Languedoc-Roussillon. The ripe fruit of a not-too-tannic California or Australian Cabernet Sauvignon, a soft, ripe Spanish, California or Washington State Merlot, or a red Côtes du Rhône are good. ★★ *red Côtes du Roussillon* ★★ *Brut Champagne*

**Oak-Smoked Ham** ❢ *lowish-tannin, light, softly fruity reds* ♀ *oaked, gently fruity whites*
Many red wines clash with, and overemphasize, the smoke in this much more strongly flavoured ham. Apart from the really delicious white pairing with oaked Rioja, Soave, Spanish Alella, and oaked Chardonnay VdP d'Oc are all quite good. There is also a star choice for red wine drinkers: Beaujolais-Villages. Gamay de Touraine, a Syrah-based Côtes du Rhône, or a light lowish-tannin California Cabernet, Merlot or Barbera are all good alternatives. ★★ *Beaujolais-Villages* ★★ *oaked white Rioja*

**CURED/DRIED HAMS** There is a huge variety of cured and dried hams. Parma ham, prosciutto crudo, jambon des Ardennes, jamón de serrano, jamón de jabugo, Speck, Westphalia ham... They may all look fairly similar, but they each behave quite differently with wines. Perversely, they generally defy attempts to match them perfectly with wines of their own nationality. The delicate flavours of Italian hams, including Parma ham and Alpine Speck, are easily swamped by any wine, although rosés, with their more delicate fruit, tend to find some successes.

**Jambon des Ardennes** ! *Beaujolais* ? *dry rosés* ? *highish-acid, dry or off-dry whites*

This is a quite smoky ham, with a sweetish, herby cure. Demi-sec (medium-dry) Chenin Blanc-based whites from the Loire go very well, and even a dry Chenin vin de pays or Anjou Blanc Sec is quite good. Or try Rioja rosado or Beaujolais-Villages. ★ *Anjou Blanc Demi-sec.*

**Parma Ham** ? *unoaked, gently fruity whites, with a touch of sweetness*

TRADITIONAL PARTNER *Lambrusco Secco*

For the perfectionist, the local dry Lambrusco tastes a little too strong and bitter with Parma ham. Other reds are also too strong, and most Italian whites are too dry, but Favorita goes reasonably well. Demi-sec Anjou Blanc or Chenin vin de pays are both stars. German Riesling Halbtrocken is an adequate match. ★★ *Anjou Blanc Demi-sec*

VARIATIONS Traditionally served with medium-sweet Lambrusco, Parma Ham with **melon** is perfect with Mosel Riesling Kabinett. Using Honeydew melon, any German Riesling Kabinett is good, but Mosel-Saar-Ruwer Kabinett is a superstar. With Charentais or Galia melon, Anjou Blanc Demi-sec is brilliant. Ruby port is a complementary flavour, although a little too sweet. Medium-sweet red Lambrusco has the right level of sweetness, but tastes slightly bitter in this context. ★★ *Mosel Riesling Kabinett*

**Spanish Jamón** ! *lowish-tannin, medium- to full-bodied fruity reds with good acidity* ? *dry rosés*

Spanish Jamón has a broader, richer, more intense flavour which makes it easier to match with wines than Italian or French hams. Single-vineyard Valpolicella is a star, hot-country Merlots are quite good, and the jamón makes an adequate match with Spanish rosados, young Rioja, or Tempranillo and Garnacha reds from other parts of Spain. ★★ *single-vineyard Valpolicella.*

### Tyrolean Speck ▮ dry rosés

Rosés go well with the delicate meat of Tyrolean Speck (the local red Schiava is so pale as to be virtually pink). ★★ *Rioja rosado.*

### Westphalia Ham ▮ *lowish-tannin, medium-bodied fruity reds with good acidity* ▮ *dry rosés* ♀ *highish-acid, medium-dry whites*

Westphalia ham, with its sweetish/salty cure and flavours of pepper and juniper, goes quite well with a local German Riesling Halbtrocken, but an inexpensive Australian medium-dry Riesling is much closer to a match. The star, however, is an Italian red – Valpolicella Classico; its flavours are just right. Beaujolais-Villages and Rioja rosado are also good. ★★ *Valpolicella Classico*

### PORK PIE ▮ *low- to medium-tannin, medium- to full-bodied, fruity reds* ♀ *gently flavoured whites*

The fresh, bright Italian fruit of Dolcetto is lovely, and the southern French Fitou has just the right flavour to complement the fatty pork filling. A light Zinfandel or Shiraz also works. Of the whites, a really ripe and fruity hot-climate Chardonnay is nearly as good as the red stars, and Soave, unoaked white Rioja or Champagne Blanc de Blancs are all good. ★★ *Dolcetto* ★★ *Fitou*

### PORK WITH PRUNES AND CREAM
♀ *fairly high- to high-acid, medium-dry or medium whites*

TRADITIONAL PARTNER *Vouvray Demi-sec*

With a sauce incorporating the sweetness of prunes, tomato paste, a demi-sec wine, *and* cream, this Loire speciality is a wine-killer unless the wine has enough sweetness and acidity to balance the sauce. The local Vouvray Demi-sec goes superbly, and Anjou Blanc, Coteaux du Layon, Coteaux de l'Aubance or Coteaux de Saumur, all in their demi-sec versions, are all well matched. German Riesling Spätlese or a not-too-sweet Late Harvest Riesling from California, north-west USA or South Africa make good but less perfectly matched alternatives. ★★ *Vouvray Demi-sec*

**PORK RILLETTES** ❢ *low-tannin, unoaked or subtly oaked reds* ♀ *medium-weight to full whites with good but not high acidity*

TRADITIONAL PARTNER *Chinon or St-Nicolas-de-Bourgueil*
Fat and tannin do not get on well, so mature reds are often the answer for this very French dish, a delicious, rough, fibrous, very fatty pâté. The Loire reds, mature Chinon or Bourgueil from a ripe year, are fine, but the stars are mature California Cabernet, a really superb partner for pork rillettes, and mature red Bordeaux, which is nearly as good. The fruit and high alcohol of red Châteauneuf-du-Pape balance the fat in the dish, and the lighter Syrahs of the Rhône – Crozes-Hermitage, St-Joseph or, better still, a good Syrah vin de pays, are delicious, as is Shiraz (though a little strong). Chablis Premier or Grand Cru is the star white, and several other whites are very good: try Italian Favorita, Australian Marsanne, South African Colombard, ripe, hot-climate Chardonnays, or a fine Burgundy from a ripe year, especially if mature. ★★ *California Cabernet* ★★ *Chablis Premier Cru*

**PORK SAUSAGE** see **SAUSAGES**

**ROAST PORK** ❢ *fairly full, low- to medium-tannin reds* ♀ *dry, fairly bland, medium-acid whites*
Red wines are the ideal choice for roast pork *without* apple sauce. (See VARIATIONS for apple sauce.) The richer of the Beaujolais crus (Moulin-à-Vent, Morgon and Côte de Brouilly) are a wonderful accompaniment. The flavour of Crozes-Hermitage, St-Joseph and Syrah vins de pays or Syrah-based Côtes du Rhône also makes a star match, though these wines can be a little too powerful (unless served with wild boar or free-range pork). Australian Shiraz is nearly as good, but again a bit strong. The flavour of Oregon or New Zealand Pinot Noir is lovely, though sometimes a little strong, and light, untannic red Burgundy works well. The savoury fruit of southern Italian Cirò Riserva goes deliciously. Portuguese Alentejo red is good, Ribatejo red and Bairrada pleasant. Apart from Chablis Premier Cru, whites are less brilliant. A fine, rich white Burgundy goes well, cheaper Chablis and Burgundy less so. Or you can try Bordeaux or Chilean Sauvignon, Alsace Pinot Blanc, or Australian Verdelho. ★★ *Moulin-à-Vent* ★★ *Chablis Premier Cru*

VARIATIONS Nothing can match the stunning partnership of pork and **apple sauce** with a good German Riesling Kabinett from the Mosel-Saar-Ruwer. With pork alone, the same wine is a little too sweet, but still pleasant. The apple sauce makes all the selected wines for roast pork above taste flat, except for Australian Verdelho, which improves dramatically. ★★ *Mosel-Saar-Ruwer Riesling Kabinett*

SALAMI ❗ *a few low-tannin, not-too-intensely flavoured reds* ♀ *bland, low- to medium-acid whites*

There are no really brilliant matches, and salami flavours vary so much throughout Italy and even within a single region that it is hard to make general recommendations. Saltier salamis can take more acid wines, and the fattier the salami, the less welcome tannin becomes. Spicy salamis from the south of Italy tend to be easier to match with wine than the milder ones of the north. No Italian wine seems to suit right across the salami board, and reds are less successful than whites. A white Dão from Portugal, southern French Terret and Hungarian Furmint all go quite well with a wide range of salamis, from meaty to fatty and from spicy to hot.

VARIATIONS Chilli-hot **Calabrese salami** is surprisingly easier to match than gentler versions: it is actively good with Chianti Classico, Rioja Crianza, a soft Navarra Tempranillo and Beaujolais crus such as Côte de Brouilly, as well as southern French or southern Italian oaked Chardonnay. ★ *Chianti Classico*. **Milano salami**, milder than Calabrese, and quite fatty, teams up half-heartedly with a good Valpolicella Classico or single-vineyard Valpolicella, Soave Classico, or a ripe Müller-Thurgau, perhaps from the Alto Adige/Südtirol. **Napoli salami** is slightly smoked, with a dash of chilli added; the best matches are with Australian Semillon-Chardonnay and California Barbera. Italian Teroldego Rotaliano or a Beaujolais cru make reasonable partners. ★ *California Barbera* ★ *Australian Semillon-Chardonnay.*

**SAUSAGES** ❢ *low- to medium-tannin reds* ♀ *dry, not-too-intensely flavoured whites*

Pork sausages are fussy. Chablis Premier Cru is the only real star, but if you want a cheaper white to go with your bangers and mash, you might try Favorita, Muscadet, Arneis, Soave, or Chardonnays, including white Burgundy. Sancerre is pleasant but other Sauvignons don't really go. Rioja, Bairrada or Valpolicella are the best bets among the reds, followed by Beaujolais (including the lighter crus such as Juliénas or Fleurie), hot-climate Merlots, red Burgundy or California Pinot Noir, and from Italy, Chianti, Bardolino, Dolcetto, Barbera or Squinzano, are also good. ★★ *Chablis Premier Cru*

VARIATIONS Sausage recipes vary, but sage tends to be a fairly dominant flavour in pork sausages. Sancerre stands a good chance of being a superstar, but other wines from the Sauvignon grape will also go well. Chablis Premier Cru and white Crozes-Hermitage go well, or try Colombard-Chardonnay. The red star is Valpolicella Classico; Chianti, Dolcetto, Squinzano and Barbera are all good. Beaujolais (especially the fuller crus) are good, as are hot-climate Merlots, red Burgundy, California Pinot Noir, Rioja Gran Reserva and Bairrada. ★★ *Valpolicella Classico*

**Black Pudding** ❢ *very low-tannin reds* ♀ *dry whites*

Black pudding, otherwise known as boudin noir, morcilla, Blutwurst, or kashanka, favours Chardonnay. Chablis at all price levels is delicious, but Chardonnays from California, Australia, New Zealand or southern France are nearly as good. New Zealand Sauvignon Blanc is also very good, and much better than other Sauvignons. Other pleasant whites are Marsanne, white Crozes-Hermitage, Alsace Pinot Blanc, Vinho Verde and South African Colombard. Black pudding makes most reds taste extra-tannic, but it behaves unexpectedly well with a light red Burgundy and a couple of other reasonably tannic reds – Dolcetto and red Châteauneuf-du-Pape. Rioja Gran Reserva also works well. ★★ *light red Burgundy* ★★ *Chablis*

**Chorizo** ❢ *reds with very low tannin* ❢ *dry rosés* ♀ *unoaked or subtly oaked fruity whites*

You will find this wonderfully flavourful, quite fatty, spicy sausage served across Spain as a pre-prandial nibble, with whatever local red, rosado or white wine is to hand. Chorizo can be accompanied quite acceptably by most unoaked Spanish whites, but the real star white match is with Australian Semillon-Chardonnay, while Australian Colombard-Chardonnay and unoaked southern French Chardonnay are nearly as successful. Rosados are ideal, both the star Rioja Rosado, and Spanish Tempranillo rosados, but good *red* matches are hard to find, since the raw fat emphasizes tannin. Red Rioja is a good flavour but can be too tannic – a mature Gran Reserva works best. Light, untannic, unoaked Tempranillos from elsewhere in Spain, such as La Mancha, are slightly soft. You have to leave Spain to find more successful reds, such as an untannic Côtes du Roussillon-Villages or Corbières, and mature Chianti Classico. A not-too-tannic California Cabernet, Barbera and Mourvèdre are all good choices. ★★ *Rioja Rosado* ★★ *Australian Semillon-Chardonnay*

**Frankfurter** ❢ *low- to medium-tannin reds, not too strong in flavour* ❢ *dry rosés* ♀ *medium- to fairly high-acid, oaked or unoaked whites*

Frankfurters have quite a delicate but smoky flavour that can be transmitted with disagreeable results to some wines. But not to Fitou, which is a brilliant match; other blended southern French reds such as St-Chinian, or Grenache-based Côtes du Rhône, also go well, as do Hungarian Merlot, mature Barbaresco and other softer Nebbiolos, Rioja Gran Reserva or Gamay de Touraine. There are other excellent dry whites: oaked white Rioja is superb, and dry (Trocken or especially Halbtrocken) German or Austrian Rieslings, Italian Pinot Grigio, Chablis Premier Cru, oaked Chardonnays – perhaps from Chile or California – are all delicious. Light, simple Sauvignons are quite good, as is Vernaccia di San Gimignano. Aligoté is a little too acid but a delicious flavour match. Rosés are a pleasant alternative – try a Bordeaux or Bergerac rosé, or Spanish Tempranillo rosado. ★★ *Fitou* ★★ *oaked white Rioja*

**Garlic Sausage (Saucisson à l'Aïl)** ❢ *medium-bodied, low-tannin, softly fruity reds* ♀ *dry, light to medium-bodied, bland whites*

The flavour of red Bordeaux is just right, but choose a soft, simple one. Once you reach cru bourgeois level, the flavour match is still excellent though the wine flavour is beginning to get a little strong. Light, untannic Cabernet Sauvignons from elsewhere are also good, and Loire Cabernet Franc-based reds such as Chinon, Saumur-Champigny or Bourgueil, or Italian Franciacorta are good, provided the tannin is not excessive. A gentle California Sangiovese also goes well. You might try Rioja Crianza, Oregon Pinot Noir, Beaujolais crus or red Corbières. Bland whites sometimes cope: Chardonnay VdP d'Oc, Soave Classico, a simple Penedés or Conca de Barberá white, Muscadet, or Burgundian or Bulgarian Aligoté. ★★ *basic red Bordeaux*

**Saucisson Sec** ❢ *a few low-tannin reds* ♀ *unoaked, bland, lowish-acid whites*

There is such variation in brand and style of saucisson sec from region to region in France that it is hard to generalize. Nothing is a perfect match, but there's a good chance of success with southern French Terret, Chablis, white Dão from Portugal, Bianco di Custoza or Australian Semillon-Chardonnay. For a red, try Coteaux du Tricastin, a Beaujolais cru such as Juliénas or St-Amour, Rioja Gran Reserva, California Barbera or hot-climate Merlot.

## SPARE RIBS WITH BARBECUE SAUCE
❢ *very fruity reds with good acidity* ♀ *medium or medium-dry, medium- to high-acid whites*

The sauce, which is sweet and fairly high in acidity, strips the fruit out of most reds and dry whites. Liebfraumilch is a brilliant match, better than much more expensive German Riesling Kabinetts from the Mosel-Saar-Ruwer. Rheingau Riesling, Spanish Alella Clásico, French Vouvray Demi-sec or Anjou Blanc Demi-sec all match very well too. Other cheaper German Rheingau wines are also good, while cheaper Mosels make nearly as good alternatives, as do medium-dry Rieslings from Australia or New Zealand (beware – some are dry). Reds able to stand up to barbecue sauce include fruity Dolcetto, Oregon Pinot Noir, Beaujolais-Villages, Zinfandel, Alentejo red from Portugal, or Valpolicella, but the sauce does them no favours. For plain spare ribs, see *Roast Pork,* and *Casseroles and Stews* if otherwise sauced. ★★ *Liebfraumilch*

## WILD BOAR see ROAST PORK and CASSEROLES AND STEWS

# Snails

## SNAILS IN GARLIC BUTTER ♥ *medium-acid, medium- to full-bodied reds* ♀ *light- to medium-bodied, bland whites*

High acid in both white or red wines is wrong with this classic dish. It's the sauce, not the bland snail meat, that needs matching. The star is a Médoc cru bourgeois, although other red Bordeaux from a ripe vintage are ideal. Other good red matches are Zinfandel, Cabernets from California, Washington State, New Zealand and Australia, red Burgundy from a good year, California or Oregon Pinot Noir, or mature Bairrada. The star white wine is the deliciously matched Bourgogne Aligoté. Other good whites are Burgundy, Chablis (an attractive flavour but a touch acid), southern French Terret, or Italian Est! Est!! Est!!!
★★ *Médoc cru bourgeois* ★★ *Bourgogne Aligoté*

# Veal

Veal is such an incredibly bland meat that the slightest sprinkle of herbs or a dash of sauce becomes the element to match. Red wines, as well as flavourful whites, are out of the question with veal, unless other ingredients in the dish, such as wine or onions, can take them on.

Calves for veal supplied to Sainsbury's are reared on British farms to the highest welfare standards. No veal is taken from foreign suppliers. Young calves are housed in large, airy barns with natural daylight and plenty of space to move freely. They are fed a milk and straw-based diet which produces pale pink flesh, as opposed to crated foreign veal which is milky white in colour.

## BLANQUETTE DE VEAU ♀ *bland or very gently flavoured whites*

It's not so much the cream and egg yolks in the sauce as the very mild flavour of the meat that makes this dish quite hard to pair with wines. The gently aromatic Italian Pinot Grigio is the answer, or a very gentle, inexpensive Alsace Pinot Gris, which also goes very well indeed, as do very gentle, unoaked Chardonnays, from both cool and warm climates. Bourgogne Aligoté tends to be better than Burgundian Chardonnay, however. You can also try southern French Marsanne, Italian Gavi, Orvieto, Soave or Bianco di Custoza. ★★ *Pinot Grigio*

## CALVES' LIVER ♥ *mature or fruity reds, with medium to low acidity and tannin* ♀ *warm-climate Sauvignon Blanc or dry Riesling*

Red wines are definitely the best choice here, with Italy leading the way. Mature Carmignano and Chianti Classico are the super-stars, with just the right level of fruit and savoury flavour to match the liver, and California Sangiovese is almost as delicious. The Nebbiolo grape of Italy (Barolo, Barbaresco) makes a delicious, savoury blend so long as the tannin is not too high, and an inexpensive Rosso del Piemonte is also very good. Two Italians from the south – Salice Salentino and Cirò Riserva – are good. A mature, not-too-tannic Bairrada from Portugal hits the spot, as do Beaujolais-Villages and a lighter-style Beaujolais cru. There are successful white wines, too. The ripe, limy fruitiness of a New Zealand or an Australian dry Riesling is a surprising hit. Alsace Riesling is pleasant, but German and Austrian Rieslings are a little too floral. ★★ *mature Carmignano* ★★ *mature Chianti Classico*

VARIATIONS With **Fegato alla Veneziana**, a delicious dish of meltingly soft fried onions and calves' liver, brightly fruity, medium-acid reds are the guide. The local Valpolicella is the wrong flavour, but another Italian, Dolcetto, is a real star (although too fruity without the onions). Shiraz and Zinfandel are both impressive matches, and Barbaresco goes well, but less well than with plain-fried liver. If you really want to drink a white wine, go for a hot-climate, not-too-acid Sauvignon Blanc. ★★ *Dolcetto*

## CHOPS IN MARSALA SAUCE ♥ *Dolcetto* ♀ *gentle, slightly aromatic whites*

Dolcetto, with its bright fruit, makes a stand as the only good red with this very slightly sweet sauce. Excellent white wine matches are very sparse, although quite a range make adequate partners. Most successful among the whites are Côtes du Rhône and Spanish Alella Clásico.

Italian Favorita, Arneis or Gravina, Australian Colombard-Chardonnay, German Silvaner Trocken or Halbtrocken, southern French Marsanne, or a warm-climate Sauvignon Blanc all make pleasant alternatives. ★ *Dolcetto* ★ *white Côtes du Rhône* ★ *Alella Clásico*

## OSSO BUCO ♀ *full-bodied, fruity whites, with good acidity*

TRADITIONAL PARTNER *Lombardy whites*

Something rather fruity and gutsy is needed for the gelatinous richness of this cut of veal, with its sauce acidified by white wine, gently sweetened with carrot and tomato, and flavoured with orange and lemon zest. Reds are too tannic, and most Italian whites are too thin and neutral. Of the native wines, however, gently aromatic Arneis from Piemonte is good, as are highish-acid Chardonnays from Alto Adige/Südtirol, Trentino, or Piemonte. Crossing into France, Chardonnay VdP du Jardin de la France or Champagne Blanc de Blancs are equally good. But for a star choice, turn to Australia and a Reserve Semillon, which has precisely the right fruitiness and flavour. Australian Marsanne is excellent, and Semillon-Chardonnay is very good. There's a surprisingly good match with German Silvaner Trocken or Alsace Sylvaner, and Viognier finds one of its rare successful food partners. Dry Rieslings from New Zealand, Australia, Alsace or Germany work quite well too. ★★ *Australian Reserve Semillon*

## SALTIMBOCCA ♀ *unoaked dry whites*

TRADITIONAL PARTNER *Frascati*

This Roman dish of veal rolled up with ham and sage is fairly hard to match. Some Italian whites stand up to it in a fairly neutral sort of way: Frascati, Favorita, Cortese, Frascati, Vernaccia or Soave Classico. However, the aroma of a white Côtes du Rhône or Viognier chimes in well with the sage; white wines from Penedés or Conca de Barberá in Spain are good; and Muscadet and Chablis are reasonable alternatives. ★★ *white Côtes du Rhône*

**VITELLO TONNATO** ♀ *bland or very gently aromatic whites*
TRADITIONAL PARTNER *Northern Italian whites*
Cold and bizarrely yet pleasantly sauced with tuna, anchovies, lemon juice, capers and mayonnaise, this traditional dish of Lombardy, in northern Italy, is hard to please. Red wines simply clash. However, several Italian whites make very agreeable matches: Arneis especially, and Cortese, Gavi, Frascati, Est! Est!! Est!!! and Vermentino are all fine, but some others, including Soave, clash with the raw egg yolk of the mayonnaise. The local sparkling rosé goes well, though it, too, reacts slightly to the egg yolk. Outside Italy, good choices are Australian Colombard-Chardonnay or southern French Terret, and German Silvaner Trocken or Alsace Sylvaner are quite good options. ★ *Arneis*

**WIENERSCHNITZEL** ♀ *very bland, unoaked, gently flavoured, medium-acid whites*
TRADITIONAL PARTNER *Austrian Weissburgunder (Pinot Blanc)*
Wienerschnitzel, egged and breadcrumbed and sprinkled with lemon juice, goes with very similar wines to plain veal, but it can take slightly more flavour and slightly higher acidity. Vienna's home-grown Grüner Veltliner is a reasonable match, but a number of foreign whites are better: try gentle Italian whites, especially Vernaccia di San Gimignano, Pinot Bianco, and Gavi, a not-too-aromatic Sauvignon Blanc from Chile or elsewhere, simple white Burgundy (either Chardonnay or Aligoté) or inexpensive, light European Chardonnays (including VdP or northern Italian examples). ★ *Vernaccia di San Gimignano*

# Venison

Venison is a rich, earthy meat with a slightly wilder, 'darker' flavour than hung beef, and a dense, unfatty texture. Quite a challenge to match with wines. Pinot Noir is the only real hope, and it tends to make a better match still once you add marinades and sauces. In fact marinades are the secret – brightening and transforming venison into moister, more exciting flavour combinations. Marinated venison is the cue for savoury, meaty reds, made from grapes such as Syrah, Nebbiolo, Pinot Noir and Zinfandel.

## CASSEROLES AND STEWS ▪ *full-bodied, flavourful, fruity reds*

The fine-tuning of the wine choice depends on the ingredients, but red wine will almost certainly be part of the marinade/cooking liquid, and will make the venison infinitely more amenable to the wine in your glass. Marinated and cooked in red wine, olive oil, onion, garlic, carrot, celery, juniper and herbs, with caramelized onions and bacon in the sauce, a Côtes du Rhône Syrah offers exactly the right flavour. Southern French Syrah vins de pays might also be wonderful, but many Syrahs of the northern Rhône taste inappropriately 'medicinal'. Australian Shiraz alone is not quite right, but Shiraz-Cabernet blends are delicious and Australian Cabernet is lovely, despite its mintiness. California, Washington State, New Zealand, Chilean and Argentinian Cabernets are all excellent, and mature fine red Bordeaux from a ripe year works very well. Ripe, hot-climate Merlots are quite good. The other super-star is Zinfandel, oaked or not, which is a brilliant match. The ripe fruit of northern Italian Dolcetto is excellent, as is a modern, fruity Alentejo red from Portugal. A not-too-tannic Pinot Noir also makes a lovely match, whether from Oregon, California, Australia or Burgundy. ★★ *Côtes du Rhône Syrah* ★★ *Zinfandel*

## ROAST VENISON ▪ *low-tannin, mature reds, especially Pinot Noir*

A lot of red wines are too brightly fruity, too tannic, too acid or simply the wrong flavour for plain-roast venison or venison steaks. Mature wines are better than young ones. Even Pinot Noir is not a stunning match. Burgundy is the best choice, whether an easy, soft Côte de Beaune, or an older, slightly pruny Côte de Nuits, but keep the tannins low. Other Pinot Noirs – from Oregon, California, Australia or New Zealand – are pleasant, as are southern Rhône reds such as Côtes du Ventoux or Côtes du Rhône. A marinade and sauce makes all the difference. See *Casseroles and Stews* above. ★ *soft red Burgundy*

# Furred Game

Hare and rabbit are not easy meats to match when plainly roasted, and become much more wine-friendly when cooked in a casserole or served with a sauce. Although rabbit is technically a white meat, it actually finds most of its partners among the gentle red wines, low in tannin.

## Hare

Dark, rich, earthy and gamy hare is very hard to match without the help of a sauce. Most wines are too bright, too tannic or too fruity. But add a sauce, or cook it in a stew, and the story changes dramatically.

### CASSEROLES AND STEWS ❢ *medium- to full-bodied, ripely fruity reds*

It depends on the ingredients, but a casserole of hare cooked in red wine with onions, garlic, bacon, thyme, oregano and bay leaves is easy to match with wines. Ripely fruity reds are the answer. Choose from Gamay-based wines including Beaujolais and the Beaujolais crus; California, Australian or Chilean Cabernet, Merlot or Pinot Noir; Australian Cabernet-Shiraz; Chianti, and Côtes du Rhône or Provençal reds.

### JUGGED HARE ❢ *medium- to full-bodied, fruity reds*

Even with quite a high dose of lemon-peel, this is quite easy to pair up. Amarone della Valpolicella makes a brilliant match. Rhône reds succeed – Côtes du Ventoux is a delicious match, the best of a good bunch, and Côtes du Rhône is good. The ripeness of Australian, California or other hot-country Merlots work extremely well, and the sweet/sour character of Zinfandel chimes in with the citrus tang. Pure Spanish Tempranillo is a lovely flavour. The fresh, lively, savoury flavour of Pinot Noir works, particularly lowish-tannin Burgundies. ★★ *red Côtes du Ventoux*

## Rabbit

Rabbit is not just furry chicken when it comes to finding matching wines. It has a stronger and very particular character that makes it a much better match for reds than for whites.

## CASSEROLES AND STEWS

The choice of wine depends on the recipe.

VARIATIONS Rabbit cooked in **white wine, onion, celery, garlic, carrot and thyme** goes well with red wines – Cahors, young red Rioja, Oregon Pinot Noir, red Burgundy and Australian Shiraz-Cabernet, or Spanish Tempranillo rosados. With **white wine, onion and tomato**, try Alsace Pinot Gris, Australian Shiraz or Shiraz-Cabernet, Oregon Pinot Noir or red Rioja Reserva. For rabbit cooked in **red wine**, serve an Australian or California Pinot Noir, Cabernet, Shiraz or Cabernet-Shiraz, or a Beaujolais cru or Rioja Crianza.

### RABBIT IN CIDER ▮ *low- to medium-tannin, fruity reds* ▮ *dry Grenache rosés* ♀ *lightly aromatic, dry or off-dry whites*

Cider goes well, as you might guess, but wines work, too. If the cooking cider was medium or sweet, go for a South African Chenin or a Rioja Rosado. Cooked in dry cider, rabbit is also a brilliant match for Grenache/Garnacha rosés (Rioja or Navarra rosados work well). Lots of untannic, bright reds go well, too. Young Rioja or Navarra reds, low-tannin Chilean, California, New Zealand or Australian Cabernet, and untannic, fruity red Bordeaux all go very well indeed. Oregon, California or Australian Pinot Noir are excellent, better than red Burgundy, which is good, too. Whites are much trickier: best are Sancerre from a ripe vintage, or Italian Lugana. ★ *Navarra or Rioja rosado* ★ *South African Chenin*

### RABBIT WITH MUSTARD ▮ *low-tannin reds* ♀ *dry, gently fruity, highish-acid, unoaked whites*

This dish finds no absolutely perfect matches, but it goes well with the pleasantly earthy flavour of a dry German Silvaner or Alsace Sylvaner, and gentle Bordeaux Blanc (Sauvignon-Semillon blend). Unoaked Chardonnays and Italian Vernaccia make reasonable matches. Best of the reds is a light, inexpensive, if a little too tannic, Australian Shiraz-Cabernet. ★ *German Silvaner Trocken*

# ETHNIC DISHES

Yes, you *can* drink and enjoy wine with Chinese, Indian and Thai food. And we believe it matches better than lager or jasmine tea, provided you choose the *right* wine. We cannot pretend to have done justice to national cuisines as diverse as these in a few short pages. But we have tasted widely – more dishes than could be included in this book – and have come up with some solutions to the main challenge: finding a wine that suits a whole range of dishes.

Chinese, Indian and Thai diners all dip communally into five or more dishes simultaneously. A wine that suits one mouthful might not suit the next. The solution is to find a 'bridging wine' that can cope with the lot. We have suggested a clutch of such wines for each of the three cuisines.

As for spicing and 'heat', they are not usually a problem. Most of the herbs and spices used in these cuisines find good wine partners. There's not even a problem with chilli – it may burn your tongue, but it doesn't affect the taste of wine. Fizzy drinks accentuate the chilli burn, however, so it may be best to avoid lager, fizzy water and sparkling wines with the hottest foods.

## Chinese Dishes

Chinese food (in its usual British manifestation at least) tends to be either supremely bland, quite sweet or very sweet, and any meal is likely to include a mixture of all three types of dishes. A Chinese family would typically eat at least three but probably four or five different dishes simultaneously, plus one or two soups, at both lunch and dinner (the advised etiquette is one dish per person plus one extra, with everyone communally dipping in). That makes life difficult for the wine drinker. The bland and the *slightly* sweet dishes have a few wine styles in common: Valencia or Yecla dry whites, Champagne, German Halbtrocken wines (made from Riesling or Silvaner, for example), and inexpensive Australian Rieslings all have the right flavours and a matching tiny touch of sweetness (whatever the label says about being 'dry' or 'brut').

But the sweetest dishes – the pork spare ribs and the sweet and sours – cause problems. They make those useful, drier, bridging wines (such as Champagne, German Halbtrockens and Valencia dry white) taste unpleasantly dry and fruitless. It is best to avoid these dishes if you don't want to spoil the wine.

The most common solution for the Chinese is to drink soup *with* the main dishes to quench the thirst and rinse out the flavours between mouthfuls of different dishes. Jasmine tea is an alternative, yet it lacks the acidity really to match most dishes, and like red wines, often tastes too tannic. Sauces are nearly always the main thing to match. If eating sweet and sour pork or prawns, you will find appropriate advice under *Chicken*.

## BEEF DISHES
### Beef with Green Peppers in Black Bean Sauce ♀ *dry or nearly dry whites*
Very slightly sweet, quite savoury, slightly gingery, and slightly bitter from the black beans, this goes well with wines with a touch of sweetness, such as Australian Verdelho or German Halbtrockens (made from Riesling or unspecified grape varieties). Even the slightly sweeter German Kabinetts or QbAs (including Liebfraumilch) go positively well. Dry whites from Valencia in Spain are pleasant alternatives. ★★ *Australian Verdelho* ★★ *German Riesling Halbtrocken*
### Beef and Mangetout in Oyster Sauce ♀ *bland whites*
This rather bland dish calls for similarly bland wines. Although nothing goes positively well, Muscadet, Soave, Pinot Grigio, Yecla, Valencia dry white, simple, light, or unoaked, not-too-acid Chardonnays, perhaps from Italy or the south of France, are all acceptable. Reds are too tannic.
### Beef with Onions and Ginger ❢ *Beaujolais* ♀ *not-quite-dry whites*
The sweetness of this dish ideally requires a slightly sweet wine, but a few dry whites go surprisingly well: try Frascati, Bordeaux, Bergerac or Duras Blanc. The flavour of Riesling goes well: best of all is a Mosel Riesling QbA or Kabinett, which has just the right touch of sweetness and acidity, but other German QbA or Kabinett Rieslings or not-quite-dry Rieslings from Australia (most of the cheaper ones) also do well. Simpler

German wines, with no grape variety mentioned on the label, are also likely to work, especially those from the Mosel region. And Beaujolais, including the crus such as Moulin-à-Vent, is also a pleasant match, though other reds tend to be too tannic. ★★ *Mosel Riesling or cheaper QbA*

## CHICKEN DISHES
### Chicken with Bamboo Shoots and Water Chestnuts ♀ *bland whites with low to medium acidity*
Nothing is good with the very delicate flavours of this dish, but Baden Dry, Bordeaux Blanc, Yecla or Valencia dry whites from Spain are acceptable.
### Chicken with Cashew Nuts ♂ *dry rosés* ♀ *dry or nearly dry whites*
Despite the red peppers, ginger and chilli used in the sauce, chicken with cashew nuts is very gently flavoured. It finds its best partners in Albariño, Yecla, and Valencia dry whites. Penedés rosados from Spain, or southern French rosés made from Cinsault are as good, or try Australian Riesling. ★ *Spanish Albariño* ★ *Valencia dry white*
### Chicken Chow Mein ♀ *bland, dry or medium-dry, not-too-acid whites*
Mainly infuenced by garlic, ginger and sugar, with mangetout, oyster sauce and mushrooms, this goes very well with white Châteauneuf-du-Pape, and adequately with Piesporter Michelsberg and other simple German QbAs, German Silvaner Trocken or Halbtrocken, Viognier, Frascati, Pinot Grigio, Vernaccia, Yecla, Valencia dry or medium-dry whites. ★ *white Châteauneuf-du-Pape*
### Sweet and Sour Chicken ♀ *medium-dry to medium-sweet whites*
With its considerable sweetness and vinegary acidity, the sauce strips the fruit from dry wines. It's best to avoid sweet and sour dishes if you want to choose one drier wine to accompany several dishes. If you are serving sweet and sour on its own, Mosel Riesling Auslese and Hungarian Tokay 3 Puttonyos are just right, Vouvray goes quite well, and Liebfraumilch is so very nearly sweet enough that it makes an adequate match. ★ *Mosel Riesling Auslese* ★ *Tokay 3 Puttonyos*

## DUCK DISHES
### Peking Duck ♂ *Cinsault rosés* ♀ *a few dry whites*
Many wines taste too acid, too dry or too bland against

the sweetness of the sauce that lines the pancakes. Even adequate wine partners are rare, but a basic Champagne works well, as do Tuscan Vernaccia-Chardonnay blends, white Châteauneuf-du-Pape and Cinsault rosés, even though they're dry. ★ *Champagne*

## PORK DISHES
**Pork Spare Ribs** ♀ *high-acid, sweetish whites*

It's hard to find a wine with the right balance of flavour, sweetness and acidity for these sweet-sauced ribs. An off-dry Vouvray might hit the spot, or you can try a squat-bottled Vinho Verde. This dish is a killer for dry wines, and one best avoided if you want to drink one wine with a spread of dishes. ★ *Vouvray Demi-sec*

**Szechuan-style Pork** ♀ *a few gently aromatic whites* ♀ *Syrah rosés*
Szechuan-style Pork has quite a gingery flavour, with chillies and green peppers. It finds better wine partners with Riesling and Silvaner than with cheaper, basic German wines. Champagne Blanc de Noirs is also pleasant, as is a not-quite-dry Hungarian Furmint, inexpensive Australian Riesling, and Syrah rosés. ★ *German Riesling or Silvaner Kabinett Halbtrocken*

## SOUPS
**Hot and Sour Soup** ♀ *medium- to high-acid whites with a touch of sweetness*

English Seyval Blanc (dry or medium-dry) makes a lovely partnership for this slightly sweet-sharp, chilli-rich soup. The next best choices are squat-bottled (slightly sweetened) Vinho Verde, VdP des Côtes de Gascogne, Bianco di Verona, Spanish Yecla or Valencia, Hungarian Furmint and white Côtes du Rhône. ★★ *English Seyval Blanc*

**Sweetcorn Soup with Chicken** ♀ *medium-dry whites*

Any chicken flavour in this simple soup is over-powered by the wine-unfriendly sweetcorn, which makes most wines taste too dry and acid. Australian Verdelho, generally very slightly sweet, is the real star, but Bianco di Verona and South African Colombard are also pleasant partners, as is Champagne. ★★ *Australian Verdelho*

Sweetcorn Soup with Crab ♀ *medium-dry whites*
There's more of a balance between fish and sweetcorn flavour than in the chicken version of this soup, but the sweetness is the same. Australian Verdelho slightly overpowers, but the flavour is good, or try Champagne.

Won Ton Soup ♀ *blandest of bland, dry, low-acid whites*
Like most Chinese soups, this is really bland – chicken stock with a few floating vegetables and minced-prawn-stuffed pasta parcels. Nothing but Yecla or Valencia whites from south-east Spain seem bland enough to accompany it without overwhelming the soup entirely. ★ *Yecla or Valencia dry white*

SPRING ROLLS ♀ *bland whites*
These nicely crunchy vegetable parcels, although the fillings vary, are very mildly flavoured, and hard to match to wine. The best choices are bland whites; try Rueda or Albariño from Spain, or Frascati from Italy.

# Thai Dishes

It's quite difficult to find perfect partners for the complex flavours of Thai food, but they do exist. The frequent tartness (from lemon and lime) calls for wines with fairly high acidity – but not excessively so, because the acidity in Thai food, like everything else apart from the super-charged chilli, is delicately balanced. The same goes for sweetness. Sweet-sour *Chinese* food may call for something full-bloodedly sweet, but sweet-sour Thai dishes require only a touch of sweetness in the wine (a German Kabinett may be too sweet, a German Halbtrocken just right). And the herbs so generously used in Thai cooking – lemon grass, coriander, basil and ginger – all go well with wine. Some wines don't turn up their noses even at the slightly rotty, salty fish sauce and fermented fish paste so beloved of the Thais – and in any case, Thai dishes often contain no more than a hint of these.

The main trouble with finding a suitable wine for a Thai meal is the wide range of dishes served simultaneously. There is a little clutch of wines that successfully matches a wide range of Thai dishes. Best bet of all are the Sauvignon Blancs of the Upper Loire: Sancerre, Pouilly-Fumé, Menetou-Salon, Quincy or Reuilly, especially ones from a good vintage. (More acidic French Sauvignons such as Sauvignon de St-Bris or Sauvignon de Touraine are too acidic, and New World and other European ones are less good.) Other grapes that can bridge a lot of dishes are Aligoté, Colombard (including VdP des Côtes de Gascogne), Pinot Blanc, inexpensive Pinot Gris, plus Muscadet Sur Lie, Champagne, rosés made with Cabernet and one red, Beaujolais-Villages: these may well go adequately even if not included in the entries below.

For dishes with more marked sweetness, such as satay, or the two famous noodle dishes, mee grob and pud Thai, the ideal partner would be not-quite-dry Riesling, or Champagne Brut (which always has a little sweetness). These dishes will make most of the drier wines listed above taste dull – though Sancerre and the like cope better than the rest.

Beer, with its bitter hoppiness and low acidity, is much less appropriate than a well-chosen white wine, and jasmin tea likewise lacks acidity, rarely positively goes, and its tannin often slightly clashes, as does that of red wine.

A word about spellings – there is no official standard for anglicized spellings. Gaeng, translatable as 'any dish cooked in a sauce', but often meaning 'curry', may also be written Kaeng, Gang or in various other ways. Where possible, we have given major variations.

## CURRY DISHES
### Beef in Peanut Curry (Panang Neuk)
♀ *dry, not-too-acid whites*
Beef in dry, aromatic peanut curry with coconut milk and herbs, spices, hot chillies and sweet basil meets its best match in a simple, dry Alsace Tokay-Pinot Gris. Soave, California Chardonnay and other New World Chardonnays also go very well, and Sauvignon Blancs make pleasant partners. ★ *Alsace Tokay-Pinot Gris*

## Green Curry (Gaeng Kiew/Khiaw Wan) ♀ *a few whites*

Thai green (khiaw) curry is hot, sour and slightly sweet (wan), with lots of coconut and other flavours, including lemon grass, coriander, fish sauce, lime and caraway seeds. It is very difficult to match well with wine. No wines are perfect, but nearest to success are Vernaccia di San Gimignano, Australian and New Zealand Semillon or Sauvignon or blends of the two. Reds are too tannic, beers inappropriate.

## Mussalman Curry (Gaeng Massaman/ Musman/Mus-Sa-Man) ♀ *fruity, dry or medium-dry whites*

This is a mild, slightly sweet Muslim curry from South Thailand, made with peanuts, cardomom, star anise, coconut, fish sauce, lemon, sugar, lemon grass, paprika and lime leaves. Two wines are stars, Hungarian Furmint, and Rueda from Spain. Next best options are white Châteauneuf-du-Pape, VdP des Côtes de Gascogne, Aligoté, Alsace Tokay-Pinot Gris, inexpensive Chardonnay from Chile, California or other New World countries or Riesling, especially one with some sweetness, such as a German QbA. You can also try Semillon-Chardonnay, Marsanne, Italian Lugana or Champagne. Red wines clash. ★★ *Rueda* ★★ *Hungarian Furmint*

## Red Curry (Gaeng Phed/Ped) ♀ *dry, fairly bland whites*

Red (phed) curry is quite hot, pepped up with lime juice and fish sauce, and scented with lemon grass, basil, creamed coconut, ginger, garlic and lime leaves. It goes well with Yecla, Valencia, Penedés or Conca de Barberá whites from Spain, Aligoté from Burgundy or Bulgaria, and Gavi or Tuscan blends of Vernaccia-Chardonnay. Or try Rieslings, German Silvaner Trocken and Alsace Sylvaner. ★ *Aligoté* ★ *Valencia dry white*

## Roast Duck Curry (Gaeng/Kaeng/Gang Ped Ped Yaang) ♀ *dry or ideally not-quite-dry, fairly high- to high-acid whites* ♟ *dry to medium-dry rosés*

Hot (ped ped) and full of fascinating flavour, roast duck curry is based on green curry (see above), with lime leaves, coconut milk, fish sauce, chillies and coriander added to the pot. There are lots of good wine partners to follow the two star choices, VdP des Côtes de Gascogne and Bordeaux Rosé. Champagne Blanc de Noirs is nearly as good, and other very good matches include Semillon-Chardonnay, Aligoté, Müller-Thurgau (including Baden Dry), squat-bottled Vinho Verde, Sauvignons, especially from the New World, and Rieslings, ideally with a touch of sweetness such as German Kabinetts, though dry ones are also pleasant. Reds are too tannic, but rosés work very well: those made from Cabernet are excellent, and Cinsault rosés are very good. ★★ *Bordeaux rosé* ★★ *VdP des Côtes de Gascogne*

## FISH CAKES (TOD MUN PLA) ♀ *Cinsault rosés ♀ a few dry whites*

Thai fish cakes have an impressively concentrated fish flavour and slight vinegary touch. A few dry whites work quite well. Best bets may be Australian Semillon-Chardonnay, Aligoté, Sancerre, Pouilly-Fumé or Menetou-Salon from the Loire, and Hungarian Furmint. Cinsault rosés are also acceptable. That's if you eat it plain. If the fish cakes are served with a sweet sauce, we give up.

## KING PRAWNS (GOONG PAO)

'Goong pao' are King prawns (goong), grilled or barbequed (pao) in their shells, and served with a variety of sauces, of which two are included here.

### King Prawns with Fish Sauce ♀ *dry, fairly bland whites with medium to high acidity*

This is the famous Thai fish sauce, salty and slightly 'rotty' in flavour. Served with the prawns, it finds a very good match with Chardonnays, especially oaked ones and those from warmer climates. Muscadet Sur Lie is pleasant, but its cheaper Loire cellar-mate, Gros Plant, is even better. Alsace Sylvaner or German Silvaner Trocken are the other best choices. Reds taste disgustingly tannic. ★ *oaked Chardonnay*

VARIATIONS **Tamarind sauce**: add tamarind and lots of chilli to the fish sauce, and it obliterates the prawn flavour, but finds some lovely wine matches. The three star whites are Gros Plant, Muscadet Sur Lie, and dry Vinho Verde. The dish goes very well with unoaked Chardonnays, Bourgogne Aligoté, and French Sauvignons, including

Sancerre and Bordeaux Blanc, and is pleasant with Australian or New Zealand Riesling, Baden Dry, South African or Australian Colombard or squat-bottled (sweeter) Vinho Verde. Reds are too tannic. ★★ *Gros Plant* ★★ *Muscadet Sur Lie* ★★ *dry Vinho Verde*

## NOODLE/STIR-FRY DISHES
### Hot Thai Noodle Salad (Yum Woon Son)
♀ *dry, fairly bland whites with fairly high acidity*

'Yum' is 'salad', and 'woon son' are 'transparent noodles', which are dressed in this traditional Thai salad with chicken and shrimps, fresh herbs (coriander especially), chillies, lots of lemon juice, and a hint of fish sauce. Pinot Blanc makes a brilliant match, and there are other good white partners: simple Chablis, Aligoté, Muscadet Sur Lie, Bordeaux Blanc, white Côtes de Duras, or Bergerac. ★★ *Austrian or Alsace Pinot Blanc*

### Noodles and Beansprouts (Mee Grob/Krob)
♀ *slightly sweet, medium- to high-acid whites*

There's a lovely texture contrast in this national dish between the crunchy beansprouts and crispy, light noodles soaked in a sweet-sour syrup. The acidity (sourness) of the noodles is not very pronounced, and many wines taste too acid as well as too dry. The best choices, medium-dry English white, inexpensive Australian Riesling, or even Champagne, are slightly too acid, but have the right sweetness and flavour to complement the dish.

### Special Thai Noodles (Pudd/Pad Thai)
♀♀ *fruity or slightly sweet rosés and whites*

Good wine partners are sparse for this most famous of the Thai noodle dishes, which incorporates shrimps or prawns, sometimes chicken or pork, bean curd, bean sprouts, ground peanut, egg and chopped salted turnips. The slight sweetness of the dish makes a German Riesling Halbtrocken a good choice, and German QbAs or Kabinett wines from a ripe year also go well (though they are a touch on the sweet side). ★ *Mosel Riesling Halbtrocken*

### Stir-fry Pork (Pud Prik Moo) ♀ *dry, bland, not-too acid whites, and Sauvignon Blanc*

'Moo' means pork(!), here hotly stir-fried with chillies (prik), basil and noodles (pud). This is not a very flavoursome dish, and goes adequately with blander whites, including Baden Dry, white Côtes du Rhône and southern French Béarn. Ripe Sauvignons are best (but not New Zealand or California Sauvignons), with Sancerre and Menetou-Salon from the Loire the closest to perfect matches. ★ *Menetou-Salon* ★ *Sancerre*

### Stir-fry Squid (Plamuek Pudd Tao Jiew) ♀ *fairly bland, gentle whites*

Aligoté is best with this stir-fried (pudd) squid (plamuek) with soya bean pickle (tao jiew), fresh ginger, and fish sauce, but the top Loire Sauvignons – Menetou-Salon, Sancerre or Pouilly-Fumé – also go well. Vermentino chimes in, and southern French Picpoul, Soave and Australian Semillon are pleasant. ★ *Bourgogne Aligoté*

### SATAY ♀ *nearly dry whites*

Lemon-grass scented, Thai mixed meat kebabs are served with two sauces: one a sweet, oily peanut sauce, the other a harder-to-match syrupy sauce with onion and cucumber. The sweetness in both calls for a corresponding sweetness in the wine, found in German Riesling Halbtrocken; German Riesling Kabinett or QbA wines work, though both are a touch too sweet. A few drier wines are pleasant: Australian Semillon-Chardonnay, Spanish Rueda, Pinot Blanc or Weissburgunder or Sancerre. ★ *German Riesling Halbtrocken*

### SOUPS
### Lemon and Chicken Soup (Tom Yum Gai) ♀ *bland, medium- to high-acid whites*

German Silvaner Kabinett Trocken and VdP des Côtes de Gascogne are stars with this hot and sour soup. Alsace Sylvaner, South African or Australian Colombard, Béarn from southern France, or Italian Gavi work well. ★★ *VdP des Côtes de Gascogne* ★★ *German Silvaner Kabinett Trocken*

### Prawn and Lemon Soup (Tom Yum/ Yam/Yaam Goong/Kung) ♀ *bland, dry, not-too-acid whites*

Hot and sour prawns in spicy lemon soup is delicious with Vernaccia di San Gimignano and Valencia dry white from Spain. Southern French Picpoul makes a good alternative. ★★ *Vernaccia di San Gimignano* ★★ *Valencia dry white*

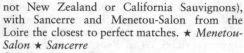

## SQUID SALAD (YAM PLA MUEK)
♀ *fairly high-acid dry whites*
This hot (very) and sour squid salad with lemon juice and a dressing containing coriander and lemon grass needs wines with the acidity to balance the lemon juice. It goes extremely well with the honeyed, grassy flavour of Gavi, but nearly as well with Vermentino or Australian or New Zealand Semillon-Chardonnay. ★ *Gavi*

# Indian Dishes

We tend to stick to lager in Indian restaurants, but the right wine goes infinitely better. Lager has a bitterness from the hops and often a fruity flavour that has no affinity with Indian food – it's not horrid, just not especially good. And lager's 'fizz' (like that of sparkling water or wine) accentuates the chilli-burn. With still wines, chilli is no problem. It may set your tongue alight, but it won't affect the actual taste of the wine. (However, chutneys and relishes are wine-killers and are best avoided if you care about your wine.)

Most of the herbs and spices used in Indian cookery – plus ginger, garlic and onions – are fairly wine-friendly (see *Herbs, Spices and Flavourings* on page 141 if your dish is dominated by a particular herb or spice). Some very powerfully spiced dishes may obliterate a lot of wines, but some wines, especially the aromatic whites such as Viognier or Sauvignon Blanc, are up to the job. And by no means all Indian food is hot and super-spicy. Most of the dishes we tasted found a good range of potential partners.

The problem is that you probably won't be eating just one particular dish – Indian meals tend to be a spread of many different dishes, and the wine needs to bridge the lot. Reds may be a problem in this respect, since many Indian dishes overemphasize the tannin in red wines. But a few reds are less tricky: the best choices to partner a selection of dishes are often Loire reds such as Chinon or St-Nicolas-de-Bourgueil, Italian Franciacorta or very light Sangiovese, inexpensive Shiraz, and light Tempranillo and young Rioja from Spain. Rosés can make easier matches, and there's guaranteed to be a white wine partner. Best bridging whites may be VdP des Côtes de Gascogne, Viognier, or New World Sauvignon Blancs. These wines often went adequately well even with the dishes below for which they are not specifically mentioned.

The following can be only a glimpse into the many different regional cuisines of India. We have chosen heavily from the rather generalized, standardized Indian repertoire of most Indian restaurants in the West. Most of the dishes were chicken-based, but the sauces are the dominant feature, and any meat – chicken, beef, or lamb or (at home in India) goat – in the same sauce will partner similar wines.

**BALTI** A balti is a wok-like cooking pot used in northern India or any dish that is prepared and served in one. Ingredients will vary enormously. See also *Chicken Tikka Balti*.

**Chicken Balti** 🍷 *not-too-fruity dry rosés*
♀ *dry, quite bland, medium to highish-acid whites*
The Sainsbury's chicken balti is very mildly spiced, the flavour dominated by onions and tomatoes, with lemon juice, vinegar and yoghurt adding to the acidity. Apart from the two good matches with white Corbières and VdP des Côtes de Gascogne, it's worth trying white Côtes du Rhône, Bordeaux Blanc and southern French Terret. Penedés rosados from Spain, Cinsault rosés, and very light reds are acceptable. ★ *white Corbières* ★ *VdP des Côtes de Gascogne*

**Vegetable Balti** 🍷 *dry rosés* ♀ *dry, fairly bland, highish-acid whites*
No wine goes better than adequately with Sainsbury's medium-spicy vegetable balti, whose main flavours are onion, tomato and cumin. Reds are too tannic or fruity, and many whites are too fruity, aromatic or oaky. Italian Favorita and South African Colombard made the most acceptable matches, with Chablis, unoaked northern Italian Chardonnay, Soave, Rueda and southern French Syrah rosé bringing up the rear.

**KORMA** 🍷 *light reds* ♀ *dry whites*
Korma is any dish in which meat is braised with a small amount of liquid – the ingredients vary. Sainsbury's Chicken Korma makes no stunning wine matches but lots of good matches with white

wines: Viognier or New World Sauvignon Blanc, Alsace Pinot Gris, VdP des Côtes de Gascogne, South African or Australian Colombard or Australian Semillon-Chardonnay. Amongst reds, Australian Coonawarra Cabernet is a surprising success, or try very light Shiraz, Zinfandel, Pinot Noir or Tempranillo. ★ *Viognier* ★ *Chilean Sauvignon Blanc*

**MADRAS** Madras is a city in south-east India, where they typically use a mix of fairly hot spices and cook to a thick sauce.
**Chicken Madras** ♀ *a few dry whites*
Many dry whites are simply the wrong flavour for this combination of spices and flavourings. The best choice is Rueda from Spain. There are plenty of pleasant matches, too: try Vinho Verde, Muscadet, Lugana, Australian or New Zealand Riesling, not-too-acid Sauvignons, dry Muscat, Italian Gravina, VdP des Côtes de Gascogne or Viognier. Reds clash. ★ *Spanish Rueda*

**MAKHANI** see **TIKKA**

**MASALA** see **TIKKA**

**PASANDA** ♥ *light reds* ♥ *dry rosés* ♀ *unoaked, dry whites*
A Pasanda is a quite sharp and mildly spiced yoghurt and cream-based sauce generally thickened with ground cashew nuts and almonds. The perfect partner with chicken, beef or lamb Pasanda is red Rioja Crianza, but it goes well with soft, fruity Pinot Noirs and light Italian Sangioveses, as well as with Cinsault and Syrah rosés and, for a white, VdP des Côtes de Gascogne or Hungarian Furmint. ★★ *red Rioja Crianza*

**ROGAN JOSH** ♀ *light, dry, highish-acid whites*
The yoghurt and tomato in the thick sauce of this lamb dish from northern India demand white wines with a fairly high acidity. Best bets are Italian Pinot Grigio and lightly oaked Chardonnay VdP d'Oc. But satisfying pairings can also be found with Vernaccia and Gavi from Italy, Sauvignons from Australia and New Zealand, dry German whites from Baden, and the aromatic Viognier. ★ *Pinot Grigio* ★ *lightly oaked Chardonnay VdP d'Oc*

### SAAG ALOO ♀ *bland, low-fruit whites with medium acidity*

Saag aloo, which comes from northern India, is a gently flavoured dish of spinach (saag) with potatoes (aloo), onion, garlic, and spices including ginger, coriander, paprika and cardamom. No wine is perfect, but it finds pleasant matches with several bland Italian whites: Soave, Frascati and Pinot Bianco, as well as Pinot Blancs from elsewhere. Breaking the low-fruit rule, Australian Semillon and Semillon-Chardonnay go quite well. The spinach unpleasantly emphasizes the tannins of red wines.

### TANDOORI ♥ *very light reds, especially Loire Cabernets* ♥ *dry rosés* ♀ *unoaked, dry whites*

A tandoor is a tall, cylindrical clay oven with a searingly hot charcoal or wood fire. Tandoori meat is always marinated in yoghurt and spices before cooking, and dyed bright red or orange with vegetable colouring. Traditionally, tandoori is served with pickled onions, which are wine-killers. No wine is perfect, although a number work well. The best choices are Loire Cabernets such as Chinon, or Franciacorta Rosso, and Bordeaux Blanc is a good white partner.

### TARKA DAL ♀ *bland, low-acid, unoaked whites*

It's the deliberately well-fried garlic (by Western standards, over-fried to burning point) that dominates this bland dish of mushy red split lentils (dal) cooked also with onion, turmeric, green chillies, cardamom seeds, fresh tarragon and coriander. The charred garlic flavour clashes with some wines, and many wines taste far too acid, as the dish has no obvious acidity of its own. However, there are good matches with bland Frascati and Sicilian whites, and with white Châteauneuf-du-Pape, though this is perhaps too expensive a partner. Spanish Yecla or Valencia dry white, Australian or New Zealand unoaked Chardonnay or Semillon-Chardonnay blends all work well. Reds clash. ★ *Frascati* ★ *Sicilian white*

**TIKKA** Tikka simply means 'boneless pieces' and can refer to meat or fish cooked in a variety of ways.

**Chicken Tikka** ▮▮ *Spanish reds or rosados made from Tempranillo* ♀ *fairly bland, dry whites*
Sainsbury's example of chicken marinated in yoghurt and spices and cooked in a tandoor (clay oven) is more chilled and spicy than most Tandoori chicken, and is attractively minty and sharp in flavour. Italian Pinot Grigio is by far the best, but Sancerre is nearly as good, making a lovely flavour match though a little too acid. Other Sauvignons (except for the too-tropical-fruity New Zealand examples) are also very pleasant. Other reasonably pleasant matches are with Soave, Vernaccia, Bordeaux Blanc, and simple Chardonnays. Spanish Tempranillo reds work well: try red Rioja Crianza or La Mancha or Valdepeñas Cencibel. ★ *Pinot Grigio* ★ *Sancerre*

**Chicken Tikka Balti** ▮ *savoury reds* ▮ *dry rosés* ♀ *fairly flavourful, dry to medium-dry whites*
The Sainsbury's version of Chicken Tikka Balti is easy to match. This is perfect with California Pinot Noir or red Rioja Crianza, but also good with other savoury reds (especially Pinot Noir, Sangiovese and Tempranillo), as well as a number of dry rosés made from these grapes, Spanish rosés and dry whites, especially Viognier, Pinot Grigio and Favorita. ★★ *California Pinot Noir* ★★ *red Rioja Crianza*

**Chicken Tikka Makhani** ▮ *gentle Shiraz* ♀ *dry whites*
'Makhani' means 'butter', and this rather dry, savoury dish is also quite creamy, and flavoured with yoghurt, spices, and lots of tomato and onion. Apart from dry Muscat and Sancerre, best white matches are with other Loire Sauvignons such as Pouilly-Fumé, Menetou-Salon or Sauvignon de Touraine, or Austrian Grüner Veltliner, German or Austrian Riesling Trocken, white Châteauneuf-du-Pape, or VdP des Côtes de Gascogne are good alternatives. ★ *dry Muscat* ★ *Sancerre*

**Chicken Tikka Masala** ▮ *light reds* ♀ *dry whites*
'Masala' means 'spice mix'. The Sainsbury's version of chicken Tikka Masala has a very thick, creamy, yoghurty sauce, gently gingery and chillied, with cumin the dominant flavour. Again, whites are best. VdP des Côtes de Gascogne is by far the ideal partner, but Australian or South African Colombard are also very good, as are

southern French or Australian Marsanne. Dry Muscat co-exists in an interesting way, both the food and wine making their own impression. For a red, try Italian Franciacorta or a Loire Cabernet such as Saumur-Champigny or St-Nicolas-de-Bourgueil. ★★ *VdP des Côtes de Gascogne*

**TUPLI** A tupli is an octagonal-shaped saucepan used in north central India.
**Chicken Tupli** ❗ *light, low-tannin reds* ♀ *dry, highish-acid whites*
The Sainsbury's version we tasted is quite limy in flavour, with some yoghurt in the sauce. It is dominated by the perfume of cardamom and cumin. Nothing goes brilliantly, but pleasant choices include Australian Semillon, Austrian dry Riesling, Bordeaux Blanc and simple white Chardonnays for whites. Cinsault or Syrah rosés are enjoyable; and, for reds, Loire Cabernets such as Chinon or St-Nicolas-de-Bourgueil, Italian Franciacorta red, young Tempranillo from Spain, light Zinfandels, and light, warm-climate Cabernet Sauvignons are all pleasant.

**VINDALOO** 'Vin' means 'vinegar', not 'hot', but as vindaloo dishes are a speciality of southern India, where they like their curries hot, there's usually plenty of chilli to accompany the gentle vinegar flavour.
**Chicken Vindaloo** ♀ *dry, fairly to very flavourful whites with medium acidity*
This may be a 'vinegar' dish, but so mildly so that many whites, including Loire Sauvignons, taste too acid for the sauce. Riper New World Sauvignons have the right flavour – the star choice is the very aromatic style of Sauvignon Blanc from New Zealand. Austrian Grüner Veltliner is also very good. Some of the aromatic grapes, Gewürztraminer, Viognier and Italian Favorita, are good, and a few blander whites such as simple, unoaked Chardonnays, South African or Australian Colombard or Colombard-Chardonnay blends, and Bianco di Verona also work well. ★ *New Zealand Sauvignon Blanc*

# EGGS AND EGG DISHES

Old wine and food lore would have us believe that it's impossible to find wines to match egg dishes. Wrong! White wines, particularly the gentle Chardonnay grape, often provide a pleasant foil. It's the simpler versions of Chardonnay that match most egg dishes, or subtle, delicate Chardonnays that have a buttery flavour from malolactic fermentation (see page 226). Strong oak and fruit flavours are less likely to work. Egg yolk has a slight tongue-coating effect (especially when well-cooked), but even when pure and undiluted by other ingredients, this is not disagreeable, maybe taking just a very slight edge off the quality of white wines. Red wines *are* difficult, and you won't find many matches with reds here. Egg yolk accentuates the tannin of red and rosé wines; hard-cooked yolk is even crueller than runny or raw yolk. Light Beaujolais or other Gamay wines are the exception. But there are a few dishes with additional flavouring ingredients that can make a bridge, even with red wines.

## BAKED EGGS (OEUFS EN COCOTTE)

🍷 *Beaujolais* 🍸 *dry, unoaked or subtly oaked, still or sparkling whites, especially Chardonnay*

Simply but deliciously baked in a little double cream, baked eggs are fairly wine-friendly. Any white Burgundy will go well, unless excessively oaky, but as the creaminess detracts slightly from the quality of the wine, avoid expensive ones. Crémant de Bourgogne is good, and better than Champagne. Chablis Premier Cru is also a star, simple Chablis very good, and California, Chilean and Australian Chardonnays match the flavour well, though they are rather dominant. Otherwise, white Lugana from northern Italy makes for a deliciously creamy blend of flavours, and Beaujolais-Villages or the lightest of the Beaujolais crus (such as Regnié, Chénas or Chiroubles) make very pleasant red wine partners, their tannin just mildly emphasized by the egg yolk and cream. ★★ *simple white Burgundy*

## EGGS BENEDICT 🍸 *still and sparkling, unoaked whites with good but not too high acidity*

Stars with this super-rich, hollandaise-topped version of bacon or ham and egg on toast are dry Rieslings from New Zealand or Chile. (Australian Riesling may be too rich, those from Alsace too lean, German or Austrian ones too perfumed.) Simple, unoaked, not-too-acid white Burgundy is good, as are simple Chardonnays from elsewhere. For a celebration brunch, Champagne Blanc de Blancs makes a good partner, as do cheaper alternatives such as sparkling Chardonnays from Italy or Australia, Crémant de Bourgogne or Cava (but not sparkling Saumur or Blanquette de Limoux). ★★ *New Zealand Riesling*

### EGGS FLORENTINE ♥ *unoaked or subtly oaked Zinfandels* ♀ *unoaked, simple Chardonnays with good acidity*

The really lovely pairing for this dish is with inexpensive Chardonnays from northern Italy (Piemonte, Trentino or Alto Adige/Südtirol) or a simple Chardonnay VdP du Jardin de la France. Chablis, though it has the correct acidity, tastes too grassy and honeyed, and, like many other white Burgundies and New World Chardonnays, often has a buttery flavour from malolactic ermentation (see page 226), which is not appropriate here. The only other white that comes near to a match is Aligoté. Reds do have a role here: the blackberry-sharp flavour of Zinfandel works well, and a light, easy Côtes du Rhône red is pleasant. ★★ *Chardonnay del Piemonte*

### EGG MAYONNAISE see *Sauces, Dressings and Relishes: Mayonnaise*

### OMELETTES Omelette clashes with oak and tannin. You really need to consider the fillings to find a complementary wine.
#### Arnold Bennett ♀ *dry whites*

White Burgundy, dry Vinho Verde and Muscadet are all successful, if not perfect, matches with this open omelette topped with smoked haddock, cream and Parmesan cheese. If you really want to splash out, the only star match is a really dry Champagne (but beware – even those marked '*sec*' or '*brut*' have a distinct dash of sweetness). ★★ *Champagne Brut*

**Cheese Omelette** ♀ *fairly low-acid, unoaked dry whites*
No wine is a star with a Cheddar omelette, but Australian Chardonnay, white Côtes du Rhône or not-too-aromatic Sauvignons from Chile, California or Australia all work.
VARIATIONS Using **Gruyère** try Australian Chardonnay, white Côtes du Rhône or hot-country Sauvignons.

**Ham (or Bacon) Omelette** ♀ *unoaked dry whites*
Nothing is perfect, but nearest to a match are Italian Pinot Grigio, Lugana, white Dão, white Côtes du Rhône, Cheverny or California Chardonnay.

**Mushroom Omelette** ❢ *Garnacha* ♀ *bland, unoaked whites; Chardonnays*
Two whites are nearly perfect: Lugana and Chardonnay VdP d'Oc. Spanish reds or rosados made from Garnacha are also very good matches. Otherwise, try not-too-acid Chardonnays from California, Australia or Chile, Frascati, Pinot Grigio or white Dão. As an alternative red, Oregon Pinot Noir is a good flavour, though the tannin is a touch high.
★ *Lugana* ★ *unoaked Chardonnay VdP d'Oc*

**Plain Omelette** ♀ *dry, unoaked, simple whites*
Adequate partners on an appropriate budget to suit the simplicity of this dish are a simple Pinot Grigio, white Corbières, white Côtes du Rhône or white Dão from Portugal.

**Spanish Omelette (Tortilla)** ♀ *bland dry whites*
TRADITIONAL PARTNER Spanish white
Some recipes include onions as well as potato and garlic, others do not, but in either case modern white La Mancha is probably the best Spanish option, while a simple white Burgundy or white Côtes du Rhône also go quite well. Bourgogne Aligoté and Spanish whites from Penedés or Conca de Barberá are good choices with an onion-based tortilla; one without onions is good with a finer white Burgundy or a very light La Mancha red. ★ *white La Mancha*

**PANCAKES** The eggs in pancakes are well-cooked and less threatening to any potential wine partners than many other egg dishes. Once again it is the filling that dominates the wine match. See also *Puddings and Desserts*

**Chicken and Mushroom Pancake** ❢ *very soft, light reds* ♀ *gentle whites*
Any gentle, unoaked European Chardonnay will be good, complementing both the chicken and mushroom well. Next choice is Bourgogne Aligoté, Jurançon Sec or white

Corbières, with Frascati or inexpensive red southern French vins de pays adequate options.
★★ *unoaked southern French Chardonnay*

**Seafood Pancake**
Most wines are too flavourful for pancakes stuffed with seafood in a gentle white sauce. Bordeaux Blanc or VdP des Côtes de Gascogne are the best bets, especially if the filling contains any lemon juice.

**QUICHES AND TARTS** Set egg custard is quite difficult to match well, whether it is made with cream or milk or a mixture of both. Chardonnays often come to the rescue, while reds tend to be too strong and tannic. See also *Vegetables: Onion.*

**Asparagus Quiche** ♀ *unoaked or very subtly oaked European Chardonnays*
Chardonnay is the only really good partner. White Burgundies are the star choice, with northern Italian Chardonnays (Piemonte, Trentino or Alto Adige/Südtirol) and Loire Chardonnay (VdP du Jardin de la France) coming out a good second best. Chablis and Chardonnay VdP d'Oc are less successful. ★★ *Montagny Premier Cru*

**Broccoli Quiche** ♀ *unoaked or very subtly oaked European Chardonnays*
As well as similar Chardonnays to the dish above, broccoli quiche pairs off adequately with Frascati, VdP des Côtes de Gascogne or South African Colombard. ★ *Mâcon-Villages Blanc*

**Cheese and Onion Quiche** ♀ *unoaked Chardonnays*
Reds are too strong and tannic and many whites taste too acid for this type of quiche. It makes adequate matches with Italian Chardonnays and Chardonnay VdP du Jardin de la France, white Burgundies (including quite fine ones), basic Chablis (but not Premier or Grand Cru) and unoaked Australian Chardonnays (California Chardonnay tends to be too oaky). Choose a higher-acid Chardonnay if tomato is a major element.

**Quiche Lorraine (d'Alsace)** ♀ *a few, low- to medium-acid, dry whites*

TRADITIONAL PARTNER Alsace Tokay-Pinot Gris

The authentic Alsace recipe for Quiche Lorraine, a creamy quiche made without cheese, finds very few good partners. The rich and spicy Tokay-Pinot Gris of Alsace, the home of Quiche Lorraine, whether dry or slightly sweet, is definitely a success. But from farther afield, in Italy, Frascati makes a nice, gentle match, and northern Italian Lugana or a gently oaked white Rioja are both adequate. ★ *Alsace Tokay-Pinot Gris*

VARIATION The lighter, cheesy (and unauthentic) version (made with **onions, bacon, Gruyère, single cream** and **milk**), is perhaps what the non-French more often serve as 'Quiche Lorraine'. This quiche is a little easier to partner with whites, and even a few reds work. As well as simple Chardonnays from northern Italy or the Loire, it goes adequately well with Chablis Premier Cru, oaked or oak-fermented white Rioja, Favorita, or Chilean Sauvignon. Of the reds, Beaujolais-Villages or mature Bairrada blend in pleasantly.

## Spinach and Gruyère Quiche ♀ *dry, unoaked or subtly oaked whites*

Nothing is absolutely perfect, but Bourgogne Aligoté comes closest to a match, followed by northern Italian Lugana, both wines attractively boosting the Gruyère flavour. Some other Italian whites, especially Soave and Favorita, are modestly successful. Some Chardonnays are adequate, particularly Chablis Premier Cru and Australian Reserve Chardonnay. The tannin in red wines clashes with the spinach. ★ *Bourgogne Aligoté*

## SCRAMBLED EGG AND SMOKED SALMON
♀ *unoaked or subtly oaked whites, especially Semillon*

For a delicious lunch-time treat or light supper, serve scrambled egg and smoked salmon with a simple, inexpensive Australian Semillon – it makes one of those really great food-and-wine partnerships, where each enhances the flavour of the other to create a better whole. Any rich, ripe Australian Semillon, whether young or mature, will make a good partner. Australian blends of Semillon-Chardonnay are also extremely good, but are less stunning. Bourgogne Aligoté and subtle California Chardonnay go quite well. Most other combinations clash gently, and all reds are much too tannic. ★★ *inexpensive Australian Semillon*

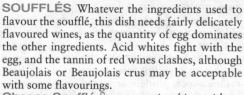

**SOUFFLÉS** Whatever the ingredients used to flavour the soufflé, this dish needs fairly delicately flavoured wines, as the quantity of egg dominates the other ingredients. Acid whites fight with the egg, and the tannin of red wines clashes, although Beaujolais or Beaujolais crus may be acceptable with some flavourings.

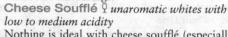

**Cheese Soufflé** ♀ *unaromatic whites with low to medium acidity*

Nothing is ideal with cheese soufflé (especially if made with Cheddar); most whites taste too acid, while reds are too tannic. Chardonnays make the best matches, so long as the acidity is not too high. Choose one from a warm climate without too obvious an oak flavour: a subtle, buttery California Chardonnay, or a ripe, unoaked Chardonnay from Italy, Eastern Europe, Burgundy or the south of France. Otherwise, try Italian Lugana, or Australian or French Marsanne. ★ *subtle California Chardonnay*

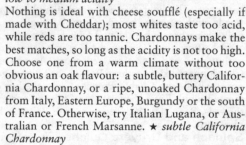

**Spinach Soufflé** ♥ *Beaujolais* ♀ *subtle, lowish-acid whites*

Perked up with a little Parmesan, spinach soufflé is even more difficult to match with wine than cheese soufflé. Subtle California Chardonnay and white Burgundy are almost as good as the star wine, South African Colombard. The tannin in most reds clashes with the spinach, but red or white Beaujolais make adequate matches. ★ *South African Colombard*

**SPAGHETTI CARBONARA** see *Pasta*

**TARTS** see **QUICHES**

**TOAD-IN-THE-HOLE** ♀ *whites with low to medium acidity, not too strongly flavoured or brightly fruity*

The star choice with this dish is white Côtes du Rhône, with Chablis Premier Cru next best, if you want to turn your toad into a prince. Or you might try a fizzy Spanish Cava, Spanish rosado, Italian Chardonnay or a simple La Mancha red. ★★ *white Côtes du Rhône*

# PASTA, PIZZA AND RICE DISHES

Pasta, pizza dough and rices are really the background to any dish; they may form the bulk of the dish, but their role in determining the choice of accompanying wine is not a dominant one. It is the sauces, toppings and stuffings that are the elements to match. It is worth remembering, however, that pasta and pizza dough act to subdue the flavour of the sauces and stuffings, so that gently flavoured wines are often the best partners. And watch out for cheeses as they will influence the wine choice too.

## Pasta

Served alone, pasta is very bland, even when coloured with spinach or tomato. And the pasta will tone down the overall flavour of even quite flavourful accompanying sauces or stuffings. It's often the fairly bland whites, therefore, that fit the bill. Gentle red wines sometimes work, but red wine drinkers should beware dishes that contain Ricotta and Mascarpone cheeses. Both cheeses emphasize the tannin in most red wines to the point of unpleasantness. If you love drenching your pasta dish in freshly grated Parmesan, that, too, will influence the wine choice. Refer to *Cheeses* and pick a wine that will go with both it and the pasta dish itself.

**CANELLONI** It is hard to generalize about canelloni, so diverse are the possible fillings. Here are two versions to give guidance. For other preferred ingredients, look them up and then select a wine that makes the best compromise.
**Beef Canelloni** 🍷 *light to medium-bodied, savoury or fruity reds* 🍷 *dry Syrah rosés*
Tomato, onions and cheddar are likely to be the dominant flavours in a beef canelloni sold ready-made in the supermarket. This combination makes excellent matches with light Sangioveses, single-vineyard or Classico Valpolicella, and the lightest Pinot Noirs. Dry red Lambrusco is very good, too, as are California Syrah and Merlots from Chile and Romania. Reds from Languedoc-Roussillon are mostly acceptable, and light Zinfandels and oak-aged Spanish Tempranillos make pleasant matches. Or you can

try Crozes-Hermitage, Cabernet Sauvignon from Coonawarra in Australia, New Zealand Cabernet Sauvignon and dry Syrah rosés. ★★ *Valpolicella Classico* ★★ *Sangiovese delle Marche* ★★ *Sangiovese di Romagna*

### Spinach and Ricotta Canelloni
♀♀ *dry and off-dry whites and rosés, with fairly low acidity*

This delicate dish, of stuffed canelloni served on a thin layer of tomato sauce and topped with white sauce, is a tricky one. Tannins clash – only the very lightest of reds might work; a southern French rosé is pleasant, however. Basic Beaujolais works, and that's about it. Turning to the white wines, many dry whites are too acid or too fruity. The closest to a perfect match is with South African Sauvignon Blanc, a lightly perfumed wine with lowish acidity. A number of other wines can also be pleasant: try modern white Dão, Sicilian white, Bianco di Verona, Gravina, Pinot Bianco and Pinot Blanc, or white Côtes du Rhône. ★ *South African Sauvignon Blanc*

## LASAGNE
### Beef Lasagne ♀ *medium-weight, fruity, fairly low-tannin reds* ♀ *a few fairly aromatic, dry whites*

Fruity reds are the ideal partners for a meat-based lasagne. They suit the white sauce, and the Parmesan-topped combination of tomato and herbs. They also match the minced beef, red wine and vegetables very well. Barbera d'Alba comes closest to perfection, and light, fruity vins de pays Merlots from the south of France, and Crozes-Hermitage all strike the right chord. Teroldego Rotaliano, red Côtes du Rhône, Australian Shiraz, gentle red Bordeaux and Valdepeñas Reserva all have enough fruitiness to make decent red matches. Most whites are too acid or too fruity, but a Chilean Sauvignon Blanc is a good solution, followed by Viognier. ★ *Barbera d'Alba*

### Vegetable Lasagne ♀ *medium-bodied, savoury or Cabernet-based reds* ♀ *light, dry or dryish, highish- to high-acid whites*

The herby and tomato flavours of most vegetable lasagne recipes call for matching acidity in the wine. As well as the star choice, VdP des Côtes de Gascogne, Soave and Cortese, Vinho Verde, Sancerre, and southern French Picpoul are all very good. Some reds – young Spanish Valdepeñas, Chianti, New Zealand and Chilean Cabernet Sauvignon – work very well too. Or you can try Bordeaux Blanc, Sauvignon de St-Bris, Alsace Riesling, white Châteauneuf-du-Pape, Viognier, or Favorita among whites, and even a soft, young red Bordeaux is a pleasant partner.
★ *VdP des Côtes de Gascogne*

## MACARONI CHEESE ♀ *oaked or unoaked dry whites with low to medium acidity*

Wines don't have a high success rate with this dish. Reds fail to make the grade, clashing with the cheese sauce. The sauce also causes problems for many white wines, leaving them tasting thin and acid. A number of whites do survive quite successfully, however: Australian Semillon, or a dry Semillon-based Bordeaux Blanc, are by far the best choices. Otherwise, a number of blander whites make adequate partners: try Italian Gavi, Lugana, Soave, or Sicilian white, oaked or unoaked white Rioja, white Côtes du Rhône, or dry German Pinot Blanc or Austrian Grüner Veltliner.
★ *Australian Semillon*

## PASTA WITH GARLIC AND OLIVE OIL see
*Herbs, Spices and Flavourings: Garlic*

## PASTA WITH MUSHROOMS AND GARLIC
♀ *low- to medium-acid, dry whites*

Needless to say, there are many variations to this dish, and the choice of wine will alter according to the main ingredients. Red wines do not work, clashing with the fat in the cream and/or cheese.

VARIATIONS With **common mushrooms, mascarpone, parmesan, parsley** and **garlic**, Frascati is much the best choice, but you can also try Sicilian white table wine or Penedés or Conca de Barberá whites from Spain. Even the lightest reds become too tannic and unpleasantly bitter with the sauce. ★ *Frascati*. With **porcini** (cèpes, boletus), **garlic, cream** and **parsley** you really need low-acid, bland, dry whites. Best bets are Frascati, white Franciacorta, Pinot Grigio, Verdicchio, southern French Terret or

Marsanne, although none is a star choice. A simple, very light southern French red vins de pays, such as VdP de l'Ardêche, can overcome the problem of tannins clashing with the sauce.

## PASTA WITH PESTO ¶ *a few soft reds* ♀ *dry, not-too-fruity, not-too-acid whites*

Three white wines are stars with this popular pasta dish. Dry Alsace Tokay-Pinot Gris and Hungarian Furmint, with their slightly musky flavours, make delicious combinations; and rich, lightly oaked Chardonnays, especially from Australia, are just as good – choose one that is not too high in acidity. (Burgundian and California Chardonnays are not recommended, as the buttery flavour of malolactic fermentation – see page 226 – does not work well with the sauce.) No other whites are remotely as good, though some of the more neutral Italian whites are acceptable. Reds are not really successful, but you might try Barbera or a soft, young Rioja or Cencibel from the centre of Spain. ★★ *Alsace Tokay-Pinot Gris* ★★ *Hungarian Furmint* ★★ *lightly oaked Australian Chardonnay*

## PASTA WITH SMOKED SALMON AND CREAM ♀ *dry, lightly oaked or unoaked whites*

Red wines and sweetish white wines are completely out of the question when serving smoked salmon. A little oak flavour in the wine helps the matching, complementing the smoky flavour in the salmon. Whites made from Chardonnay are best, with gentle white Burgundies the top choice, and Chardonnays from the south of France nearly as successful. Unoaked white Rioja and Sicilian whites are also pleasant. ★ *white Burgundy*

## PASTA WITH TOMATO SAUCE see *Sauces, Dressings and Relishes: Tomato Sauce*

## RAVIOLI/TORTELLONI/CAPPELLETTI

Fillings vary from recipe to recipe, supermarket to delicatessen. Here are a few possibilities:

**Pork and Beef Ravioli** ¶ *dry rosés* ♀ *dry, low-acid, bland whites*

There is no really happy partnership to be made with this dish. Most whites are too acid, aromatic or flavourful. Sicilian white table wine, inexpensive Alsace Pinot Blanc, or Cinsault rosé, are three acceptable possibilities.

**Spinach and Ricotta Ravioli** ♀ *very bland whites with low acidity*

The greatest success is with whites from Penedés or Conca de Barberá in Spain. Otherwise, try Frascati, a basic Rosso di Verona, or a Douro white from Portugal. Most other whites are too brightly fruity, too acid, too aromatic or simply too flavourful for these delicate pasta parcels; and the spinach clashes with almost all red wines, making them taste more bitterly tannic than they really are.
★ *Penedés white*

**Wild Mushroom, Garlic, Parmesan and Ricotta Ravioli** ¶ *soft reds* ♀ *dry, low-acid, bland whites*

Again, the combination of ingredients in the filling make good partners hard to find. Apart from a soft, gentle Sangiovese delle Marche, good red partners are scarce. As for white wines, only the blandest of styles will succeed.
★ *Sangiovese delle Marche*

## SPAGHETTI

There's quite a difference between the traditional Italian meat sauce, known as ragu, and the very herby, tomato sauces often cooked by us 'foreigners', or bought ready-made at the supermarket. Not surprisingly, the wine requirements will be quite different, too.

**Spaghetti Bolognese** ¶ *light- to medium-bodied, fruity or savoury reds* ¶ *dry rosés* ♀ *dry, neutral whites*

If you buy a ready-made spaghetti bolognese or make your own to a recipe from an English cookery book, it is likely to be much herbier, more tomatoey, and sweeter in flavour than the classic Italian ragu (see below). It can therefore handle wines with more fruit and personality, both whites and reds. Australian Shiraz is the star choice, and California Syrah, Crozes-Hermitage and the lighter style of Zinfandel all make delicious matches. Other southern French Syrahs, South African Shiraz, Merlots from Chile, South Africa, Romania and California, or Italian Barbera and Cirò will also make very good partners. Whites and rosé wines make no more than adequate partners, but

South African Sauvignon or Colombard, VdP des Côtes de Gascogne, modern whites from Penedés in Spain, basic white Verona table wine or dry southern French or Bordeaux rosés are all enjoyable options. ★★ *Australian Shiraz*

VARIATIONS **Ragu**, the traditional Italian meat sauce used in spaghetti alla Bolognese, is made with minced beef, bacon, onion, carrot, celery, tomato, red wine and milk. It is very mildly flavoured, and can cope with only very gentle wines, of which Bianco di Custoza is the star white, and Bordeaux rosé (or clairet) comes a close second. Decent white matches are also found with Gavi, Sicilian white wines, VdP des Côtes de Gascogne and South African Colombard. No reds shine, but a few make reasonable matches: Montepulciano d'Abbruzzo, Australian Shiraz, lighter red Bordeaux, Crozes-Hermitage and gently fruity southern French reds. ★ *Bianco di Custoza*

**Spaghetti alla Carbonara** ♀ *not-too-acid, bland, dry or dryish whites*
This rich dish is hard to match with wine. It is not surprising, with eggs, pancetta or bacon, garlic and Parmesan cheese all vying for attention. The blander whites, particularly from Italy, make the best partners. A simple Sicilian white table wine comes closest, or you can try a Tuscan Vernaccia-Chardonnay blend, Bianco di Verona, Valdadige Bianco, and Pinot Grigio, or Bordeaux Blanc or Aligoté. Most reds taste super-tannic but Valpolicella is passable. ★ *Sicilian white*

**Spaghetti alla Vongole (Cockles)** ♀ *dry, fairly neutral, highish-acid whites*
The cockles (vongole) in this recipe clash with red wines, and whites have to be virtually bone-dry to succeed. Sauvignons and Rieslings are too fruity, and Chardonnays too honeyed, so the stage is set for fairly neutral dry whites. Dry Sicilian white is the best choice, followed by a modern Tuscan Vernaccia-Chardonnay blend, and Terret from the south of France. Other possible partners are Verdicchio, basic white table wines from northeast Italy, Austrian Grüner Veltliner and unoaked white Rioja. ★★ *dry Sicilian white*

# Pizza

Your pizza can be 'deep pan' or 'thin and crispy'; it makes little difference to the wine match, except that the thicker base will subdue the topping flavours slightly more. The type of cheese used does have a strong influence. The Italians tend to use Mozzarella, very occasionally pepped up with a little grated Parmesan. Then there are the extras – mushrooms, seafood, anchovies, various salamis, and herbs. We have included a simple, authentic Italian Pizza Napoletana, and a typical supermarket pizza. For other toppings, look the ingredients up in the relevant sections, and select a wine that makes the best overall compromise.

## CHEESE AND TOMATO PIZZA ♥ *light to medium-bodied, savoury reds* ♀ *fairly neutral, highish-to high-acid whites*

This is the standard pizza as you would buy it ready-to-bake in the supermarket. It is topped with Cheddar as well as Mozzarella, and given a generous sprinkling of dried herbs. Cheddar and herbs have strong flavours that welcome more flavourful wines than the Napoletana (see below). A standard, off-dry white from northern Italy leads the way, followed by Vernaccia di San Gimignano, Bordeaux Blanc and Aligoté among whites, and Valpolicella Classico, Copertino and Valdepeñas Reserva in the reds, all of which go well. Several other gentle whites are fine, such as Bianco di Custoza, Pinot Grigio, Valdadige Bianco, northern Italian Chardonnay, Sicilian white, southern French Terret and Australian Semillon. A gentle, basic red Chianti can work as well. ★★ *Bianco di Verona*

## PIZZA NAPOLETANA ♥ *dry rosés* ♀ *dry, highish-acid, fairly neutral whites*

The authentic Pizza Napoletana is a simple dish, made with just olive oil, tomato, oregano and Mozzarella on a pizza base. And it can only cope with fairly simple white wines – reds are overpowering. A fresh, modern Italian Vernaccia-Chardonnay blend is almost perfect, and a decent Frascati is nearly as good. After that come wines such as Verdicchio, Vernaccia di San Gimignano, Sicilian white, white Corbières and South African Sauvignon Blanc. Dry rosés from Spain and the south of France are also pleasant. ★ *Tuscan Vernaccia-Chardonnay*

# Rice and Grains

Rice and grains have a fairly neutral flavour. Brown rice has much more flavour than white rice, and bulgar or cracked wheat more than cous-cous. But they all usually bow to the influence of other ingredients in a dish.

## COUS-COUS ! *light, not-too-tannic Shiraz* ♀ *fruity medium-acid rosés* ♀ *fruity, hot-climate Chardonnays*

The flavour and fruitness of oaked or unoaked Australian Chardonnays are just perfect with cous-cous, and California and Chilean Chardonnays are also excellent, while Australian Semillon-Chardonnay and New Zealand dry Riesling both go quite well. Rosés from Bergerac, Bordeaux, Provence or Tavel are good, but reds are mostly too strong, tannic and/or oaky. A light, inexpensive, not-too-tannic Australian Shiraz is fine, however. ★★ *Australian Chardonnay*

## KEDGEREE ♀ *light, unoaked, dry whites with good acidity, especially Sauvignon Blanc*

Kedgeree is usually made with haddock, chopped hard-boiled egg, onion and lashings of butter. Light, fresh Sauvignon Blanc is the first choice, and the acidity and character of Burgundian Aligoté ring in a perfect alternative. Bordeaux Blanc made with Sauvignon, Bergerac Sec, or Côtes de Duras are also very good. Kedgeree can take only the lightest dash of oak. ★★ *VdP d'Oc Sauvignon Blanc* ★★ *Bourgogne Aligoté*

## NUT CUTLETS/NUT ROAST ! *very gentle, low-tannin reds* ♀ *gentle, not-too-acid, not-too-fruity whites*

Recipes vary, but your average nut cutlet is not the most tasty of dishes. Wines that are aromatic, tannic or acid are too powerful. A gentle, savoury red such as Sangiovese delle Marche is just the thing; a Sangiovese di Romagna almost as good. Soft, ripe Merlot from the south of France, or Bulgaria, Romania or Chile also make pleasant partners. Of the whites, try Côtes du Rhône, Hungarian Furmint, Soave, Australian Marsanne, northern Italian table wines and Rueda. ★★ *Sangiovese delle Marche*

**PAELLA** Paella, like pizza, has almost infinitely variable ingredients. The base is always rice, but the flavourings vary. You can stick to seafood, or make it with meat alone. And in Spain there are as many ways to cook a true Paella alla Valenciana as there are cooks making them.

**Paella alla Valenciana** 🍷 *dry rosés* 🍷 *gentle, fruity to fairly neutral, oaked or lightly oaked whites*

The usual version of this paella is made with pork, chicken and prawns, and includes saffron in the seasoning. Around Valencia, the locals would probably start with a bottle of the local sparkling wine, Cava, and continue with a dry rosado. Add a lightly oaked white Rioja to the list and you have three very good, if not quite perfect, choices. Other contenders are Rueda, Bianco di Verona, Soave and lightly oaked Australian Chardonnay. Reds are too strong.
★ *Cava* ★ *Spanish rosado* ★ *oaked white Rioja*

## RISOTTO

**Mushroom Risotto (al Funghi)** 🍷 *a few very gentle, light reds* 🍷 *dry, low- to medium-acid, bland whites*

This delicious combination of rice, porcini (cèpes, boletus), shallot, dry white wine, butter, meat stock and Parmesan, is not easy to partner with wine. Most whites taste too acid. However, Frascati, Verdicchio, Bianco di Custoza, white Franciacorta, Gravina, unoaked white Rioja or Rioja Crianza, Alsace Pinot Blanc, or Australian and French Marsanne are all enjoyable choices. A very gentle, light, soft red, such as a VdP de l'Ardêche red, can be a pleasant partner.

**Risotto al Bianco** 🍷 *unoaked, bland, dry whites*

This is a simple but delicious risotto made with chicken stock, onion, garlic, and grated Parmesan. But it doesn't suit many wines. Reds are too tannic, and many whites taste too acid, too fruity, too grassy or too honeyed. Pleasant whites are Vernaccia, Pinot Bianco, Bianco di Custoza, Bianco di Verona, Soave, Spanish Conca de Barberá or Penedés white, Austrian Pinot Blanc or Grüner Veltliner, white Côtes du Rhône or Australian Semillon.

VARIATIONS With **chicken**, the choices remain the same.

### Risotto alla Milanese ♀ *dry, unoaked, low- to medium-acid whites*

Rice, beef stock and marrow, onion, saffron, Parmesan and butter are used in this Milanese version of risotto. White wines are the best, with Verdicchio, southern French Terret, not-too-fruity, unoaked European Chardonnay, and Chablis all good partners. Next best are Sicilian white table wines, Gravina, white Côtes du Rhône, southern French or Australian Marsanne or Australian Riesling. Most reds are too strong and tannic, but a very soft, gentle Merlot vin de pays, or an Austrian Zweigelt stand up well. ★ *Verdicchio*

### Seafood Risotto (alla Marinara) ♀ *dry rosés* ♀ *dry, fairly bland, highish-acid whites*

Frascati's gentle, creamy flavour is easily the best match for mixed seafood risotto. Next in line come dry rosés from Italy, the south of France, Spain and South Africa. Gentle whites work too: try Lugana, Pinot Grigio, Sicilian white, Tuscan Vernaccia-Chardonnay blends, Bordeaux Blanc, Aligoté, Chablis, Australian Semillon or a not-too-aromatic South African Sauvignon. Reds are too tannic, too acid or just clash. ★★ *Frascati*

### STUFFED VINE LEAVES (DOLMADES)
♀ *a few high-acid reds* ♀ *dry, high-acid whites*

Retsina is not the answer for dolmades; dry English wine is the best bet. Its high acidity and sharp fruit match the tangy vine leaf extremely well. Next best are dry Rieslings from Alsace, Australia or New Zealand, or Bourgogne Aligoté. Lambrusco Secco, Valpolicella Classico and Dolcetto are all acceptable reds. ★★ *dry English white*

### TABBOULEH ♀ *dry, fairly high-acid whites*

Lots of mint, parsley and spring onion are mixed with cracked wheat in this salad; the gently grassy flavour of Bordeaux Blanc is perfect, emphasizing the mint. Other good matches are with Sancerre and New Zealand Sauvignon, Alsace and Chilean Rieslings, Soave, VdP des Côtes de Gascogne, Alsace Pinot Blanc and South African Colombard. All reds are too strong. ★★ *Bordeaux Blanc*

# VEGETABLES, VEGETABLE DISHES AND SALADS

Unless a salad or vegetarian dish is the centrepiece of your meal, you will probably want to match the meat, fish and/or sauce instead. But wines make many delicious matches with vegetables and salads. There may be a wine that goes well with both the vegetables and the meat you plan to serve. It is certainly worth avoiding the clashes some vegetables make with certain wines, and taking into account the natural sweetness of many vegetables, and the sharpness of salad dressings.

## Vegetables and Vegetable Dishes

White wines tend to go better than reds with vegetable dishes. Celery, spinach and black olives, in particular, emphasize the tannin in reds, making them seem tougher than they really are. Many vegetables, especially root vegetables, are naturally slightly sweet: onions, garlic, carrots, parsnips, turnips and swedes will all add sweetness to a dish. Such dishes will respond well to wines with a touch of sweetness, or very bright fruit. Certain vegetables are simply not very wine-friendly, but even fennel, parsnip, and artichokes find the occasional agreeable partner.

### ARTICHOKES

**Globe Artichokes** 🍷 *Cinsault rosés* 🍷 *dry whites*
With wine, artichokes create a weird, slightly metallic, slightly sweet sensation that still lingers long after you have swallowed. Some wines react more strongly than others: Rueda, Pinot Blanc and Albariño are particular culprits. It is not a nasty taste, but it certainly detracts from the wine's quality, so it is best to drink inexpensive wines with artichokes. Dry Riesling from Australia, however, is not affected, and goes rather well with artichokes served either plain or with an olive oil vinaigrette. Muscadet, Chablis, Champagne, Austrian Grüner Veltliner, or a dry English Seyval Blanc are good alternatives, as is a Cinsault rosé. ★ *Australian dry Riesling*

**Jerusalem Artichokes** see *Soups*

**ASPARAGUS** Green asparagus, cut after it has grown above ground, has a stronger, grassier character than white asparagus, with its sweeter, and more delicate flavour. See also *Soups*.

**Green Asparagus (plain or with melted butter)** ♀ *unoaked or subtly oaked dry whites*
Chardonnays and Sauvignon Blancs are especially suited to the intensely grassy, honeyed flavour of green asparagus, particularly when it is served with melted butter. The most concentrated ones –

top white Burgundies, New World Chardonnays and New Zealand Sauvignons – are too much, but the star choice, a mature, oaked white Graves from Bordeaux, is perfect. Other gentle Bordeaux or Chilean Sauvignons, and lightly oaked or unoaked Chardonnays, are also appropriate.

Chablis and Chardonnay VdP d'Oc are excellent alternatives. Spanish Rueda is also delicious, and dry German Riesling and Pinot Blanc make reasonable matches. ★★ *mature oaked white Graves*
VARIATIONS With **hollandaise**, New Zealand Sauvignon Blanc is a superb match, Chablis Pre-

mier Cru very good; with **vinaigrette**, Chablis or Sancerre are brilliant, New Zealand Sauvignon and Alsace Riesling good.

**White Asparagus** ♀ *unoaked, ripely fruity Chardonnays, with low to medium acidity*

All Sauvignon Blancs become too brightly grassy for white asparagus. Ripely fruity Chardonnays, mainly from the New World, match the sweetness in the vegetable; an unoaked Australian Chardonnay is far and away the best choice. See also *Eggs: Quiches.* ★★ *unoaked Australian Chardonnay*

## AUBERGINE
**Aubergine dip (Melitzanosalata)**
❢ *Beaujolais* ♀ *dry whites, especially Sauvignons*
TRADITIONAL PARTNER *Greek white*

New Zealand Sauvignon Blanc is perfect with this creamy dip. Other Sauvignons, including Sancerre, Chilean Sauvignon and Bordeaux Blanc, are good. Southern Italian Gravina is a surprising success, as is simple Chablis. Beaujolais-Villages is a rare good red match. ★★ *New Zealand Sauvignon Blanc*

## Baked Aubergine with Parmesan (alla Parmigiana) *♥ Beaujolais ♀ Sauvignon Blanc, New World dry Riesling, a few simple Italian whites*

The really brilliant match with this northern Italian speciality is with Sauvignons from Touraine in the Loire, but other Sauvignons also go well, including Sancerre and Pouilly-Fumé, and New Zealand or Chilean Sauvignons. Dry Rieslings from Australia, New Zealand and Chile are a success; or try Lugana, Orvieto, Soave Classico, or Hungarian or Alsace Pinot Gris. For a red, a Beaujolais-Villages or light Beaujolais cru is fine, but the local Lambrusco Secco is too acid, and other reds are too tannic. ★★ *Sauvignon de Touraine*

## Fried/Grilled Aubergines, or Fritters *♀ dry whites*

This rich, unctuous vegetable tastes fantastic with the crisp, green fruit of Jurançon Sec and is nearly as wonderful with Alsace Tokay-Pinot Gris and Chablis. Oaked European and California Chardonnays and Frascati make passable partners. For recipes that add lemon juice – a stimulating contrast with aubergine's opulent flesh – the higher-acid, more aromatic Sauvignons come into their own, with Touraine, Upper Loire, and even New Zealand Sauvignons making good partners. Jurançon Sec is still good. Reds tend to overpower. ★★ *Jurançon Sec*

**AVOCADO** Avocado may not find many brilliant partners, but it rarely clashes with white wines. Dressings help by raising the acidity level. See *Salads: Vinaigrettes.*

## Avocado, Mozzarella and Tomato Salad see *Salads*

## Avocado with Prawns *♀ bland dry whites with medium to high acidity*

Simple Chablis is a star, and a few other whites make reasonable matches: Vernaccia, Verdicchio, Sauvignon de Touraine, Alsace Pinot Blanc, and Spanish Rueda. Reds are too tannic. ★★ *Chablis*

## Avocado with Vinaigrette *♀ unoaked or very subtly oaked dry whites*

European Chardonnays work well, especially simple Chablis, but white Burgundies are also very good, and mature white Burgundies are quite delicious. Aromatic Sauvignons such as Sauvignon de Touraine and New Zealand Sauvignon taste good, and Frascati works well.

Or try Muscadet Sur Lie or Vernaccia di San Gimignano. ★★ *Chablis* ★★ *mature white Burgundy*

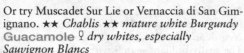

**Guacamole** ♀ *dry whites, especially Sauvignon Blancs*

TRADITIONAL PARTNER *beer or Spanish white*

Chilean and New Zealand Sauvignons are both especially delicious with this Mexican dish; Sancerre and Sauvignons from the Bordeaux area also go well. (Higher-acid Sauvignons, such as Sauvignon de Touraine are adequate.) Next best are fine white Burgundies, simple Chablis, or Champagne Blanc de Noirs. Reds are too tannic. ★★ *Chilean or New Zealand Sauvignon Blanc*

## BEANS
**Bean Salad** see *Salads*
**Beans in Tomato Sauce (Fagioli all'Uccelletto)** ❢ *low-tannin reds with not-too-bright fruit, especially mature* ♀ *dry whites*

TRADITIONAL PARTNER *Chianti*

Sauvignon Blanc is a wonderful flavour for this sage-laced Florentine dish, but some Sauvignons are too acid, while others are too aromatic or too bland. Chilean Sauvignon just hits the spot. Other good white matches are with Rueda, Conca de Barberá or Penedés whites from Spain, or South African Colombard. A simple Alsace Tokay-Pinot Gris goes very well; and Pinot Grigio fairly well. Among Italian reds, best match is Salice Salentino from southern Italy. A good, mature, low-tannin Chianti goes quite well, or you can try a mature Vino Nobile di Montepulciano or Rosso di Montalcino. ★★ *Chilean Sauvignon Blanc*

## BEETROOT see *Soups*

## CABBAGE
**Red Cabbage with Apple and Onion**
♀ *medium-dry to medium whites with fairly high to high acidity*

Gently stewed in the traditional German or Polish way, adding apple, onion, red wine, a touch of brown sugar and vinegar, juniper and coriander seed to the red cabbage, this dish varies slightly in flavour, sweetness and acidity – but it is always hard to match. Try a medium English wine, or an Alsace Gewürztraminer.

**Sauerkraut** ♀ *very high-acid dry whites*
TRADITIONAL PARTNER *Mosel Riesling Trocken*
Even quite a lot of very high-acid dry whites taste soft next to Sauerkraut. A Riesling Trocken from the Mosel-Saar-Ruwer is the only star match, but other German Riesling Trockens also go well. Alsace Riesling works modestly well but Austrian, Australian and New Zealand Rieslings do not. Most reds taste flat, but Teroldego Rotaliano has a very pleasantly complementary flavour. See also *Pork: Choucroute*. ★★ *Mosel Riesling Trocken*

**CARROT** see *Soups* and *Salads*

**CAULIFLOWER CHEESE** ♀ *unoaked, dry to medium whites*
The cooked Cheddar makes finding a matching wine for this winter-warming dish very difficult. Reds are too dry and tannic for the cheese. Whites are the answer, although no wine is perfect. Best hopes are Spanish Rueda, South African Chenin Blanc, Bianco di Verona, Liebfraumilch or other simple, inexpensive German wines such as Piesporter Michelsberg or Niersteiner Gutes Domtal.
VARIATIONS A cheese sauce made with **Gruyère** makes things easier. Of the whites, Rieslings go well, from German Riesling Trocken to dry Australian Riesling. With reds, avoid tannin and oak. Best are Montepulciano d'Abruzzo, Beaujolais-Village or southern French Gamay vin de pays. ★ *German Riesling Trocken.*

**CELERY** ♀ *a few dry, unoaked whites*
Serving celery with cheese is not helpful – it makes most reds taste nastily tannic, and no whites match well, though you might try a simple, unoaked Chardonnay, an inexpensive Rhine Riesling or Bordeaux Blanc. See also *Soups*.

**CHICK PEAS**
**Felafel** ♀ *a very few whites*
The strong flavour of cumin and coriander seed is very difficult to match. Verdicchio is much the best choice, or you might try a medium English wine. Reds are too tannic. ★ *Verdicchio*

**Hummus** ♀ *high-acid, unoaked, bland whites*
Hummus needs a wine with enough acidity to balance its lemon juice content. The earthy flavours of chick peas and sesame seed purée (tahini) don't call for a particularly refined style of wine, and nothing aromatic, too fruity or too oaky will work. Best is the sharp, lemony flavour of Portuguese Vinho Verde. Dry English Seyval Blanc wines, with their fairly neutral taste and highish acidity, are quite good. ★★ *Vinho Verde*

## COURGETTE
The very delicate flavour of courgette (and marrow) is overwhelmed by wine or other food flavours. For Stuffed Courgette or Stuffed Marrow, look up the relevant stuffing ingredients.

## COUS-COUS (VEGETABLE) see *Rice and Grains*

## CRUDITÉS WITH DIPS
The dips are usually the things to match, but sweet peppers and celery crudités need to be taken into account when choosing the wine. See *Sauces* for individual dips, or look up the ingredients of the dip.

## CUCUMBER see *Salads* and *Soups*

## FELAFEL see CHICK PEAS

**FENNEL** ♀ *dry whites with medium acidity*
The gently aniseedy flavour of fennel is very difficult to match to wine. Spanish Rueda, Italian Gravina and Rieslings are often the best bet. See also *Salads* and *Soups*.

## JERUSALEM ARTICHOKES see *Soups*

**LEEKS** A little touch of sweetness in a wine goes down well with leeks. Australian Riesling matches extremely well, and Spanish Rueda and Italian Soave are good, despite being dry. See also *Soups*.

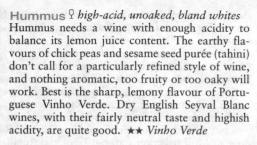

**Leeks in Cheese Sauce** ♀ *bland, dry or dryish whites with low to medium acidity*

Brilliant with a simple Australian Semillon, this dish is otherwise very hard to match. Many whites taste too fruity, or too acid for the combination of cooked Cheddar and leeks. Reds simply don't work. Adequate matches can be found with white Côtes du Rhône, dry Saumur or Anjou Blanc, Bianco di Verona and Frascati Superiore.
★★ *inexpensive Australian Semillon*

VARIATIONS Wrapping the leeks in **ham** doesn't make things any easier. The Australian Semillon is acceptable, or you can try Italian Gravina or Frascati, white Penedés or Conca de Barberá from Spain, or white Côtes du Rhône.

**LENTILS** see *Soups*

**MARROW** see **COURGETTE**

**MUSHROOMS** Mushrooms are fairly picky about their wines. Some overemphasize the tannin in red wines, making the wine taste more bitter than it actually is – choose wines with no more than modest tannin. Mush-rooms rarely clash with white wines, but most whites are still too bright, fruity and/or acidic to make really good matches. The more exotic varieties of mushroom find more wine partners, especially reds, although they still cannot cope with more than modest tannins – more mature reds with their lower tannins might therefore be best. Other ingredients in the dish will widen the choice of wines. See also *Soups* and *Eggs*.

**Cèpes/Porcini/Boletus** ♥ *low-tannin, not-too-fruity, savoury reds, especially if mature* ♀ *a few blandish whites*
Very mature Spanish Valdepeñas Reserva or Gran Reserva is a superstar, and other mature Spanish Tempranillos are also good. Not-too-tannic, mature New World Pinot Noir also goes superbly, better than red Burgundy. Southern Italian Cirò or Cirò Riserva and really low-tannin Nebbiolos make a superb flavour match; mature red Bordeaux, ripe Merlots and Cabernets, and Austrian Blauer Zweigelt all marry well. Vernaccia and Gavi make attractive white partners. ★★ *Valdepeñas Reserva* ★★ *California Pinot Noir*

**Chanterelles** ♀ *unoaked, fairly bland whites*
Simple Chablis is best, and finer Chablis (Premier Cru) is good, if too intensely flavoured. Muscadet and simple

white Burgundies make pleasant partners. Other simple, unoaked Chardonnays – from Hungary, Italy or southern France – make gently pleasant matches. White Rioja, oaked or unoaked, clashes horribly, and reds don't work. ★ *Chablis*

**Common Mushrooms (Fried)** ♥ *a few mature reds* ♀ *unoaked, not-too-acid or brightly fruity dry whites*

White Burgundy is the best choice, but other not-too-fruity Chardonnays work. Rueda, Pinot Grigio, dry German Riesling and southern French Picpoul are all possible. Mushrooms unpleasantly emphasize the tannin of most red wines, and frying them makes little difference. They have some affinity with the following mature reds: Cahors, Pinot Noir, Italian Cirò, Merlot and Austrian Blauer Zweigelt. ★ *white Burgundy*

VARIATIONS The combination of acidity and sweetness in **mushrooms à la Grèque** calls for care in the wine-matching. Reds don't work at all. Among whites the gentle flavour and crisp acidity of Bordeaux Blanc is very good, as is the steely Sauvignon from St-Bris, in northern Burgundy. Off-dry wines from Germany are pretty good, particularly Kabinetts made from Riesling, and basic QbA wines from the Mosel-Saar-Ruwer. ★ *Bordeaux Blanc*

**Morels/Morilles** ♥ *soft, gentle reds*

Whether fresh or dried, morels have a very delicate flavour that is easily swamped by wine. Pinot Noir is much the best flavour, but it must be a very soft, untannic one (and not red Burgundy). Gentle, southern French Gamay works and the flavour of Cabernet Sauvignon is good, though strong. Alsace Riesling and Bordeaux Blanc are possible whites. ★ *Pinot Noir VdP de l'Aude*

**Oyster Mushrooms** ♀ *low-acid, fairly neutral whites*

Oyster mushrooms are quite delicately flavoured, and there's little difference in taste between the grey and yellow versions. Reds are almost uniformly too tannic. The best whites are the neutral ones: Bordeaux Blanc, Picpoul, Bianco di Verona and white Châteauneuf-du-Pape.

**Shitake** ❣ *low-tannin reds* ♀ *a few whites*
Shitake mushrooms, with their lovely, naturally garlicky flavour, are difficult to match. Northern Italian Lugana blends in beautifully, and dry German Rieslings are good (but not dry Rieslings from the New World). The flavours of Pinot Noir, Cabernet Sauvignon and Sangiovese are good, but choose low-tannin ones. ★★ *Lugana*

**OLIVES (BLACK AND GREEN)** ♀ *fino and manzanilla sherry; dry, fairly high-acid whites*
In the south of Spain, they serve olives with chilled fino or manzanilla sherry; the combination is perfect with both black and green olives. It is the salty tang of dry sherry that chimes in so well. Otherwise, olives are very hard to match with wine – highish-acid dry whites are acceptable, but reds don't work. ★★ *fino or manzanilla sherry*

**Tapénade** ♀ *fino and dry amontillado sherry; dry, fairly high- to high-acid whites*
Chilled fino and manzanilla sherries are just as good when the olives are blended with thyme and olive oil in this salty Provençal spread/dip. Dry amontillado sherry is nearly as good, and various highish-acid whites work very well, including Champagne, sparkling Saumur, Australian dry Riesling and Sancerre. Reds clash. ★★ *fino sherry*

**ONION** Onion, especially when cooked, is very white-wine friendly. Dishes containing lots of cooked onion have a natural sweetness that needs a corresponding sweetness or ripe fruit in the wine.

**Cooked Onion** ❣ *a very few reds* ♀ *dry to medium-dry fruity whites*
Cooked onion goes well with a big range of whites. Alsace Pinot Blanc is a super-star, and a not-too-grand Gewürz-traminer from Alsace or elsewhere matches brilliantly, better than an Alsace Reserve or Grand Cru (though these also go well). Sauvignon de St-Bris is wonderful, other Sauvignons good, and Alella Clásico from Spain is another delicious partner. Marsanne, from France or Australia, goes well, as does Australian Verdelho, Viognier, dry Muscat, VdP des Côtes de Gascogne and Hungarian Furmint. Among reds, the Beaujolais crus (Fleurie, Regnié etc) and gentle, low-tannin Pinot Noirs are best, followed by Cahors, Chianti, Cirò and Naoussa, but many reds taste too austere. ★★ *Alsace Pinot Blanc*

VARIATIONS With **raw onion**, Sancerre is best, followed by Verdicchio. Australian Semillon, Spanish Rueda and simple, inexpensive Alsace Gewürztraminer are pleasant. ★ *Sancerre*

### Alsace Onion Tart (Tarte à l'Onion à l'Alsacienne) ♀ *dry whites with medium acidity*

TRADITIONAL PARTNER *Alsace Pinot Blanc*

As an alternative to the local choice, Alsace Pinot Blanc, top-quality Alsace Reserve or Gewürztraminer Grand Cru make a delicious accompaniment to this rich but delicate tart made with lots of cream. A modest Gewürztraminer or a dry Muscat also go quite well. Simple white Burgundy or Furmint from Hungary are good, and VdP des Côtes de Gascogne, Chilean Sauvignon, Australian Semillon or Verdelho, German Morio-Muskat or Rueda from Spain, are all possible partners. ★★ *Alsace Pinot Blanc*

### Provençal Onion Tart (Pissaladière) ♀ *light, highish-acid, fairly fruity whites*

It's the anchovy decoration that causes the problems when matching wines with this tasty dish. The best match is with the soft, greengagey fruit of Italian Lugana; other decent matches are with modern Sauvignons and, occasionally, Chardonnays. Sauvignons from New Zealand and Chile, and fruity Chardonnays from Hungary and the south of France are acceptable. Sweetness and too much acidity clash. Reds are hopeless. ★ *Lugana*

### PEPPERS (CAPSICUM) Sweet peppers

come in three different colours depending on how ripe they are. Green peppers are the least ripe – grassy and acid in flavour. As they ripen, turning yellow and then red, they become sweeter and less grassy. Cooking peppers emphasizes their natural sweetness, although green peppers are never very sweet. See also *Soups: Gazpacho.*

### Green Peppers (cooked) ❗ *bright, fruity or grassy reds* ♀ *bright, fruity, or herbaceous whites*

Cooked green peppers find a number of partners. The juicy-fruity Teroldego Rotaliano leads the way, followed by Cabernet Franc-based Loire reds. Of the whites, gentle Gewürztraminers and dry Muscats are best, and New Zealand Sauvignon Blanc, Bordeaux Blanc and warm-climate Sauvignons are pleasant. ★★ *Teroldego Rotaliano*

VARIATIONS **Raw green peppers** are almost impossible to match. Only the grassiest reds, such as Cabernet Franc-based Loire reds or some coolish-climate Merlots, can cope.

**Yellow Peppers (cooked)** ▮ *fruity reds* ♀ *dry whites*
Teroldego Rotaliano and Australian Shiraz are both stars. Warm-climate Cabernets, Merlots and Shiraz, or blends of those grapes, are successful, and Merlots from anywhere, and red Bordeaux, go fairly well. Gentle Gewürztraminers, dry Muscats and less aromatic Sauvignons are good. ★★ *Australian Shiraz* ★★ *Teroldego Rotaliano*

VARIATIONS The best match for **raw yellow peppers** is grassy Merlot. Rueda white is fine. ★ *cool-climate Merlot*

**Red Peppers (cooked)** ▮ *low-tannin, fruity reds*
♀ *aromatic, dry whites*
The Beaujolais crus (Côte de Brouilly, St-Amour, Fleurie etc) are really delicious, and Australian Shiraz is also a star. Red Navarra Crianza, especially if pure Tempranillo, is another superb partner. Ripe, fruity warm-climate Cabernets go very well indeed. Few whites work well, but dry Muscat and Gewürztraminer are delicious, Viognier is good, and New Zealand Sauvignon Blanc is pleasant. ★★ *Côte de Brouilly*

VARIATIONS Avoid very tannic reds with **raw red pepper**. Beaujolais crus are stars; and soft, low-tannin Australian Cabernet, ripe, low-tannin Merlots, or Viognier are pleasant. ★★ *Côte de Brouilly*

**Stuffed Peppers**
The ideal wine partner depends partly on the stuffing ingredients, but the peppers themselves are likely to be fairly dominant. For the most successful combination, find a compromise between the wines that go with the relevant colour of cooked pepper (above) and the stuffing.

**RATATOUILLE** ▮ *gentle, unoaked, low-tannin, southern French reds* ♀ *unoaked, aromatic dry whites with fairly high to high acidity*
TRADITIONAL PARTNER *Provençal red*
New Zealand Sauvignon Blanc is a super-star with this dish, and Sancerre, Pouilly-Fumé, Reuilly, Menetou-Salon and Quincy are nearly as good. (Warmer-climate Sauvi-

gnons taste flat alongside ratatouille, and many other French ones, from Touraine, Haut-Poitou or St-Bris, taste too acid.) Next best are Rieslings, especially from New Zealand, Australia and Chile, though Alsace, German and Austrian dry Rieslings are also pleasant. VdP des Côtes de Gascogne and South African Colombard go well, as does dry Vinho Verde. Muscadet Sur Lie, Alsace Pinot Blanc, Aligoté, Viognier and Crémant de Bourgogne are all worth trying. Avoid Muscat and Gewürztraminer. Some inexpensive southern French reds work: Côtes du Rhône, Provence, or Languedoc-Roussillon reds such as Corbières. ★★ *New Zealand Sauvignon Blanc*

## RED CABBAGE see CABBAGE

## SAUERKRAUT see CABBAGE

## SPINACH
Spinach is a difficult vegetable to partner. Many dry wines seem sweet and even the mildest reds seem very tannic. Two Italian whites provide the answer: the star choice, Frascati, and Soave. Spinach makes a simple Frascati taste better than it really is, while itself remaining unchanged in flavour. Soave is quite good. See also *Soups; Eggs: Quiches and Tarts, Soufflé* and *Eggs Florentine; Pasta: Ravioli, Canelloni.* ★★ *Frascati*

## STUFFED VINE LEAVES (DOLMADES)
see *Rice and Grains*

## SWEETCORN
Sweetcorn, whether frozen, out of a tin, or served on the cob with the traditional melted butter, is surprisingly difficult to partner with wine. Australian Verdelho, which has bags of ripe fruit without being actually sweet, works quite well, as does Champagne, which is rarely bone-dry. Reds are totally wrong, and most other whites are either too dry, too sweet, too acid, or too bland.

TOMATO see *Soups*, *Salads* and *Sauces*

# Salads

Salads usually call for white wines. For the majority of us who like to add dressings – especially vinaigrette – the wines will need to have highish acidity. Many vegetables used in salads (such as carrots, beetroot or red peppers), whether cooked or raw, have a certain natural sweetness, and respond well to a touch of sweetness in the accompanying wine. Tomatoes, however, despite their sweetness, prefer dry wines. Yoghurt dressings are very difficult to match with wine, cream less so. For oil and vinegar/lemon/reduced-wine dressings, see *Sauces: Vinaigrette*.

## AVOCADO, MOZZARELLA AND TOMATO SALAD (INSALATA TRICOLORE) ♀ *dry whites with good acidity*

It is quite hard to match all the elements of the popular avocado, mozzarella and tomato salad. No wine is perfect with everything, but simple Chablis goes well, as do white Burgundies, from young to mature, simple to fine. New Zealand Sauvignon Blanc works well, and Verdicchio, though a bit strong and bright for the avocado, goes well with everything else and slips down with the avocado. You could also try southern Italian Gravina. ★ *Chablis*

## BEAN SALAD ♥ *soft, unoaked Spanish reds* ♥ *dry rosés* ♀ *crisp, fruity, medium- to fairly high-acid dry whites*

Cooked dried beans, dressed in olive oil, wine vinegar, parsley and onion, make a wonderfully delicious contrast with Sancerre or New Zealand Sauvignon Blanc. Spanish Rueda, made from the local Verdejo grape or from Sauvignon, is also a star. Chablis goes well, or you could try Alella Clásico, or other Spanish whites, or VdP des Côtes de Gascogne, Australian Semillon or Semillon-Chardonnay blends. Most reds taste too tannic, but a soft, simple, unoaked Tempranillo or Cencibel from Spain goes quite well. Some rosés are pleasant: Rioja or Navarra, or South African Shiraz rosé. ★★ *Rueda* ★★ *Sancerre*

## BEETROOT SALAD ♀ *medium-dry to medium-sweet whites with fairly high acidity*

Dry whites taste acid with this dish, made with an olive oil vinaigrette, so you should look for something with a touch

of sweetness. The star match is with white Lambrusco, and Rhine Riesling Kabinett is next best. Mosel Riesling Kabinett is quite good, and Anjou Blanc Demi-sec and Spanish Alella Clásico are pleasant partners. Other possible white matches include sparkling wines made from the Champagne grapes, which are almost always slightly sweetened even if they claim to be 'brut' (dry).
★★ *white Lambrusco*

### CAESAR SALAD ♀ *dry whites*
The very lightly boiled egg in the dressing for this green salad (made with garlic croutons, grated Parmesan, Worcester sauce, olive oil and lemon juice) has a strong influence on the wine choice – it clashes with reds, but rarely bothers whites. The real stars are Frascati and Aligoté, but several other whites go well: white Burgundy, simple Chablis, VdP des Côtes de Gascogne, Bordeaux Blanc, Chilean Sauvignon Blanc and other warm-climate Sauvignons, Verdicchio, Champagne and Crémant de Bourgogne. ★★ *Aligoté* ★★ *Frascati*

### CARROT SALAD ♀ *dry to medium whites with fairly high acidity*
The sweetness and flavour of carrot, coupled with the acidity of the olive oil dressing, are quite hard to match. The tiny touch of sweetness in brut Champagne hits the spot, although price-wise this is hardly appropriate. A more budget-orientated medium English wine (but not Müller-Thurgau) often works, and demi-sec Anjou Blanc or Chenin vins de pays are pleasant. Aligoté surprisingly works despite its dryness. Otherwise, Bordeaux Blanc, Alsace Riesling, Austrian Riesling Trocken and Alella Clásico make adequate partners.

### COLESLAW ♀ *high-acid whites with a touch of sweetness*
A more appropriately priced choice than Champagne, which works exceptionally well, is inexpensive (slightly sweetened) Vinho Verde, also a very good match indeed. Other good matches are with Liebfraumilch, Piesporter Michelsberg or

other inexpensive German wines, medium-dry English wines, Alella Clásico or Vouvray Demi-sec. ★ *Vinho Verde*

## CUCUMBER SALAD ♀ *dry whites with medium to highish acidity, especially Chardonnay*

A cucumber salad, made with cream and dill, finds star partners in Chablis, California Chardonnay and Crémant de Bourgogne. White Burgundy and other European Chardonnays are good too, although Australian and New Zealand ones taste too fruity. Bordeaux Blanc and Lugana are both good, Anjou Blanc and Favorita adequate. Reds taste too tannic. ★★ *Chablis* ★★ *California Chardonnay*
VARIATIONS Turkish **Cacik** is a quite salty cucumber salad, dressed with yoghurt, mint and garlic, and is tricky to match, but some high-acid whites chime in adequately with the saltiness as well as the flavour. Try Gros Plant, Muscadet, VdP des Côtes de Gascogne and Cheverny. The Greek version, **Tzatziki**, made with grated cucumber, Greek yoghurt, garlic, olive oil and a little vinegar, is very hard to match. Inexpensive South African Colombard is perhaps the most appropriate choice.

## GREEK SALAD ♀ *bland whites with fairly high to high acidity*

TRADITIONAL PARTNER *Retsina*
Nothing goes perfectly with Greek salad, though Retsina is up among the best matches. Other good matches are Muscadet Sur Lie, Spanish Rueda and Chardonnay VdP du Jardin de la France. Or try Gros Plant, Cheverny (Touraine), Sancerre, or a Beaujolais as a possible red. ★ *Retsina*

## GREEN SALAD ❢ *a few very light, low-tannin reds* ♀ *high-acid dry whites*

Lettuce of whatever type (as opposed to more bitter chicory or endive) has little effect on white wines. The salad-dressing is the thing to match. With a simple olive oil dressing, the best white choices are Bourgogne Aligoté and a VdP des Côtes de Gascogne. Most reds taste slightly bitter, but a few very light reds can cope: try Lambrusco Secco and Valpolicella. For different types of dressings, see *Sauces: Vinaigrettes.* ★★ *Bourgogne Aligoté* ★★ *VdP des Côtes de Gascogne*

## PEPPER SALAD see PEPPERS

**SALADE NIÇOISE** ♀ *highish-acid dry whites*
Nothing makes as delicious a match as Cheverny (from Touraine), but there are plenty of good partners: Muscadet, white Corbières, Soave, Vinho Verde, Chardonnay VdP du Jardin de la France, northern Italian Chardonnays, and white Burgundy, including fine ones (but not Chablis, which has too honeyed a flavour). ★★ *Cheverny*

**TOMATO SALAD** ♀ *dry whites with fairly high to high acidity, especially Sauvignon Blanc*
Best matches to accompany a simple tomato salad with an olive oil vinaigrette are Sauvignon Blancs: Sauvignons de Touraine, du Haut Poitou or de St-Bris are excellent, and Sancerre and Chilean and New Zealand Sauvignons are very pleasant. (Sauvignons from Bordeaux, Duras, Bergerac and South Africa tend to be too soft.) Muscadet, Cheverny, Spanish Rueda and Italian Lugana are a success, and Champagne, Aligoté, VdP des Côtes de Gascogne and Chablis all make adequate partners. ★★ *Sauvignon de Touraine*

VARIATIONS With **raw onions**, a match is harder to find. Sauvignons still work, though not nearly as well. The best match is with VdP des Côtes de Gascogne, with Muscadet runner-up. ★ *VdP des Côtes de Gascogne*. With **basil**, things do not improve, as this herb finds very particular wine partners. Lugana is the best choice, and there are adequate pairings with sharp, cool-climate Sauvignons, Chablis, Champagne, Aligoté and Muscadet. ★ *Lugana*. With **mozzarella and basil**, nothing goes brilliantly with all the elements, but Verdicchio is good, simple Chablis and white Burgundies make pleasant partners, and cool-climate Sauvignons are fine. ★ *Verdicchio*

**WALDORF SALAD** ♀ *medium-dry whites with medium acidity*
Many whites taste too acid and/or fruitless. Nothing is perfect, but Liebfraumilch, hock or basic German Rhine wines (such as Niersteiner Gutes Domtal) hit the spot for sweetness, acidity and flavour, and Anjou Blanc Demi-sec is fine.

# HERBS, SPICES AND FLAVOURINGS

Herbs, spices and other flavourings are, of course, only elements in a dish, and other more substantial ingredients will also influence the wine match. But a small sprinkling of herb goes a long way, and often it will dominate the overall flavour. There are some excellent wine and herb matches that can act as a bridge between the wine in your glass and the main ingredient of the dish.

This section also includes spices and flavourings used in puddings and desserts, such as vanilla and peppermint. Some flavourings will obviously appear in both savoury and sweet dishes – the relevant wine partners for the sweet dishes are listed separately.

## ALMOND
SWEET Sweet Muscats are the perfect complement to almonds in puddings and desserts. ★★ *sweet Muscats*

## BASIL ♀ *dry whites*
Basil goes well with a lot of white wines. One of basil's best matches is with Gravina, from southern Italy, an extraordinary white wine that actually *tastes* of basil. Equally pleasurable is rich, buttery, top-class California Chardonnay, and not far behind comes soft, Chardonnay-based Crémant de Bourgogne fizz. Among the best matches are good white Burgundy, Chablis and South African Colombard, Victoria Chardonnays and Hunter Valley Semillons from Australia. Bourgogne Aligoté, VdP des Côtes de Gascogne and Bordeaux Blanc are as good. Also pleasant are Verdicchio, Sauvignon Blanc, Semillon-Chardonnay and Champagne. See also *Pasta: Pesto*. ★★ *Gravina* ★★ *top-class California Chardonnay*

## CAPERS ♀ *fairly high- to high-acid dry whites*
The flavour of capers is unavoidably dominated by the vinegar in which they are pickled. It is therefore the vinegar that dictates the choice of wine. Sancerre and Pouilly-Fumé (especially from a cool vintage) hit the spot abso- lutely, with their high acid and grassy flavour, but most other Sauvignon Blancs don't match. Other reason-able white partners are South African Colombard, VdP

des Côtes de Gascogne, Spanish dry whites from Penedés and Conca de Barberá, and unoaked Italian Chardonnay. ★ *cool-vintage Sancerre*

### CARAWAY SEED ♀ *dry, unoaked whites, especially Sauvignon Blanc*

Sauvignon Blanc is the grape variety for caraway: riper New World Sauvignons are the best partners, although New Zealand Sauvignon is altogether too strong. Sancerre, Pouilly-Fumé and Sauvignon de Touraine make other very good pairings, as does unoaked white Rioja. Next come a host of other dry whites, including Terret, Picpoul, Bordeaux Sauvignon and basic Bordeaux Blanc, English Seyval Blanc, Rueda and Vernaccia di San Gimignano. ★★ *Chilean or Australian Sauvignon Blanc*

### CARDAMOM ▮▮ *a few reds and rosés* ♀ *whites*

Exotically perfumed cardamom goes brilliantly with a rich, white Châteauneuf-du-Pape or oaked Chardonnay from Chile or Australia. It also goes well with California Chardonnay, Australian Semillon-Chardonnay, Viognier, Sancerre from a ripe vintage, Spanish Rueda, and New World Sauvignon. High-acid Loire Sauvignons, however, make a bitter combination. Or you can try dry Muscat, Bordeaux Blanc, white Côtes du Rhône, Terret, or Spanish Yecla. Reds and rosés are less ideal, but there is some affinity between cardamom and a handful of red grape varieties: Merlot, Shiraz, Pinotage and very light Pinot Noirs such as red Sancerre. Beaujolais clashes. ★★ *white Châteauneuf-du-Pape* ★★ *oaked Australian, Chilean or New Zealand Chardonnay*

### CHERVIL ♀ *dry Spanish rosés* ♀ *dry, fairly bland whites*

The gently honeyed flavour of Hungarian Furmint works extremely well, as do two Italian whites – Verdicchio and Gravina. Gavi and Lugana, German Silvaner Trocken, Alsace Sylvaner, VdP des Côtes de Gascogne, Sancerre and New Zealand

Sauvignon Blanc are all pleasant. From Spain, Penedés and Conca de Barberá whites are possible, and a dry Spanish rosé is another good alternative. ★ *Hungarian Furmint*

## CHILLI
Although a variety of flavourful chilli peppers exists, they are rare, and the common, small, pointed red or green ones give little actual flavour, whether fresh, dried or powdered. What they do give you, of course, is a hot, burning sensation in the mouth. Chilli has no effect on the flavour or structure (tannin etc) of a wine served with it, although sparkling drinks – whether Champagne, lager or sparkling mineral water – tend to emphasize the burning sensation. So any wine that partners the other ingredients in the dish will be fine with the chilli. You may feel, however, that a burning tongue takes your mind off the complexities of a fine wine; if so, choose something not too grand.

## CHIVES ♥ *unoaked reds* ♀ *unoaked, dry whites*
Used in moderation, chives can be ignored when choosing a wine. They neither actively clash with wines (except slightly with oak, which is best avoided) nor do they really complement most wines. There are some white wines that make pretty good matches – the best are Bordeaux Blanc and Sancerre; Pouilly-Fumé is also a good choice. Of the reds, chives make pleasant partners with the flavour of Pinot Noir (including red Burgundy) and with Beaujolais. ★ *Sancerre* ★ *Bordeaux Blanc*

## CINNAMON
SWEET Cinnamon goes deliciously with sweet Rieslings, especially those from Germany, and quite well with Sauternes, Barsac and other sweet Bordeaux wines, which work better than sweet Semillons from elsewhere. It is generally quite wine-friendly (but best avoided with Hungarian Tokay, Italian Vin Santo and Recioto di Soave, and sweet Champagne). ★★ *sweet German Riesling*

## COCONUT ♥ *a few low-tannin, low-fruit, ideally mature reds* ♀ *lots of whites*
Coconut in savoury dishes manages pretty well with a host of dry whites, but occasionally makes a really unpleasant clash – Terret and Seyval Blanc in particular – resulting in a flavour like sour milk. White Châteauneuf-du-Pape,

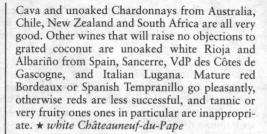

Cava and unoaked Chardonnays from Australia, Chile, New Zealand and South Africa are all very good. Other wines that will raise no objections to grated coconut are unoaked white Rioja and Albariño from Spain, Sancerre, VdP des Côtes de Gascogne, and Italian Lugana. Mature red Bordeaux or Spanish Tempranillo go pleasantly, otherwise reds are less successful, and tannic or very fruity ones in particular are inappropriate. ★ *white Châteauneuf-du-Pape*

## CORIANDER
**Coriander Leaf** ♀ *dry, fairly neutral whites*
Dry German wines perform extremely well with coriander leaf: the star is dry Baden white, and Silvaner Trocken is almost as good. Other highly successful matches are with Müller-Thurgau and South African Colombard. These wines really enhance the coriander flavour. Coriander leaf also relates very well to whites as diverse as Retsina, Conca de Barberá and Penedés whites from Spain, Verdicchio and Furmint. Soave and Alella are pleasant. More aromatic grapes such as Sauvignon and Riesling are inappropriate, as are red grapes. ★★ *Baden Dry*

**Coriander Seed** ♀ *fairly bland whites*
Coriander seed has an utterly different flavour from the leaf, and the best wine partners are mostly quite different, too. The star, Bianco di Custoza, makes a lovely, lemony combination; the fruitiness of Lugana goes well. A third Italian wine, Cortese, and coriander are mutually enhancing. Hungarian Furmint, South African Sauvignon and Spanish Rueda all work equally well. Gavi, Sicilian white table wine, Australian or Bordeaux dry Semillon, Pinot Blanc, Austrian Grüner Veltliner, and Chablis are fine. Even the lightest of red wines, however, tastes nastily bitter. ★ *Bianco di Custoza*

## CUMIN ♀♀ *a variety of whites and reds*
Cumin finds no stunning partners, but goes quite well with a variety of wines. Frascati and oaked white Rioja are the best white matches,

followed by Viognier or Condrieu, Chardonnay, Pinot Blanc, Penedés white, southern French Terret, white Corbières and Sicilian white. Passable red partners are Italian Valpolicella, Salice Salentino, Copertino, Franciacorta, or Sicilian reds, and young Tempranillos or Cencibels from Spain, as well as Beaujolais. ★ *Frascati* ★ *oaked white Rioja*

## DILL ♀ *aromatic to neutral dry whites, especially Sauvignon Blancs*

You can't go far wrong with Sauvignon Blanc and dill, as long as you steer clear of the most exotically fruity styles (New Zealand Sauvignons are a bit too strong). Good, crisp, grassy Sauvignons from St-Bris and the Loire regions (Sancerre, Pouilly-Fumé, Sauvignon de Touraine, etc), and from Chile, are delicious. Bordeaux and South African Sauvignons are very good, too, on a par with VdP des Côtes de Gascogne and a clutch of Italian whites: Favorita and Cortese from Piemonte and Gravina from the south, as well as the Portuguese Trincadeira das Pratas. Reds are unpleasantly tannic. ★★ *Chilean Sauvignon Blanc*

## GARLIC
### Cooked Garlic ♥ *very varied reds* ♥ *dry and off-dry rosés* ♀ *dry, highish-acid whites*

It's just as well that cooked garlic can match as many wines – both reds and whites – as it does, considering the number of recipes in which garlic appears. The savoury, figgy-sweet Cirò from southern Italy is the undisputed star, a brilliant match, but there are many to follow it. The lighter Beaujolais crus, Portuguese reds from the Ribatejo and Oeste regions, the lighter Cahors, and Pinot Noirs from Australia, New Zealand, California and the south of France are almost as good as Cirò. Other reds worth considering are lighter red Burgundies, Rioja, Navarra and Valdepeñas Crianzas, Merlots from Chile, Australia and California, Australian Cabernet Sauvignons, and Syrahs from California. Of the whites, California Chardonnay and Spanish Rueda match nearly as brilliantly as Cirò. Chilean Sauvignon, Vernaccia di San Gimignano, Aligoté, Picpoul, Hungarian Furmint and German Riesling Trocken also make admirable matches. Spanish dry rosado and rosés from around the Bordeaux region are successful, too. ★★ *Cirò*

**Raw Garlic** ♥ *soft, fruity reds* ♀ *dry, fruity rosés* ♀ *fairly bland whites*

Raw garlic is much less positively wine-friendly, but it goes adequately with many wines, and rarely clashes with the rest. The best white matches are with fairly bland wines: the star is Rueda, and Valencia or Yecla whites, also from Spain, are nearly as good. Pleasant white matches include English Seyval Blanc, Riesling, Sauvignon Blanc, Aligoté, Chablis, Champagne, Châteauneuf-du-Pape, unoaked Chardonnay, Pinot Blanc, Lugana, Penedés white and Cava. Cinsault Rosé is also a star choice, and red Burgundy is nearly as good. Other Pinot Noirs are quite successful too. There are also pleasant matches with a host of other reds from Beaujolais-Villages to Coonawarra Cabernet, and fine mature red Bordeaux, Barossa Shiraz and South African Pinotage. ★ *Rueda* ★ *Cinsault Rosé*

**GINGER** ♥ *a few low-tannin reds* ♀ *a variety of whites*

Surprisingly, in view of its strong flavour, ginger rarely clashes with white wines, nor does it swamp or upset their flavour. Italian Pinot Grigio is positively delicious with ginger, and Alsace Pinot Gris a good match. Next best are Viognier, Gewürztraminer, New Zealand Sauvignon Blanc and Soave, followed by Chablis and other simple Chardonnays, Sancerre and other Sauvignon Blancs, Bordeaux Blanc, white Corbières, dry Muscats, Vernaccia di San Gimignano, Favorita, Baden Dry, South African Colombard, and Spanish whites from Penedés. Reds are more difficult. Ginger sometimes over-emphasizes their tannin, or makes them taste a little coarse (avoid Valpolicella, Chianti, Beaujolais and oaked reds). But ginger is good with the lightest of Sangioveses – Sangiovese delle Marche and Sangiovese di Romagna – and with a few other reds: light Côtes du Rhône, Côtes du Roussillon or simple southern French vins de pays. ★★ *Pinot Grigio*

SWEET Sweet Rieslings are the star with ginger in puddings, but there are other pleasant matches with sweet Semillons – including Sauternes and

Barsac – and with Recioto di Soave. Asti goes pleasantly, though other Muscats seem to have the wrong flavour. Sweet Loires clash. ★★ *sweet Rieslings*

## HAZELNUT

SWEET Hazelnut is a difficult flavour to match and when toasted it reacts differently to wines. Provided the flavour of the pudding or dessert is quite strong, Australian Rutherglen Liqueur Muscats go very well (though less well if the nuts are toasted). Muscat de St-Jean-de-Minervois and Setúbal are pleasant (less good with toasted nuts), but other Muscats have no particular affinity. Austrian Bouvier/Pinot Gris/Pinot Blanc Beerenauslesen are other possibilities, and sweet Loires – Vouvray or Coteaux du Layon – go modestly well with toasted hazelnuts. ★ *Australian Rutherglen Liqueur Muscat*

## HONEY

SWEET Honey is generally not objectionable with sweet wines, but it has particular affinity only for sweet wines from the Loire. ★ *Vouvray Moelleux*

## JUNIPER ❗ *a variety of reds and rosés* ♀ *a few whites*

Juniper is not especially wine-friendly, but some wines are pleasant with it – reds slightly better than whites. Best are California or Oregon Pinot Noir, South African Pinotage and Shiraz (better than the fruitier Australian ones), followed by Beaujolais, red Bordeaux, Syrah, Zinfandel, Tempranillo, Rioja, Côtes du Rhône, and other Pinot Noirs. Rosés made from the same grapes are also good. Among whites, Chardonnays have most affinity with juniper, and Douro whites from Portugal, and Spanish Yecla and Valencia dry whites are all pleasant. ★ *California Pinot Noir*

## LEMON GRASS ♀ *most whites, particularly Sauvignon Blancs and Rieslings*

Lemon grass is the most white wine-friendly herb of the lot: its lively, lemony taste goes well with a vast range of white wines, and injects character into bland wines (Frascati clashes, however). Sauvignon Blanc is the most successful: Sancerre and New Zealand Sauvignon are the outright winners, and Sauvignons from St-Bris in Burgundy, Chile and South Africa are very good, too. Australian and

German Rieslings, dry and off-dry, are likewise successful. Viognier and Favorita, with their very aromatic flavours, make excellent pairings, as does the dry Vernaccia di San Gimignano. Other very good matches include oaked white Rioja, Soave, Vinho Verde, mature Alsace Riesling, Rueda, Lugana, VdP des Côtes de Gascogne and Picpoul. Even a few very light reds will work – Sangiovese from the Marche or Romagna in Italy, or a young Valdepeñas from Spain. ★★ *Sancerre* ★★ *New Zealand Sauvignon Blanc*

**LEMON ZEST** ♀ *whites, ideally aromatic ones*
Lemon zest rarely has the magical, enlivening effect of lemon grass (see above) on white wines, but does combine well with many. Austrian Riesling Kabinett is the star among Rieslings, and Gewürztraminer, Muscat and Sauvignon Blanc are also very good, and Viognier very pleasant. Of the less aromatic grapes, the best are South African Colombard and VdP des Côtes de Gascogne, and a number of other wines go very pleasantly: dry Vinho Verde, Spanish Albariño and Portuguese Alvarinho, Rueda, Vernaccia di San Gimignano, Gavi, Lugana, Bordeaux Blanc, Terret, Muscadet Sur Lie, Hungarian Furmint and Australian Verdelho. Reds are out, as they tend to clash and/or taste more tannic than they really are. ★★ *Austrian Riesling Kabinett*
SWEET Sweet Muscat has a real flavour affinity with lemon zest. Moscatel de Valencia is utterly delicious, but there are also star matches with Muscat de Beaumes-de-Venise, Muscat de St-Jean-de-Minervois and Muscat de Rivesaltes. Asti and Moscato d'Asti go very well, and California Orange Muscat is very pleasant. Sweet Hungarian Tokay is a surprise hit with lemon, and the flavour of sweet Riesling works very well. ★★ *Moscatel de Valencia*

**LIME ZEST** ♀ *a variety of whites*
Lime is the wine-lover among citrus zests. Australian Riesling and Muscadet Sur Lie make brilliant flavour matches, and Chenin Blanc is also

excellent (try a Saumur or Anjou Blanc Sec, Savennières or South African Chenin). So too are expensive, dry Vinho Verde, VdP des Côtes de Gascogne, Australian Verdelho or South African Colombard. Plenty of other whites go very well: Rueda, Lugana, Gavi, dry Muscat, Sauvignon Blancs from the Loire or the New World, Terret, and Gros Plant. There is a slight clash with Aligoté, Chardonnay and Viognier. Reds become very tannic with lime zest. ★★ *Muscadet Sur Lie* ★★ *Australian Riesling*

SWEET Some sweet Rieslings are quite wonderful with the complex and delicious flavour of lime zest, and the combination is always at least pleasant. Light Muscats – such as Asti, California Orange Muscat or Muscat de St-Jean-de-Minervois – are pleasant but can bring out a slight bitterness in the lime. Sweet (*riche*) Champagne and Recioto di Soave go pleasantly. Sauternes and other botrytized Semillons taste very bitter. ★★ *sweet Mosel Riesling*

## MARJORAM see OREGANO

## MINT ❗ *various reds* ♀ *dry whites*
Mints do vary, but concentrating on common mint, this is fairly wine-friendly, and rarely clashes. The brilliant red match is with a modern, fruity Corbières, which explodes in a crescendo of minty flavour. Pinot Noir, including red Burgundy, also works well. Cabernet Sauvignons are fine, the minty Australian ones from cooler areas matching a little better than others. Other pleasant red matches are with Teroldego Rotaliano, Fitou, Côtes du Roussillon-Villages and other southern French appellations, and Zinfandel. White stars are Côtes du Rhône and gentle Sauvignons such as Bordeaux Blanc, and common mint also goes well with Est! Est!! Est!!!, white Rioja whether oaked or not, and dry German or Austrian Rieslings. ★★ *fruity, modern red Corbières*

VARIATIONS **Apple mint** is much gentler and less aromatic than common mint, and it is delicious used in cooking. But it is not quite so wine-friendly – some reds seem too tannic, and white wines are no more than adequate. The best matches are with Tempranillo-based oak-aged Spanish reds. There are fairly good matches with low-tannin Sangioveses, Barbera, Greek Naoussa, Beaujolais-Villages and red Corbières, and low-tannin Pinot Noir and Shiraz. Of the whites, try Bordeaux Blanc, white Côtes du Rhône,

Austrian Grüner Veltliner, Vernaccia, and Rueda from Spain. ★★ *red Rioja Crianza*

**MUSTARD** see *Sauces, Dressings and Relishes*

### NUTMEG
SWEET Nutmeg tastes bitter with many sweet wines (for example Rieslings, most Muscats and sweet Champagne). However, fortified California Orange Muscat and Italian Vin Santo both pleasantly emphasize the nutmeg flavour while retaining their own character. ★★ *fortified California Orange Muscat* ★★ *Vin Santo*

### ORANGE ZEST ♀ *a variety of whites*
Nothing goes perfectly with orange zest, but there are a lot of fairly good white matches. The stars are Muscat and Chardonnay; Gewürztraminer, Riesling, Australian Verdelho, expensive dry Vinho Verde, Spanish Rueda, and VdP des Côtes de Gascogne all go well. There are also pleasant matches with Viognier, Lugana, Favorita, Arneis, Spanish Albariño and Portuguese Alvarinho. ★ *dry Muscat* ★ *simple Chardonnay*

SWEET How appropriate that fortified California Orange Muscat should be a superb match with orange zest. Next best are Asti and Muscat de St-Jean-de-Minervois. Sweet German Rieslings don't work, but Late Harvest or botrytized Rieslings from South Africa, California or Australia are acceptable. Sauternes and other sweet Bordeaux are pleasant, as are sweet Loire whites such as Vouvray, sweet Champagnes, or heavier Muscats such as Australian Liqueur Muscat or Setúbal if the orange flavour is very strong. ★ *California fortified Orange Muscat*

### OREGANO/MARJORAM ❢ *grassy and savoury reds* ♀ *bland whites*
Oregano and (to a lesser extent) marjoram have a bitterness that is hard to match. Go easy with both these herbs. Good white matches with oregano are rare: some – especially the aromatic grapes – really emphasize the bitterness. Spanish

Rueda is, however, very good, and southern French Terret and fino sherry both work well too. Good red matches are more abundant, but beware the bitter touch here, too, if you use a lot of herb. The star red is Merlot, as its grassy flavour works well with the herb. Warm-climate Pinot Noirs are also good. Barolo and other Nebbiolos have a complementary flavour, though other ingredients will need to cope with the tannin. Montepulciano d'Abruzzo and Rosso Conero blend in well too. Or try a light Spanish Tempranillo or warm-climate Cabernet Sauvignon. ★★ *Merlot* ★★ *Rueda*

## PARSLEY
### Curly Parsley ♀ *a very few whites*
Go easy on this herb – curly parsley has a positive affinity with very few wines. As well as the very good matches with Hungarian Furmint and Vernaccia di San Gimignano, it goes pleasantly with Soave, Bianco di Verona and Bordeaux Blanc. White Châteauneuf-du-Pape greatly emphasizes the parsley flavour. Some reds survive (without really matching), while others taste much more tannic than they really are. Merlots, even very gentle ones, are best avoided for this reason. ★ *Hungarian Furmint* ★ *Vernaccia di San Gimignano*
### Flat-leaved Parsley ♀ *dry, unoaked whites*
Flat-leaved parsley, usually the type preferred by cooks in continental Europe, has a similar, yet stronger flavour than the curly version. It behaves quite differently with wines, however. A surprise match is with aromatic Viognier or Condrieu (neither of which work with curly parsley). It also goes positively well with the bland flavour of whites from Valencia or Yecla in south-east Spain. Other wines with which it has reasonable affinity are Soave, Vernaccia di San Gimignano, Sauvignon Blancs including Sancerre, Semillon or Semillon-Sauvignon blends, Spanish whites from Conca de Barberá or Penedés, and South African Colombard. Reds tend to taste slightly coarser, or very much more tannic than they really are. ★ *Viognier* ★ *Valencia dry white*

## PEPPERMINT
SWEET A strong peppermint flavour in a pudding will kill all wines, and even gentle peppermint tastes foul with certain wines (such as sweet Loires, Recioto di Soave or sweet

Jurançon). But a mild peppermint flavour blends in really well with the flavour of sweet Muscat, especially those from Beaumes-de-Venise or Rivesaltes. Sauternes survives with peppermint.
★★ *Muscat de Beaumes-de-Venise*

### ROSEMARY ♀ *reds, especially Burgundy and Bordeaux* ♀ *dry, bland whites*
Rosemary's strong flavour overpowers lots of wines and finds no affinity with many others, but there are few actual clashes with either reds or whites. The star choice is fine red Burgundy, especially Gevrey-Chambertin, which is really delicious with rosemary, and the grassiness of red Bordeaux is nearly as good. Other Pinot Noirs, Zinfandels, Shirazes, Merlots, Cabernet Sauvignons, Cencibel/Tempranillos, and Montepulciano d'Abruzzo and Rosso Conero are all pleasant choices. The best whites are Frascati, Bianco di Custoza, Arneis and Viognier, with runners-up Pinot Blanc, Spanish Albariño or Portuguese Alvarinho, white Corbières and Austrian Grüner Veltliner all good alternatives.
★★ *Gevrey-Chambertin*

### SAFFRON ♀ *dry Grenache rosés* ♀ *dry whites*
The faintly smoky flavour of Austrian Grüner Veltliner comes out on top, but unoaked Australian Chardonnay is not far behind. Other good matches can be made with Lugana, and Cava and Rueda from Spain. Several other crisp dry whites work reasonably well, too: try Muscadet, VdP des Côtes de Gascogne, unoaked Italian Chardonnay, Chilean Sauvignon Blanc, Chablis Premier and Grand Cru and Alsace Pinot Blanc. Gentle southern French dry rosés made from Grenache are acceptable. ★ *Austrian Grüner Veltliner*

### SAGE ♀ *low- to medium-tannin reds*
♀ *Sauvignon Blancs and other aromatic whites*
Sauvignon Blancs are the great stars with sage – all are good, though New Zealand ones are slightly too ripely fruity and aromatic. Sage also goes pleasantly with Rueda, Conca de Barberá

and Penedés whites from Spain, Alsace Tokay-Pinot Gris, Viognier, Gewürztraminer, dry Muscat, Arneis, and Frascati Superiore. Dry rosés made from Cabernet Sauvignon also make interesting partners. Red wines are not so easy to match. Sage unpleasantly emphasizes the tannin of Pinot Noir, the Beaujolais crus and Lambrusco, and tends to create bitter flavours with Cabernet Sauvignons and red Bordeaux. There are some brilliant matches with Italian reds, however: Chianti Classico and fine but not-too-tannic Tuscan Sangioveses, especially if mature, Cirò or Cirò Riserva, and Barbera d'Alba all emphasize the sage flavour and are themselves enhanced by the sage. The same goes for Dolcetto: it is a lovely flavour for the herb, provided the other ingredients in the dish can cope with the tannin in the wine. ★★ *Chilean Sauvignon Blanc*

### SORREL ♀ *fairly high- to high-acid dry whites*

The very distinctive, almost metallic, acid flavour of sorrel in fact goes well with Chenin Blanc, particularly from the Loire (Anjou or Saumur Blanc Sec, sparkling Saumur, Savennières) which have the right acidity. Cool-climate Sauvignon Blancs go well, especially from New Zealand, the Loire or Sauvignon de St-Bris. In Tuscany, Vernaccia di San Gimignano has the right flavour, and enough acidity if the sorrel is well-diluted in a sauce. Other pleasant matches are with VdP des Côtes de Gascogne, Chablis, Rueda, Gavi, dry Rieslings, Hungarian Furmint, Terret, Muscadet and dry Vinho Verde. Bordeaux Blanc is fine with a sauce lightly flavoured with sorrel. ★ *Saumur and Anjou Blanc Sec* ★ *Sauvignon de St-Bris*

### TARRAGON ♀ *selected whites*

White wines have to be carefully selected, but there are quite a lot of fairly good matches to be found. Gentle warm-climate Sauvignon Blancs are the best choice, especially those from Chile and South Africa. Viognier, dry Muscat wines, dry German Riesling, VdP des Côtes de Gascogne, Chenin Blanc, or southern Italian Gravina are nearly as good. Or you could try Aligoté, Sauvignon de St-Bris, Bordeaux Blanc, southern French whites such as Terret and Picpoul, Bianco di Custoza, Lugana, Soave, basic whites from Sicily and the Veneto, Vinho Verde, and Spanish Rueda. Reds do not work with this herb. ★ *gentle Sauvignon Blancs from Chile and South Africa*

### THYME ♥ *a variety of reds, especially if mature* ♀ *very few low-fruit whites*

Thyme chimes in much better with the flavours in red wine than white, and copes well with tannin. It has a particular affinity with some reds: the Tempranillo/Cencibel grape of Spain is a hit, especially if oak-aged – go for a Crianza or Reserva from Rioja, Navarra, Ribera del Duero or Valdepeñas, or an up-market, oaked Cencibel from La Mancha. Red Bordeaux is good, too, especially if mature. The main Greek reds – Naoussa, Goumenissa and Nemea – are all very complementary. Many whites are too fruity, but Soave is in fact a star choice, while white Côtes du Rhône and white Corbières all match positively well, and VdP des Côtes de Gascogne and Aligoté are both quite successful. ★ *red Rioja Crianza* ★ *mature red Bordeaux* ★ *Soave*

### VANILLA

SWEET Even quite a strong vanilla flavour is fairly wine-friendly, though there are no really stunning matches. Sweet Loires such as Vouvray or Coteaux du Layon are very complementary, and work especially well if the pudding also contains some acidity, such as added lemon juice. The lighter Muscats go pleasantly, as does Recioto di Soave, and Australian botrytized Semillon is fine (but Sauternes doesn't work). ★ *sweet Muscats* ★ *Recioto di Soave* ★ *sweet Loires*

### WALNUT

SWEET Even plain walnuts go much better with sweet wines than with dry wines, although the tannin in the nut skin clashes with some sweet wines (such as sweet Loires or Hungarian Tokay). Sweet sherry is a great success, whether an inexpensive cream sherry or a fine (but sweet) old oloroso, and amontillados (not dry ones) are pleasant too. Otherwise, sweet Muscats, from Asti to Australian Rutherglen Liqueur Muscat, make reasonable partners. Greek Mavrodaphne of Patras goes really quite well, and Marsala is pleasant. ★ *sweet oloroso sherry*

# SAUCES, DRESSINGS AND RELISHES

A dish is often dominated by the sauce or dressing that accompanies it. Rather than match the wine to the meat, fish or vegetables (though the latter also often make their own demands in the dish), you are looking to find a wine partner for the sauce. Sauces and relishes high in acidity or sweetness – mint or barbecue sauce, bottled sauces such as ketchup and brown sauce, pickles and chutneys – are particularly difficult to pair with wine. The sweet, high-acid wines that do work are probably completely inappropriate for the meat or cheese they are to be served with. If you want to give your wine the best chance to taste good, these sauces and relishes should be avoided altogether.

### AÏOLI (GARLIC MAYONNAISE) ▼ *Beaujolais-Villages* ♀ *fairly bland, dry whites*
Adding lots of garlic to mayonnaise (see *Mayonnaise* below) makes it far more wine-friendly. Aligoté from Burgundy or Bulgaria goes very well indeed, as does gently oaky white Rioja. Several other whites are fairly successful, including Chardonnay del Piemonte, Chardonnay VdP d'Oc (unoaked is best, but any will work), white Corbières, dry Vinho Verde, unoaked white Rioja and Est! Est!! Est!!!. Reasonable white partners are Muscadet, Bordeaux Blanc, white Châteauneuf-du-Pape or Côtes du Rhône, Soave, Lugana, Gavi, Conca de Barberá and English Seyval Blanc. Spanish *rosados* tend to go well, and Beaujolais-Villages unexpectedly makes a really good red wine match. ★★ *Aligoté* ★★ *white Rioja Crianza*

### APPLE SAUCE ♀ *fairly high-acid whites*
The wine match depends on how much sugar you add to the apple – it's best to add a minimal amount, unless you are happy to drink a fairly sweet wine. You should also consider the meat the apple sauce is to accompany. Apple sauce with just a touch of added sugar goes really superbly with the highish acidity of Riesling Kabinetts from the Mosel-Saar-Ruwer (which also go well with both pork and goose). Fruity Australian Verdelho is also brilliant. See also *Meat: Roast Pork* and *Puddings: Apple*. ★ *Mosel Riesling Kabinett*

### BARBECUE SAUCE ♥ *bright, fruity reds* ♀ *medium-dry or medium whites*

Although many dry whites taste flat and fruitless with this sweetish sauce, it makes a really brilliant match with Liebfraumilch or inexpensive Rhine wines such as Niersteiner Gutes Domtal. It is also excellent with German Riesling Kabinetts, but Trocken and Halbtrocken Rieslings are too dry. From Spain, Alella Clásico, with its touch of sweetness, is another good choice, as is a demi-sec Vouvray from the Loire. Among dry whites, really fruity Rieslings from New Zealand, Australia or Chile go surprisingly well, as does unoaked white Rioja. Some reds clash disgustingly, but a number of bright, fruity ones can cope: best are Dolcetto, a really modern, fruity Côtes du Roussillon or Oregon Pinot Noir, with Zinfandel, Beaujolais-Villages, Portuguese Alentejo, Valpolicella and Teroldego Rotaliano bringing up the rear. ★★ *Liebfraumilch*

### BÉARNAISE SAUCE ♥ *light Beaujolais* ♀ *high-acid whites with a touch of sweetness*

Béarnaise sauce is really hollandaise sauce dressed up with chervil, tarragon, thyme and bay. It is a brilliant match for German Riesling Kabinett, whether from the Mosel-Saar-Ruwer or the Rhine. Inexpensive, slightly sweet Riesling from Australia makes an adequate partner, but other Rieslings are too dry or too sweet. South African Colombard goes well, Soave and Bordeaux Blanc adequately. For Béarnaise sauce served with beef, a Beaujolais-Villages or one of the lightest of the crus (Regnié, Chiroubles, Chénas or Brouilly) is the best solution: it is not an ideal match, but not a battle either. ★★ *German Riesling Kabinett*

### BEURRE BLANC ♀ *crisp, high-acid whites*

With beurre blanc, it's the vinegar in the sauce you have to balance – although you can soften this element by making the sauce with reduced white wine. High-acid wines such as Portuguese dry Vinho Verde and Champagne Blanc de Blancs solve the conundrum. Ripe, fruity Chardonnays (perhaps from California, Chile or Australia), Sancerre and Sauvignon de Touraine are almost as good, with dry German Riesling, off-dry Vinho Verde and Bianco di Custoza just a whisker behind. Chablis Premier Cru and dry Rieslings from Alsace, Australia, New Zealand and Chile are worth trying, too. ★★ *Champagne Blanc de Blancs* ★★ *dry Vinho Verde*

**BREAD SAUCE** 🍷 *soft, fruity reds* 🍷 *high-acid, fairly neutral whites*

Bread sauce is bland, and aromatic whites and tannic reds completely overpower it. Soft red wines from Minervois, in the south of France, make a delicious match, and the smooth, fruity flavours of Australian Cabernet and Shiraz suit it well. Gentle whites such as Bordeaux Blanc, Muscadet, Côtes de Gascogne and unoaked white Rioja and Navarra are just as successful. Otherwise, it's worth trying a fruity Côtes du Rhône red, Australian Merlot or basic white Burgundy. ★★ *red Minervois*

**BROWN SAUCE (BOTTLED)**

This is a wine-killer. It is far too vinegary for any wine.

**CHEESE SAUCE (MORNAY)** 🍷 *various reds* 🍷 *dry whites*

For a cheese sauce made with Cheddar, the star wine, an oaked Australian Chardonnay, is a stunning complement. Chablis Premier Cru comes a very modest second, leading other Chardonnays. Sancerre is a very good partner, and other French Sauvignon Blancs are quite good. New Zealand Sauvignon is too vegetal and tropical-fruity, however. Medium-dry (squat-bottled) Vinho Verde and dry Muscat go well; and Gewürztraminer is pleasant. Cooked Cheddar in a sauce copes better with tannic reds than when it is eaten alone. Australia comes up with the real winners: Australian Cabernet, Shiraz and Cabernet-Shiraz are all excellent partners, but you should also enjoy Barbaresco, soft red Burgundy, Oregon or California Pinot Noir, red Côtes du Rhône (not made by carbonic maceration – see *Tannin* page 221), young Chianti or Barbera. ★★ *oaked Australian Chardonnay* ★ *Sancerre*

VARIATIONS When made with **Gruyère**, the cheese sauce becomes harder to match but oaked – or unoaked – Australian Chardonnay is still a very good choice, as are

Chardonnays from other countries, but particularly from warm climates. German Riesling Halbtrocken is a success, and adequate matches are found with Sancerre, Champagne and Australian Semillon. Many reds taste too tannic. Best bet is Australian Shiraz or young Rioja, or you can also try Barbera, warm-climate Merlot, Australian Cabernet, Oregon Pinot Noir, Côtes du Rhône or Crozes-Hermitage. ★★ *Australian Chardonnay*

## CHILLI SAUCE see *Herbs, Spices and Flavourings*

## CHUTNEY
Really sweet/salty chutneys, such as mango chutney, find no wine partners at all; they strip the fruit out of many wines, especially reds. The same goes for chutneys with a very high vinegar content. Gentler ones, however, including popular brand name chutneys, may go quite well with sweet white wines such as Coteaux du Layon, Sauternes or Graves Supérieures, or with port, all of which have a balance of sweetness and sharpness. These wines may also be appropriate for chutney served with cheese.

## CRANBERRY SAUCE
Don't serve cranberry sauce with a good wine – or ideally with any wine at all. It strips the fruit out of reds and dry whites. It does sweeter wines no favours, though it goes passably with sweet German Riesling or Scheurebe Auslesen.

## CREAM SAUCES
Reds taste very tannic and nasty with cream or crème fraîche, and even rosés taste bitterly tannic. Whites cope, however, even with pure cream, although the cream slightly coats the tongue, and takes a very subtle edge off the quality of white wines. High-acid wines cut through this coating, but may taste too acid unless there are sharp ingredients in the sauce. Avoid Muscadet, which makes a bitter clash, and Aligoté, which makes the cream taste strangely sour.

## CUMBERLAND SAUCE ♀ *high-acid, sweetish whites*

Vouvray or Montlouis Demi-sec are stars, and other sweet Loire whites also go well: try Coteaux du Layon, Coteaux de l'Aubance, or Coteaux de Saumur. Rheingau Riesling Kabinett works well too. Port is too strong, despite the generous dollops of port and redcurrant jelly in the sauce.
★★ *Vouvray Demi-sec* ★★ *Montlouis Demi-sec*

## DEVILLED SAUCE ♀ *high-acid, sweetish whites*

Devilled sauce varies in flavour according to which recipe you follow. Made with English mustard, vinegar, capers, Worcester sauce and sugar, this is a killer for dry white and red wines. Vouvray Demi-sec is your best bet and demi-sec Champagne also has the right sweetness and acidity to make a complementary flavour, although the bubbles make the sauce seem even more peppery. If just based on mustard, Worcester Sauce and tomato ketchup, and used to coat grilled meat, devilled sauce goes well with Australian Shiraz. See also *Chicken: Devilled Chicken*.

## FRUIT SAUCE (BOTTLED)

The very high acid and sweetness of fruit sauces overpowers almost all wines. Vouvray Demi-sec or Montlouis Demi-Sec, with their touch of sweetness, can cope, but the sauce does them no favours.

## GARLIC MAYONNAISE see AÏOLI

## HOLLANDAISE SAUCE ♀ *crisp, dry, highish-acid whites*

Hollandaise sauce neutralizes the aroma and dulls the flavour of a lot of white wines, and the egg in it is mouth-coating. Whites with highish acidity and enough flavour can cope. The star choice is New Zealand Sauvignon Blanc – its faintly asparagus-like flavour echoes the delicious partnership of fresh asparagus with hollandaise sauce. Chablis Premier Cru is very good, as is German Riesling Halbtrocken. Other wines made from Sauvignon, such as Sancerre, or from Chardonnay (try Mâcon-Villages), are good. Further possibilities include Vinho Verde, Alsace Riesling, Frascati, German Silvaner, Liebfraumilch and Hock. Forget reds with hollandaise. See also *Eggs and Egg Dishes: Eggs Benedict*. ★★ *New Zealand Sauvignon Blanc*

## HORSERADISH SAUCE

A tiny touch of horseradish sauce will strip all or some of the fruit out of both red and white wines. Even the few red wines that stand up to it best – such as California Cabernet Sauvignon, Dolcetto or Bairrada – lose an edge of quality. Horseradish sauce is to be avoided if you care about the taste of your wine.

## MAYONNAISE ♀ *dry whites with fairly high acidity (but not Sauvignon Blanc)*

Nothing goes positively well with mayonnaise. White wine partners are rarely horrid, though Sauvignons tend to clash with the egg. Verdicchio and Muscadet Sur Lie may be the best bet, but the match will also be influenced by whatever the mayonnaise is accompanying – eggs, salmon or seafood, for instance. Adding garlic, herbs or other ingredients to mayonnaise often makes it far easier to pair with wine. See also *Aïoli* and *Salsa Verde; Shellfish and Seafood: Crab, Langoustines, Lobster, Prawns.*

## MINT SAUCE/JELLY

Mint sauce and mint jelly are best avoided: both are wine killers, stripping wines of their fruit.

## MORNAY see CHEESE SAUCE

## MUSTARD

Mustards vary enormously, from dry to sweet, through mildly flavoured to tongue-searingly hot, and gently vinegary to extremely tart. Some contain herbs and other flavourings. Mustard sauces vary, not least in the type of mustard they contain. They can often be surprisingly mild, and need very gentle whites. With the following entries, we have simply listed the red and white wines that complement particular kinds of mustards especially well.

### Dijon Mustard

This is the magic mustard as far as red wine is concerned. Dijon has the remarkable ability to soften the tannin of tough red wines, and to make quite modest reds taste special. Beware of very soft reds, however, as the mustard can soften them out of existence. The tannin-neutralizing effect of Dijon works in a sauce, too, but to a more limited extent. *Reds:* Barolo and Barbaresco, the Beaujolais crus (Morgon, Fleurie, Côte de Brouilly, etc), warm-climate Cabernet Sauvignons, Valpolicella, young Spanish Tempranillo, Cencibel or Tinto Fino, red Burgundy and other Pinot Noirs. *Whites:* Crémant de Bourgogne, Champagne, Vinho Verde and Gros Plant. ★★ *Morgon*

### English Mustard

'Hot' English mustard is perhaps best avoided if you are drinking wine, but some wines can stand up to the challenge quite well. *Reds:* Tempranillo/Cencibel, red Burgundy and other Pinot Noirs, and red Bordeaux. *Whites:* Alsace Pinot Blanc or Chablis.

### English Wholegrain Mustard

This goes far better with wine than plain English mustard, especially with dry whites. *Whites:* Muscadet, Chablis, VdP des Côtes de Gascogne, New Zealand Sauvignon Blanc and other very fruity New World Sauvignons, Chilean, New Zealand and Australian Riesling, Bulgarian or Bourgogne Aligoté, and South African Colombard. Vinho Verde, whether dry or not. *Reds:* unoaked, fruity Zinfandel, Valpolicella, red Bordeaux and Lambrusco. ★★ *light, fruity Zinfandel*

### French Mustard

The dark brown style of French mustard, with its origins in Bordeaux, and usually labelled simply 'French mustard', is quite picky in its choice of wine partners. *Reds:* Zinfandel and fruity, warm-climate Cabernet Sauvignons. *Whites:* unoaked Bordeaux Blanc, Muscadet and Aligoté, most Sauvignon Blancs and Vinho Verde. ★★ *unoaked Bordeaux Blanc*

**PESTO** see *Pasta*

**RAGU** see *Pasta*

**SALSA VERDE** ♀ *unoaked, dry, bland whites with high acidity*

TRADITIONAL PARTNER *northern Italian whites*

Txacoli from the Basque country of Spain makes a stunning partner for this mayonnaise-based relish, which is thickly flavoured with parsley, rocket, garlic, spring onion, mustard and anchovies (recipes vary and may contain other salad greens, capers or bread). If Txacoli proves hard to track down, next best are Aligoté from Bulgaria or Burgundy, dry Vinho Verde, Chablis, or Frascati, which somehow makes a lovely match despite its lowish acidity. Other possible choices are southern French Terret, white Corbières, Cheverny, simple white Burgundy, Chardonnay del Piemonte and Soave Classico. ★★ *Txacoli*

## SOY SAUCE
Whether light or dark, salty soy sauce gets along with wines in general in the same way that salt does: not really changing the wine/food match unless used in excess. A high dose of soy sauce on a dish, like a generous measure of salt, has an affinity with high-acid wines; too much may clash with very tannic red wines. Wines that go especially well with the flavour of soy sauce are Australian Semillon and Riesling, and the fuller Beaujolais crus such as Morgon, Côte de Brouilly or Moulin-à-Vent. ★★ *Australian Semillon*

## SWEET AND SOUR SAUCE ♀ *sweetish whites with good acidity*
This is a tricky customer. Many whites that apparently fit the bill are turned to water by sweet and sour sauces. The real goodies are Vouvray or Montlouis Demi-sec, and German Riesling Spätlese (but not Trocken), especially from the Mosel-Saar-Ruwer. ★ *Vouvray Demi-sec*

## TARTARE SAUCE ♀ *very high-acid dry whites*
Tartare sauce is pretty tart and difficult to match. Nothing is perfect, but it goes well with Muscadet and the most sharply acid of the French Sauvignons: Touraine, Haut-Poitou and vins de pays from the Loire. ★ *Sauvignon de Touraine*

## TOMATO SAUCE (COOKED) ♀ *crisp, fairly fruity, highish- to high-acid whites*
Home-made tomato sauce (with onion, garlic,

bay leaf, thyme and marjoram) is best matched by the fruity, gentle flavour of Italian Bianco di Custoza. The flavour of Sauvignon Blanc goes well with the fairly high-acid tomato, so Sancerre and fruity Sauvignons from the south of France are almost as good. Otherwise, try off-dry Vinho Verde, Soave Classico, Gewürztraminer or Vernaccia. White Zinfandel is also good. ★★ *Bianco di Custoza* VARIATIONS Add **basil** to the sauce and Bianco di Custoza is the only wine that really works. ★ *Bianco di Custoza*

**Tomato ketchup** ♀ *high-acid, sweetish whites*
Wine-buff ketchup-lovers can swoon over the brilliant match with a sweetish German Silvaner Spätlese (beware Spätlese Trocken, which is dry). Best alternative is an inexpensive Mosel, such as Piesporter Michelsberg, or a medium English Müller-Thurgau or Rivaner. ★★ *German Silvaner Spätlese*

**WINE-BASED SAUCES** The precise match will depend on the other sauce ingredients, as well as the dish it is served with, but wine in a sauce is usually the magic link to a vast choice of wines. (See *Cooking with Wine*.)

**Madeira Sauce**
Madeira comes in various styles from nearly dry to luscious, and you need to match the sweetness of the sauce with sweetness or very ripe fruit in the wine. White wines tend to be too bright and acidic. *Reds:* savoury-fruity Pinot Noir from California, Oregon or Australia, or warm-climate Cabernet Sauvignon.

**Marsala Sauce**
Marsala in a sauce is hard to match. *Reds:* Dolcetto. *Whites:* best are Côtes du Rhône and Alella Clásico, or try Italian whites Gravina, Favorita or Arneis, dry Silvaner/ Sylvaner from Germany or Alsace, southern French Marsanne, or a warm-climate Sauvignon Blanc.

**Red Wine Sauce**
Fruity reds taste wonderful with a rich red wine sauce. *Reds:* best choice is Beaujolais, Australian Shiraz or Shiraz-Cabernet, ripe Cabernet, Merlot or Pinot Noir from warm climates, Chianti Classico and reds from Provence, the Rhône or elsewhere in southern France.

**White Wine**
These sauces can be quite high in acidity, unless diluted by a hefty dose of stock or water, and if so you will need a high-acid white to match.

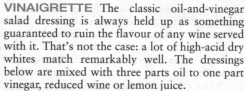

**VINAIGRETTE** The classic oil-and-vinegar salad dressing is always held up as something guaranteed to ruin the flavour of any wine served with it. That's not the case: a lot of high-acid dry whites match remarkably well. The dressings below are mixed with three parts oil to one part vinegar, reduced wine or lemon juice.

**Hazelnut Oil with Lemon Juice** ❢ *a few unoaked, light reds* ♀ *high-acid, dry whites*
Aligoté from Burgundy or Bulgaria is the best match, but a hazelnut-oil dressing also marries well with Cheverny, Muscadet, Alsace Pinot Blanc or Italian Pinot Bianco and Soave. A few reds can be paired with the hazelnut flavour – Merlot, the fuller Beaujolais crus such as Morgon, and Dolcetto. ★★ *Bourgogne Aligoté*

**Olive Oil and White or Red Wine Vinegar** ❢ *low-tannin reds with highish acidity* ♀ *high-acid whites*
As well as the excellent matches with Bourgogne and Bulgarian Aligoté, there are other first-class matches with Soave, Crémant de Bourgogne, Muscadet, Chablis and Sancerre. Also quite good are Chablis Premier Cru, New Zealand Sauvignon, Alsace Riesling, VdP des Côtes de Gascogne and Vinho Verde. Champagne, Retsina, South African Colombard, Chilean and Austra-lian Rieslings are adequate partners. Best reds are Lambrusco and warm-climate Cabernet Sauvignons, or you can try red Burgundy, the fuller Beaujolais crus, unoaked Tempranillo, Italian Dolcetto and southern French Merlot. ★★ *Bourgogne or Bulgarian Aligoté*

VARIATIONS When you add **Dijon mustard**, the dressing becomes much harder to match. The relatively neutral, high-acid flavour of a Muscadet Sur Lie is a brilliant match here, Alsace Riesling is a star, and Aligoté is fine. Of the reds, warm-climate Cabernets are nearly as good as the Riesling, with unoaked Tempranillo and Italian Dolcetto good alternatives. ★★ *Muscadet Sur Lie*

**Olive Oil and Balsamic Vinegar** ❢ *highish-acid, low-tannin, fruity reds* ♀ *high-acid, sweetish or fruity whites*

The stars, Champagne and Vinho Verde, and Crémant de Bourgogne, New Zealand Sauvignons and Chilean and Australian Riesling all have the sweetness or the aromatic fruit to match the characterful vinegar. Retsina is a success, and VdP des Côtes de Gascogne is good. Some reds are good: try richer Beaujolais crus, unoaked Tempranillo, red Burgundy, dry red Lambrusco and southern French Merlot. ★★ *Champagne* ★★ *Vinho Verde*

### Olive Oil with Lemon Juice ❢ *light, highish- to high-acid reds* ♀ *dry, high-acid whites*

The softer flavour of lemon juice creates a few more wine matches than a vinegar-based dressing, but it's a close-run thing. Best is the crisp, lemony flavour of unoaked Chardonnay – Chablis and Crémant de Bourgogne are especially good. Soave, Aligoté, VdP des Côtes de Gascogne, and Bordeaux Blanc are also excellent. Red Burgundy is excellent, and Valpolicella, dry red Lambrusco, Italian Dolcetto and southern French Merlot are good alternatives. ★★ *Chablis* ★★ *Crémant de Bourgogne*

### Olive Oil and Reduced White Wine
❢ *light, unoaked, fruity reds* ♀ *medium-acid, dry whites*

This is the solution if you want to serve softer, lower-acid whites, or reds to flatter other ingredients on your plate. Substitute the wine vinegar with white wine that has been boiled down to get rid of the alcohol and to concentrate the acidity. The resulting dressing is much less sharp than either vinegar- or lemon-based ones, and demands softer, gentler wines. More reds than whites match well, with Valpolicella Classico leading the way, and very successful pairings with gentle Australian, California and Chilean Cabernets, and southern French Merlot. Other good red matches come from the heavier Beaujolais crus, unoaked Spanish Tempranillo and red Burgundy. Bordeaux Blanc is the star white, with unoaked whites from Rioja and Penedés almost as successful. Sauvignons are very satisfactory partners, too, particularly those from New Zealand and Chile, and Chablis Premier Cru is also very good. ★★ *Valpolicella Classico* ★★ *Bordeaux Blanc*

### Walnut Oil and Lemon Juice ♀ *high-acid dry whites*

Nut oils are harder to match with wine than olive oil. This dressing goes very well with Cheverny and Alsace Riesling, as well as Bordeaux Blanc, which is very good despite its lower acidity. VdP des Côtes de Gascogne, South African Colombard and Aligoté are also fair. ★ *Bordeaux Blanc*

# CHEESES

Wine and cheese, eggs and bacon, strawberries and cream. All perfect partners? No. *Most* cheeses can make marvellous matches with wines. But to assume that any cheese will go with any wine could not be more wrong. Some strong blue cheeses resist all attempts at being paired off. Several really characterful cheeses clash with or spoil most wines. Yet some of the most flavourful and pungent cheeses find heaps of good partners. The French consider a meal incomplete unless it has incorporated a cheese course with a glass of red wine, but the best option is often a white wine – and sometimes even a sweet white wine! Tannin in red wine often spoils a match, so mature reds are frequently more successful than young ones.

Matching the acidity level of wine and cheese is often important. The trickiest thing is to serve one wine with a platter of different cheeses. You can sometimes find a wine that can match them all – red Rioja Gran Reserva would be an excellent choice, as it complements so many cheeses, and it's the perfect partner to many. Otherwise, it might be better to serve one good cheese, and partner it with a wine that is really suitable.

## Hot Cheese Dishes

Red wines are less appropriate here because cooked cheese emphasizes the wine's tannin.

### FONDUE ♀ *dry whites, especially Sauvignon*
TRADITIONAL PARTNER *Swiss white*

Fondue is fairly easy to match with wine (including high-acid Swiss wines) as the recipe includes white wine. Aromatic Sauvignon Blancs from warm climates, especially Chile or a cooler part of Australia, are the stars. New Zealand Sauvignons also make a wonderful, if sometimes over-aromatic, accompaniment. Loire Sauvignons are all pleasant, if a touch too high in acidity. Almost all southern French, California and Australian Sauvignons are too soft and gentle. Warm-climate

Chardonnays, oaked or unoaked, match pleasantly to well, as do warm-climate dry or nearly dry Rieslings, from Chile or Australia. ★★ *Chilean Sauvignon Blanc*

**RACLETTE** ♀ *whites with low to medium acidity*
TRADITIONAL PARTNER *Swiss white*
Supping a Swiss white wine with their raclette, the Swiss probably never spare a thought for the wine's high acidity, which makes it far from ideal for this low-acid cheese, though not a clash. No wine in fact is perfect, and all reds are too tannic. The best matches are with warm-climate Chardonnays, ideally unoaked, all the better if they have the buttery flavours of malolactic fermentation (see page 226). White Corbières is also good, as is the southern Italian Gravina. ★ *California or Chilean Chardonnay*

# Hard Cheeses

On the whole, hard cheeses are easier to match than creamy, soft or blue cheeses, but even so there are some difficult customers. Low-tannin (which often means mature) reds tend to be best. If the cheeses are cooked, choose reds even lower in tannin.

**CAERPHILLY** ❢ *low-tannin, not-too-fruity, medium-to full-bodied reds*
This gentle, chalky/curdy cheese finds no match as good as red Rioja Gran Reserva. Mature red Bordeaux, Corbières and California Syrah all go quite well. Caerphilly also makes adequate matches with Dolcetto, Vino Nobile di Montepulciano, Barbera, warm-climate Merlot, Coteaux du Tricastin and Oregon Pinot Noir. Whites are generally a disaster, but New Zealand Sauvignon (unlike other Sauvignons) copes. ★★ *red Rioja Gran Reserva*

**CANTAL** ❢ *mature, savoury reds with lowish tannin*
♀ *a few dry whites*
The best partner is red Rioja Gran Reserva – much better than younger Riojas. Quite good are red Burgundy, southern Italian Cirò Riserva or mature Vino Nobile di Montepulciano, a gentle Australian Cabernet Sauvignon (even a young one), and Greek Naoussa. Whites are not generally a success, but northern Italian Favorita and Alsace Riesling are pleasant. ★ *red Rioja Gran Reserva*

## CHEDDAR (MATURE FARMHOUSE)

❢ *mature, full-bodied, lowish-tannin reds* ♀ *a few medium-sweet to sweet whites*

The lovely, pungent fruitiness, acidity and creaminess of fine mature Cheddar finds many more good matches than milder versions. The star is a southern Italian red, Salice Salentino; other successful red wines are Rosso di Montalcino, mature Vino Nobile di Montepulciano, or mature Spanish Ribera del Duero. Not quite as good but still pleasant are any style of Zinfandel, mature Chianti Classico or Rufina, Carmignano or California Sangiovese, Rosso Conero or Montepulciano. (But avoid Pinot Noir or Cabernet Sauvignon-based wines.) The savoury flavour of many Portuguese reds works so long as the tannin is not excessive; even a 20-year-old tawny port makes a good, though very strong, match. As a white partner, sweetish Alsace Gewürztraminer Vendange Tardive goes surprisingly well. ★★ *Salice Salentino*

VARIATIONS With **medium Cheddar**, Salice Salentino is still far and away the star choice, but other reds – Rioja Gran Reserva, mature Ribera del Duero and Vino Nobile or Rosso di Montalcino – marry well. ★★ *Salice Salentino*. With **mild Cheddar**, red Rioja Gran Reserva makes the only good match apart from the excellent Salice Salentino. Arruda, Bairrada, Chianti or mature Ribera del Duero are acceptable. ★★ *Salice Salentino*

## CHESHIRE ❢ *full, fairly fruity, lowish-tannin reds*

This delicate, gently fruity cheese responds well to good fruit in a wine, but no wine is quite perfect. An untannic California Cabernet is the closest to a star match, although Australian Cabernet can be too fruity and minty. Oregon or California Pinot Noirs are also good, as is Syrah and Shiraz. Cheshire makes no really good matches with whites, but Sauvignon Blancs go adequately (not the more acid Loire-style), as do Bourgogne Aligoté, Italian Cortese and German Riesling Spätlese. ★ *California Cabernet Sauvignon*

## CHÈVRE see GOATS' CHEESE

## DOUBLE GLOUCESTER ❢ *full, not-too-fruity, preferably mature reds*

Southern Italian Cirò Riserva is the only star, but Italian Rosso Conero or Montepulciano d'Abruzzo, and southern French St-Chinian also make lovely, savoury red wine matches. Reasonable partners are Sangioveses from California or Italy, Zinfandel, mature red Bordeaux, Portuguese Arruda, Rioja Gran Reserva or mature Ribera del Duero. Whites do not work. ★★ *Cirò Riserva*

## EDAM ❢ *full, not-too-fruity reds*

Nothing is absolutely perfect, but the savoury flavour of the top Greek reds – Nemea, Naoussa and Goumenissa – all work well. Rioja Gran Reserva is also good (though a little too strongly flavoured) and so is a gentle Australian Shiraz (if slightly too fruity). Vino Nobile di Montepulciano is pleasant. Other acceptable reds are Rioja Reserva, mature red Burgundy, Australian Cabernet, mature Dão, Cirò, Salice Salentino, St-Chinian or Côtes du Roussillon-Villages. If you really want to drink white, white Burgundy and Sauternes are adequate. ★ *Greek Nemea*

## EMMENTAL ❢ *unoaked reds, preferably mature*

Pick your wine carefully for this interesting, fruity, slightly granular cheese, because it makes a distinctly vomitty-tasting combination with some wines, both white and red. Nothing is ideal, but there are several pleasant matches, headed by Barbera d'Alba. California Barbera, Shiraz (provided it's not too oaky) and southern French Syrah work well, as do the lighter northern Rhônes – St-Joseph and Crozes-Hermitage. Mature Ribera del Duero also works well. (Avoid Cabernet Sauvignon, Merlot or red Bordeaux.) Whites do not work. ★ *Barbera d'Alba*

## GOATS' CHEESE

Really hard, dry, granular goats' cheeses with powerfully goaty flavours find no really perfect partners. Many wines are overwhelmed, some wines nastily emphasize the goatiness, others simply clash. (The clash with Beaujolais, Sangiovese, Syrah, Amarone della Valpolicella and Sauternes is foul.) Cheese flavours vary, but Alsace Pinot Blanc may be best, with Bourgogne Aligoté, and two reds

– Australian Coonawarra Cabernet Sauvignon and Zinfandel – coming in close behind. Or try red Rioja Gran Reserva, or southern Italian Aglianico del Vulture. A few whites succeed: unoaked white Rioja, Lugana, German Riesling Kabinett, or a high-acid, aromatic Sauvignon. See also *Soft Cheeses*. ★ *Alsace Pinot Blanc*

## GOUDA (MATURE) ♥ *medium- to full-bodied reds* ♀ *sweet whites*

Mature Gouda has a delicious, concentrated, savoury flavour, and goes well with a wide range of red wines. (It is also a good match for lager.) An equal star with red Rioja Gran Reserva is a mature Vino Nobile di Montepulciano. Younger Rioja, Navarra, Ribera del Duero, Valdepeñas and full-bodied wines made with Tempranillo are good, as are Cirò, Salice Salentino, and full-bodied Sangioveses (including Chianti Classico) from Italy. Many southern French reds are successful, the Greek Naoussa is good, as are Portuguese Arruda and modern Bairrada. Or you can try Washington State Late Harvest Riesling, or Sau-ternes or Graves Supérieures (all sweet) from Bordeaux. ★★ *Rioja Gran Reserva* ★★ *mature Vino Nobile di Montepulciano*

VARIATIONS **Young Gouda** peacefully co-exists with most reds, although it may be obliterated by the fullest and most concentrated. Australian Shiraz makes a superb partner, and French Syrah is good, too. Chianti also goes well, as do the Greek reds Goumenissa and Nemea. Among whites, the flavour of Gewürztraminer is good, if a bit strong; gently aromatic Favorita from northern Italy makes a pleasant partner. ★★ *Australian Shiraz*

## GRUYÈRE ♥ *medium- to full-bodied, not-too-tannic reds* ♀ *gently aromatic whites*

Good red Italian partners to follow the star, Dolcetto, are Rosso Conero and Montepulciano d'Abruzzo. Gruyère is a superb match with many good Spanish reds, too: Rioja Gran Reserva, mature Ribera del Duero, Navarra or Valdepeñas, Penedés or Costers del Segre. Greek

Naoussa is as good. Red Bordeaux goes well, as does Beaujolais, especially the crus (Fleurie, Regnié and so on), and simple Rhône or southern French reds such as Côtes du Roussillon-Villages or Côtes du Ventoux. From Portugal, try Douro reds. The star white is Mosel Riesling Kabinett, which deliciously emphasizes the cheese character. Rieslings from New Zealand, Australia and Chile are also good (and better than Alsace). Simple, unoaked European Chardonnays match well, and South African Colombard and northern Italian Favorita also go well.
★★ *Dolcetto* ★★ *Mosel Riesling Kabinett*

**JARLSBERG** ❢ *full, low-tannin, unoaked, not-too-fruity reds* ♀ *dry whites, especially New World Riesling*
Beware: despite its mild flavour, this Norwegian cheese is tricky to match. It strips the fruit out of some wines, and clashes with others. However, there are still lots of successes to be found. Jarlsberg tastes delicious with dry Chilean Riesling, the superstar white, and New Zealand and Australian (dry) Rieslings also work well. Fine white Burgundy (but not Chablis) is another excellent choice, yet New World Chardonnays are a flop. Sauvignon Blanc is fairly successful, riper ones matching better than Loire Sauvignons. Of the reds, mature Ribera del Duero reds are excellent with Jarlsberg; it is also very good with other mature Spanish reds. From Portugal, Douro reds and modern Bairrada are successful, and good red Bordeaux pairs off well. Soft, easy, unoaked Zinfandels are the best American bet. ★★ *Chilean dry Riesling*

**LANCASHIRE** ❢ *medium- to full-bodied reds* ♀ *whites with good acidity*
Lancashire's acidity allows it to chime in with a number of quite acid white wines – but nothing is a super-star. Champagne is in fact the best, followed by sweet Bordeaux such as Sauternes or Graves Supérieures. Adequate whites include Aligoté, Chilean, New Zealand or Australian (dry) Riesling, gentle European Sauvignon Blancs, and some medium English whites. Some reds clash (especially Merlot) or taste bitterly tannic, but Australian Cabernet and Pinot Noir from Oregon, California or Australia are quite good, and fair matches can be found with Dolcetto, Rioja Reserva and Gran Reserva, mature Portuguese Borba, Faugères and mature red Bordeaux. ★ *Champagne*

## MANCHEGO ❗ *medium- to full-bodied, savoury, not-too-fruity or tannic reds*

TRADITIONAL PARTNER *Valdepeñas red*

California Sangiovese is a real hit with this slightly grainy sheeps' cheese from central Spain, but the local Valdepeñas red is very good as well, as is red Rioja Gran Reserva. Wines made from Syrah in the northern Rhône (such as Crozes-Hermitage or St-Joseph), or Shiraz in Australia, are also very good, as are ripe but not-too-tannic southern French reds such as Faugères. Red Bordeaux from the classic Médoc villages (Margaux, St-Julien, Pauillac, St-Estèphe) work well, as do Cabernets from California and Bulgaria. And Oregon Pinot Noir and light styles of Zinfandel are also good. A few dry whites also make the grade – unoaked white Rioja or other Viura or Macabeo whites from Spain, Italian Pinot Grigio and Retsina. ★★ *California Sangiovese*

## PARMESAN REGGIANO ❗ *full-flavoured, not-too-tannic reds* ♀ *a few dry whites*

Fresh Parmesan is highly regarded in Italy as a cheese to serve at the close of a meal – together with a bottle of fine red wine. And many of the best matches do seem to be with Italian reds, from the marvellous pairing with Aglianico del Vulture, to very good matches with Amarone della Valpolicella, Brunello di Montalcino, Chianti Classico, Vino Nobile di Montepulciano and even a light Sangiovese di Romagna. Rioja Reserva, Crozes-Hermitage, southern French reds, and Australian Cabernets also measure up very well. South African Colombard and soft white Burgundies are very good; Mosel Riesling Kabinetts and gentle Italian whites such as Lugana are pleasant. ★★ *Aglianico del Vulture*

## RED LEICESTER ❗ *medium- to full-bodied, low-tannin, not-too-fruity reds*

Red Leicester is a red wine cheese, but not easy to partner. The pairing with red Rioja Gran Reserva is delicious. Australian Shiraz is next best, although Crozes-Hermitage and St-Joseph work fairly well, as do southern French Syrah vins de pays, or other Syrah-based reds. Mature red Bordeaux is pleasant, and Italian Cirò (young or Riserva) goes well. ★★ *red Rioja Gran Reserva*

### SMOKED CHEESE (BAVARIAN)

This is incredibly difficult to partner with wine, many clashing with the smoke or making the cheese taste fatty, and nothing is perfect. Sweet Bordeaux (from Graves and Sauternes) is the closest to a match. Mosel Kabinett wines go well, as does dry Alsace Gewürztraminer. (Gewürztraminer Vendange Tardive makes a reasonable if slightly too sweet match, despite being less sweet than the Bordeaux wines.) Australian Shiraz is perhaps the only red contender. ★ *Graves Supérieures (sweet)* ★ *Sauternes*

### WENSLEYDALE

This gentle, crumbly, curdy, buttery cheese has quite high acidity, and is a challenge to match. There are few foul clashes, but most wines are too strong, too acid, too sweet, too aromatic or the wrong flavour. Rheingau Spätlese makes the only good match, but a handful of reds work: Corbières, mature red Bordeaux, Rioja Reserva or Gran Reserva, and California Syrah. ★ *Rheingau Spätlese*

# Soft Cheeses

White wines often go better than reds with creamy or curdy cheeses. Brie or Camembert, especially when mature, are infamously tricky to match well with wine, but they do find reasonably good partners. Other strong cheeses, however, such as Munster, are wonderfully compatible with a variety of wines.

### BEL PAESE ❢ *medium-bodied, highish-acid reds*
♀ *unoaked, dry Chardonnays; other crisp whites*
This soft, relatively bland Italian cheese is bowled over by many wines. Most reds are much too tannic, but the soft, fruity, highish-acid flavour of California Barbera suits it well, as does light California Pinot Noir. Gentle but aromatic Australian Sauvignon Blanc is a good white partner. Unoaked Chardonnays, such as Chablis and northern Italian Chardonnays, also work well. Or try a lively Alsace Riesling or Hungarian Pinot Gris. ★★ *California Barbera*

## BOURSIN ▮▮ *light to medium-bodied, Cabernet-based reds or rosés* ♀ *crisp, dry, unoaked whites*

The quite powerful herbiness of this cream cheese favours wines with grassy, herbaceous flavours. The star wine, Sancerre, is delicious, and other crisp and unoaked New Zealand and Bordeaux Sauvignons are very good as well. Alsace Riesling is another excellent match, Alsace Gewürztraminer, also works well, and crisp whites, such as Muscadet, southern French Terret and Italian Vernaccia, all do a good job. Even the fragrant Viognier matches up. A brilliant red wine choice is the ripe, smooth, blackcurranty fruit of mature California Cabernet Sauvignon, and Coonawarra Cabernet, red Bordeaux and Loire reds are pleasant. Crisp, modern rosés also work well. ★★ *Sancerre*

## BRIE (PASTEURIZED) ▮ *gentle, savoury reds* ♀ *highish-acid, unoaked whites*

Pasteurized Brie, with its smooth, buttery, flavour, is hard to pair with wines. Most whites are too fruity or too acid, most reds too tannic. The exception is the gentle, savoury flavour of mature Ribera del Duero. Adequate choices include Rioja Reserva, Côtes du Roussillon-Villages or Beaujolais-Villages. Among whites, try any unoaked southern French Chardonnay or Sauvignon de Touraine. ★ *mature Ribera del Duero*

VARIATIONS A good **unpasteurized Brie** goes positively well only with a ruby, premium ruby or Late Bottled Vintage (LBV) port. Brie's rich farmyardy flavour overwhelms many wines, but aromatic Australian Sauvignon Blanc or a neutral Italian white such as Frascati are acceptable, as are red Bordeaux, Châteauneuf-du-Pape, or Bairrada from Portugal. ★ *LBV port*

## CAMEMBERT (PASTEURIZED)

▮ *medium- to full-bodied, savoury reds* ♀ *crisp, dry whites*

Gentle, pasteurized Camembert is easily overwhelmed by wine. The best matches are with

reds, the star a straightforward Chianti and, surprisingly, the much more powerful Châteauneuf-du-Pape is also excellent. Beaujolais-Villages, red Burgundy, Côtes du Roussillon-Villages and Australian Cabernet-Shiraz are all acceptable. Also adequate are a variety of crisp whites – Sauvignon de Touraine, Chilean Sauvignon, Chablis, southern French and northern Italian Chardonnay, South African Colombard or modern white Rioja. ★ *Chianti*
VARIATIONS The more intensely farmyardy flavour of **unpasteurized Camembert** is what drives it into the arms of red Burgundy: it's a case of matching rotty flavours. Otherwise, partnering wines are similar to the pasteurized version, or try a drop of LBV port. ★★ *red Burgundy*

CHAOURCE ❢ *medium-bodied, Cabernet-based and savoury reds* ♀ *highish- to high-acid whites*
TRADITIONAL PARTNER *Champagne*
Champagne (both white and rosé) goes remarkably well with Chaource. It's the high acidity that pairs well with the mild, creamy cheese. English off-dry wines, New Zealand Riesling, and Italian Lugana are successful, too. Fewer reds match: highish-acid Loire reds make the only good connections, though California Cabernet Sauvignon and Pinot Noir, red Burgundy, and oak-aged Spanish Tempranillo reds are acceptable. ★★ *Champagne*

CHAUME ❢ *medium- to full-bodied, savoury reds* ♀ *gentle, crisp, lightly aromatic whites*
This pleasantly creamy, lightly farmyardy cheese is fairly easy to match with wines. Arneis, with its gentle, crisp, aromatic flavour, is a winner, but Alsace Gewürztraminer, white Trincadeira das Pratas and dry Spanish rosés are all good as well. Best reds are Burgundy, Châteauneuf-du-Pape, Cabernets from Australia and California, and Greek Nemea. ★★ *Arneis*

CHÈVRE see GOATS' CHEESE

FETA ♀ *highish- to high-acid whites*
Yes, Retsina goes with feta, but Alsace Riesling is much better. Both belong to a fairly wide group of white wines (reds do not work) that can cope with this salty, high-acid, white Greek cheese. Rieslings from Alsace (the star) and the Mosel, Chardonnays from Burgundy and California,

Sauvignons from Bordeaux and Chile, are all good. So are Muscadet, dry Muscat from the south of France, Soave Classico, and Penedés and Conca de Barberá whites. ★★ *Alsace Riesling*

## GOATS' CHEESE ♥ *medium- to full-bodied, not-too-tannic reds, especially Pinot Noir* ♀ *dry rosés* ♀ *dry to off-dry, unoaked whites*

Highish-acid, gentle goats' cheese (sometimes named Cendré) goes well with a surprising array of wines. All unoaked Sauvignons are very good; the softer style from the south of France or Chile is just as delicious as a higher-acid Sancerre; a super-aromatic one from New Zealand is nearly as good. Dry, nearly dry or Halbtrocken Rieslings are a success, whether from Alsace, Australia, New Zealand or Germany (though the floweriness of German ones may be a bit overpowering). The aromatic Gewürztraminer works well. The blander Terret, Est! Est!! Est!!!, Vernaccia and gently aromatic Arneis all match quite well. Spanish Tempranillo or Garnacha rosados are a success, as are Provençal and Tavel rosés. Red Burgundy and other Pinot Noirs are delicious, and low-tannin Cabernet Sauvignons, hot-climate Merlots, Chianti, Bairrada, Rioja Gran Reserva, and Loire Cabernet Francs are all good. ★★ *Sancerre*

### Crottin de Chavignol ♥ *light, low-tannin reds* ♀ *Tempranillo rosado* ♀ *aromatic, dry whites*

This pungent cheese needs a pungently aromatic, unoaked Sauvignon Blanc: both Sancerre and New Zealand Sauvignon are superstars, but softer Sauvignons from Bordeaux, Côtes de Duras, Australia, California or Chile rarely have enough character. German Riesling Halbtrocken also makes a superb match, and Alsace Riesling copes. Best red is Saumur-Champigny, but Zinfandel, Cirò and Chianti are good, as are Spanish Tempranillo rosados. ★★ *Sancerre*

## MILLEENS ♥ *savoury, medium-bodied reds* ♀ *honeyed, slightly aromatic dry whites*

An Irish cheese with a gloriously fruity, farmyardy flavour, Milleens is just right to partner a soft, savoury red Burgundy from the Côte de Beaune, especially Volnay. The Nebbiolo grape from Piemonte and Sangiovese from Tuscany work very well in their richest, most savoury incarnations – Barolo and Brunello di Montalcino. Côte de Brouilly and other fuller Beaujolais crus are also excellent. A touch of honey in some dry whites echoes the fruitiness of the cheese: that's why Soave Classico, Chablis Premier Cru and Hungarian Pinot Gris all work well. ★ *Volnay*

MOZZARELLA ♀ *delicately flavoured whites*
Nothing seriously clashes with Mozzarella, but most flavours are too strong. Whites from southern Burgundy (Montagny the most successful, or Mâcon or Côtes Chalonnaise, for example) are best of all, but some other Chardonnays are adequate: you can try California Chardonnay or Chablis Premier Cru. Alsace Pinot Blanc is also an acceptable choice. Frascati, Pinot Bianco, and Verdicchio are best of the Italian whites. Reds are universally too strong and tannic. But it is worth noting, for cooked dishes with other ingredients that tame the tannin, that Dolcetto is a delicious flavour with Mozzarella. Sauvignon is also too powerful, but again the flavour matches, which is useful for Mozzarella-topped tomato and onion-based dishes. ★ *Montagny Premier Cru*

MUNSTER ❢ *medium- to full-bodied, not-too-oaky reds* ♀ *dry or nearly dry, aromatic whites*
TRADITIONAL PARTNER *Alsace Gewürztraminer*
It is amazing how many excellent wine matches are possible with this super-characterful, strong-smelling cheese, though there are also plenty of clashes. Munster can span the whole range of Alsace white wines – the Gewürztraminer is nearly a star, and Pinot Gris is also very good. Other whites include German Riesling Kabinett, German Silvaner Trocken, Hungarian Pinot Gris, Italian Arneis or Favorita, VdP des Côtes de Gascogne. But the star is California Syrah; it makes a stunning red match (much better than Rhône Syrah), and Australian Shiraz goes pretty well, especially if not too oaky. Red Rioja Reserva and Gran Reserva are also excellent, and so is red Burgundy, so long as the tannin level is low. New World Pinot Noirs may be a little too fruity, but also good. (Cabernet, Chardonnay and Sauvignon Blanc do not work.) ★★ *California Syrah*

### NEUFCHÂTEL-EN-BRAY ! *medium- to full-bodied reds* ♀ *not-too-aromatic whites with good acidity*

This Normandy cheese seems quite delicate in a Camembert-like way, but in fact it stands up to quite strong wine flavours, and finds many more successful partners than Camembert. The high acidity and flavours of ideally not-too-tannic red Burgundy (including fine, rich ones) are perfect. Ripe, fruity Australian Cabernet is also excellent, and California and other warm-climate Cabernets are good, better than red Bordeaux. From Italy, Montepulciano d'Abruzzo and Rosso Conero both make really delicious matches, and from Spain, Rioja Crianza and Garnacha wines go well. Northern Rhônes (Crozes-Hermitage or St-Joseph) are a success. Several whites work well: German Silvaner Trocken or Alsace Sylvaner, Chablis Premier Cru, northern Italian Chardonnay, Chardonnay VdP du Jardin de la France, Hungarian Furmint and Sauvignon Blanc. ★★ *not-too-tannic red Burgundy*

### PONT L'EVÊQUE ! *full-bodied, mature reds* ♀ *a few dry, gently aromatic whites*

The savoury flavour of Rioja Reserva, Gran Reserva or mature Ribera del Duero, Navarra or Valdepeñas reds links in beautifully to the slightly farmyardy flavour of this cheese. Red Burgundy tends to be too acid, but Pinot Noirs from Oregon, California or Australia work well. California Barbera is a lovely flavour match; Sangiovese and Syrah from California are both pretty good. Cabernet Sauvignons work, especially if mature, and/or not too tannic. Two obscure white pairings are with Portuguese Trincadeira das Pratas and mature Australian Semillon. ★★ *red Rioja Reserva*

### PORT-SALUT ! *low-tannin, low-fruit reds* ♀ *a very few unoaked, low-acid whites*

This very mild cheese may be swamped by many reds, but it can stand up to a few specific strong flavours in matching wines. Valpolicella is a real super-star. Other stars are Chianti, mature

Cabernet Sauvignons from warm climates, or red Bordeaux from a ripe year. Untannic red Burgundies are quite good, as are Greek Nemea and southern Italian Cirò. Among whites, southern French Terret and Hungarian Furmint are also pleasant matches. ★★ *Valpolicella*

# Blue Cheeses

Blue cheeses may look similar, but they vary immensely in strength and character – and in their compatibility with wine. The bluest-tasting, such as Danish Blue and Bleu d'Auvergne, are wine-killers, clashing foully with everything. Several others fail to make a really star match. Reds tend to be best, but as with other types of cheeses the tannin needs to be low. Dry whites rarely work, but sweet and fortified wines sometimes go brilliantly.

### BLEU D'AUVERGNE
Dry whites, sweet whites, fortified wines – all are steamrollered by the pungency of the blue mould. If you want to drink wine with your cheese, do not choose this one.

### BLUE BRIE ❢ *highish-acid, not-too-tannic reds* ♀ *New Zealand Riesling*
Reds with the bite of highish acidity are definitely the best choice, led by gentle, mature red Bordeaux (preferably from a ripe vintage). Others that make pleasant matches are mid- to light-weight Beaujolais crus (Côte de Brouilly, Juliénas, St-Amour, etc), Anjou or Touraine Gamay, Côtes du Rhône, and Cabernet Sauvignon, Barbera and Zinfandel from California. The New Zealand Riesling is unusual in making a spritely match; most other whites are either too strong, too sweet or too feeble. ★ *mature red Bordeaux* ★ *New Zealand Riesling*

### BRESSE BLEU ❢ *light reds*
Easy-drinking Juliénas, a Beaujolais cru, is best with this, the most mild-mannered of the creamy blue cheeses. Côte de Brouilly is very good (and a few notches heavier in the Beaujolais crus). Acceptable red matches are with Beaujolais-Villages, Côtes du Rhône, Côte de Beaune, Barbera (from Italy and California) and Zinfandel. Whites (with the exception of an adequate pairing with New Zealand Riesling) don't work. ★★ *Juliénas*

## CAMBOZOLA ❢ *medium-bodied, highish-acid reds*

This is the creamiest of the blue Brie-style cheeses, and is too creamy for dry or sweet whites. No red wine is absolutely perfect, but several match very well. California Zinfandel is the star choice, but close behind come the more substantial Beaujolais crus (Morgon, Moulin-à-Vent, Chénas, Juliénas, etc), Anjou Gamay, Côtes du Rhône and mature red Bordeaux from ripe vintages. Young red Bordeaux and California Cabernet are respectable matches, as are lighter styles of Beaujolais crus and Beaujolais-Villages, red Burgundies and Côte de Beaune reds. The Barbera grape, with its highish acidity, is a satisfactory partner – be it from California or Italy – as is Chianti. ★ *California Zinfandel*

## DANISH BLUE

A corrosively pungent blue cheese, Danish Blue is the most completely wine-resistant cheese. Not one to include on the cheese platter.

## DOLCELATTE ❢ *medium-bodied, fruity reds*

Dolcelatte has a farmyardy character that sets it apart from most other creamy, gentle blue cheeses, but makes it harder to match with wine. Whites don't work. Among reds, the almost pruny flavour of Rioja Gran Reserva, as well as its oaky, savoury taste, makes it the best companion for this cheese. Other pleasant pairings are found with the heavier Beaujolais crus (Morgon, Moulin-à-Vent, etc), Coonawarra and California Cabernet Sauvignon and good basic tawny port (10-year-old tawny is too intense). ★ *red Rioja Gran Reserva*

## GORGONZOLA

Gorgonzola is an aristocrat among the crowds of ordinary, creamy blue cheeses. It has a much more complex, interesting flavour, quite fruity, almost nutty. Its blue character blends perfectly with the creaminess. All this makes it quite difficult to match. The complex flavours of fine,

mature red Bordeaux come closest to a perfect pairing. Reasonable white matches are with the really ripe fruit of Australian Marsanne, the overt sweetness of Sauternes, Barsac or Graves Supérieures, and basic tawny port.
★ *mature red Bordeaux*

## ROQUEFORT ❢ *fruity and savoury reds* ♀ *sweet whites, especially botrytized; some fortified wines*
TRADITIONAL PARTNER *Sauternes*

The combination of Sauternes and Roquefort is one of the great, traditional pairings of French gastronomy – the attraction of opposites – and it works brilliantly. Somehow, the intensely salty, vigorous blue flavour of the cheese makes a wonderful combination with the opulently sweet white wine. Apart from this classic combination – Sauternes' neighbour, Barsac, is as perfect – Roquefort is also excellent with California botrytized Semillon (Australian ones tend to be too pungent and sweet). Other sweet wines from around the Bordeaux region (Monbazillac, Ste-Croix du Mont, Cadillac, Loupiac, Graves Supérieures) can work brilliantly, too. Fortified wines are good: from Madeira, try sweet Malmsey, or medium-sweet Bual. Another unexpected success is with dry fino and Manzanilla sherries. Port is less successful. Roquefort makes short work of all dry whites. A few reds with good, ripe, fruity flavours do work, however: try Zinfandel, mature red Bordeaux, Rioja Reserva and Gran Reserva, and Chianti Classico. ★★ *Sauternes* ★★ *Barsac*

## STILTON (BLUE) ❢ *medium-bodied, highish-acid, fruity reds; aged tawny port and aged Bual Madeira*

The 'port and Stilton' tradition at the end of a formal British dinner is absolutely right. But the port should be aged tawny (10- or 20-year-old). It's the nutty, creamy flavour of tawny port that works best with salty blue Stilton. Ruby, LBV (Late Bottled Vintage) and vintage character ports are really too sweet. The nutty, tangy flavours of old Bual Madeira are also excellent, and old Verdelho is not far behind. Less good, but still very pleasant, are a few reds: Côtes du Rhône, Chianti and California Barbera. Dry whites are not a lost cause: highish-acid whites like Chilean, New Zealand and South African Sauvignon Blanc, and Alsace, Australian and New Zealand Riesling are perfectly pleasant. ★★ *10-year old tawny port*

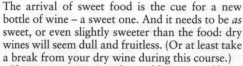
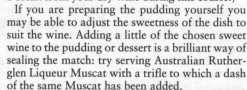
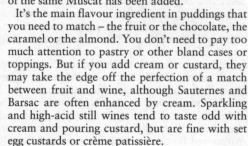

# DESSERTS, PUDDINGS AND FRUIT

The arrival of sweet food is the cue for a new bottle of wine – a sweet one. And it needs to be *as* sweet, or even slightly sweeter than the food: dry wines will seem dull and fruitless. (Or at least take a break from your dry wine during this course.)

If you are preparing the pudding yourself you may be able to adjust the sweetness of the dish to suit the wine. Adding a little of the chosen sweet wine to the pudding or dessert is a brilliant way of sealing the match: try serving Australian Rutherglen Liqueur Muscat with a trifle to which a dash of the same Muscat has been added.

It's the main flavour ingredient in puddings that you need to match – the fruit or the chocolate, the caramel or the almond. You don't need to pay too much attention to pastry or other bland cases or toppings. But if you add cream or custard, they may take the edge off the perfection of a match between fruit and wine, although Sauternes and Barsac are often enhanced by cream. Sparkling and high-acid still wines tend to taste odd with cream and pouring custard, but are fine with set egg custards or crème patissière.

## Fruits and Fruit Desserts

Many fruits have high acidity, and this, as well as the sweetness and the specific flavour, is a very important aspect to match with wine. Sweet Rieslings are the ideal partner for a wide variety of fruits, and Asti is also a good all-rounder. So either of these is a good choice for fresh fruit salads. Some fruits are difficult to match with any wine – bilberries, cherries, pears and pineapples are best avoided if you want to show off a special sweet wine. Whether the fruit is stewed or served as a pie, however, the same wines usually match. See also *Ice Creams and Sorbets*.

**APPLE** Sweet wines made from Riesling, Semillon, Muscat and Chenin Blanc tend to be the best choices with both eating and cooking apples.

## Apple Pie/Charlotte/Crumble/Tart or Stewed
♀ *sweet, medium- to high-acid whites*

German Riesling Beerenauslese is a star with apple pie (ours was made with Bramley apples); an Auslese is pleasant, though not quite sweet enough, unless you are really miserly with the amount of sugar you add to the apple. Botrytized Rieslings, particularly from Napa Valley in California, are pretty good. Sweet, more expensive Loire wines such as Coteaux du Layon, Quarts de Chaume or Bonnezeaux all make good matches, as does Asti or Sauternes. Or you can try sweet Jurançon, sweet Anjou Blanc or Austrian Müller-Thurgau Beerenauslese. ★★ *Mosel Riesling Beerenauslese*

VARIATIONS With added **cinnamon** the Riesling Beerenauslese and botrytized Rieslings are still brilliant, and Sauternes and Recioto di Soave are pleasant, but the sweet Loire wines are the wrong flavour. ★★ *Riesling Beerenauslese*. With **clove**, again the Riesling Beerenauslese and botrytized Riesling are stars, but other wines tend to clash. ★★ *Riesling Beerenauslese*. With **lemon zest** the sweet Rieslings still shine, and even slightly less sweet Rieslings – German or Austrian Auslesen or Washington State Late Harvest Rieslings – are quite successful. Asti is good. Adding lemon zest is a good trick if you want to tailor an apple dish to a less sweet wine. ★★ *sweet Rieslings*

## Apple Strudel ♀ *very sweet whites, especially Riesling*
TRADITIONAL PARTNER *Austrian Riesling Beerenauslese*

This Austrian pastry roll, stuffed with apples, buttered breadcrumbs, walnuts, lemon zest, cinnamon and raisins, must have been designed for Rieslings. The best we found was a Washington State Late Harvest Riesling, but Austrian or German Riesling Beerenauslesen and botrytized Rieslings from elsewhere are also excellent. Austrian Müller-Thurgau Trockenbeerenauslese and the more affordable Moscatel de Valencia, Muscat de St-Jean-de-Minervois or Muscat de Beaumes-de-Venise are all pleasant. ★★ *Washington State Late Harvest Riesling*

## Apple Tart with Crème Patissière ♀ *sweet, not-too-high-acid whites, especially Semillon*

Sweet Semillons are the star choices: Australian botrytized Semillon or a good, ripe Sauternes or Barsac are better than the lighter, slightly less sweet wines from the surrounding areas of Bordeaux. ★ *Australian botrytized Semillon* ★ *Barsac* ★ *Sauternes*

**Baked Apple** ♀ *sweet, quite high-acid whites*

We tried two different versions of baked Bramley apple, one with brown sugar, butter and raisins, the other with honey, sultanas and cinnamon, and neither found a good wine partner. The first went pleasantly with German Riesling Beerenauslese, and the cinnamon version was fine with either the Beerenauslese or with Sauternes.

**Tarte Normande** ♀ *medium- to high-acid sweet whites*

This dish is a delicious combination of Frangipane (a cooked paste of almonds, eggs, butter, flour and sugar) on a pastry base, topped with glazed apples. It is lovely with sweet Semillons (including sweet Bordeaux) because of the apples, and with a light, sweet Muscat à Petits Grains, which complements the almonds (fortified Muscats are too strong). Asti and Clairette de Die are pleasant though a touch too acid, as are sweet Loire whites such as Vouvray Moelleux or Coteaux du Layon. ★ *Graves Supérieures* ★ *southern French Muscat à Petits Grains*

**Tarte Tatin** ♀ *sweet, not-too-high-acid whites*

If the star, the wonderful Austrian Müller-Thurgau Trockenbeerenauslese, is unavailable, other good partners for this delicious, upside-down, caramelized tart are an Austrian Riesling Beerenauslese, or a not-too-acid botrytized Riesling from California's Napa Valley or elsewhere. For a cheaper choice, Recioto di Soave works well, as do the lighter fortified Muscats, especially Muscat de Saint-Jean-de-Minervois. ★★ *Austrian Müller-Thurgau Trockenbeerenauslese*

## APRICOT

**Apricot Pie/Crumble/Tart or Stewed**
♀ *highish-acid, botrytized whites*

Australian botrytized Semillon and Mosel Riesling Beerenauslese are stars with cooked apricots; California and Australian botrytized Rieslings are next best. Unfortified southern French Muscats and fortified California Muscats are worth trying, as are Asti, Sauternes, and Austrian or German Müller-Thurgau Beerenauslesen or Trockenbeerenauslesen. If the amount of sugar in the pie is low, Asti is best. ★★ *Australian botrytized Semillon* ★★ *Mosel Riesling Beerenauslese*

## BANANA
**Banoffee Pie** ♀ *very sweet, botrytized Chardonnay or fortified Muscat, and very sweet Tokay*
The sugary sweetness of toffee, and the fruity sweetness of banana, combine to create a dish that needs a really sweet wine. Best is botrytized Australian Chardonnay. Since this is rarely made and difficult to find, it's fortunate that Hungarian Tokay 5 Puttonyos is nearly as good. Sweet fortified Muscat (Beaumes-de-Venise) or unfortified sweet Muscat is also pleasant. ★★ *Australian botrytized Chardonnay* ★ *Hungarian Tokay 5 Puttonyos*
**Flambéed Banana with Rum** ♀ *very sweet whites*
Bananas cooked with brown sugar, raisins, and a splash of rum need a very sweet matching wine, and one that can stand up to the rum. Recioto di Soave fits the bill almost perfectly, and Austrian Beerenauslesen are good. Asti, Australian botrytized Semillon, Moscatel de Valencia and Muscat de Beaumes-de-Venise are all satisfactory alternatives. ★ *Recioto di Soave*

## BLACKBERRY & APPLE PIE/CRUMBLE OR STEWED ❢ *Black Muscat* ♀ *very sweet, high-acid whites, especially Riesling*
A high-acid Mosel Riesling of Beerenauslese level is a perfect match – the botrytis is flattering to the fruit, Riesling has the right acidity, and Beerenauslese is the right sweetness level. If this is too expensive, skimp on the amount of sugar added to the fruit, and serve a Mosel Riesling Auslese. California botrytized Riesling is satisfactory, as is Australian botrytized Semillon. If you like your pie very sweet, with lots of added sugar, a California Black Muscat is the answer. ★★ *Mosel Riesling Beerenauslese*

## BLACKCURRANT see also *Ice Creams and Sorbets*
**Blackcurrant Cheesecake** ♀ *sweet Muscats*
The combination of high acidity tamed by a lot of sugar makes this dish difficult to pair off perfectly. Wines based on Chenin Blanc, Semillon and Riesling don't really work,

so turn to the faithful Muscat. California Black Muscat or fortified Orange Muscat (most other fortified Muscats are a bit heavy, however), and other unfortified sweet Muscats are all pleasant.

### Blackcurrant Mousse ♀ high-acid, fairly sweet to sweet whites

Asti is a lovely choice with this mousse made with cream, crème de cassis and eggs. Botrytized Rieslings and Semillons are nearly as good (Sauternes and other sweet white Bordeaux have the wrong flavour). Recioto di Soave is fine, as are German or Austrian Riesling or Müller-Thurgau. Just choose the sweetness level – Auslese, Beerenauslese or Trockenbeerenauslese – according to how sweet the mousse is. ★ Asti

### Blackcurrant Pie/Crumble ♀ high-acid sweet whites with not too much botrytis

Asti is far and away the best partner for cooked blackcurrants. Most botrytized wines taste bitter, though German and Austrian Riesling or Müller-Thurgau Auslesen are good. ★ Asti

## BILBERRY/BLUEBERRY/WIMBERRY PIE ♀ botrytized Rieslings and Semillons

The acidity and sweetness of these delicious, dark berries is not very high, and the flavour is quite subdued. Many sweet wines are too strongly flavoured, others clash. You might be satisfied with Australian botrytized Semillon, German or Austrian Riesling Auslese, Washington State, New Zealand or South African Late Harvest Rieslings, but nothing is a real success.

## FRESH FRUIT SALAD ♀ sweet whites with good acidity, especially Rieslings and Asti

Sweet Rieslings and Asti will happily accompany a very wide range of fruits. When served with a mixed fruit salad, though, the choice of wine really depends on the dominant fruit. Beware cherries, pineapple and pear – they are particularly wine-unfriendly, and it's probably best not to include these in a fruit salad if you have a fine sweet wine. Bananas, fresh figs and kiwi fruits match sweet Rieslings. German or Austrian Rieslings are good all-round choices; they need to be of at least Auslese level if the salad is not too sweet, or Beerenauslese for a sweeter one. If a Beerenauslese is too expensive, look to Australia, New Zealand, South Africa or California for slightly more affordable botrytized Rieslings, which also work very well with fresh fruit salads. To help the match – and if your wine is not too fine and expensive – pour a little into the fruit salad as well. See also individual fruit entries. ★★ *Asti* ★★ *sweet Riesling*

## GOOSEBERRY
**Gooseberry Fool** ♀ *very sweet botrytized whites*
The creaminess of gooseberry fool makes it a good match with Australian botrytized Semillon; Mosel Beerenauslese is also a good choice. ★ *Australian botrytized Semillon*
**Gooseberry Pie/Crumble** ♀ *sweet Mosel Rieslings*
Gooseberries have a piercing acidity that survives cooking and that makes this fruit very difficult to match to wine. The only match we found was Mosel Riesling Auslese. It's not quite perfect – not *quite* sweet enough for a pie or crumble – but the flavour is good, and you can help the match if making the dish yourself by going easy on the sugar. ★ *Mosel Riesling Auslese*

## LEMON see also *Ice Creams and Sorbets*
**Lemon Cheesecake** ♀ *sweet high-acid whites*
Australian botrytized Semillon is the closest to a success, and Asti is the only really pleasant alternative. ★ *Australian botrytized Semillon*
**Lemon Meringue Pie** ♀ *very sweet, botrytized whites or lighter Muscats*
There's more sweetness than acidity to most lemon meringue pies, which is why Rieslings are not successful. Asti and Moscatel de Valencia both marry well with the lemon. Sauternes and Barsac are more surprising – and successful – choices. ★ *Asti* ★ *Moscatel de Valencia*
**Lemon Tart (Tarte au Citron)** ♀ *very sweet, botrytized, high-acid whites*
This tart, with its creamy, very lemony filling, demands acidity and sweetness, and the Austrian Müller-Thurgau Beerenauslese fits the bill very well. New Zealand Late Harvest Riesling is very good, too, but may not be *quite* sweet enough, and Muscat de St-Jean-de-Minervois is another successful combination. Otherwise, there are

pleasant pairings with Asti, Australian botrytized Semillon and California fortified Muscat. ★★ *Austrian Müller-Thurgau Beerenauslese*

## MANGO ♀ *very low-acid, sweet whites*

Gentle, fortified or unfortifed Muscats are best with unsweetened mango. Asti or Moscato d'Asti are pleasant, as are the gentlest of botrytized Semillons, such as Graves Supérieures. In a sweeter dish enlivened with a little lemon juice, the flavour of sweet Riesling goes brilliantly, especially South African Late Harvest Riesling, with Australian botrytized Riesling a close second. Botrytized Semillons and Asti are pleasant. ★ *botrytized Riesling*

## MELON
### Cantaloupe ♀ *fairly sweet to very sweet Rieslings*

High-acid Rieslings from the Mosel scoop the pool with Canteloupe at several levels of sweetness, and you can also make a good match with late-picked Rieslings from Washington State and New Zealand. Austrian Müller-Thurgau Trockenbeerenauslese is also pleasant. The traditional partner, ruby port, is no more than adequate, while 10-year-old tawny port is too nutty. ★ *Mosel Riesling Spätlese, Auslese and Beerenauslese*

### Charentais ♀ *fairly gently flavoured, fairly sweet whites*

Sweet wines from the Loire are by far the best. Sweet Muscats go pleasantly, though the flavour tends to be a little too strong. ★ *Vouvray Moelleux* ★ *Coteaux du Layon*

### Galia ♀ *sweet (moelleux) Loire wines, very light, sweet Muscats; 10-year-old tawny port*

We found no perfect partner, but there's a decent range of pleasant matches. From the Loire, Vouvray Moelleux and Coteaux du Layon are perfectly respectable. Asti works, and 10-year-old tawny port comes into its own as well.

### Honeydew ♀ *gentle, low-acid sweet Muscats*

Almost all wines taste too strong and/or acid for this gentle flavour. Muscat de St-Jean-de-Minervois comes closest to a match.

## NECTARINE see PEACH

## ORANGE
### Caramelized Oranges ♀ *very sweet whites, particularly Muscats*
Asti provides exactly the right combination of grapy sweetness and lively acidity. But there are several other wines that work very well, starting with fortified Orange Muscat from California. Sauternes, Barsac (and other sweet white Bordeaux), Australian botrytized Semillon and California and Australian botrytized Riesling are also very good. Other satisfactory wines are Riesling Auslese, Vouvray Moelleux, Moscatel de Valencia and Muscat de St-Jean-de-Minervois. ★★ *Asti*
### Crêpes Suzette ♀ *very sweet whites*
It's the sweet, orangey-flavoured sauce and orange zest that create the problems with Crêpes Suzette. Nothing is perfect, but the light, frothy flavours of Asti come closest. Late-harvest Rieslings from Washington State and New Zealand are the other main contenders. Moscatel de Valencia is quite good, though a little too alcoholic. ★ *Asti*
### Orange Bavarois/Mousse/Soufflé/Tart ♀ *sweet Muscats*
Asti hits the right note for these gently flavoured, creamy orange desserts. Muscat de Beaumes-de-Venise is a pretty good choice, too. Other Muscats – both fortified and unfortified – such as Muscat de St-Jean-de-Minervois and sweet southern French Muscats, are pleasant partners. The surprise match comes with 10-year-old tawny port, which is perfectly agreeable, though somewhat strong. ★★ *Asti*
### Orange Cheesecake ♀ *very sweet but gentle, fortified or sparkling Muscats*
You need to select wines that will match the sharp flavour of the orange as well as the creaminess of the cheesecake, and that probably means Muscat. Light, lively Asti is the most successful, with Muscat de St-Jean-de-Minervois next best. Australian botrytized Riesling copes adequately, too. ★ *Asti*

## PASSION FRUIT
### Passion Fruit Fool ♀ *high-acid sweet whites*
Nothing goes really well with passion fruit fool, but sweet Loire wines (such as Vouvray Moelleux), Moscatel de Valencia or Australian botrytized Semillon all make adequate partners.

### PEACH/NECTARINE ♀ *high-acid, fairly sweet whites, especially Riesling*

Though nectarines tend to have slightly higher acidity, the wine matches are the same. Rieslings are spot on with peaches and very nearly as good with nectarines. German or Austrian Auslesen are likely to be the right sweetness for the raw fruit, and South African or New Zealand Late Harvest Rieslings also go very well. Sweetened cooked, tinned peaches or peach desserts can take the extra sweetness of a Beerenauslese or Australian botrytized Riesling. Clairette de Die is good, and Asti pleasant. ★★ *Mosel Riesling Auslese*

### PEAR
### Pears in Red Wine ♀ *sweet and very sweet whites, not Muscat*

Raw pear will kill any wine, but the red wine syrup (made with cinnamon, cloves, orange and lemon zest) that the pears are poached in helps a little, although no wine is more than adequate. Rieslings work best, from the sweetest California and Australian botrytized Rieslings, to the much more acidic Mosel Riesling Beerenauslese. Sweet (moelleux) Vouvray, and light Recioto della Valpolicella are also pleasant, as is Asti.

### PINEAPPLE

Fresh pineapple is difficult to match with wines because of its very high acidity and natural sweetness. About the only wine that makes a decent pairing is Asti, or the less fizzy Moscato d'Asti.

### PLUM
### Plum Pie/Crumble or Stewed ♀ *sweet and very sweet Rieslings, fortified Muscats*

Riesling is perfect with plums, be they fresh or cooked, although with the latter the wine should be a notch sweeter, to balance the sugar used in the cooking. Mosel Riesling Auslese and Beerenauslese are good, but South African and Australian botrytized Rieslings are better. Some fortified Muscats are also good with cooked, sweetened plums. Moscatel de Valencia, Muscat de Beaumes-de-Venise and Muscat de St-Jean-de-Minervois are all pleasant, though Muscat isn't the *ideal* flavour. ★★ *Australian and South African botrytized Rieslings*

## RASPBERRY
**Fresh Raspberries** ♀ *fairly sweet to very sweet whites*
If you serve raspberries with a little sugar, the partnership with sweet wines is much better. California fortified Orange Muscat is the star match, with demi-sec Champagne and Mosel Riesling Spätlese and Auslese nearly as good. Asti and Lambrusco Rosso are pleasant, too, with the added attraction of serving lower-alcohol wines at the end of a meal. ★★ *California fortified Orange Muscat*
VARIATIONS Pouring **cream** over the fruit makes New Zealand botrytized Riesling the most suitable partner. Sweet Semillon is a good alternative: Sauternes, Barsac and the other sweet whites from the Bordeaux region are very good. ★★ *New Zealand botrytized Riesling*
**Raspberry Fool** ♀ *sweet whites with good acidity*
Good Sauternes or Barsac is brilliant; botrytized Semillon from elsewhere also works well. German Riesling Auslese or Washington State, California, South African or New Zealand Late Harvest Rieslings are good, as is Coteaux du Layon from the Loire. ★★ *Sauternes*
**Raspberry Pavlova**
Not easy, raspberry pavlova. Almost everything seems too acid or not sweet enough. Young Portuguese Setúbal comes nearest to a match.

## RHUBARB
**Rhubarb Fool**
Asti is the only wine that comes close to a match.
**Rhubarb Pie/Crumble/Tart or Stewed**
♀ *sweet and very sweet, high-acid whites*
Rhubarb, with its high, undisguisable acidity, even when cooked and with added sugar, needs a similar acidity in the wine. Asti is very good, and Riesling Auslese from the Rheingau or Pfalz, Australian and California botrytized Rieslings are also successful. Mosel Riesling Beerenauslese, sweet (unfortified) southern French Muscats and Moscatel de Valencia are all acceptable partners, but nothing else really works. ★ *Asti*

## STRAWBERRY

**Fresh Strawberries** ♀ *gently flavoured, fairly sweet, not-too-acid whites*

Even when sprinkled with sugar, strawberries are overwhelmed by the sweetest of wines, and by many sweet wine flavours. Clairette de Die is the best, light partner, and an unfortified southern French Muscat à Petits Grains goes very well, provided the strawberries are ripe and sprinkled with sugar. There are pleasant matches with Recioto di Soave, demi-sec Champagne, Alsace Tokay-Pinot Gris Vendange Tardive, and pink or red Lambrusco. ★ *Clairette de Die*

VARIATIONS If you enjoy your strawberries doused in **cream**, see *Strawberry Mousse* below for matching wines.

**Strawberry Ice Cream** see *Ice Creams and Sorbets*

**Strawberry Mousse/Bavarois/Fool**
♀ *sweet whites, especially botrytized Semillon and fortified Muscats*

Cream somehow makes a bridge between strawberries and wine, especially botrytized wines (but sparkling wines, including Clairette de Die and sweet Champagne, taste wrong). Unfortified southern French Muscat à Petits Grains makes a wonderful accompaniment, and California, New Zealand or Australian botrytized Semillons are nearly as good, and Sauternes and Barsac match deliciously. It's partly the oak in these Semillons that goes so well – lesser sweet Bordeaux, such as Graves Supérieures, lack this oak, and so are not quite so good. Mosel Riesling Beerenauslese and other very sweet Rieslings are very pleasant. So are fortified Muscat de Beaumes-de-Venise or Muscat de St-Jean-de-Minervois, though both are a little too powerful. ★★ *botrytized Semillon* ★★ *Sauternes* ★★ *southern French unfortified Muscat à Petits Grains*

## SUMMER PUDDING ♀ *high-acid, very sweet whites*

The high acidity of the blackcurrants, blackberries, redcurrants, raspberries and strawberries all packed into the pudding dominates the choice of partnering wine; the bread casing plays no part in the wine match. High-acid Riesling strikes the most appropriate chord, but you need a wine of Beerenauslese level to cope with the sweetness of the pudding. So the winner is Mosel Riesling Beerenauslese, followed – at a distance – by a sweet (moelleux) Coteaux du Layon from the Loire, and Hungarian Tokay 5 Puttonyos, which both make pleasant partners. ★ *Mosel Riesling Beerenauslese*

# Other Puddings and Desserts

Sweet Muscat is often the perfect partner for puddings and desserts that contain no fruit – it is brilliant with many flavours, from almond to chocolate, caramel to coffee. But Muscat comes in many guises – delicate or strongly flavoured, dry, fairly sweet or rich and sticky, so you need to choose fairly carefully. Few puddings defy matching with any wines, but meringue is a tough one, bread-and-butter pudding is tricky, and pecan pie does no favours to a fine sweet wine. Adding cream can help with the more difficult customers – Sauternes and Barsac are particularly enhanced by cream.

### ALMOND DISHES see also CHOCOLATE: SACHERTORTE
**Almond Tart (Pithivier)** ♀ *sweet, fortified Muscats, some other sweet whites*
This French-style almond tart, with its sweet filling, demonstrates how well sweet Muscats partner almond dishes. Moscatel de Valencia has just the right balance of sweetness and acidity, and young Setúbal or Muscat de Beaumes-de-Venise are almost as good, as is Australian botrytized Riesling. California botrytized Riesling and Australian botrytized Semillon are next in line, along with very sweet (moelleux) Loire whites. Asti is also a pleasant, light alternative. ★★ *Moscatel de Valencia*
**Baclava** ♀ *very sweet fortified Muscats*
It's the sugar syrup in which baclava is soaked that dictates which wines will work. The actual flavour (apart from sweetness) of this sticky Middle Eastern creation is very gentle, so you can't go for too strongly flavoured a

wine. The gently nutty flavour of old Setúbal is a star choice, much better than the strong fruit of, say, a Muscat de Beaumes-de-Venise. Moscatel de Valencia is nearly as good as the Setúbal, but few other wines really work. ★★ *20-year-old Setúbal*

## Bakewell Tart ♀ *very sweet whites*

Icing sugar and almond essence are the main ingredients to match here. The lively acidity of Asti, the star choice, cuts through and balances the sweetness in the tart. Other good matches are even sweeter botrytized Australian Semillons or Rieslings. Greek Muscat from the island of Samos works pleasantly, and the ultra-sweet, treacly Pedro Ximénez sherry makes a rather wonderful combination, if a bit too serious a wine for a tart with a glacé cherry on top. ★★ *Asti*

VARIATIONS The inhabitants of Bakewell in Derbyshire will assure you that the town houses no tarts, only **Bakewell puddings**: puff pastry filled with a wonderful, rich, soft, baked filling of eggs, sugar, butter and ground almonds (and no flour or icing). Only Muscat works, and apart from Moscatel de Valencia from south-east Spain or Setúbal from Portugal (the young one rather than the 20-year-old), you can try Muscat de Beaumes-de-Venise, or Muscat de Rivesaltes. (Australian Liqueur Muscats are too strong.) ★ *Moscatel de Valencia* ★ *young Setúbal*

## Tarte Normande see APPLE

## BLACK FOREST GÂTEAU see CHOCOLATE

## BREAD-AND-BUTTER PUDDING ♀ *not-too-acid sweet whites*

Only one wine goes *really* well – German Scheurebe Trockenbeerenauslese is delicious with a creamy version. Recioto di Soave or California and Australian botrytized Semillon are adequate. ★★ *German Scheurebe Trockenbeerenauslese*

## CHEESECAKE see also BLACKCURRANT, LEMON and ORANGE

**Sticky Toffee Cheesecake** ♀ *assorted very sweet whites*

The oaked, slightly savoury flavour of Recioto di Soave works very well with this sweet toffee cheesecake. Muscat de St-Jean-de-Minervois and Australian botrytized Riesling are very good as well, and Asti is acceptable. ★★ *Recioto di Soave*

**CHOCOLATE** Although chocolate overpowers many sweet wines, it is not as impossible to partner with wine as many might think. The answer lies with sweet Muscat; it is a really complementary flavour that sticks up for itself. Which style of Muscat to serve will depend on the sweetness, the acidity, and the intensity of flavour in the particular chocolate dish.

**Black Forest Gâteau** ♀ *sweet Muscats with fairly high acidity*

The black cherry jam in this popular German recipe calls for good acidity in the matching wine. Moscatel de Valencia is a star, and sweet, unfortified southern French Muscat à Petits Grains also works very well. Asti, however, is *too* acid. ★★ *Moscatel de Valencia*

**Chocolate Bavarois** ♀ *sweet whites, including botrytized and especially Muscats*

Bavarois is made with custard and whipped cream and set with gelatine, and tends to have a gentler flavour than mousse. The lighter Muscats – unfortified southern French Muscats, Muscat de St-Jean-de-Minervois, Australian and California Orange Muscats – go very well, as does Asti if the bavarois is not too sweet. Heavier Muscats from Australia or Valencia in Spain are pleasant. So, too, are Recioto di Soave, Sauternes or simpler sweet white Bordeaux, Australian botrytized Semillon, 10-year-old tawny port or LBV (Late Bottled Vintage) port. ★★ *California Orange Muscat*

**Chocolate Gâteau (also Chocolate Roulade)** ♀ *sweet Muscats*

After the perfect partner, an Austrian Müller-Thurgau Trockenbeerenauslese, sweet Muscats are the best choice. Which one depends on the sweetness or bitterness of the chocolate. With a low-sugar, bitter-chocolate gâteau or roulade, California Orange Muscat is very good, but the fortified southern French, Australian and Spanish Muscats are too strong and sweet. These sweeter Muscats are better with sweeter gâteaux (which includes most bought ones). ★★ *Austrian Müller-Thurgau Trockenbeerenauslese*

**Chocolate Ice Cream** see *Ice Creams and Sorbets.*

**Chocolate Mousse** ♀ *very sweet, not-too-acid Muscats*

Moscatel de Valencia comes closest to perfection with a rich, sweet, dark chocolate mousse. Australian Rutherglen Liqueur Muscat and Australian or California Orange Muscat, despite the latter's acidity, are also pleasant. LBV (Late Bottled Vintage) port is surprisingly good, too – not a marriage, but the peppery fruit sets off the intensity of the chocolate very well. ★ *Moscatel de Valencia*

VARIATIONS A lighter, **milk chocolate** mousse is brilliant with Asti: the bubbles in the wine match the chocolate froth, and the acidity cuts through the richness of the dish. Other good Muscats are Muscat de Beaumes-de-Venise, de Rivesaltes or de St-Jean-de-Minervois, as well as Sauternes or botrytized Semillon. ★★ *Asti*

**Chocolate Profiteroles with Cream**
♀ *sweet, unfortified Muscats*

The chocolate flavour in profiteroles is fairly gentle, diluted by the pastry and whipped cream. So you don't need the heaviest guns in the Muscat armoury to balance the chocolate flavour. Sweet, unfortified Muscats are best, closely followed by Australian botrytized Chardonnay. Other good choices include fortified Muscats and Asti. ★ *sweet, unfortified Muscat*

VARIATIONS Chocolate profiteroles filled with **crème patissière** are harder to match than the cream-filled version. Best bet is a California or Austra-lian Orange Muscat. Sauternes, Barsac or other sweet white Bordeaux are pleasant alternatives, as is a Greek Muscat from the island of Samos.

**Chocolate Roulade** see **CHOCOLATE GÂTEAU**

**Sachertorte** ♀ *sweet whites, including botryized, with good acidity*

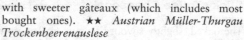

TRADITIONAL PARTNER *Coffee*
This bitter-chocolate, almond-rich Austrian cake, coated with apricot jam and more dark chocolate, goes sensationally well with Australian botrytized Semillon, which has just the right acidity level for the apricot jam. A good Sauternes or Barsac is excellent, too, and Moscatel de Valencia is very good and better than other Muscats. Recioto della Valpolicella makes a surprisingly good partner. From Austria, the best bet may be a Müller-Thurgau Beerenauslese (sweet Riesling and Weissburgunder don't work). But then you'll probably be served Sachertorte mid-afternoon, with a cup of coffee and no alcohol in sight. ★★ *Australian botrytized Semillon*

## CHRISTMAS PUDDING ♀ *very sweet Muscats, botrytized Riesling*
Asti is a revelation with Christmas pudding. In its traditional form, heavy with beef suet, the pudding can sit very heavily on the already groaning Christmas tummy. Asti is the perfect answer. It has enough sweetness to match the dried fruit, and its acidity and light sparkle enlivens and lifts the stodgiest of puddings. Fortified Muscats make very good flavour matches, too, especially Australian Rutherglen Liqueur Muscat and Moscatel de Valencia. Australian and California botrytized Rieslings are fine, too, and Australian botrytized Semillon just about copes. ★★ *Asti*

## COFFEE All sorts of sweet wines go well with the
flavour of coffee, but as with chocolate, sweet Muscats are the real stars. You just need to choose the right Muscat from the big range of possibilities to match the sweetness and intensity of your dish. The acidity level of coffee-based dishes will usually be low, so Asti is not an ideal choice. See also *Tiramisu*.
### Coffee Gâteau ♀ *sweet whites, especially Muscat*
Moscatel de Valencia is the tops with coffee gâteau, but Muscat de St-Jean-de-Minervois, Australian Rutherglen Liqueur Muscat and Greek Muscat from Samos are all very good, and other Muscats are very pleasant. Sauternes, Barsac and sweet Premières Côtes de Bordeaux all go well, too, or you can be really bold and try an inexpensive, Full Rich Madeira or an LBV (Late Bottled Vintage) port. ★★ *Moscatel de Valencia*

### Coffee Mousse ♀ *not-too-acid, sweet wines, especially Muscat*

Australian Liqueur Muscat or a light, unfortified sweet Muscat Blanc à Petits Grains from the south of France are the most delicious of all with coffee mousse, and there are very good matches with Moscatel de Valencia, Muscat de Rivesaltes or de St-Jean-de-Minervois, and California Orange Muscat. Muscat de Beaumes-de-Venise is pleasant. Malaga, Malmsey and LBV (Late Bottled Vintage) port, Australian botrytized Semillon and Austrian Müller-Thurgau Trockenbeerenauslese are also good, or try a sweet Champagne, Sauternes, a Bual, Malmsey or Full Rich Madeira, a 10-year-old Tawny port or Vieux Rivesaltes. ★★ *Australian Rutherglen Liqueur Muscat*

### Coffee Profiteroles ♀ *sweet, low-acid whites, especially fortified Muscats*

With coffee profiteroles (especially if filled with crème patissière) you need to serve low-acid sweet whites, especially fortified Muscats. Sauternes or Barsac from a ripe year, and Austrian Müller-Thurgau Beerenauslese or Trockenbeerenauslese are quite good. ★★ *Moscatel de Valencia* ★★ *Muscat de St-Jean-de-Minervois*

### CRÈME BRÛLÉE ♀ *sweet, not-too-acid Muscats and Semillons*

Australian botrytized Semillon makes a great match with crème brûlée. Sauternes or botrytized Semillon from California or New Zealand are also very good indeed. The caramel flavour in crème brûlée also goes well with Muscat, and best is Muscat de St-Jean-de-Minervois. ★★ *Australian botrytized Semillon*

### CRÈME CARAMEL ♀ *not-too-acid sweet whites, especially Muscat and Semillon*

The gentlest of the sweet Muscats (with the exception of high-acid Asti) are best with crème caramel. If an unfortified version proves hard to find, go for Muscat de Beaumes-de-Venise, Muscat de St-Jean-de-Minervois, or Muscat de Rivesaltes, all of which are a touch too strongly flavoured, but good all the same. Botrytized Semillons, including Sauternes and Barsac, are also pleasant. ★ *sweet, unfortified southern French Muscat à Petits Grains*

## CUSTARD Egg custards are hard to match well with wine. The fizz in sparkling wines and high acid in still or sparkling wines clash with unset versions.

### Baked Egg Custard ♀ *whites of similar sweetness*
Very gentle Muscats – Asti, Moscato d'Asti or Muscat de St-Jean-de-Minervois – are pleasant, as are Late Harvest Rieslings, but nothing goes very well.

### Crème Anglaise/Home-made Pouring Custard ♀ *sweet Muscats or Rieslings*
It's worth avoiding fizzy wines and the unpleasant sensation they create when serving a home-made custard with a pudding. High acidity is not ideal either, but it's best to match the acidity of the pudding or pie. The flavours of Muscat and sweet Riesling work quite well.

### Floating Islands (Îles Flottantes) ♀ *sweet Muscats*
Caramel is the dominant flavour in this sweet sea of crème anglaise topped with floating 'islands' of caramel-covered, poached whipped egg white. Muscat de Beaumes-de-Venise is much better than any other Muscat. High acidity and sparkling wines clash with the egg. ★ *Muscat de Beaumes-de-Venise*

## MERINGUE AND CREAM ♀ *very sweet whites with not-too-high acidity*
Nothing really goes with meringues, served plain or with cream. Australian Liqueur Muscats and Portuguese Moscatel de Setúbal just about cope. See also *Raspberry Pavlova*.
VARIATIONS Adding **hazelnuts** does not help – Australian Liqueur Muscat is the only acceptable partner.

## MINCE PIE ♀ *very sweet, highish-acid whites*
The sweetness level in mince pies is intense, but that can be balanced by any number of wines; it's the acidity in the mince meat that makes good wine matches so hard to find. Australian botrytized Semillon does the trick extremely effectively, and the other satisfactory pairing is with 20-year-old Setúbal from Portugal. With a few less sweet mince meats, Asti works very well. ★★ *Australian botrytized Semillon*

## MOUSSE (AND COLD SOUFFLÉ) see individual fruits or flavourings.

## PANCAKES see ORANGE: CRÊPES SUZETTE

## PECAN PIE ♀ *low-acid sweet whites*
Recioto di Soave and Australian botrytized Semillon come closest to partnering this delicious, densely nutty American pie, but they don't *really* work. Sweet Muscats simply clash.

## RICE PUDDING ♀ *sweet whites, ideally with low acidity*
Rice pudding is very soothing, and can cope well with acidity as well as wines sweeter than itself. Fortified French Muscats or Recioto di Soave are best, and sweet Jurançon and California or Australian Orange Muscat are pleasant. ★★ *Recioto di Soave* ★★ *Muscat de St-Jean-de-Minervois*

## RUM BABA ♀ *very sweet, not-too-acid whites*
Nothing goes well with the rum that dominates in this dish. Good, sweet Sauternes is acceptable, but is rather wasted on rum baba. Inexpensive Moscatel de Valencia is also a pleasant partner. Add a dash of the Moscatel to the syrup, along with the rum, and it will make a closer match.

## SACHERTORTE see CHOCOLATE

## SAVARIN ♀ *sweet, not-too-acid Muscats*
This is a very sweet dish, a syrup-soaked, slightly lemony yeasty ring. It makes most sweet wines taste too acidic. Spanish Moscatel de Valencia or Greek Samos Muscat come closest. To make it more wine-friendly, fill the centre with fruit, and/or add lemon juice or even sweet wine (if so, add less sugar) to the syrup.

## SHERRY TRIFLE ♀ *inexpensive medium-dry to sweet sherries*
If you haven't made the trifle yourself and therefore don't know what sweetness of sherry was

tipped over the sponge, the best answer is to serve an inexpensive sherry somewhere between medium-dry and sweet, perhaps an amontillado. (Older, finer sherries taste too nutty and strong, dominating the overall flavour of the trifle.) The best alternative is sweet Muscat – especially Australian Rutherglen Liqueur Muscat and Muscat de St-Jean-de-Minervois. Recioto di Soave is another pleasant option. If you are making the trifle yourself, add a dash of any of the above wines to the trifle, and they will perform even better. ★ *inexpensive medium-sweet sherry*

**SOUFFLÉ** To find a wine match for soufflé, look up the individual flavourings, such as chocolate, lemon or orange.

**TIRAMISU** ♀ *sweet to very sweet, not-too-acid whites*
Tiramisu is a real heart-stopper, a wickedly delicious Italian dessert, combining coffee and coffee liqueur, Marsala, Mascarpone cheese, egg yolks, cream and cocoa. Fortified Muscats have a complementary if slightly overpowering flavour, and a good Sauternes or Barsac works quite well, too. Hungarian Tokay 5 Puttonyos is also very good indeed, though a little too assertive, with Recioto di Soave and Banyuls from southern France nearly as successful. Marsala and LBV (Late Bottled Vintage) port both make pleasant partners. ★★ *Moscatel de Valencia*

**TREACLE TART** ♀ *very sweet whites*
There are no absolutely perfect wine partners, but several wines go very well with treacle tart. The high acidity of Asti successfully cuts the sweetness, and Australian, New Zealand or California botrytized Riesling perform the same trick. Very sweet Tokay makes an unexpectedly good flavour match, and Muscats are pleasant alternatives. ★ *Asti* ★ *Tokay 5 Puttonyos*

**TRIFLE** see **SHERRY TRIFLE**

**ZABAGLIONE**
Wines either taste too acid with zabaglione, or they form a slightly eggy clash. Even Marsala, which is in the dish, tastes too strong and nutty when drunk neat alongside. In any case, since zabaglione comes in a glass and is frothily liquid, it's almost a drink in itself.

# Ice Creams and Sorbets

A chilled palate can't appreciate wine, so the theory goes. Wrong. It's one of the great myths that ice cream and wine don't go. Just make sure that the wine is well chilled to show at its best. Sparkling wines clash slightly with the cream in ice cream, but are fine with sorbet. Bear in mind that sorbets will perhaps be sharpened with lemon juice.

## ICE CREAMS

### Chocolate Ice Cream ♀ *sweet, not-too-high-acid whites, especially fortified Muscats*

A pale, milk-chocolate ice cream is at its best with California fortified Orange Liqueur Muscat, and is pleasant with Moscato d'Asti (but not Asti fizz), Sauternes and other sweet white Bordeaux, Lambrusco Rosso and an inexpensive sweet Madeira. ★ *California fortified Orange Muscat*
VARIATIONS With **dark chocolate** ice cream, much stronger wines are good, and dark, sweet and fortified wines are particularly delicious. The stars are a fine Marsala or Muscat de St-Jean-de-Minervois. There are very good matches, too, with sweet Madeiras, ideally five-year-old Bual or Malmsey. LBV (Late Bottled Vintage) port goes well, and better than finer ports, though these are pleasant too, and sweet Malaga is good. Sweet oloroso sherries, even quite fine ones, are very pleasant. California fortified Orange Muscat is enjoyable, and other sweet, strongly flavoured Muscats go pleasantly. Recioto della Valpolicella is a surprising success, its tannin somehow cancelled out by the dark chocolate. ★ *fine Marsala* ★ *Muscat de St-Jean-de-Minervois*

### Strawberry Ice Cream ♀ *light, sweet whites*

The delicate flavour of strawberry ice cream finds no ideal partners, but sweet Loires, including Coteaux du Layon and Vouvray Moelleux, are very good choices. Otherwise serve very light sweet Muscats (but not Asti), or an Austrian

Beerenauslese cocktail of Bouvier, Pinot Gris and Pinot Blanc. ★ *Coteaux du Layon*

## Vanilla Ice Cream

Perhaps the myth that ice cream doesn't go with wine is based on people's bad experiences with vanilla ice cream. It is true that most wines clash or fail miserably to match. But in south-west Spain they serve vanilla ice cream with wonderfully gooey, intensely flavoured Pedro Ximénez (PX), the sweetest and darkest of sherries; sometimes sultanas that have been soaked in the PX are added. It is a wonderful combination. And Australian Rutherglen Liqueur Muscat works in a similar way. ★★ *PX sherry* ★★ *Australian Rutherglen Liqueur Muscat*

## SORBETS

### Blackcurrant Sorbet ♀ *sweet Rieslings*

German or Austrian Riesling Beerenauslesen, although just right for sweetness, are very expensive, and Auslesen are not sweet enough. Botrytized Rieslings, especially from South Africa or Australia, are just as good, and somewhat cheaper. ★ *South African botrytized Riesling*

### Lemon Sorbet ♀ *sweet whites with good acidity*

The star choice is Australian botrytized Semillon. That apart, best partners are Tokay 5 Puttonyos and Moscatel de Valencia, the latter especially if the sorbet is quite sweet. Muscat de St-Jean-de-Minervois is quite good, and there are also good matches with South African, New Zealand or California Late Harvest Riesling and German Riesling Beerenauslese. ★★ *Australian botrytized Semillon*

### Mango Sorbet ♀ *sweet, not-too-acid Riesling, Muscat and Semillon*

Riesling is a lovely flavour with mango, but has too high an acidity for the plain fruit. But South African botrytized Rieslings, closely followed by those from Australia, are very successful with mango sorbet, which often has a dash of lemon juice, upping the acid to match the wine. ★★ *South African botrytized Riesling*

### Peach Sorbet ♀ *gently flavoured, sweet whites, especially Muscat*

Sweet Muscats are the best flavour, if often too strong, and gentle Moscato d'Asti is best of all. Or try Australian botrytized Riesling or Recioto di Soave. Sweet Muscat and Semillon are not as good, but make pleasant matches, and Lambrusco Rosso is surprisingly good. ★ *Moscato d'Asti*

# MATCHING FOOD TO WINE STYLES

 We have eaten our way through every food and dish in this book. And tasted with each one a tableful of wines wines chosen from the 250 bottles open (at any one time) in our kitchen. In the charming manner of all wine writers and merchants, we then spat them out. This was rarely, we hasten to say, because the combination of any wine with food was unbearably vile. More by way of protection for our livers and brains from the rigours of tasting scores of wines every evening for months – over 28,000 mouthfuls of different wine and food combinations.

Of course, we wouldn't normally go about our eating and drinking in such an obsessive way. You *can* enjoy a good wine that does not relate to the food on your plate, and appreciate both in their own right, without considering the combined effect. But for this book we set out to find the food and wine combinations that *really* work, and that will positively add to your (and our) mealtime pleasure.

This section of the book will lead you simply through all you need to know to make your own choices. What matters is not just the *colour* of the wine, but its taste. In the seach for ideal wine and food partners, you first need to think about the most basic elements in your food and wines (saltiness, sweetness, acidity, bitterness – tannin – and so on) and whether they will match up.

You are probably quite clued up on the food flavours, particularly if you have prepared the meal yourself. Once you've chosen the dish, imagine how it will taste. Is it at all sharp (perhaps from lemon juice, or wine or fruit in a sauce)? Is it at all sweet? (It's easy to forget the natural sweetness of vegetables such as carrots, onions, or courgettes.) Food with even a tiny touch of sweetness needs an echo of that sweetness in the wine, or at least a fruitiness so vibrant that you could mistake it for sweetness. A dry, not-so-fruity wine will taste dull and even less fruity alongside sweetish food. And food with a bite of acidity needs a wine with the right degree of sharpness if it is not to taste flat and dull.

You may not be so well acquainted with the flavours in your wine, however. How fruity is it? How intensely flavoured? How acidic? These are all essential guides to a wine's food-partnering potential. What you are after is a wine with a 'structure' corresponding to that of the food – the right level of body and intensity of flavour, the right acidity, sweetness and fruit, and, in the case of red wines, an appropriate amount of tannin (the bitterness that comes from the red grape skins – a positive attribute for red wines if not present in excess, see page 220).

Most wines with the right basic 'structure' for a particular type of food will go adequately to well with it, neither overpowering the flavour of the food, nor being overpowered themselves. If you were served them at a dinner party you probably wouldn't give the matter a second thought. But at this point, for the perfectionist – at home or with a restaurant wine list in hand – comes the chance for fine tuning, for finding a wine with the right 'structure' and the specific flavour that chimes in beautifully with the flavour of the food.

Three elements are important here: above all the grape variety or varieties from which the wine was made; the climate; and the stamp of the grape-grower and winemaker. The winemaker may have added oak flavour from oak barrels, for example, or introduced 'boiled-sweet'-like flavours in red wines from carbonic maceration (see page 221), or 'buttery' flavours from a second malolactic fermentation (see page 226); and much more.

Twenty years ago, it was much easier to predict how a wine from a certain place would taste. Winemakers made the best of local conditions – climate, traditional local grape varieties – and of the vine-growing and wine-making techniques handed down by their fathers. You could be pretty sure that a red wine made in a hot climate – southern France or Australia, for example – from super-ripe fruit would be big, dark and alcoholic, with low acidity. A red wine made in a cool climate like New Zealand would be thin and pale, with tart acidity from the under-ripe fruit.

It's no longer so clear-cut. Modern technology and know-how has swept through much of the wine-making world, and can compensate for local shortcomings. A maker of red wines in the hot south of France can analyse his grapes and pick them when they are just ripe – and fast, because he does it by machine. He's probably heaved out his father's vines and planted something fashionably flavourful, such as Syrah or Cabernet. And he has learnt at college how to improve on his father's old ways in the cellar. He might even add a little acidity before he ferments. His New Zealand counterpart, meanwhile, has learnt to train his vines in such a way that the maximum sunlight is used for ripening, with the result that New Zealand reds can nowadays be rich and ripe.

But even if the contrasts from region to region and country to country are less stark than they used to be, climate is still a good starting point when guessing how a wine might taste. That New Zealand red will never be *as* rich and ripe as the one from the south of France. And grape variety is a major clue. Cabernet Sauvignon may taste mintier in Australia, more blackcurranty in Bulgaria and grassier in New Zealand, but the fundamental flavour and character of the grape variety still peeps or bulges out from whatever local form the climate, vine-grower and winemaker have imposed upon it.

This chapter helps you to recognize and understand the aspects of a wine's structure, and how they matter when matching wine with food. It should also arm you with clues as you face the wine shelf or wine list, and help you to pick out from a world of wine *the* one with the flavour and structural characteristics to achieve that perfect partnership.

## Fruitiness

'Simply bursting with fruit,' chorus the wine-writers; 'packed with ripe blackcurrants, strawberry, black cherry, greengages and a tiny hint of grapefruit and lemon.' We may not all be so verbose, but if given a choice of two wines, most of us would pick the fruitier one.

Fruit is synonymous with good, modern wine-making, and any young wine should be fruity. If not, something has gone wrong. Grapes picked at their ideal point of ripeness, neither too early nor too late, have the greatest potential fruit. Ferment that grape-juice into wine, and you should have a fruity wine, though the flavours will not longer be grapy, having changed in the fermentation. Of course, some grape varieties make fruitier wines than others. There's only a certain amount of fruit that even a wizard winemaker can extract from the Italian Trebbiano, for example, or Spain's Airén and Macabeo, or the Melon grape of the Muscadet region.

If you are drinking wine on its own, as an aperitif, say, or at a party, the more fruit the better. But *masses* of bright, modern fruit is not always ideal when drinking wine with food. Plain fish or chicken, for example, do not generally make a good match with vibrantly fruity wines. Low-fruit Italian wines, such as Frascati or Soave, many of which do not shine alone, are often brilliant with fish.

As wines age, the fruit gradually mellows and fades – this may take one year or 20 years, depending on the grape variety, its origin, and how the wine was made. The mellower fruit of a more mature wine often blends better with subtly flavoured food than those explosive fruit cocktails of the young guns.

Where super-ripe fruit, with its apparent sweet note, is a really *positive* asset, however, is with savoury food that contains a hint or more of sweetness. A medium-dry or medium-sweet wine is a perfect choice to accompany pork served with prunes and cream. But if you really prefer to drink a dry wine at this stage in a meal, an exceptionally fruity wine will also hit the spot.

### VERY FRUITY WHITES
**Dry**

AUSTRALIA Most South Australian and New South Wales *Chardonnay*.
FRANCE Condrieu, *Viognier* Vins de Pays.
NEW ZEALAND *Sauvignon Blanc*.

**Sweet**

AUSTRALIA Rutherglen *Muscats*.
CANADA Ice wine.
FRANCE Bordeaux: Cadillac, Cérons, Graves Supérieures, Loupiac, Monbazillac, Sauternes and Barsac, Ste Croix du Mont; fortified *Muscats*.

### FAIRLY FRUITY WHITES
**Dry**

ARGENTINA *Torrontes*.
AUSTRALIA Western Australian and Tasmanian *Chardonnay, Marsanne, Sauvignon Blanc, Chenin Blanc* and *Riesling*.
CHILE *Chardonnay* and *Sauvignon Blanc*.
ENGLAND *Ortega* and *Schönburger*.
FRANCE Alsace *Gewürztraminer*, dry white Bordeaux, expensive white Burgundy, Loire: Pouilly-Fumé, Sancerre, Sauvignon de Touraine.
GERMANY Dry wines.
HUNGARY White wines.
PORTUGAL Vinho Verde labelled *Loureiro, Trajadura* or *Alvarinho*.
NEW ZEALAND Most *Chardonnay, Chenin Blanc* and *Riesling*.
SOUTH AFRICA *Chardonnay, Sauvignon Blanc, Chenin Blanc (Steen)* and *Colombard*.
USA California *Chardonnay* and

*Sauvignon Blanc.*
Sweet
FRANCE Loire: Bonnezeaux,
Chaume, Quarts de Chaume,
Coteaux du Layon.
GERMANY Most medium-dry
and sweet whites.
**LOW FRUIT WHITES**
FRANCE Basic Burgundy,
Chablis, Champagne, Loire:
Anjou Blanc, *Gros Plant*,
Muscadet, Savennières,
Vouvray; Rhône: basic white
Côtes du Rhône, Crozes-
Hermitage, Châteauneuf-
du-Pape; most southern
French whites.
Most AUSTRIAN, BULGARIAN,
ENGLISH, ITALIAN,
PORTUGUESE, ROMANIAN,
SPANISH and SWISS whites.
**VERY FRUITY REDS**
*(Wines not made by carbonic
maceration – see page 221)*
AUSTRALIA *Shiraz, Merlot,*
Coonawarra and Maclaren Vale
*Cabernet Sauvignon.*
ITALY Teroldego Rotaliano,
*Dolcetto.*
*(Wines made by carbonic
maceration – see page 221)*
FRANCE Beaujolais: Beaujolais,
Beaujolais Villages, some
Beaujolais crus – Brouilly,
Chénas, Chiroubles, Côte de
Brouilly, Fleurie, Juliénas,
Regnié; some Côtes du Rhône.
**FAIRLY FRUITY REDS**
ARGENTINIA Most reds.
AUSTRALIA Most *Cabernet
Sauvignon, Pinot Noir* and
*Grenache.*
BULGARIA *Cabernet Sauvignon*
and *Merlot.*

CHILE *Cabernet Sauvignon*
and *Merlot.*
FRANCE Burgundy, some
Beaujolais crus – Morgon,
Moulin-à-Vent, St-Amour; Côtes
du Frontonnais, Loire:
Bourgueil, Chinon, St-Nicolas-
de-Bourgueil, Saumur-
Champigny; Rhône: Côte Rôtie,
Crozes-Hermitage, Hermitage,
St-Joseph.
ITALY Bardolino,
*Montepulciano*, Rosso Conero,
Valpolicella.
NEW ZEALAND *Merlot,
Pinot Noir* and *Cabernet
Sauvignon.*
OREGON *Pinot Noir* and
*Zinfandel.*
PORTUGAL Most Alentejo,
Bairrada, Douro, Oeste and
Ribatejo reds.
ROMANIA *Cabernet Sauvignon*
and *Merlot.*
SOUTH AFRICA *Merlot, Pinot
Noir* and *Pinotage.*
SPAIN Some modern-style
*Tempranillo* and *Cencibel* wines.
USA: California *Cabernet
Sauvignon, Pinot Noir,
Zinfandel* and *Merlot.*
**LOW-FRUIT REDS**
FRANCE Bordeaux,
Châteauneuf-du-Pape, some
Côtes du Rhône, most southern
French reds.
Most GERMAN and ITALIAN
reds.
PORTUGAL Algarve, Colares,
most Dão reds.
Most SPANISH reds.
SOUTH AFRICA *Cabernet
Sauvignon.*
USA California *Petite Syrah.*

# Aroma

Some wines have a fragrance that leaps from the glass. Some smell of very little. 'So what?' you might ask, 'we're talking about eating and drinking, not sniffing.' But think how much less you can *taste* when you have a cold and your sense of smell is out of action. Our mouths and tongues can sense only a small range of basic 'structural' tastes – sweetness, acidity, bitterness and saltiness. They also react to oiliness, metallic sensations and register 'pain' in reaction to the burn of chilli peppers or alcohol. All the subtleties of the food we taste are in fact detected by our nose as the food vapours waft up the passage from the back of the mouth to the nose. Aroma, then, refers not only to the smell, but to all the flavours in a food that the tongue cannot pick up.

All those wine-writers' tasting notes (blackcurrant, tarry, apricotty, petrolly, lemony, flowery, grassy, farm-yardy, even 'wet dog') are in fact aromas, vapours, 'tasted' by the nose. And the comparisons with the smells and tastes of foods and other things are not just figments of an over-active imagination. Green peppers and blackcurrants can be shown to contain some of the same volatile, aromatic compounds as Cabernet Sauvignon, for instance, and the Chinese fruit, lychee, contains some of the same chemical compounds as the Gewürztraminer grape.

A wine's particular aroma, and how strong that aroma is, depends first on the grape variety, and then on how and where the grapes were grown, and how the wine was made. Some grape varieties, such as Gewürztraminer or Muscat, are highly aromatic, while others (particularly some whites), such as the Italian Trebbiano or the Spanish Airén, have hardly any aroma at all. Modern wine-making methods can imprint a little aroma on to the blandest of wines: usually a peardroppy, appley aroma from cool, temperature-controlled fermentation. Fruity reds for drinking young can be given a great burst of juicy fruit aroma by carefully keeping the grapes whole and allowing the juice to ferment inside each individual grape. Traditional variations of this method – known as 'carbonic maceration' – are practised in the Beaujolais region and at some wineries in Rioja.

A wine's individual cocktail of aromatic flavours is very important in determining how well it will go with a certain food or dish. Wines with a lot of aromatic character over-power delicately flavoured foods. It's no use serving a Gewürztraminer or a New Zealand Sauvignon Blanc with a delicately flavoured fish if you want to taste the fish. Equally, flavourful food overwhelms wines that lack aroma. That is simple enough.

What is not so easy is matching the specific aromatic flavour of a wine to the particular flavour of a dish to find the perfect wine and food partnership. This is why we ended up tasting every dish mentioned in this book (see pages 6–203) – just to be sure.

Grape variety is obviously the biggest clue of all to find-ing the right wine (see *Grape Varieties*, page 231), and wines made with the same grape variety share a similar blend of aromas. So, once you have worked out the best choice of grape – whether aromatic or bland – to match your chosen dish, you can predict that if, for example, a Burgundian Chardonnay tastes delicious with baked monkfish, so might a California or an Italian Chardonnay.

## VERY AROMATIC WHITES

ARGENTINA *Torrontes*.

CHILE Casablanca *Sauvignon Blanc*.

ENGLAND *Ortega, Schönburger*.

FRANCE Condrieu, *Viognier* Vins de Pays.

GERMANY *Ortega, Riesling, Schönburger*.

ITALY Alto Adige/Südtirol *Rosenmuskateller* and *Goldmuskateller*, Asti Spumante.

NEW ZEALAND Marlborough *Sauvignon Blanc*.

PORTUGAL Vinho Verde labelled *Alvarinho, Loureiro* or *Trajadura*.

SPAIN *Albariño*.

USA Washington State and Finger Lakes *Riesling*.

EVERYWHERE *Gewürztraminer, Viognier* and dry and sweet *Muscat*.

## QUITE AROMATIC WHITES

AUSTRALIA *Riesling*.

CANADA Ice wine.

ENGLAND Most whites.

FRANCE Alsace *Riesling*, white Bordeaux, Loire: Sancerre, Pouilly-Fumé, Sauvignon de Touraine.

GERMANY *Riesling, Müller-Thurgau* and *Scheurebe*.

ITALY *Arneis, Favorita*.

NEW ZEALAND Most *Sauvignon Blanc* and *Riesling*.

PORTUGAL *Treixadura*.

SOUTH AFRICA *Riesling*, Durbanville and Constantia *Sauvignon Blanc*.

SPAIN *Godello, Torrontes*.

USA California *Riesling*.

## UNAROMATIC WHITES

AUSTRALIA Most *Chenin Blanc, Sauvignon Blanc,* and *Semillon*.

FRANCE Alsace *Pinot Blanc, Sylvaner* and *Tokay-Pinot Gris*,

Burgundy, Champagne, Châteauneuf-du-Pape, Côtes du Rhône, Loire: Anjou and Saumur Blanc, Muscadet; most southern French whites.
GERMANY *Silvaner* and *Ruländer*.
SOUTH AFRICA *Chenin Blanc, Colombard* and most *Sauvignon Blancs*.
EVERYWHERE *Chardonnay*.

**BLAND WHITES**
FRANCE Bordeaux Blanc, *Gros Plant*, Muscadet.
Most whites from AUSTRIA, BULGARIA, CYPRUS, GREECE, HUNGARY, ITALY, PORTUGAL, ROMANIA, SPAIN, and SWITZERLAND.

**AROMATIC REDS**
AUSTRALIA *Shiraz*.
FRANCE Beaujolais: Beaujolais, Beaujolais Villages, Beaujolais crus (Brouilly, Chénas, Chiroubles, Côte de Brouilly, Fleurie, Juliénas, Morgon, Moulin-à-Vent, Regnié, St-Amour); Gamay de l'Ardêche,

Gamay de Touraine, *Syrah*.
ITALY *Dolcetto*.
USA Young *Zinfandel*.
EVERYWHERE *Wines made by carbonic maceration (see page 209).*

**FAIRLY AROMATIC REDS**
AUSTRALIA *Pinot Noir* from the Adelaide Hills, Eden Valley and Tasmania.
FRANCE Alsace *Pinot Noir*, red Burgundy, modern Côtes du Rhône, Loire: Bourgueil, Chinon, St-Nicolas-de-Bourgueil; Lubéron, Roussillon.
SOUTH AFRICA *Pinotage*.
SPAIN *Tempranillo/Cencibel*.
EVERYWHERE *Cabernet Sauvignon* and *Cabernet Franc*.

**FAIRLY BLAND REDS**
FRANCE Inexpensive Bordeaux and Burgundy, much northern and southern Rhône, most southern French reds.
Most reds from CYPRUS, EASTERN EUROPE, GERMANY, GREECE, ITALY, PORTUGAL, SOUTH AFRICA and SPAIN.

# Body

A big, fat California Chardonnay would overwhelm prawns served without a dressing or sauce. A Muscadet Sur Lie would taste thin and feeble beside a roast chicken plumped up with a richly flavoured sage-and-onion stuffing. You need to balance the 'weight' or 'body' of the wine and food. Flavoursome food needs a punchy wine.

And that punch is mainly created by alcohol, recognised by the sensation of fullness in your mouth. (A sip of any de-alcoholised wine will show you just how weedy wines taste without it.) How full a wine will feel depends on the amount of alcohol in it: wines containing under 10.5 per cent alcohol taste light – German wines, for example – and full from about 12.5 per cent alcohol upwards.

How much alcohol a wine contains is determined principally by the ripeness of the grapes when harvested, since it is the grape sugar that is converted to alcohol during fermentation. And the more sunshine there is, the riper the grapes. So hotter countries, such as Chile or Spain, tend to produce wines that are higher in alcohol than those made in more temperate places such as New Zealand or the Loire Valley in France.

Needless to say, it's not quite as clear-cut as that. Hilly or mountainous parts of hot countries are cooler and produce lighter wines. And grape-growers in cooler climates can get richly ripe grapes from vines grown on south-facing slopes that are exposed to the sun all day, or trained on super-modern trellises that let in the maximum sunlight. Growers in hot countries try to pick white grapes early before they become too rich in sugar and potentially over-alcoholic; winemakers in colder regions often add sugar or grape concentrate to boost the alcohol level artificially. But there's still a strong tendency for hotter countries to produce fuller wines, and for cooler countries or regions to produce lighter ones.

Fortified wines are especially full-bodied because they contain a good dose of added alcohol. Some sweet or sweetish wines (such as Asti or German Kabinetts) have low alcohol and light body because not all their sugar was converted to alcohol. Sugar also gives a heavier feeling in the mouth, so the sweeter a wine is, the fuller it will tend to feel and taste. To a certain extent, the weight of the sugar counter-balances the lightness of alcohol of a fine German wine.

## FULL WHITES

AUSTRALIA, CHILE and USA: California (except for 'jug' or mass-produced wines) most medium to expensive whites. FRANCE Expensive Alsace *Tokay-Pinot Gris* and *Gewürztraminer*, very expensive white Bordeaux, and very sweet wines such as expensive Sauternes or Barsac, very expensive white Burgundy, white Châteauneuf-du-Pape, white Côtes du Rhône, Condrieu. GREECE Most whites. SPAIN Expensive, oaked white Rioja. *Chardonnays* from all but the coolest spots of ARGENTINA, AUSTRALIA, BULGARIA, CHILE, ITALY, MEXICO, PORTUGAL, SOUTH AFRICA, SPAIN, USA: California. Sweet fortified *Muscats* from AUSTRALIA, southern FRANCE, GREECE, SPAIN.

## MEDIUM-BODIED WHITES

AUSTRALIA Most whites from Western Australia, Tasmania.

AUSTRIA Most whites.

FRANCE Moderately priced Alsace, Bordeaux: Bordeaux Blanc, sweet wines such as inexpensive Graves Supérieures, Monbazillac, Sauternes, Ste-Croix-du-Mont; moderately priced white Burgundies and *Aligoté*, Loire: Anjou Blanc, Pouilly-Fumé, Sancerre, Sauvignon de Touraine, sweet, inexpensive Coteaux du Layon; Provençal whites, many *vins de pays* from the southern half of France.

HUNGARY Most whites.

ITALY Most whites other than Chardonnays.

PORTUGAL and ROMANIA Most whites.

SPAIN Most whites except for the most expensive.

USA California *Gewürztraminer, Sauvignon Blanc, Riesling, Chenin Blanc*. New York State *Chardonnay*. Washington State *Chardonnay, Semillon, White Zinfandel*. Inexpensive wines from ARGENTINA, CHILE and SOUTH AFRICA.

## LIGHT WHITES

FRANCE Muscadet, inexpensive *vins de pays* from the northern half of France, VdP des Côtes de Gascogne.

GERMANY Most are fairly light but *Kabinett* wines are especially light, particularly those from Mosel-Saar-Ruwer.

ITALY Asti.

PORTUGAL Vinho Verde.

SPAIN Ribeiro, Valdeorras. Most whites from ENGLAND, LUXEMBOURG, SWITZERLAND.

EVERYWHERE De-alcoholised wines.

## FULL REDS

AUSTRALIA Barossa *Grenache* and expensive *Shiraz*.

FRANCE Very expensive Bordeaux, Rhône: Châteauneuf-du-Pape, Cornas, Côte Rôtie, Hermitage.

ITALY Amarone della Valpolicella, Barbaresco, Barolo, Brunello di Montalcino.

SPAIN Priorato.

USA Most expensive *Zinfandels;* California Amador County *Zinfandel*.

## MEDIUM-WEIGHT REDS

AUSTRALIA Most reds.

CALIFORNIA *Cabernet, Merlot, Pinot Noir* and *Petite Syrah*.

FRANCE Most Bordeaux, most Burgundy, some Beaujolais crus – Morgon, Moulin-à-Vent, St-Amour; Loire: Bourgueil, Chinon, St-Nicolas-de-Bourgueil, Saumur-Champigny; Rhône: some Côtes du Rhône, Crozes-Hermitage, St-Joseph; most southern French reds.

ITALY *Barbera*, Chianti Riserva, *Dolcetto, Lagrein Dunkel, Montepulciano* d'Abruzzo, Torgiano, most middle to southern Italian reds.

LEBANON Château Musar.

NEW ZEALAND *Cabernet Sauvignon, Merlot* and *Pinot Noir*.

Most reds from PORTUGAL and SPAIN.

Reds from ALGERIA, CHILE, CYPRUS, EASTERN EUROPE, GREECE, and SOUTH AFRICA.
LIGHT REDS
FRANCE Alsace *Pinot Noir*, Beaujolais: Beaujolais, Beaujolais-Villages, some crus – Brouilly, Chénas, Chiroubles, Côte de Brouilly, Fleurie, Juliénas, Regnié; Loire: Anjou Rouge, Cabernet Rouge d'Anjou, Sancerre Rouge; most Côtes du Frontonnais, some Côtes du Rhône.
GERMANY Reds.
ITALY Many central northern and north-eastern reds, such as Lago di Caldaro, Bardolino, Valpolicella.
SWITZERLAND Reds.

# Dryness and Sweetness

With puddings and desserts, your task is wickedly simple: find a wine that is as sweet as the food. It can even be slightly sweeter. Wines with less sweetness than the food will lose their attraction, tasting dull or dry. (Sweet wines tend to be expensive, so it's better to err on the sweeter side and make sure you can really taste them!) But beware super-sweet wines – they can overpower a pudding that is not as sweet and leave you with an unimpressive match.

It's not only in really sweet foods and out-and-out dessert wines that sugar plays a part in our diet, however. Many vegetables have a sweetness of their own – think of new potatoes, courgettes, carrots, tomatoes, onions. Dishes such as soups or casseroles that are heavily influenced by 'sweet' vegetables often go well with a wine that has its own touch of sweetness – such as an Australian Riesling, a South African Chenin Blanc, or a Vinho Verde, slightly sweetened as it often is for export markets. Savoury foods cooked with fruit – raisins, orange, apple, apricot, prunes and the like – also call for a corresponding sweetness in the wine. A really ripe, fruity wine can fulfil the same role. Australian, California or Chilean wines, both white and red, often have this 'sweet' quality of fruit but are in fact completely dry.

Cheese also has a surprising affinity for sweet, medium or medium-dry white wines (after all, port is sweet). The saltier the cheese, the better the match. Sauternes, for instance, makes the most delicious combination with Roquefort – much better than any red wine. Slightly sweet English and German wines go quite well with lots of cheeses. Wines that are sweet because of the effects of botrytis (*see below*) have a special affinity with cheese because of the pungent tang of the botrytis. Liver (including *foie gras* and its pâté) is the other savoury food that makes a surprisingly good match with sweet wine.

There are no easy geographic clues to the degree of sweetness in white wines. Hotter climates, where grapes normally ripen more fully, stand a better chance of making very sweet wines naturally, but some intensely sweet wines are made in good, hot vintages in the generally coolish climates of Germany and the Loire Valley in France. Even super-cool England made some impressively sweet wines after the hot summers of 1989 and 1990. The most helpful guide is the information given on the bottle label.

Words to look for on **French** labels are *moelleux* and *doux,* both meaning 'sweet'; *demi-sec,* meaning 'medium' or 'medium-dry'; and *sec* ('dry'). In Alsace, *Sélection de Grains Nobles* ('very sweet') and *Vendange Tardive* ('late harvest') are often, in practice, 'sweetish', though confusingly some Alsace *Vendange Tardive* wines are dry, because they have been left to ferment for longer until all or nearly all the sugar has turned to alcohol. Champagne has other variations, with the driest wines labelled *ultra-brut, brut zero* or *brut sauvage*. *Brut,* on its own, can mean anything from 'completely dry' to just 'off-dry', while *sec* is definitely sweetish. Sweet Champagnes are sometimes labelled *demi-sec* or *riche*. *Botrytis* indicates 'sweet' or 'very sweet' (and usually very fine) wines. (Botrytis is the Latin name for 'noble rot'. It is a fungus that thrives on hot, misty autumnal mornings; it sucks out moisture from the grapes, concentrates sugar and acidity, and adds an attractive, pungent tang of its own.)

In **English**-speaking countries, 'late harvest' means anything from 'fairly sweet' to 'very sweet'.

In **Germany**, *Trocken* means 'dry' and *Halbtrocken* 'medium-dry'. Without either of these clues on the label, a basic *Qualitätswein bestimmtes Anbaugebiet* (QbA) – including all the ubiquitous Niersteiners, Piesporters and Liebfraumilchs – can be assumed to be medium to medium-dry. *Landwein* is a type of table wine (*Tafelwein*) that is always dry or medium-dry. *Kabinett* wines tend to have just a touch of sweetness, *Spätlese* implies a very obvious sweetness but not enough for any pudding or dessert, and *Auslese* enough sugar to accompany a dish such as unsweetened raspberries. *Beerenauslese* is quite definitely sweet, and a good match for many puddings. *Trocken-*

*beerenauslese* is 'super-sweet', and *Eiswein* (harvested in early winter, while the grapes are frozen) is a super-sweet wine with especially zingy acidity.

**Austria** uses the same classifications, but you can add on a few notches more of sugar: an Austrian *Beerenauslese*, for example, tends to be slightly sweeter than a German one. Austria has one additional level of sweetness, called *Ausbruch*, tucked in between *Beerenauslese* and *Trocken-beerenauslese*. Both Germany and Austria produce a lot of dry wines at a basic level: wine you buy by the glass in either country will tend to be dry.

In **Italy**, *abboccato* means 'medium dry'; *amabile*, 'medium' or 'medium-sweet'; *dolce* indicates 'sweet'; *secco*, 'dry'; *vin santo* or *vino santo* may be a dry or sweet wine. In **Spain**, *dulce* is 'sweet', *seco* 'dry', *semi-dulce* 'quite sweet', *semi-seco* 'medium' and *abocado* 'medium-dry'. In **Portugal**, *doce* means 'sweet', *seco* 'dry'. Wines made from the Muscat grape (Moscatel in Spain and Portugal, Moscato in Italy) tend to be very sweet, but beware – there are some bone-dry ones.

Most red wines are dry. It's usually only with fortified wines, such as port, that you find sweetness. But there are a few exceptions, such as Recioto della Valpolicella, made from super-ripe grapes near Verona, in Italy, (Amarone della Valpolicella, however, is dry and *very* alcoholic). As with white wines, some reds made in hot places, such as Australia and California, give the impression of sweetness through the ripeness of their fruit flavour although they are in fact bone-dry.

### DRY WHITES AND ROSÉS

FRANCE Alsace (except for Vendange Tardive and Sélection de Grains Nobles wines), Bergerac Sec, Bordeaux Blanc Sec, all white Burgundy (Meursault, Beaujolais Blanc, Chablis, Mâcon, etc), Champagne Brut, white Châteauneuf-du-Pape, white Côtes du Rhône, Condrieu, Jurançon Sec, Loire: Anjou Blanc Sec, *Gros Plant*, Menetou-Salon, Muscadet, Pouilly-Fumé, Sancerre, *Sauvignon* du Haut-Poitou, *Sauvignon* de Touraine; most white vins de pays (unless the label says 'medium-dry'), anything that says 'blanc sec', Bordeaux rosé, Tavel rosé.
GERMANY Trocken wines, Landwein.
GREECE All whites and rosés.
HUNGARY Tokaji Szamorodni.
ITALY Alto Adige whites, Bianco di Custoza, *Chardonnay*, Est! Est!! Est!!!, Frascati, Gavi, *Malvasia, Pinot Grigio, Pinot*

*Bianco*, *Prosecco*, Soave, *Trebbiano*, Tocai, *Verdicchio*, *Verduzzo*, *Vernaccia*, and most other whites that do not specify sweetness (see below).

LUXEMBOURG All whites.

PORTUGAL Bairrada Branco, Dão Branco, Douro Branco, Vinho Verde as sold in Portugal, selected (usually more expensive) exported Vinho Verde (most are sweetenened up for 'foreign' tastes), most other white wines unless they come in bulbous Mateus-type bottles.

SPAIN All white and *rosado* table wines except the few marked 'dulce' or 'semi-seco', fino and Manzanilla sherries as sold in Spain (sometimes they're sweetened up for export markets), Amontillado seco and Oloroso seco sherries. *Chardonnay, Marsanne, Sauvignon Blanc, Verdelho, Viognier* from AUSTRIA, AUSTRALIA, CANADA, CHILE, HUNGARY, NEW ZEALAND, SOUTH AFRICA, USA: California, Oregon, Washington State.

## MEDIUM-DRY WHITES

AUSTRIA and GERMANY Halbtrocken, Kabinett, Landwein.

FRANCE Champagne Demi-sec, Vouvray Demi-sec.

SOUTH AFRICA Inexpensive *Chenin Blanc*.

## MEDIUM WHITES

FRANCE Champagne Demi-sec, Anjou Rosé.

GERMANY QmP Spätlese and all QbA wines such as Liebfraumilch, Piesporter Michelsberg, etc, except those marked 'Trocken' or 'Halbtrocken'.

HUNGARY Tokaji Aszú 3 Puttonyos.

ITALY Orvieto Abboccato.

PORTUGAL Most white ports, *Verdelho*, Madeira, Mateus and other commercial rosés.

SPAIN Medium Amontillado sherry.

## FAIRLY SWEET WHITES

AUSTRIA Spätlese and Auslese.

ENGLAND Late-harvest wines.

FRANCE Alsace Vendange Tardive, Jurançon Moelleux.

GERMANY Auslese.

HUNGARY Tokaji Aszú 4 Puttonyos.

ITALY Marsala, Recioto di Soave, Vin Santo.

PORTUGAL Bual Madeira.

AUSTRALIA, CANADA, NEW ZEALAND, SOUTH AFRICA, USA Late-harvest *Riesling, Chenin Blanc* and *Semillon*.

## VERY SWEET WHITES

AUSTRIA Ausbruch, Beerenauslese, Eiswein, Trockenbeerenauslese.

FRANCE Alsace Sélection de Grains Nobles, Bordeaux and surrounds: Cadillac, Cérons, Loupiac, Monbazillac, Premières Côtes de Bordeaux, Sauternes and Barsac, Ste Croix-du-Mont; Loire: Bonnezeaux, Coteaux du Layon, Montlouis Moelleux, Quarts de Chaume, Vouvray Moelleux; Rhône: Vin de Paille; Muscat de Beaumes de Venise, Muscat de Frontignan, Muscat de Lunel, Muscat de Rivesaltes, Muscat de St-Jean du Minervois.

GERMANY Beerenauslese, Eiswein, Trockenbeerenauslese.

GREECE *Muscats* from Samos, Limnos and Patras.

HUNGARY Tokaji Aszú 5 Puttonyos and above.

PORTUGAL Moscatel de Setúbal, Malmsey Madeira.

ROMANIA Cotnari, *Tamaiioasa*.

SPAIN Cream and Oloroso sherry, Málaga, Moscatel de Valencia.

AUSTRALIA, CANADA, NEW ZEALAND, SOUTH AFRICA and USA Late harvest *Riesling, Chenin Blanc* and *Semillon*.

BOTRYTIZED WINES

AUSTRIA Ausbruch, Beerenauslese, Trockenbeerenauslese.

FRANCE Alsace Sélection de Grains Nobles, Bordeaux and surrounds: Cadillac, Cérons, Graves Supérieures, Loupiac, Monbazillac, Premières Côtes de Bordeaux, Sauternes and Barsac, Ste Croix-du-Mont; Loire: Bonnezeaux, Coteaux de l'Aubance, Coteaux du Layon, Montlouis Moelleux, Quarts de Chaume, Vouvray Moelleux.

GERMANY Beerenauslese, Trockenbeerenauslese.

HUNGARY Tokaji Aszú 5 Puttonyos and above.

ITALY *Muffa nobile* wines.

ROMANIA Cotnari, *Tamaiioasa*.

AUSTRALIA, CANADA, NEW ZEALAND, SOUTH AFRICA and USA Botrytized *Riesling*, *Chenin Blanc* and *Semillon*.

SWEET RED WINES

FRANCE Banyuls and other southern French fortified *Grenaches*.

GREECE Mavrodaphne of Patras.

ITALY Recioto della Valpolicella.

PORTUGAL Port.

# Acidity

Suck a lemon. Bite into a gooseberry. That sourness is acidity. For something to have acidity is not necessarily a bad thing. All fruits contain acidity, though it may not be mouth-puckeringly obvious. Natural grape acidity is vital to all wine styles, especially to whites – dry and sweet – and rosés, but is important for reds as well.

In the right proportions, acidity gives wine its tang, bite, freshness, and crispness. In excess, it can make wine taste tart, aggressive and sour, but too little leaves a wine flat, flabby and boring. However, just as it's easier to eat a bowlful of otherwise too-tart gooseberries or blackcurrants if they are well-laced with sugar, so too does sweetness in a wine help to counterbalance the acidity.

When the food itself contains some acidity – maybe in the form of fruit, or lemon juice, vinegar, or wine or cider used in the cooking, acidity in the wine becomes vitally important. You need to try to match the two. High-acid foods, such as taramasalata, duckling with orange sauce, a dressed salad or a lemon tart, need accompanying wines with a good tang of matching acidity. Wines with medium or low acidity will taste dull even if they are delicious when served alone

So how do you find a wine with the required acidity? Not so many years ago you could safely apply logic to the question. As fruit ripens and gets sweeter, it gradually loses acidity; so wines grown in hot climates were low in acidity, while those from cool climates were much more tangy. Although it's still a helpful guide, the edges of this theory have been blurred as modern grape-growing and wine-making practices spread across the wine-making world.

Many winemakers in hot countries now pick their grapes early while the grapes still have good acidity, or they add acid to the fermenting juice. Hot-country vineyards planted at high altitudes in any case produce grapes with higher acidity than those nearer to sea level. Cool-climate vines with the good fortune to be planted on slopes exposed to the sun, and/or on modern trellises, become riper and less tart than those grown on flat ground. Winemakers in cooler countries, such as New Zealand or England, are legally permitted to de-acidify their grape juice with additives.

Acidity also varies from vintage to vintage – low in hot years, high in cooler years. Grape varieties ripen in different ways, too, some retaining much more acidity than others under the same climatic conditions. Good acid retainers include white Rhine Riesling, Chenin Blanc, Colombard, Ugni Blanc, and the red Carignan.

## DRY WHITES WITH HIGH ACIDITY

ENGLAND.

FRANCE Alsace: Crémant d'Alsace, *Riesling*, Champagne; Loire: Cheverny, *Gros Plant*, Muscadet, sparkling Saumur, Vouvray (still and sparkling).

GERMANY Mosel-Saar-Ruwer *Riesling*.

LUXEMBOURG.

PORTUGAL Vinho Verde.

## SWEET WINES WITH HIGH ACIDITY

FRANCE Vouvray

GERMANY All Eiswein, Mosel-Saar-Ruwer *Riesling*.

## DRY WHITES WITH FAIRLY HIGH ACIDITY

AUSTRIA *Grüner Veltliner*.

CANADA.

FRANCE Burgundy: *Aligoté*, Chablis; Loire: Anjou Blanc, Pouilly-Fumé, Sancerre,

*Sauvignon* de Touraine; Savoie, VdP des Côtes de Gascogne, VdP du Jardin de la France.

GERMANY Rheinhessen, Rheingau, and Pfalz *Rieslings*.

ITALY Alto Adige, Bianco di Custoza, Soave, *Trebbiano*.

NEW ZEALAND Marlborough *Chardonnay, Riesling, Sauvignon Blanc*.

SPAIN Galicia, Rueda.

**SWEET WHITES WITH FAIRLY HIGH ACIDITY**

FRANCE Bonnezeaux, Coteaux du Layon, Quarts de Chaume.

GERMANY Rheingau, Rheinhessen and Pfalz *Rieslings*.

NEW ZEALAND *Riesling*.

**DRY WHITES WITH MEDIUM ACIDITY**

FRANCE Alsace: *Gewürztraminer, Muscat, Pinot Blanc*, and *Sylvaner*; Blanquette de Limoux; Bordeaux Blanc, Jurançon, white Burgundy other than *Aligoté* and Chablis.

GERMANY Baden, Franken, *Müller-Thurgau*.

ITALY Frascati.

SPAIN Penedés, Rioja.

AUSTRALIA, CHILE, SOUTH AFRICA and USA: California *Chardonnays*.

**SWEET WHITES WITH MEDIUM ACIDITY**

FRANCE Clairette de Die, Sauternes and Barsac, Monbazillac.

ITALY Asti Spumante.

**WHITES WITH LOW ACIDITY**

BULGARIA.

EASTERN MEDITERRANEAN.

FRANCE Rhône.

GREECE.

NORTH AFRICA.

SPAIN La Mancha, Valencia, Valdepeñas and the rest of the south.

**REDS WITH HIGHER THAN USUAL ACIDITY**

ENGLAND Reds.

FRANCE Loire: Anjou Rouge, Bourgueil, Chinon, St-Nicolas-de-Bourgueil, Saumur-Champigny; Champagne: Ambonnay, Bouzy Rouge.

GERMANY *Dornfelder*.

ITALY *Barbera, Dolcetto*.

PORTUGAL Red Vinho Verde.

# Tannin

Remember the bitter, mouth-furring shock when you accidentally bite on a grape pip? Or the astringent, mouth-puckering taste of the skin of certain table grape varieties? That's tannin. You will also find it in many red wines.

The main reason for its presence is that the tannic grape skins are in fact the source of colour. When making red wines, the skins and pips are left to soak in the fermenting juice for days (sometimes for weeks) until a sufficient depth of red colour has been extracted. White wines are nearly tannin-free as the juice is only in contact with the skins for a very short time. Any noticeable tannin in a white wine can be a sign of clumsy handling or over-rough pressing of the grapes. Rosé wines contain a little tannin from their short stay on the skins to obtain their soft colour.

Tannin is rather like medicine: it may taste disagreeable at first, but it can do red wine a power of good. It not only gives them a firmer taste, but more importantly it is a vital preservative. Red wines that are designed for drinking in five to ten years' time (usually the more expensive ones) are often undrinkably tannic when first made. The tough tannin also masks the wine's fruit.

Winemakers who want super-tannic wines leave in the stalks too – the result is even more bitter. But as the wine ages, and develops interesting, mature flavours, the tannins diminish and soften, and the fruit gradually shines through. Wines – red, rosé and white – can also leach tannins out of oak barrels (see Oak, page 224).

The amount of tannin in a wine also depends on the grape variety. Some are naturally more tannic than others. Cabernet Sauvignon, Syrah, the Nebbiolo of northern Italy and the Baga of Bairrada in Portugal have a lot, for instance, while Gamay (the grape of Beaujolais) has very little. Even the same grape variety planted in different places or from different vintages can be more or less tannic. In dry vintages, when the grapes have remained small due to lack of water, there's a higher ratio of skin and pip to juice, and the wines can be very tannic.

But for inexpensive red wines intended for drinking young, you don't want noticeable tannins. Luckily winemakers have ways and means of getting lots of colour out of their grapes without too much unwanted tannin. They can use the Beaujolais method, known as carbonic maceration, and ferment the juice inside *whole*, unsplit grapes, so avoiding the tannic outer skins; or they can quickly heat the grape/juice mix before fermentation begins; or by various means keep the skins constantly mixed in with the juice, rather than floating, as they naturally tend to do, on top. This helps, because the colour starts to emerge immediately fermentation begins, but the tannins remain locked up for a few days in the skins until there is more alchohol in the juice (alcohol acts as a solvent on tannin).

The softest, fruitiest reds of this type taste good alone, without food. But reds in which the tannin is really noticeable (the majority) will probably taste better and softer with food. Tannin reacts with food in different ways, but, in the main, the higher the tannin content of a red wine, the more difficult it is to match with food. Certain foods are particularly difficult with tannin, and strongly emphasize the tannin in wines in a very unpleasant way. Egg yolks are notorious in this respect, but you will find similar reactions if you serve any red wines (even low-tannin ones) with melted cheese, celery, spinach or black olives.

White meats (chicken, turkey and suchlike) cooked plainly can only cope with low-tannin wines; and the same guide applies to most red meats. A tannic red wine *can* be served successfully with meat – white or red meat – if there is a sauce, especially a red-wine sauce, to bridge the gap between wine and food. Fatty meat (particularly pork fat and cold lamb fat) reacts strongly to tannin as well. Several herbs (cumin, garlic, marjoram, mint, thyme, oregano and rosemary) cope well with tannic reds, but most others heighten tannin's bitter effect.

## TANNIC REDS

FRANCE Expensive red Burgundy, Rhône: expensive Châteauneuf-du-Pape, Cornas, Côte Rôtie, Hermitage; expensive Cahors.

ITALY Barbaresco, Barolo, Brunello di Montalcino.

PORTUGAL Bairrada, Colares, Dão.

USA California expensive *Cabernet Sauvignon*.

EVERYWHERE Most expensive (too-) young reds.

## REDS WITH MEDIUM TANNIN

FRANCE Bordeaux, mid-price Burgundy, some Beaujolais crus – Morgon, Moulin-à-Vent, St-Amour; Rhône: Crozes-Hermitage, St-Joseph, some Côtes du Rhône; Loire: Bourgueil, Chinon, St-Nicolas de Bourgueil, Saumur-Champigny; most southern French reds.

ITALY Amarone della Valpolicella, *Barbera*, Chianti Riserva, *Montepulciano* d'Abruzzo, Torgiano, most southern Italian reds.

SPAIN Priorato, Toro. Most other reds.

Most reds from ARGENTINA, AUSTRALIA, CHILE, CYPRUS, EASTERN EUROPE, GREECE, NEW ZEALAND, SOUTH AFRICA and the USA: California and Oregon.

## LOW-TANNIN REDS

FRANCE Alsace *Pinot Noir*, Beaujolais: Beaujolais, Beaujolais-Villages, some Beaujolais crus – Brouilly, Chénas, Chiroubles, Côte de Brouilly, Fleurie, Juliénas, Regnié; some Côtes du Rhône, most Côtes du Frontonnais.

GERMANY *Pinot Noir*.

ITALY Bardolino, Lago di Caldaro, *Lambrusco*, Valpolicella.

SPAIN Most reds.

# Intensity of Flavour

How well a wine stands up to very flavourful food is not just a matter of body, ie how full or weighty the wine feels in the mouth due to alcohol or sugar (*see Body, page 209*). You need also to consider the intensity of the wine's flavour. Quite light-bodied wines can sometimes be very richly flavoured, while big, heavy wines can be rather subdued. It depends partly on the grape variety – some are more flavoursome than others (*see Grape Varieties, page 231*). But it is also a question of the *quality* of the grapes.

Pampered grapes of a good variety, favoured by the weather, can make wines with stunning intensity of flavour. A really concentrated flavour is a sign of a fine wine – which need not necessarily cost the earth. Such wines often come from vineyards where the grape yield is low, so that all the goodness and ripening powers are poured into a tiny crop. Different methods of training the vines can produce wines of varying intensity.

Good, intense grape flavours can be lost if the grapes are poorly handled or the wine is carelessly made, but good wine-making can enhance the flavour and make it more complex. If the grapes were watery and short on flavour in the first place, there is little a winemaker can do to boost it. Special yeasts and careful wine-making help a little, and using oak can enhance the flavour, though at the risk of swamping the basic taste of the wine itself.

So how do you pick out an intensely flavoured Mosel Kabinett and not a feeble one, or a richly flavoured red Rhône rather than an unremarkable version from the same village? Price may be an indication – intensely flavoured wines can command higher prices. In cooler climates, the better vintages are likely to produce more intense flavours, so a vintage chart will provide some clues (though it is worth bearing in mind that good growers often produce more intense wines in 'poor' years than poor growers in the 'vintage of the century').

The best indicator of intense, concentrated flavours is the name of a grower reputed for painstaking grape-growing and wine-making. However, a list of all the conscientious producers in the world would fill several chapters here. If your dish is very richly flavoured and merits a particularly concentrated wine, look up the region in a reliable reference book, and search out the star producers.

# Oak

Oaky flavour in wine has become very fashionable, but distinctly oaky wines rarely go positively well with food. Oak flavour is rather like make-up. Discreetly applied, it can flatter. Over-done, it doesn't work. Good wine is oak-matured to add complexity to the eventual result, not to leave you with a glassful of strong oak flavours. Powerful oak flavour will fade somewhat with time, but some wines are so very oaky that they never let the flavour of the wine shine through.

Most wine that is to be oak-aged is put into oak barrels after it has finished fermenting. Some wines are actually fermented in oak, which gives a much subtler, more complex set of flavours. How long the wine spends in the barrels – from a few weeks up to two years or more – depends on the style (and ultimate cost) of the wine. Barrels made of new oak are very expensive (and French oak is twice the price of American). For oaked wines to be sold at low prices, winemakers can achieve that oaky flavour more cheaply by suspending oak chips or oak powder (in large 'tea-bags') in the wine. From these or from the insides of oak barrels, the wine leaches flavour and wood tannins. You also often find a savoury, sometimes rather meaty, flavour in oak-aged wines that comes from the gradual exposure of the wine to air during its time in barrel.

Barrels give up a lot of flavour and tannin to the first wine they hold. There is less flavour left in the wood for the next wine, and by the sixth or seventh year the inner surface has nothing left to offer. Italian reds made following traditional methods, such as most Barolo, Barbaresco, Brunello di Montalcino and Chianti, are aged in big, old, barren wooden vats that have no oak flavour left to give.

Winemakers have a choice of oaks, so there is not just one 'oak taste' to recognise. American oak (used a lot in Spain, and occasionally in Australia and the USA) tends to taste strongly of vanilla or sometimes coconut. French oak, from forests in the Vosges, Alliers, Tronçais or Nevers, tends to be subtler, with a gentler vanilla flavour, and sometimes with toasty, smoky notes as well.

You can find oak in some whites or reds from most wine-making countries and regions nowadays. Even in Germany and the Muscadet region, once strictly new-oak free areas, some producers are making smart, fashionable, oaked wines. Certain grape varieties are more likely to be oaked than others: Chardonnay is the commonest white candidate. Many red varieties are often oaked, especially Cabernet Sauvignon and Pinot Noir. Rieslings and Chenin Blancs and light Italian whites are rarely oaked.

It's easier with New World than with European wines to establish without tasting whether, and how much, a wine is oaked. Australians, New Zealanders, North Americans, South Africans and export-minded Chileans and Argentinians all tend to fill their back labels with juicy details of their wine-making, and if they used oak, they will say so. European back labels tend to be more poetic than informative, even if you speak the language, though British supermarket back labels are often more useful. In general, wines that are bottled and sold young for early consumption are less likely to have oak flavours than those that are sold later, or destined to be matured before drinking.

For a meal, we would rarely seek out an overtly oaky wine, but smoky, toasty oak flavours do have a special affinity with smoked meat or fish. A subtle layer of oak doesn't interfere with most foods, but out-and-out oakiness is a killer.

### VERY OAKY WHITES
BULGARIA Reserve *Chardonnay*.
USA California some *Chardonnay*.
FRANCE Bordeaux: expensive Graves and Pessac-Léognan, expensive Sauternes and Barsac.
SPAIN Traditional white Rioja, oaked table wines.

### GENTLY OAKED WHITES
FRANCE Expensive white Burgundy.
ITALY Expensive *Chardonnay*.
Most *Chardonnays* from AUSTRALIA, CHILE, NEW ZEALAND, SOUTH AFRICA and USA: California.

### UNOAKED WHITES
AUSTRALIA Most *Semillon*.
FRANCE Alsace whites, most Bordeaux Blanc, inexpensive white Burgundy, most Chablis, Champagne, Loire whites, white Rhône, southern French whites.
NEW ZEALAND *Sauvignon Blanc* and *Semillon*.
SOUTH AFRICA *Sauvignon Blanc, Chenin Blanc* and *Colombard*.
Most whites from AUSTRIA, EASTERN EUROPE, ENGLAND, GERMANY, ITALY, LUXEMBOURG, PORTUGAL, SPAIN and SWITZERLAND.
EVERYWHERE Most *Riesling*.

### VERY OAKY REDS
AUSTRALIA Expensive *Cabernet Sauvignon* and *Shiraz*.
BULGARIA Reserve reds.
FRANCE Expensive Bordeaux, Rhône: most Hermitage and Côte Rôtie.

ITALY Most expensive Vini da Tavola.

SPAIN Traditional Rioja and Ribera del Duero, oaked table wines.

USA California expensive *Cabernet Sauvignon* and some *Zinfandel*.

### GENTLY OAKED REDS

FRANCE Mid-range Bordeaux, expensive red Burgundy.

PORTUGAL A few modern-style reds.

SPAIN Crianza and Reserva wines from Rioja, Ribera del Duero, Navarra and Penedés.

USA California *Pinot Noir*, most *Cabernet Sauvignon* and *Zinfandel*; Oregon *Pinot Noir*.

Most reds from AUSTRALIA, CHILE, NEW ZEALAND, and SOUTH AFRICA.

### UNOAKED REDS

FRANCE Alsace *Pinot Noir*, basic Bordeaux, inexpensive red Burgundy, Loire reds, most red Rhônes apart from Hermitage and Côte Rôtie, most southern French reds.

GERMANY Most reds.

ITALY Most mid-priced reds.

SPAIN Vino Joven, most La Mancha and Valdepeñas reds.

Most reds from ARGENTINA, CYPRUS, EASTERN EUROPE, GREECE, NORTH AFRICA and PORTUGAL.

Some inexpensive reds from CHILE and SOUTH AFRICA.

# Buttery (Malolactic) Flavours

At some point between the fermentation that converts grape juice into alcoholic wine and the onset of the following summer, many wines go through a second, gentler fermentation. This is known as a 'malolactic fermentation'. Lactic bacteria convert the sharp, appley-tasting malic acid in the wine into much softer lactic acid. The effect of this process on the wine is to soften the acidity and to leave a characteristic buttery, butterscotchy flavour. The butteriness goes unnoticed in the bundle of flavours in a red wine, but it can be an important flavour element – sometimes very strong, sometimes subtle – for whites, particularly Chardonnays.

Once upon a time, before winemakers understood the techniques of wine-making as well as they do now, most wines would have gone through the malolactic fermentation more or less undisturbed. Today, winemakers decide how much of the buttery flavours they want in their white wines, and tweak the wine-making recipe accordingly. They can stop it happening completely by filtering out the lactic bacteria, by stunning the bacteria with sulphur dioxide, or by keeping the wines chilled. But many actively want the softened acidity and the buttery complexity.

White wines made from Riesling, Sauvignon Blanc, Chenin Blanc, and most of the Germanic grapes are rarely put through a malolactic fermentation. Plenty of Chardonnays have the buttery malolactic flavour, but it is hard to tell which without opening the bottle and tasting, or taking advice from a wine merchant or importer.

You are on fairly safe ground with white Burgundy, which almost always goes through a malolactic fermentation, except in the ripest, hottest years when growers want to retain as much as possible of the natural acidity. In Australia, New Zealand, California and South Africa, the top Chardonnays will almost certainly have had some malolactic fermentation, even if only a small part of the blend has gone through the process.

This buttery flavour can be quite an important element in a wine's match or clash with food. Balance is crucial. If the wine is too buttery or strongly butterscotchy, it can ruin the chances of a decent wine and food match. (A lobster served without dressing will be swamped, for instance.) But with creamy, buttery, eggy, or fatty dishes and sauces, the buttery flavour can help bridge the gap between the flavour of a white wine and the food. It also blends deliciously with roast chicken or monkfish fried simply in butter and oil.

**VERY BUTTERY WHITES**
AUSTRALIA, NEW ZEALAND and USA: (California) some expensive *Chardonnays*.

**MODERATELY BUTTERY WHITES**
FRANCE Expensive white Burgundy, most Chablis.
Most *Chardonnays* from AUSTRALIA, NEW ZEALAND, SOUTH AFRICA and USA: California and Oregon.

**LIGHTLY BUTTERY WHITES**
FRANCE Inexpensive white Burgundy, Limoux *Chardonnay*.

Most *Chardonnays* from CHILE.

**WHITES WITHOUT BUTTERY FLAVOUR**
AUSTRALIA *Semillon*.
FRANCE Alsace whites, Bordeaux, most Champagne, Loire whites, white Rhône, most southern French whites.
SOUTH AFRICA *Chenin Blanc* and *Colombard*.
Most whites from GERMANY, ITALY and SPAIN.
Whites from AUSTRIA, ENGLAND, EASTERN EUROPE, PORTUGAL and SWITZERLAND.

# Age and Maturity

Not all wines age gracefully. Most cheaper whites, made for early drinking, are distinctly wrinkly by the end of their first year. Inexpensive reds may last a year or two longer, especially if they have the preserving benefit of some tannin. The bright, fresh, fruity flavours of well-made wines of this 'drink-me-quick' style go with many foods. But the subdued fruit and more complex flavours of a wine that has benefitted from aging often have a better relationship with subtle food flavours.

How wines change as they age depends on the grape variety, and how it was grown and made into wine. Concentrated, intensely flavoured wines (see page 223) age better than delicate flavoured ones, especially if they start out in life with high acidity and/or strong tannin. Broadly speaking, finer (affordable but not the cheapest) red wines gradually mellow, taking on savoury and then pruney flavours, and the tannins soften. In white wines, the colour deepens, acidity seems to soften, flavours become more complex and, over a long period of maturation in bottle, sweet wines actually become drier.

There is a limited number of grapes that make wines actually *worth* aging. Even then it depends on the quality of the individual wine. Fine Cabernet Sauvignon-based wines demand to be aged, for instance, but there's no point expecting much positive development out of an inexpensive Cabernet Sauvignon from Bulgaria that was designed to be drunk young.

You can hope for good things from expensive examples of wines based on, or made entirely from, Chardonnay, Chenin Blanc, Gewürztraminer, Pinot Gris, Riesling and Semillon among whites; and Baga, Cabernet Sauvignon, Merlot, Nebbiolo, Periquita, Pinot Noir, Sangiovese, Syrah, Tempranillo and Zinfandel among reds. How long you can age wines also depends on the grape variety, the vintage, and how the grapes were grown and the wine made. (See the opposite page for a basic guide.)

However, you shouldn't expect mature examples of these fine bottles to be easy to obtain. Walk into your local supermarket or off-licence and you'll find lots of young, inexpensive wines, and maybe some finer wines as well. But there won't be many wines over, say, ten years old (and most will be under three). If you want to drink mature fine wine, the best thing to do is to buy it by the case when it's young (maybe even before it has left the producer – *en primeur*), keep it in a cool, dark place, and forget about it for several years. Then you can try it, bottle by bottle, until you feel it has come to its peak. But don't keep it for *too* long: you might miss it at its best.

Even with these more expensive wines, though, you have to make your own decision as to whether you prefer the fresh, fruity flavours of young wines, or the increase in complexity and subtlety that can come with time spent aging in the bottle. It's all a matter of individual taste: older isn't necessarily better. But it might in some cases mean a better match with food.

## WHITES TO DRINK VERY YOUNG

CHILE *Chardonnay*.

EASTERN EUROPE Most whites.

FRANCE Alsace *Sylvaner* and *Pinot Blanc*, basic dry Bordeaux, Burgundy: inexpensive whites, Mâcon-Villages, St-Véran; dry Loire whites, all white Rhônes apart from Hermitage, most southern French whites.

GERMANY Tafelwein, Landwein and inexpensive QbAs.

ITALY Most whites.

PORTUGAL Whites.

SPAIN Most unoaked whites.

Most *Chardonnay*, dry *Chenin Blanc* and *Colombard* from ·

SOUTH AFRICA.

SWITZERLAND Whites.

EVERYWHERE *Sauvignon Blanc*.

## WHITES TO AGE FOR A FEW YEARS

AUSTRALIA Mid-price *Chardonnay* and *Riesling*, expensive *Chardonnay*, *Marsanne*.

AUSTRIA Sweet whites.

CHILE Reserve *Chardonnay*.

ENGLAND Most whites.

FRANCE Alsace *Riesling, Tokay-Pinot Gris* and *Gewürztraminer*, mid-price white Burgundy, inexpensive Chablis, most non-vintage Champagne, sweet Monbazillac.

GERMANY Riesling QbAs and most Spätlese and Auslese wines.

ITALY Recioto di Soave (sweet).

SPAIN Crianza and Reserva whites.

NEW ZEALAND *Chardonnay* and *Riesling*.

SOUTH AFRICA *Riesling*.

USA California, Oregon and Washington State *Chardonnay*.

## WHITES TO MATURE FOR A LONG TIME

### Dry

FRANCE Bordeaux: expensive Graves, Pessac-Léognan; expensive white Burgundy, expensive Chablis, vintage Champagne, white Hermitage.

SPAIN Expensive Rioja Gran Reserva.

### Sweet

AUSTRALIA *Semillon*, expensive *Riesling*.

FRANCE Alsace Sélection de Grains Nobles and Vendange Tardive wines made from *Riesling, Tokay-Pinot Gris* and *Gewürztraminer*, expensive Sauternes and Barsac, sweet white Loires.

GERMANY expensive *Riesling* Spätlese, Auslese, Beerenauslese and Trockenbeerenauslese wines.

HUNGARY Tokay.

ROMANIA Sweet wines.

SOUTH AFRICA Late Harvest and Noble Late Harvest *Riesling* and *Chenin Blanc.*

## REDS TO DRINK YOUNG

AUSTRALIA and NEW ZEALAND Inexpensive *Cabernet Sauvignon* and *Merlot.*

EASTERN EUROPE Most reds.

FRANCE Alsace *Pinot Noir*, basic Bordeaux, Beaujolais, Beaujolais-Villages, basic red Burgundy, Côtes du Frontonnais, most Côtes du Rhône; Loire: Anjou Rouge, Sancerre Rouge; most inexpensive southern French reds.

SOUTH AFRICA Inexpensive reds.

USA Inexpensive *Zinfandel*, jug wines.

Reds from AUSTRIA, GERMANY and SWITZERLAND.

Basic ITALIAN and SPANISH reds.

## REDS TO AGE FOR A FEW YEARS

AUSTRALIA *Pinot Noir* and *Merlot*, mid-price *Cabernet* and *Shiraz.*

CHILE Expensive *Cabernet.*

FRANCE Mid-range Bordeaux, mid-range Burgundy; Loire: Bourgueil, Chinon, St-Nicolas-de-Bourgueil, Saumur-Champigny; Rhône: Crozes-Hermitage, St-Joseph; Bandol, expensive Corbières, expensive Faugères, Fitou, expensive Minervois, expensive Côtes du Roussillon.

GREECE Reds.

ITALY Most mid-price reds.

NEW ZEALAND Expensive reds.

NORTH AFRICA Reds.

PORTUGAL Alentejo, Bairrada, Dão, Douro, Oeste, Ribatejo and Setúbal reds.

SPAIN Most Crianza, Reserva and Gran Reserva wines.

SOUTH AFRICA Expensive *Pinotage, Merlot, Cabernet* and *Shiraz.*

USA *Petite Syrah;* California: Most *Cabernet, Merlot* and *Pinot Noir.*

## REDS TO AGE FOR A LONG TIME

AUSTRALIA Expensive *Cabernet* and *Shiraz.*

FRANCE Expensive Bordeaux, expensive Burgundy, Rhône: Châteauneuf-du-Pape, Cornas, Côte Rôtie, Hermitage; expensive Cahors, Madiran.

ITALY Amarone and Recioto della Valpolicella, Aglianico del Vulture, Barolo, Barbaresco, Brunello di Montalcino, Chianti Riserva.

LEBANON Chateau Musar.

PORTUGAL Colares.

SPAIN Expensive Reserva and Gran Reserva Rioja and Ribera del Duero.

USA California *Cabernet* Reserve and expensive *Zinfandel.*

# GRAPE VARIETIES

 What a wine tastes like depends largely on what grape (or grapes) it's made from. Wherever in the world you grow Chardonnay, it should taste like Chardonnay, influenced by climate and wine-making, certainly, but recognizably Chardonnay all the same. So if a light, unoaked Italian Chardonnay goes with cod, for instance, should an oaky Australian one work as well? Well, not necessarily, but it's worth trying other *light* Chardonnays instead. Most New World wines are helpfully labelled with their grape varieties, but many famous European wines are not. And many wines are blends of two or more varieties. The reference panels at the end of each grape variety below list major wines (variety-labelled or not) made solely or principally with the grape in question, plus wines in which that grape is very important, taste-wise, in a blend of two or more varieties.

## White Grape Varieties

### ALIGOTÉ

Aligoté is crisp, green, light and lively. The best examples come from Burgundy; good, oak-matured ones can age. This is a really versatile grape with food, but beware cream. It partners many fish (particularly smoked fish) and seafood dishes very well. It's excellent with kedgeree, smoked salmon or smoked trout (especially if oaked) – even with steak tartare. It copes with savoury lemon sauces, many dressed salads, and garlic dishes. But the best match is with sizzling hot, fat Burgundy snails in butter and garlic. WHERE TO FIND IT Eastern Europe – Bulgaria, Moldova, Romania. France – *Burgundy. Always labelled.*

### CHARDONNAY

Chardonnay has an amazing range of flavours in its repertoire – pineapple, lemon, grapefruit, peach, apple, flowers, biscuit, honey, hazelnut, toast, vanilla (when oak-aged), butter and cream (when put through the malolactic fermentation – see page 226). No wonder it can partner so many different dishes. In cool climates (Champagne, Burgundy), Chardonnay can be steely and austere, and ages well; in hotter areas (Australia, New Zealand, California,

Chile, South Africa), it is rich, ripe and lusciously fruity, and should be drunk young. Chardonnay is best for most egg dishes, and very good with chicken dishes or guinea fowl, sweetbreads, garlic, avocado, basil and pesto. It is delicious with many sauced or plain fishes, and lobster, and oaky Australian Chardonnays go with smoked fishes.
WHERE TO FIND IT France – *Burgundy, Chablis, Champagne Blanc de Blancs. Labelled 'Chardonnay', almost everywhere. In blends: Champagne, except for Blanc de Noirs; with Colombard in Australia; a splash or a large dollop can perk up bland wines anywhere.*

## CHENIN BLANC
Western Loire Chenins range from dry, high-acid sparkling Saumur to the voluptuous dessert wines of Quarts de Chaume and Bonnezeaux, and from basic to stunning quality. In warmer climates – in Australia, New Zealand and California – Chenin produces softer, gentler dry wines. Chenin Blanc is South Africa's most widely planted grape (known there as Steen), making soft but crisp, easy-drinking, inexpensive whites.

Dry Loire Chenins partner sharper foods exceptionally well, and demi-sec Vouvray is *the* choice with Gravadlax. Honeyed and complex, but with a refreshing streak of acidity, the sweet wines of the Loire often strike just the right note of acidity with tart fruits. Lime zest goes wonderfully. Warm-climate Chenins often have a touch of sweetness that matches gently flavoured vegetable dishes, and particularly Jerusalem artichokes, and tarragon.
WHERE TO FIND IT: DRY Australian *Chenins.* France – *Anjou Blanc Sec, Coulée de Serrant, Crémant de Loire, Jasnières, sparkling Saumur, Savennières, Vouvray Sec.* New Zealand *Chenin. Some* South African *Chenins (or Steens). USA – California Chenins.* MEDIUM-DRY TO MEDIUM-SWEET France – *Anjou Blanc Demi-sec, Vouvray Demi-sec. Some inexpensive* South African *Chenins (Steen).* SWEET France – *Bonnezeaux, Chaume, Coteaux de l'Aubance, Coteaux du Layon, Quarts de Chaume, Vouvray Moelleux.* South Africa – *late-harvest Chenin.*

## GEWÜRZTRAMINER (TRAMINER)
A full-bodied and flavourful grape, with a spicily aromatic character, often likened to rose-petals or lychee fruit, Gewürztraminer can be fully dry, or very sweet; light or

full in body. Generally moderate in acidity, Gewürztraminer grown in hot climates is sometimes short on acidity. The fullest-bodied, most richly flavoured Gewürztraminers come from Alsace. Of the New World examples, the best are found in cooler New Zealand.

Gewürztraminer is too powerful and exotic for many foods, but it does make a brilliant match with cooked red peppers and onion, chicken chasseur, and some cheeses, especially Chaume, Munster, Cheddar, and several goats' cheeses. It is very good with lemon zest.

WHERE TO FIND IT *Always labelled with the variety name*. Australia. Austria. Canada. Eastern Europe *(Tramini or Traminec)*. France – *Alsace*. Italy – *Alto Adige (also Traminer)*. Germany. New Zealand. USA – *California, East Coast, Oregon, Washington*.

## GRÜNER VELTLINER
Austria's most important grape is crisp and easy-drinking, sometimes with a slightly smoky overtone to its apple and gooseberry fruit flavours. Best drunk young and fruity, it goes especially well with shellfish, especially scallops.
WHERE TO FIND IT Austria.

## MARSANNE
The main grape of white Hermitage and St-Joseph from the northern Rhône, and of both still and sparkling St-Péray, Marsanne makes big, fat wines, high in alcohol, and fruity when young and at their best. The best are heavy, peachy and toasty; the worst fat and flat. Oak can lift them. In Australia, they are usually picked earlier and can be crisper.

Southern French Marsanne, often blended with the more scented, livelier Roussanne, is a good match for trout, and Australian Marsanne is wonderful with many curries.
WHERE TO FIND IT Australia – *Victoria*. France – *white Hermitage, white St-Joseph, St-Péray*.

## MELON DE BOURGOGNE (MUSCADET)
The grape of Muscadet is pretty flavourless unless it has had the sur lie treatment. Left in contact with the yeast deposit after fermentation, the wine gains a savoury, tangy, bready flavour. Mostly designed for drinking young, it is too acid for many foods, but Muscadet is often a perfect match for seafood, especially mussels, oysters and whelks.
WHERE TO FIND IT France – *Muscadet*.

## MÜLLER-THURGAU

Germany's most widely planted and prolific grape can produce spicy, curranty, 'catty' fruit. It does this more often in England, where yields are lower and the ripening time longer. High-yielding, inexpensive German wines based on Müller-Thurgau taste of very little. A bland food wine, it does, however, enhance the flavour of coriander superbly.
WHERE TO FIND IT England. Germany. Hungary *(Rizling-Szilvani)*. Italy – *Alto Adige.* Luxembourg *(Rivaner)*. New Zealand *(Riesling-Sylvaner)*. Switzerland *(Riesling-Sylvaner)*.

## MUSCAT

The family of Muscat grapes is large, but all the members share a floral, aromatic character. Dry Muscat is difficult to pair with foods – cooked red or yellow peppers, and salmon excepted – but sweet Muscats are invaluable with puddings, as the floral, orange and almond flavours shine through the stickiest of desserts. It is often fortified.
WHERE TO FIND IT DRY France – *Alsace.* Italy – *Alto Adige, Piedmont (Goldenmuskateller and Rosenmuskateller). A few in* Portugal *and* Spain. SWEET Australia – *Rutherglen Liqueur Muscat.* Greece *(very sweet).* France – *Clairette de Die (up to 50% Muscat), Muscats de Beaumes-de-Venise, de Frontignan, de Lunel, de Rivesaltes, de St-Jean-de-Minervois.* Italy – *Alto Adige (as above), Asti Spumante, Moscato d'Asti, di Pantelleria.* Portugal – *Setúbal.* South Africa – *Hanepoot (White Muscat, Muskadel).* Spain – *Moscatel de Malaga, de Valencia.* USA – *California.*

## PINOT BLANC (WEISSBURGUNDER, PINOT BIANCO)

At its best in Alsace and northern Italy, well-made Pinot Blanc can be lovely, soft and fullish, honeyed wine with a tiny whiff of spice; simple, crisp and inexpensive whites for drinking young, both still and fizzy. In the southerly wine regions of Germany, it makes fullish whites, often dry or nearly dry. It is very occasionally oaked. A good choice with cooked onion dishes and goats' cheeses.
WHERE TO FIND IT Austria. Chile. Eastern Europe – Hungary, Slovakia *and* Slovenia. France – *Alsace (including most Crémant d'Alsace); a very little in Burgundy.* Germany – *Baden, Pfalz, the east.* Italy – *Alto Adige, Friuli, the Veneto and elsewhere.* USA – *California.*

## PINOT GRIS (TOKAY, RULÄNDER, PINOT GRIGIO)

Pinot Gris has a fat, alcoholic and meatily spicy character, with a honeyed flavour. Despite its low acidity, it can keep and mature well and, when super-ripe, it can make wonderful sweet wines. Pinot Gris needs richly flavoured foods – confit de canard and domestic duck and pork make brilliant companions for the rich, dry style of Pinot Gris. The lighter Pinot Grigio of north-east Italy rarely shines with food but is fine with many pizzas and pasta dishes, and a star with frankfurters. It is also good with mushrooms and a star with fresh ginger. A sweeter style, such as Alsace Vendange Tardive, is good with foie gras and pâté de foie gras.

WHERE TO FIND IT Eastern Europe – Hungary *(Szürkebarat), Romania, Slovenia, Slavonia.* France – *Alsace.* Italy – *Alto Adige, and the north-east.* Switzerland.

## RIESLING (RHEIN RIESLING, WHITE RIESLING, JOHANNISBERG RIESLING, RIESLING RENANO)

Rhine Riesling (German by origin) rivals Chardonnay for the title of best white wine maker in the world – and probably wins. It always has a steely streak of acidity and tends to have a very floral, lemony and limy flavour, developing a petrolly pungency as it ages (sounds foul, tastes great). The most exciting Rieslings from outside Germany, Austria and Alsace come from cooler vineyards in Australia. These are usually dry or just a touch sweetened, with heaps of fruit, good acidity and a distinctive, floral, limy character.

Dry or nearly dry Rieslings can be too perfumed and floral, or too acid, for some foods. The limy note makes them ideal with dishes containing lemon grass or lime zest. Choucroute, goose, fennel, and cooked garlic are good matches. German Riesling Kabinett and Halbtrocken are a good choice for some Chinese foods and many dressed salads. The high acid of sweet, late-picked Rieslings often stars with fruit desserts, some blue cheeses and foie gras.

WHERE TO FIND IT Australia. Austria. Canada – *Ontario.* Eastern Europe – Hungary, Romania, Slovenia. France – *Alsace.* Germany – *mainly Mosel-Saar-Ruwer, Nahe, Pfalz, Rheingau.* Italy – *Friuli-Venezia Giulia, Trentino-Alto Adige.* Luxembourg. New Zealand. Switzerland. USA – *California, Finger Lakes, Long Island, New York State, Oregon, Washington State.*

## SAUVIGNON BLANC (SAUVIGNON, FUMÉ BLANC, MUSCAT-SYLVANER)

Grown in a cool climate, Sauvignon makes delightfully sharp, tangy dry whites, with a distinctive flavour of grass, elderflowers and gooseberries. Much of the best Bordeaux Blanc is also made from Sauvignon. This is a much softer, less aromatic style of wine, especially when blended with Semillon, and/or oaked. But the world's most consistently exciting cool-climate Sauvignons come from New Zealand: tangy, super-fruity and bursting with aroma and flavour – delicious gooseberry and asparagus in less ripe years, stunning gooseberry and tropical fruit in riper vintages. Hotter countries such as California, Australia, South Africa and Chile tend to make fatter, more muted Sauvignons, with less of the acid tang, more tropical fruit and less gooseberry. These softer Sauvignons are often oaked, giving an even rounder, softer effect.

The tangy (Loire) Sauvignon goes well with dishes with high acidity, especially those containing cooked tomato. With goats' cheeses it is a match made in heaven, and is good with soft, creamy garlic and herb cheeses. The softer (Bordeaux Blanc) style is an easy match with lots of foods, especially asparagus and fish. Most Sauvignons (unless too oaky) go well with onions, herby pork sausages, many shellfish, and hollandaise sauce. It is a brilliant match for many herbs, including sage, tarragon, dill, lemon grass and mint.
WHERE TO FIND IT *TANGY STYLE* France – *Loire: Haut-Poitou, Menetou-Salon, Pouilly-Fumé, Quincy, Reuilly, Sancerre, Touraine, Vin de Pays du Jardin de la France; St-Bris.* Hungary. Italy – *Alto Adige.* New Zealand. USA – *California, Oregon, Washington State. Very few from* Australia, Chile, South Africa. *SOFTER STYLE (sometimes oaky)* France – *Bordeaux: Bordeaux Blanc, Entre-Deux-Mers, Graves; Bergerac, Buzet, Côtes de Duras, vins de pays from the south.* Hungary. Italy – *Friuli, Veneto and elsewhere.* HOT-CLIMATE Australia. South Africa. USA – *California.*

## SEMILLON

Bordeaux's most widely planted grape, Semillon, is an extraordinary, underrated grape, making delicious dry and sweet wines. (As dry Bordeaux Blanc, its fat, honeyed style is pepped up by blending in Sauvignon.) In New Zealand it becomes extremely herbaceous. Some of Australia's finest dry wines stem from this grape: in the Hunter Valley, the limy intensity of youthful Semillon matures into a big, creamy, toasty wine with ripe greengages. Sweet Semillon's honeyed character is transformed when affected by botrytis, or 'noble rot', as in Sauternes, into flavours of dried apricot, pineapple and tropical fruit, fat and opulent in style, with balanced acidity.

Dry Bordeaux Blanc is easy to partner with fish and shellfish. The rich but dry Australian Semillon copes well with spicy dishes or richly sauced fish dishes, and is brilliant with osso buco and some curries, gazpacho and leek dishes. Sweet Semillon is especially delicious with apple tart with crème patissière, apricot pie, mince pies, strawberries and cream, chocolate cake, and crème brulée. It partners many cheeses, the most famous combination being Sauternes and Roquefort.

WHERE TO FIND IT DRY Australia. Chile. France – *Bordeaux: Bordeaux Blanc, Entre-Deux-Mers, Graves, Pessac-Léognan; Bergerac, Buzet, Côtes de Duras, Côtes du Marmandais.* New Zealand. South Africa. USA – *California.* SWEET Australia. France – *Bordeaux: (often with Sauvignon Blanc) Barsac, Cadillac, Cérons, Loupiac, Premières Côtes de Bordeaux, Sauternes, St-Croix-du-Mont; Monbazillac.* USA – *California.*

## SILVANER/SYLVANER

Silvaner makes dry, high-acid wines with reasonable body, often an earthy, vegetal character, and a slightly appley flavour. In Alsace it gains a touch of spice. Its greatest attribute is acidity. With its fairly neutral flavour, Silvaner goes quite easily with foods which themselves contain acidity. It is a perfect match with carp, and rabbit in mustard sauce, and is a real discovery with coriander.

WHERE TO FIND IT Austria. Eastern Europe – Czech Republic, Hungary, Slovakia, Slovenia. France – *Alsace.* Germany – *mostly Franken and Rheinhessen.* Italy – *Alto Adige.*

## TREBBIANO (UGNI BLANC)

Italy is swamped in Trebbiano. This neutral grape has highish acidity, medium body, and very little else, although modern-style Trebbianos have a little fresh fruit. The exception in Italy is Lugana, where somehow it is transformed into a more aromatic, characterful wine. Known

as Ugni Blanc in France, it is widely used in southern French whites to bump up acidity, and turns up as Vin de Pays des Côtes de Gascogne. Its main role in France is in distillation for Cognac and Armagnac. Trebbiano's blandness makes it an easy match for white fish and fish soup.
WHERE TO FIND IT France – *Vin de Pays des Côtes de Gascogne, and blended in many southern whites; also Armagnac and Cognac.* Italy – *everywhere (but the far north and north-east), including Bianco di Custoza, Frascati, Galestro, Lugana, Orvieto and Soave.*

## VERDEJO

Spain's most interesting native white grape, found almost solely in the white wine region of Rueda, Verdejo makes crisp, fairly full, gooseberry-fruity wines with a gently nutty character. Bottles labelled 'Rueda Superior' are made with at least 60 per cent Verdejo. Too rich for some fish, Verdejo is excellent with monkfish and crab, and very good with quail. It enhances the flavour of leeks, and goes very well with garlic, asparagus, many salads, oregano, marjoram and saffron.
WHERE TO FIND IT Spain – *Rueda.*

## VERNACCIA

Various grapes go by the name of Vernaccia in Italy, but the most likely one you'll meet is the Vernaccia di San Gimignano of Tuscany. Potentially this is a fairly characterful grape, with highish, tangy acidity. Some modern Vernaccias are crisp and fairly bland, although riper, fuller – but still crisp – ones can have a creamy, nutty butteriness. It is very occasionally oaked.

Vernaccia accompanies lots of dishes well, including quail, ham, veal and sweetbreads, bouillabaise, grilled tuna, mullet, and some cooked tomato and garlic dishes. It has a particular affinity to parsley.
WHERE TO FIND IT Italy – *Tuscany.*

## VIOGNIER

Viognier makes a wonderful and characterful aperitif. It is extremely fruity and very aromatic, yet subtle – a complex and lush blend of fresh apricots, musk, blossom, peaches and almond, sometimes with a dash of honey. It gains nothing from aging, however. Expensive Viognier can be as rich and full as the fattest Chardonnay.

Viognier is not a great food wine; it clashes (sometimes quite horribly) with many foods. It comes closest to a match with lobster and crab. Herbs help: sage, cumin, cardamom, lemon grass, flat-leafed parsley and rosemary are all good. Not surprisingly, it goes quite well with Indian food.

WHERE TO FIND IT France – *Château-Grillet, Condrieu, northern Rhône, southern vins de pays*. USA – *California*.

# Red Grape Varieties

### AGLIANICO
The best of the southern Italian red grapes makes big, intense, tarry, very tannic wines with quite high acidity and moderate fruit. Very expensive ones may be oak-aged. Heavy and rich, Aglianico always needs substantial food partners. It is brilliant with Parmesan.

WHERE TO FIND IT Italy – *Aglianico del Vulture, Basilicata, Campania, Falerno, Taurasi*.

### BARBERA
Italy's most common red grape typically makes fairly light-bodied reds to be drunk young. With lots of sweet-sour plumskin-flavoured fruit, and a bit of tannin, Barbera is best with dishes that match its pricklingly high acidity.

WHERE TO FIND IT Argentina. Italy – *Alba, Asti, Campania, Emilia-Romagna, Lombardy, Monferrato, Piemonte, Puglia, Rubino di Cantavenna, Sicily, Tortona*. USA – *California*.

### CABERNET FRANC
This is the member of the Bordeaux bunch often responsible for a grassy, flowery overtone in red Bordeaux (claret). As the main grape of the red Loire appellations, in the best years Cabernet Franc makes Loire reds with a ripe raspberry aroma and chocolaty depth that can mature into rich, long-lived, savoury complexity. In cool years they can be off-puttingly grassy. Cabernet Franc is always fairly light, with medium to highish acidity, and tannin ranging from little to lots. As Cabernet d'Anjou, it also makes most of the *good* Loire rosés (dry or off-dry).

The typical grassiness of the Cabernet Franc clashes mildly with many foods. Roast beef or steaks are lovely exceptions, as are haggis and Indian food, with which a Loire Cabernet Franc does the trick.

WHERE TO FIND IT Australia. France – *Bordeaux: in most St-Émilion and Pomerol blends; Loire: Anjou Rouge Cabernet, Bourgueil, Chinon, St-Nicolas-de-Bourgueil, Saumur-Champigny.* Italy – *Alto Adige, Colli Berici, Franciacorta, Grave del Friuli, Oltrepò Pavese, Piave (all often in blends with Cabernet Sauvignon and/or Merlot).* South Africa. USA – *California.*

## CABERNET SAUVIGNON

Cabernet Sauvignon has become the world's most travelled red vine without a whisper of competition. The grape that gives flavours from grassy to ripe blackcurrants in red Bordeaux (claret), can come up with plum, blackcurrant, raisin, mint, eucalyptus, green pepper and tar in sunnier climes. In Bordeaux, it is *always* blended, with Merlot, Cabernet Franc and Petit Verdot the usual choice of partners, to make mid-weight reds with medium acidity and tannin. Elsewhere, Cabernet Sauvignon is often used alone, or blended with the other Bordeaux red grapes to give more complexity, or with local varieties to bring added character. Cabernet Sauvignon has phenomenal aging ability, developing cedary, tarry flavours in bottle, and fading elegantly into graceful old age.

Mature Cabernet Sauvignon-based wines need the simplicity of plain meat dishes, although rosemary chimes in deliciously. A ripe, fruity, beefy New World Cabernet Sauvignon is best suited to hefty stews or casseroles cooked in red wine, although it is fine with plain roast goose or lamb. It is also particularly good with Cheshire cheese and some hard goats' cheeses. Young, fruitier Cabernets are delicious with goose. Cabernet complements thyme really well, but clashes with sage. Red Bordeaux goes well with Gruyère and Manchego cheeses. WHERE TO FIND IT *In almost every country where red wine is made.*

## DOLCETTO

Dolcetto makes Piemontese reds of an exuberant fruitiness, dominated by intense, fresh plum flavours. The best, most concentrated examples of Dolcetto, made from low-yielding, fully ripe grapes, may be matured in new oak, and can age for ten years or so. Most Dolcettos are juicily fruity, lightish, quaffing reds, though, with a lively acidity, and are best drunk within two years. Dolcetto is a lovely partner for beef, and very good with herby pork sausages, veal in Marsala sauce and calves' liver and onions, sage, and Gruyère cheese.

WHERE TO FIND IT Italy – *Piemonte.*

## GAMAY

Gamay is the grape of Beaujolais, renowned for its soft, aromatic wine, light in tannin, and full of pastilly, cherry-fruit flavour. It's not all cherry pastille stuff, though. Ten Beaujolais villages ('crus') have been elected superior sources of Beaujolais; they are named on the bottle. Of these, Morgon and Moulin-à-Vent are capable of making wines with greater richness and depth than the rest.

Gamay, particularly from Beaujolais, is one of the most food-friendly grapes you'll find anywhere. The combination of light, easy fruit, low tannin and, in the 'cru' wines, a savoury, meaty character, seems to make for brilliant matches with meat dishes. Beaujolais is especially good with pork products, and is wonderful with beef and offal. It makes a delicious match for red wine casseroles, including coq au vin; it also accompanies garlic and red peppers (cooked or raw), and cooked onion. Gamay goes well with some cheeses, including Gruyère, Milleens and Bresse Bleu.

WHERE TO FIND IT Australia. Canada. France – *Beaujolais: generic, Beaujolais-Villages, the crus (Brouilly, Chénas, Chiroubles, Côte de Brouilly, Fleurie, Juliénas, Morgon, Moulin-à-Vent, Regnié, St-Amour); Loire: Anjou Gamay, Châteaumeillant, Côtes d'Auvergne, Côtes du Forez, Côtes Roannaise, Gamay de Touraine, St-Pourçain-sur-Sioule; Gaillac, Gamay de l'Ardèche.* Switzerland.

## GRENACHE (GARNACHA, CANONAU)

Blended with other varieties, but often dominating the flavour, Grenache makes many spicy, peppery reds in the Côtes du Rhône, and forms the heart of Châteauneuf-du-Pape. It reappears as lively, strawberry-scented light reds in southern France and Spain (as Garnacha), and makes most of Spain's best and fruitiest rosados. Grenache reveals its true splendour in wines made from low-yielding old vines, with magnificent concentration and power, capable of maturing for decades to raisiny richness and complexity. Grenache rosés can cope with everything from garlicky southern French fish dishes, to roast turkey and light vegetarian recipes. The fuller, spicier red wines are at their best with hearty meat and vegetable dishes.

WHERE TO FIND IT Australia – *South Australia*. France – *many southern French reds and rosés, including Bandol, Cassis, Châteauneuf-du-Pape, Coteaux d'Aix-en-Provence, Coteaux du Tricastin, Côtes de Provence, Côtes du Rhône, Côtes du Ventoux, Gigondas, Lirac, Rasteau, Tavel, Vacqueyras*. Spain – *Ampurdan-Costa Brava, Calatayúd, Campo de Borja, Cariñena, Navarra (young reds and rosados), Priorato, Rioja (wines from Rioja Baja and rosados)*. Italy – *Sardinia (Canonau)*.

## MERLOT

Merlot is the softest, fruitiest and easiest-drinking of the Bordeaux grapes, often curranty and/or grassy in flavour, and rarely making very tannic wines. It is the most important grape in the soft, drinkable wines of St-Émilion. And wherever Cabernet Sauvignon goes, Merlot is sure to follow. Seductively drinkable when young, the fruit fades gently with age, but the wines do not often gain much in complexity. In warmer climates overripe grapes can make jammy, blousy wines, but the best wines balance rich, plummy fruit with sufficient tannin and acidity.

The soft, honeyed fruit of many Merlots makes them ideal for savoury foods with an element of sweetness; goose is good, too. Cooler-climate (grassy) Merlots go very well with oregano or marjoram; light ones go well with beef.

WHERE TO FIND IT Australia. Chile. Eastern Europe – Bulgaria, Czech Republic, Hungary, Romania, Slovakia. France – *blended in almost all red Bordeaux, occasionally by itself, and southern French Merlot vin de pays*. Greece. Italy – *north-east*. New Zealand. Portugal. South Africa. Spain. USA – *California, Washington State*.

## NEBBIOLO

The hills of Piemonte are covered with Nebbiolo vines, the source of two famous wines – Barolo and Barbaresco. There are two very different styles of these great wines: the lean, tannic, traditional style, that positively *needs* aging to soften the aggressive tannins, and will then last for decades; and the richer, less brutally tannic modern wines. The latter are much more drinker-friendly, starting with more fruit and less tannin, and aging gracefully.

Nebbiolo wines are rich and savoury, with quite high acidity, ideal for heavy meat or game dishes, and kidneys. The modern, fruity, and less tannic style is delicious with roast duck, as well as poultry livers or their pâtés, or confit de canard. The flavour of oregano works well, as do some cheeses, especially Milleens.

WHERE TO FIND IT Australia. Italy – *Barbaresco, Barolo, Carema, Gattinara, Ghemme, Roero, Spanna del Piemonte, Valtellina.* USA – *California.*

## PINOT NOIR

Although a difficult customer, Pinot Noir has continued to find success away from its famous home in Burgundy. Pinot Noir can make wines that blend sweet fruit and savoury complexity more successfully than any other. It takes on intricate earthy flavours (leaf-mould, hung game, even horse manure), while the fruit changes from raspberry, strawberry, plum or cherry, to prunes and dried fruits. It can yield the lightest of delicate, savoury reds in Alsace, herbaceous cherry flavours in Western Australia, and big, jammy wines in the hotter Eastern European countries.

Because of Pinot Noir's potential subtlety and complexity, it is well suited to complex meat dishes – particularly game. The lightest styles of Pinot Noir (Alsace, for example) make excellent partners for poached salmon and sea trout; nottoo-tannic Pinots are good with garlic and onion dishes, rosemary and mint. It is one of the best red wines with cheeses, including strong goats' cheeses and ripe Camembert. Mature Pinot goes well with a variety of mushrooms.

WHERE TO FIND IT Australia. Austria. Eastern Europe – Bulgaria, Hungary, Romania. England. France – *Alsace, Ambonnay Rouge, Bouzy Rouge, all red Burgundy (except Beaujolais and Mâcon), Sancerre.* Germany – *Spätburgunder.* Italy – *Alto Adige, Pinot Nero del Trentino, Veneto.* New Zealand. South Africa. USA – *California, Oregon, Washington State.*

## SANGIOVESE

Sangiovese owes its reputation as a great Italian red grape to the wines it makes in Tuscany. Even there, it's not always great. There are different strains of Sangiovese vine, some very mediocre, others to rival the best wines in the world. Top vines can produce long-lived, concentrated reds, with substantial tannin and acidity. Good Chiantis (from the Classico or Rufina regions) start with rich plum and raspberry fruit, but highish tannin and acidity, and soften with bottle-age towards cedary, elegant flavours. Simple Chiantis are much lighter; as are the lively, easy-drinking Sangioveses di Romagna and delle Marche, still with the typical astringency found elsewhere in Italy. There are also very expensive table wines (vini da tavola) made from pure Sangiovese, sometimes cut with Cabernet Sauvignon. They start very tannic but full of rich, plummy fruit, and eventually become drinkable after many years.

The higher quality Sangioveses are good with mid-weight meat, game and offal dishes, especially calves' liver. They are also wonderful with cheeses as diverse as Cheddar and mature Gouda. The flavour of sage is delicious with Chiantis and less tannic Sangioveses.

WHERE TO FIND IT Italy – *Bolgheri, Brunello di Montalcino, Carmignano, all Chianti, Morellino di Scansano, Rosso Piceno, Sangioveses dei Colli Pesaresi, delle Marche, di Aprilia, and di Romagna, Torgiano, Velletri Rosso, Vino Nobilo di Montepulciano.*
USA – *California.*

## SYRAH/SHIRAZ

The fine, dark red Syrah, the red grape of the northern Rhône, makes rich, flavourful wines full of raspberry fruit and smoky, tarry, spicy, sometimes burnt-rubbery flavours. In their youth Syrah wines can be very tannic, softening with age to a still very fruity, leathery, smoky character. It pops up in the south of France in a much lighter style, to make single-variety Syrah vins de pays or to give a firm, flavourful boost to more feeble varieties. As Shiraz, it is Australia's most abundant red grape, offering a range of styles from light and peppery, with aromas of eucalyptus and mint in Victoria, to massively fruity, rich, softly tannic wines from old vines in South Australia's Barossa and Eden Valleys.

Syrah and Shiraz are powerfully flavoured, full-bodied wines and the food that goes with them also needs plenty of flavour. Northern Rhônes and other French Syrahs are delicious with a whole range of game birds. Syrah and Shiraz are excellent with roast turkey or pork, lamb's liver and cooked red or yellow peppers. These are good cheese wines (particularly the Shiraz), especially with Cheshire, young Gouda and Emmenthal.

WHERE TO FIND IT Argentina. Australia. France – *northern Rhône, Vin de Pays de Comtés Rhodaniennes, other southern vins de pays.* Italy – *Tuscany.* South Africa. USA – *a very little in California.*

## TEMPRANILLO (ARAGONEZ, CENCIBEL, OJO DE LIEBRE, TINTO FINO, TINTO DEL PAIS, TINTA RORIZ, ULL DE LLEBRE)

Spain's best red grape makes lovely, elegant wines in the cooler northern regions, combining wild strawberry fruit with a herby, savoury, tobacco-like character. The finest classic Tempranillo areas are the Ribera del Duero and Rioja. Tempranillo vines are sprouting everywhere, capable of making young, aromatic reds or richer wines that are often oaked. It blends well with Cabernet Sauvignon and successfully perking up lesser Spanish varieties.

The great food match for Tempranillo is lamb. Thyme and rosemary are lovely flavours, as is cooked red pepper. It is good with game, some Indian dishes, and mature Tempranillo is excellent with cèpes, and with several cheeses, including Pont l'Evêque, Brie and Cheddar.
WHERE TO FIND IT Argentina. Portugal. Spain – *La Mancha, Navarra, Penedés, Ribera del Duero, Rioja, Somontano, Valdepeñas.*

## ZINFANDEL

Zinfandel ranks as one of the world's finest grape varieties, yet is rarely grown outside California. There, 'Zin' is the most-planted black grape, much of which is turned into bland, very slightly sweet, very slightly pink 'White Zinfandel' or cheap 'jug' red. The best grapes from the best vineyards and oldest vines go to make more substantial reds, mainly designed to drink within two to six years. Good red Zinfandels vary enormously in style, from serious, elegant, oak-aged and richly fruity ones in a style rather like red Bordeaux, to light, juicy-fruity Beaujolais-style. All should be bursting with blackberry-like fruit and peppery flavour, with a firm tang of acidity.

Unoaked or not-too-oaky red Zinfandels are good with roast chicken, lamb with rosemary, venison, hamburgers, tomato dishes, and goats' cheeses. 'White Zinfandel' is a good match for tomatoes and tomato sauces.
WHERE TO FIND IT Australia – *Western Australia.* USA – *California.*

# PUTTING IT ALL TOGETHER

 Playing by the rules can take all the fun out of eating and drinking. Consider the ancient commandment concerning the serving order of wines throughout a meal: 'Dry before sweet, light before full'. The theory is that a dry wine tastes dull after a sweet one, and a light wine feeble after something more full-bodied. Yet do our taste buds rise up in revolt when we are served a rich liver pâté before grilled chicken? Or when smoked salmon is followed by a lighter, more delicate flavour such as white fish or veal? Of course not. So treat wine in the same way, and when the occasion demands it, break the rules.

## Planning the Wine List

### THE FORMAL APPROACH

It's more important to serve an appropriate wine with each dish than to worry about whether one wine might be prejudiced by the lingering taste of its predecessor. A quick bite of bread or a gulp of water, followed by the first mouthful of the next dish, and the tastebuds are back in fighting fettle. (Worried chefs sometimes serve a sorbet between two potentially conflicting dishes as a sort of mouthwash.) Even without bread and water, any initial disappointment caused by the juxtaposition of wines will only be fleeting, provided the new wine complements the new dish.

Here's an example of a brilliantly matched but sequence-busting menu, just to show how it can be done:

Foie gras canapés – *Sauternes*
Sole fillets in a delicate prawn sauce – *Bordeaux Blanc*
Roast pheasant – *Oregon Pinot Noir*
Goats' cheese, soft garlic and
herb cheese – *Sauvignon Blanc*
Chocolate mousse – *Asti Spumante*

The wines go from sweet to dry and back to sweet, from full to light to medium and finally to very light indeed, breaking almost every rule in the book. And the selection really works, because the wine and food served at each course make a perfect match.

## BRIDGING THE GAPS

You might expect a procession of wines at grand dinner parties. Even then, however, as host you might not want to introduce new wines with each course. Nor do you need to. Carefully chosen, one wine can often bridge two courses and partner each with panache. This can be the ideal solution, too, for a relaxing, informal supper, or simply to please yourself.

A fruity, dry (or sparkling) white served as an aperitif can lead on into the starter. A starter wine can also accompany the main course. If you are having cheese before pudding, or missing out on a sweet course altogether, the red or white wine served with the main course can smoothly make the leap. If you are having pudding *and* cheese, that's fine too. Sweet wines often go brilliantly with cheeses, especially with very salty ones. What *doesn't* work at all is to continue drinking the red or white *dry* wine of the main or cheese course with the pudding. The most delicious red or dry white will taste flat and dull with sweet food. Better to forget the wine and enjoy the dessert alone.

If you simply fancy one glass of wine with your meal, yet have planned a starter and main course, you will probably want to focus on matching the second dish. Look up both dishes, and see if there's any common ground. Maybe adding a stuffing, sauce or accompaniment for one of the dishes would *create* some common ground.

The easiest bridging wines are dry wines with light to medium body, gentle rather than vibrant fruit, medium acidity, gentle aroma and flavour, very subtle oak – if any at all – and light tannin in reds. Many southern French reds, Bordeaux Blanc and Italian whites are often good. You may prefer to avoid a very characterful wine, even if it goes brilliantly with the main course, and choose a gentler wine that makes an adequate pairing with the main course, but also partners what comes before or after. Or you could relish the heavenly match with the meat and put up with a slight mismatch elsewhere.

## FACING THE WINE LIST

Choosing the right wines at home, when you are serving the same dish to everyone, is all very well. Where do you start in a restaurant, with a potential clash at every course? There could be several different starters, fish here, meat there for the main course, and all sorts of different flavours to match. Again, those mild-mannered, multipurpose wines – Bordeaux Blanc, Italian whites, southern French reds – will give no offence. The odd white or red by the glass, or half-bottle, might satisfy someone whose food is really out on a limb, but there's often a very limited choice on wine lists. A good wine waiter should have some ideas on how to bridge the gaps.

## Party time

A successful party wine needs to make a hit by itself. It cannot rely on mouthfuls of crisps or peanuts, or savoury canapés to make it shine. That rules out reds with medium to high tannin and whites with high acidity. Whether dry or medium-dry, party wines need to be light and gulpable, enticingly fruity and fresh.

For whites (and especially inexpensive whites), aim for the most recent vintage. Bright, super-fruity Australian or New Zealand whites, Alsace Pinot Blanc and inexpensive Chardonnay score better than blander whites from Italy, Spain, Portugal or Eastern Europe, which tend to pall as the evening wears on. Avoid assertive wines in favour of gently aromatic wines. Drinking a really spicy Gewürztraminer, a musky, apricotty Viognier, or a fragrant, grapy dry Muscat can become a bit much after a while. Oak can also be hard to take without food, unless it is very subtle. For those with a slightly sweet tooth, German wines (QbA and Kabinett are good, fruity gulpers.

Beaujolais, Beaujolais-Villages and all the Beaujolais crus (such as Fleurie, Juliénas and Brouilly), and Gamays from anywhere, provided they are young and fresh, make good, fruity red party wines. Italy's Teroldego Rotaliano and Dolcetto make scrumptious party reds, as do inexpensive Australian Shiraz or Syrah *vin de pays*, light, low-price Merlots, modern Côtes du Rhône or Côtes du Ventoux. Eastern European wines, especially the lighter Bulgarian reds, can also be just right, but you need to pick carefully to avoid low-fruit party-poopers.

### FIZZ FACTOR

No one is likely to complain at the time if you serve Champagne throughout the party – but they may mumble later about stomach-ache. Champagne is actually rather an acid wine to drink glass after glass without substantial food.

Australian sparkling wines are often the best-value party fizzes, and kinder to the stomach because lower in acidity.

## ALCOHOL HAZE

If your guests are to remain upright throughout the proceedings, you might check the alcohol level of the wines you serve, and provide mineral water, too. You may prefer to stick to wines of 11 degrees or under. German Kabinett wines (just off-dry) are excellent for parties, often with as little as 8.6 degrees of alcohol, and other German medium or medium-dry QbA whites rarely pass 10.5 degrees.

White wines from other countries with the right levels of acidity and flavour for parties mainly start at about 10.5 or 11 degrees and may even top 14, so pick with care. Some of the lightest wines unfortunately fail the party wine test on other counts. Vinho Verde (typically around 8 degrees of alcohol) is too raspingly acid, while Asti Spumante (around 6.5 degrees) is too sweet.

## SUMMER SEASON

Lower alcohol is especially important for summer parties. A glass of wine enjoyed in the sun can seem twice as strong. If you don't feel like white wines, choose really light, aromatic reds and chill them. You could make a summer cup: an ice-cold mix of still or sparkling wine, fizzy water and fruit juice, garnished with bits of fruit. Or perhaps Buck's Fizz – traditionally half orange juice, half Champagne, but it's the quality of the orange juice you'll really notice, not that of the fizz: choose freshly squeezed orange juice and economize on a cheaper sparkling wine.

For barbecues, match the individual fish or meats, or, more importantly, the sauces. Oaky flavours go well with the smoky (sometimes, dare we say, charred) flavours of barbecued foods.

## WINTER WARMERS

Warming up your guests in winter with a mulled wine is far more effective if you don't let the mixture boil. A mulled wine or punch boiled even for a couple of minutes will send them home sober, leaving alcoholic fumes floating in the kitchen. Those wonderful aromatic flavours from the wine will also disappear.

How do you extract the flavour of the spices if you don't have a boil-up? You infuse the spices beforehand in a little pan of boiling water, strain the liquid, and add that spicy 'tea' to the pan of gently heated wine.

## STOCKING UP

You can generally count on people drinking two-thirds white, a third red. And it's worth providing some medium-dry white wine, even if you think the majority of your guests will go for dry. Half a bottle of wine per head is an average calculation of party consumption – but you know your friends.

# Serving wine

## A CHOICE OF GLASS

A good wine glass is made of plain, clear glass and has a tulip-shaped bowl – the in-curving sides trap and concentrate the wine's aromas. Somehow wine always tastes finer out of thin glass, so cut glass is not ideal. You need a glass of a reasonable size, too, to allow room above the wine for the aromas to congregate, and space to give it a good, aroma-releasing swirl without spattering yourself and your neighbours with fly-away drops.

If you are a real perfectionist, you can even buy glasses designed to show different styles of wine at their best. It's hard to believe until you actually try the experiment that the taste of the same wine will alter depending on which shape of glass you drink from. Some of these specialized glasses are almost big enough to house a goldfish. And they cost £20 to £80 a throw.

Of course you don't need a vast armoury of different glasses; one set of largish, tulip-shaped, fairly thin-walled glasses will do justice to most wines. Whatever the glass, it should be filled to no more than two-thirds capacity (goldfish bowls with little more than a normal measure in the bottom). The 'large-glass, two-thirds-full' rule goes for sherry and port, too. Nor is it always necessary to change glasses between wines, except at a very formal meal or if changing from red or dark rosé wine to white.

Careful washing, rinsing and drying is important for all wine glasses, but especially for sparkling wine glasses. Traces of detergent on the glass can prevent the expected streams of bubbles forming. Wine glasses can pass on the smell and taste of detergent and washing-up cloths to the next wine. Always rinse, and use a clean tea-towel to dry.

Wine glasses can also pick up a strong 'cupboard smell' if they are stored upside down. Better to leave them upright, gathering dust if irregularly used, and give them a quick re-wipe before using.

## TEMPERATURE

You don't have to go as far as taking a wine's temperature, but you can spoil your drinking pleasure by serving wine too warm or too cold. All whites and rosés are best chilled (*not* frozen). They taste brighter and fresher, and even quite a dull or a low-acid wine can be given a lift. But cool a wine down too far, and you risk losing some of the nuances, especially with the fullest, most alcohol-rich whites and the darkest, fullest rosés. The more alcoholic a wine is, the less easily the aromas escape from its surface, and the less apparent they will be to the drinker.

An hour in the refrigerator is about right for a good white Burgundy or a full Chardonnay, a Tokay-Pinot Gris d'Alsace or a big Australian Semillon. But lighter wines, such as Muscadet, Sancerre, New Zealand Sauvignon Blanc, German wines and Vinho Verde, will be delicious served icy-chilled from the coolest part of the fridge. Once the wine begins to warm up in the glass the aromatic subtleties will fly out.

Lighter reds benefit from cooling, too. At a party, at a picnic or when soaking up the summer sun, a cool red wine can be just the thing. Choose from Beaujolais, the lighter red Loire wines, red Alsace or Sancerre, most German reds, English or Swiss reds, and lots of central northern Italian wines such as Bardolino, Lago di Caldaro and basic Valpolicella. As with the fuller whites, cool the fuller Beaujolais crus a little less. Be careful, too, when cooling tannic red wines to serve with food. Chilling, by subduing the aroma and flavour of a wine, points up acidity and tannin. (Remember how tea tastes more tannic when cold?)

What of other reds? 'Room temperature' was always the quoted guide. That was in the days when houses had no central heating. The room temperature of the average house in the winter these days is probably a bit over-warm for wines. So serve red wines cool rather than over-warmed. You can always warm them up by cupping your hands round the glass once the wine has been poured.

What if you have unexpected visitors and the white wine

is too warm, or your full-bodied red wines are too cold? Ice buckets filled with a mixture of (lots of) ice cubes and water are a life-saver. You can also buy bottle-hugging chiller-sleeves filled with freezer fluid, which you keep in your freezer until needed. They'll chill your white wine perfectly in five or six minutes. A short spell in the freezer is also a good last resort – as long as you don't forget the bottle. Removing glass splinters from among the lamb chops is a hazardous business.

As for warming up chilly red wines in a rush – don't do anything so drastic as standing the bottle on the radiator, or right by the fire. You're far more likely to spoil the wine's more delicate flavours by any form of heating. Better to serve it cold, apologize, and let drinkers warm it up by cupping their hands around the glass.

## THE ART OF DECANTING

There are three reasons for decanting wines. First, to stop any sludgy deposit at the bottom of the bottle getting into your glass. Second, to give a wine that isn't quite ready to drink a crash course in maturation. Thirdly, to get rid of unpleasant, rubbery, eggy sulphur compounds that may be spoiling the smell and taste of your bottle of wine. The latter is rare but horrid.

Taking these three in reverse order, decanting wines can be a very effective way of removing sulphur compounds that, at their worst, make wines smell of bad eggs. These compounds – formed quite naturally if things go slightly wrong at some points in the wine-making process – are very volatile, and can be removed simply by exposing the wine to air. Pour the wine from the bottle into a decanter (or another empty and washed wine bottle, and then back into the original bottle). The eggy smell should have disappeared. If not, repeat the process.

Decanting a wine – or, rather, aerating it – can also make a young wine more drinkable if you've opened it before it is really ready to drink. Slooshing a bottle of tough young red wine into a decanter (and maybe carefully pouring it back into the original bottle) exposes it to the air and gives the wine a vastly accelerated 'aging'. This causes changes that might have taken years to happen in a tightly stoppered bottle. It's a pretty brutal process, and the results aren't nearly as subtle and complex as the normal effects of gentle bottle-aging, but it can help to subdue tough tannins and bring out hidden flavours.

Lastly, the prime reason to decant a wine (as opposed to just aerating it) is to get rid of sediment. And that almost certainly means elderly red wines. The compounds that give red wine its colour gradually clump together as the wine ages, forming ever-larger molecules. These eventually get so big that they can no longer stay dissolved in the liquid. And so they drop out of solution and form a solid deposit in the bottle. There's nothing wrong with that, and the sediment doesn't taste nasty. But it does feel sludgy or gritty, and it makes the wine look cloudy as you pour.

If you want your glass of red wine to be bright and clear, you have to pour it gently off the dregs. If you have stored your bottle on its side in approved fashion, it's worth standing it upright for a day or two if you know you will be drinking it at a particular meal. It's just that it's much easier to decant the wine if all the gunk is at the bottom of the bottle rather than spread out in a thin line along the side. The trick is to get as much clear wine as possible off the sediment. If your hand has been steady, you should end up with no more than half a glass of dregs. Don't throw them away: add them to a meat sauce or gravy to enrich the flavour.

And most importantly – decant your wine (contrary to traditional wine lore) *just before* you want to serve it. Mature wines fade quickly after decanting. Do it too early and you may lose much of the subtlety and pleasure the bottle had to offer. Really old wines can fade and die in a matter of minutes. If you are serving old vintages, decant them between courses.

---

### Red Wines to Watch

Vintage port has quite a solid sediment – sometimes known as a 'crust' – and is quite easy to decant as long as you can find a light bright enough to shine through the dark glass. In mature red Bordeaux and Rhône wines, the sediment is finer, so more inclined to cloud the wine as you pour. The most difficult is mature red Burgundy, which has very fine sediment that puffs up at the slightest tremble of your hand. The sediment in mature Australian Cabernets and Shirazes often sticks obligingly to the side of the bottle.

# COOKING WITH WINE

 Spruce up your sauces and slosh in some wine for stupendous stews, scrumptious soups, magnificent marinades, gastronomic gravies, rich risottos and casseroles of captivating consistency! Sometimes a quick splash, sometimes a glassful, sometimes a bottleful – wine can work wonders in the cooking pot, adding body or richness, acidity, colour and flavour.

Wine can enrich and revitalize all sorts of sauces. A splash of dry or sweet fortified wine – oloroso sherry, Madeira, Málaga or Marsala – a couple of minutes before the end of cooking makes for delicious flavours that go particularly well with kidneys, pork and chicken.

Apart from tasting good in its own right, a winey sauce can act as a go-between at the table, bringing together the food on your plate and the wine in your glass. The extra boost of body and flavour that wine brings to a dish also allows a partnership with fuller, more flavourful wines. Delicate foods that would be over-powered if served with a glass of red wine stand their ground when cooked in it.

But what sort of wine should you use? How good a wine? Is 'cooking wine' good enough for a grand occasion, or should you sacrifice a bottle of Gevrey-Chambertin? How much should you use? And might you be caught out by a breathalyser on the way home?

It all comes down to the separate elements of the wine's taste. Just as you need to consider the individual traits of a wine when browsing the wine list for the best match for a particular dish – assessing such things as its body, acidity and flavour, sweetness and oakiness (see pages 204-230 and below) – so, as cook, you need to consider these same facets of a wine before tipping it into your pan.

## Alcohol

You can eat Beef Bourguignonne to your heart's content without fear of the breathalyser, because alcohol is one of the first elements to be boiled off. Within a couple of minutes' cooking in an open pan, only traces remain. Even with the lid on, it will gradually escape with the steam.

Savoury sauces with added wine taste odd if the alcohol is noticeable. They are best boiled for at least a couple of minutes. If the other ingredients in your dish would suffer from this treatment, boil up the wine separately to get rid of the alcohol before adding it to the sauce.

A tang of alcohol in a *sweet* sauce for a pudding or dessert is sometimes an added pleasure. Or even *in* the dish – we all slosh neat sherry into trifle, after all. Bring a fruit salad to life with a splash of the wine you'll be serving with it. For a dramatic – and tasty – touch, instead of soaking the wall of finger biscuits for a charlotte in syrup, leave them dry. At the table, pour sweet Champagne or a sparkling wine such as Asti over the dish. The Champagne fizzes festively on the plate until the biscuits soak it up.

Alcohol is also the key to success when adding wine to marinades. Mixed with oils, herbs, spices, onions, or garlic, it unlocks the flavours from these ingredients. Where acidity only tenderizes the surface of meat and fish, alcohol penetrates the fatty tissues and carries the flavours deep into the flesh. This happens quite quickly with fish and poultry, a little more slowly with red meat.

## Cook's Tips

◆ Boil sauces for at least a couple of minutes to drive off the alcohol.

◆ *Don't* allow punches and hot wine cups to come to the boil, unless you want to turn them into soft drinks.

◆ Beware using too much wine in homemade ice creams and sorbets – the alcohol lowers the freezing point. This can result in 'slush' cream.

# Sweetness

Sugar, whether from the wine itself or from ingredients such as onions, garlic, tomatoes, carrots or fruit, plays an important part in creating the flavour of a wine-enriched sauce. Thrown together in the heat of the pan, the sugars react with the other ingredients to form a vast number of new aromatic compounds, adding complexity to the overall flavour of the dish.

Even wines that declare themselves to be dry generally contain a smidgin of sugar, though even the smartest wine-taster might not notice it. When using sweet wines in sauces, bear in mind that as you boil the sauce and reduce its volume, the sugar will concentrate and intensify the sweetness of the sauce. If you know what wine you are going to serve with the dish (maybe the one you've cooked with), you'll need to make sure that the sauce ends up with about the same sweetness as the wine you drink. This is true for savoury as well as for sweet dishes.

Sweet wine is sometimes very good in a *savoury* dish, and can link the food to a medium or even sweet wine. A classic dish in the Sauternes region of Bordeaux is chicken in a Sauternes sauce – and it works. Sweet Coteaux du Layon from the Loire tastes wonderful in (and served with) a creamy sauce for pork and prunes. You can make a quick and delicious sauce for pork chops or kidneys by bubbling up some sweet (or sweetish) fortified wine such as Madeira or oloroso sherry with the cooking juices in the pan. Drinkers of vintage port might stir in the dregs remaining after decanting.

An impressive pudding trick is to freeze cubes of very sweet wine in an ice-cube tray, and pop one into the middle of individual fruit soufflés before cooking. (The soufflé mixture should be quite dense, and the cubes must be made in a deep-freeze – even then they may be a little mushy.) The wine then melts as the soufflé cooks. When you insert your spoon, the trapped wine flows out and makes an instant sweet winey sauce. Simply serve with the same sweet wine for a perfect combination.

### Cook's Tips

◆ Remember the sweetness will intensify the longer the sauce is cooked.

◆ Add a little of the sweet wine you intend to drink to a pudding or accompanying sauce.

## Acidity

The tartness of acidity is one of the positive contributions cooks are looking for from a wine – just as they might add lemon juice or tomatoes to give the sauce a sharper edge. But you need to think carefully before reaching for a bottle of wine to add to the pot. Although water and alcohol boil off, reducing the volume of liquid, the main types of acidity found in wine – tartaric and malic acids – are not volatile, and so do not evaporate when heated.

As the liquid is reduced and concentrates, so the acidity increases and can leave you with an over-tart sauce. So white wines, which tend to have rather higher acidity than reds, need to be used with caution in cooking. You can happily tip a whole bottle of most types of red wine into the pot for a coq au vin, but the Alsace speciality coq au Riesling would taste too sharp if you used a whole bottle of Riesling, which is rather sharply acid. The solution? Use half white wine, half stock or water.

For a perfect match, it is best to aim for the finished sauce to have about the same acidity level as the wine you plan to serve with it. If you do misjudge it and overdo the acidity, you might save the dish by offsetting the acidity with something sweet, perhaps carrots or other sweet root vegetables. Enriching the sauce with cream or butter will also lessen the impact of the acidity.

Old, really past-it wine and wine sold as 'cooking wine' has often been spoiled by acetic acid, the acid of vinegar. Acetic acid, which should be present only in the most minimal quantities in drinkable wine, is known in the wine trade as 'volatile acidity'. In other words, happily for the cook, it evaporates on heating. However, it does take up to 15 minutes to boil off the amount of acetic acid you'd find in old or defective wine, so it's probably best not to use 'cooking wine' or other vinegary plonk in sauces that are cooked only briefly. But vinegary wines should pose no problem in casseroles that are cooked for an hour or more (with the lid off for a time to allow evaporation).

## Cook's Tips

◆ Don't use aluminium when cooking with wine (or other acidic ingredients). The acid easily reacts with the pan to form minute amounts of aluminium compounds. Often grey or black, these may cause slight discoloration of pale foods. Beware also of non-stick pans that have been chipped or scratched through to the metal.

◆ Remember, acidity will intensify the longer a sauce cooks.

◆ Use sharp white wine in moderation.

◆ Add something sweet, or cream, butter or bone stock if your sauce becomes too acidic in taste.

◆ Boil up a medium- to high-acid wine, and reduce its volume by about a half. Use it instead of vinegar or lemon juice for a gentler salad dressing or mayonnaise.

◆ Like any other acid substance, wine will curdle a cooking liquid containing dairy products

◆ Use vinegary wines only in dishes that will be boiled for at least 15 minutes.

◆ The acidity in a wine – in the same way as that of a lemon or lime – is an important ingredient in marinades.

## Colour

A lovely, rich, reddy-brown hue in a wine is a big plus when picking a red wine for a sauce. You can *see* the red colour attaching itself to the surfaces of meat and fish, but plenty of colour will remain in the sauce. Pears or peaches cooked in red wine gain a rosy colour as well as flavour and extra tangy acidity. White wine discolours on boiling, but this isn't a problem in a sauce. Since wines will oxidize on boiling, you can use tired wines when cooking.

## Tannin

Surprisingly, tannin is not a problem in cooking. Tannin quickly reacts with any protein, meat or fish, binding to it chemically and thereby losing most of its astringent taste. You can happily cook meat or even fish in a very tannic red wine. The sauce will be smooth and gentle, the fish or meat unharmed. Very tannic wines are often full-bodied and have plenty of other constituents to offer the dish.

## Body and Intensity

Body, namely a velvety richness of texture, is one of wine's major contributions to stews and sauces. Although the alcohol content partly determines the fullness of body (the higher the alcohol, the fuller the wine), it is irrelevant in the kitchen as the alcohol is boiled off in the cooking. What gives body to a wine-based sauce is the concentration of all those constituents of the wine that do not get carried off with the steam. Important among these is glycerine, a bi-product of fermentation that gives a velvety mouth-feel when sufficently concentrated. Red wines generally have more than whites, but sweet wines that have been affected by botrytis (see page 215) are especially rich in glycerine. All the other unvolatile components of wine, including its colour, also boil down to a richer, fuller sauce.

Rich, full-bodied, unoaked wines – the ideal wines for this job – needn't be expensive. Portugal, Romania and Bulgaria are good sources of inexpensive wines that can generally be relied upon to be full-bodied.

### Cook's Tips
◆ Choose inexpensive, full-bodied, unoaked reds for stews and casseroles.

# Fruitiness

Fruit is not important in a wine for cooking. The fruit in even the fruitiest wine is lost after a few minutes' boiling.

# Flavour and Aroma

Sadly, all the fruity, flowery, spicy aromas and flavours are among the first constituents of wine to fly off in the alcoholic steam during the first few minutes' boiling. They disappear before the alcohol, so their sacrifice is unavoidable.

You can sniff goodbye to the spice of Gewürztraminer, the grapiness of Muscat, and the raspberries of Syrah. (Some of the grassy, green pepper, blackcurrant leaf character of Cabernet Sauvignon and Merlot survives, though its only attraction in a sauce is that it makes a link with an herbaceous wine in your glass.) Some fortified wines do survive the heat of the pan: Madeira and oloroso sherry, for example, contain a lot of 'heavy' compounds, big molecules that don't get driven off by the heat. But the distinctive, tangy taste of fino, Manzanilla and Amontillado sherry is soon gone.

As we have seen, the alcohol, sugars, colour and body, thrown together in the heat with the other ingredients of the dish, create new tastes, and add layers of flavour and richness to the cooking pot. But there is a joker in the flavour pack: oak. Many of the compounds that make up oaky flavour do not evaporate when boiled, so the sauce gets oakier as it reduces. Concentrated oak flavour doesn't belong on a plate, so it's best to avoid using anything but the most delicately oaked wine for cooking.

It is with sweet dishes that you can exploit all the volatile aromas and more subtle flavours of wine, because you don't need to cook the wine that you add to many desserts. Zabaglione, syllabub and trifle are all alcoholic and all taste recognizably of the wines they contain.

In Bordeaux, the locals pour red wine, neat, over strawberries. In the sherry region of south-west Spain, they pour thick, treacly PX (Pedro Ximénez, the sweetest of sweet sherries) over vanilla ice cream. It is delicious. Few other wines in the world would have the guts to stand up to the cold shoulder of ice cream.

A splash into a pudding or dessert of the sweet wine you'll be serving with it – perhaps Beaumes-de-Venise in a chocolate mousse, a trifle or fruit salad – can really put a heavenly seal on the blend of flavours.

There is also the question of 'off' flavours and faulty wines. Luckily, most of the bad flavours and aromas of defective wines also disappear with the steam. All the smells caused by rogue sulphur compounds (rotten eggs, putrid drains, cabbages, sweaty socks...) leave with the steam. One thing boiling won't rid a wine of is corkiness and other musty smells. That musty, mouldy flavour imparted by defective corks stays for the most part: it may be slightly modified in the boiling, but your sauce will stay resolutely musty.

## Cook's Tips

◆ Don't waste complex, aromatic wines in the kitchen – lesser wine will do just as well.
◆ 'Cooking wines' rejected as faulty for drinking are fine for cooking unless corked.
◆ Avoid oaky wines for cooking.

# Draining the Bottle

The alternative to buying undrinkable 'cooking wines' or inexpensive, sound wines, is to use leftovers (or dregs from decanting). They are just asking to be cooked with.

For long-cooked stews and casseroles, you can't go far wrong, however long you store your cooking wine. The compounds formed during oxidation are all very volatile and, together with any vinegary flavours, will eventually boil off during the cooking time.

You can freeze leftovers or dregs to cook with at a later date. Most white wines freeze reasonably well, reds not too badly although they are slightly hindered by the tannin and colouring matter. Sweet wines are more difficult to freeze successfully because of the sugar content. The smart thing to do, both ridding the wine of alcohol and saving space in the freezer, is to boil the wine down by half before freezing it. Fortified wines, preserved by their higher alcohol content, keep well enough for cooking without any special attention.

## Cook's Tips

◆ Add left-over wine or the dregs from decanting to the cooking pot.
◆ You can freeze boiled-up wine in an ice-cube tray, or in yoghurt pots or larger containers to suit your needs.

# INSTANT MATCHES: FOOD TO WINE

This quick-reference directory offers instant solutions for matching food to wine. The entries are listed alphabetically as dishes or as ingredients within their food type, ie Chicken under POULTRY. Accompanying each entry you will find the best wine partners – perfect partners (★★) where they exist, otherwise the closest match (★) – and guides to the styles of red (♟), rosé (♟) or white (♀) wines that work well with that particular food.

Only the best-known dishes from the main directory are mentioned here; sauces, herbs and salad dressings, for example, have been omitted. For more detailed advice, and for many more choices of wines to serve with these and other dishes, turn to the main section (pages 6-203). For a deeper understanding of the general wine style suggestions, see *Matching Food to Wine Styles* (pages 204-230).

## SOUPS *pages 6-13*

**ARTICHOKE (JERUSALEM) SOUP**
★★ South African Chenin Blanc
♀ unoaked, medium-acid, medium-dry whites

**ASPARAGUS SOUP** ★★ New Zealand Sauvignon Blanc
♀ unoaked, dry whites, especially Sauvignon Blanc

**BEETROOT SOUP (BORSCHT)**
★ Soave ♀ crisp, fresh, unoaked dry whites

**BOUILLABAISSE** ★★ Vernaccia di San Gimignano ★★ Bergerac or Bordeaux rosé ♟ light, dry rosés
♀ unoaked, unaromatic, medium-acid whites

**CARROT AND ORANGE SOUP**
★★ Alsace Tokay-Pinot Gris Vendange Tardive ♀ a variety of medium-acid, unoaked whites

**Carrot and Coriander Soup**
★ Alsace Riesling

**CELERY SOUP** ★ Frascati

♀ dry to medium-dry whites

**CHICKEN SOUP, CREAM OF**
★★ Alsace Pinot Blanc
♀ dry, medium- to highish-acid, unoaked whites

**CLAM CHOWDER** ★ Sancerre
♀ unoaked, light, bland, not-too-fruity whites

**COCK-A-LEEKIE** ★★ off-dry South African Chenin Blanc
♟ light, softly tannic reds
♀ off-dry, gently flavoured, unoaked whites

**CRAB BISQUE** ★★ unoaked Australian Chardonnay
♀ unoaked, bland or aromatic dry whites

**CUCUMBER SOUP** ♀ a few gentle whites

**FISH SOUP** ★★ Rueda
♟ dry Grenache rosés ♀ soft, gentle whites

**FRENCH ONION SOUP**
★ VdP des Côtes de Gascogne

GAZPACHO ★★ inexpensive Australian Semillon ♀ dry whites with medium to high acidity

**Seville-style Gazpacho** ★★ inexpensive Australian Semillon

**LEEK AND POTATO SOUP** ★ inexpensive Australian Semillon ♟ dry Syrah rosés ♀ unoaked whites

**LOBSTER BISQUE (BISQUE D'HOMARD)** ★ Cinsault rosé ★ Arneis ♟ dry Cinsault rosés ♀ dry, medium-acid whites

**MINESTRONE SOUP** ★ Soave ♟ Dolcetto ♀ dry, not-too-fruity, not-too-acid whites

**MUSHROOM SOUP** ★★ modern Douro white ♟ soft, savoury low-tannin reds ♀ dry, fairly neutral whites

**ONION SOUP** ★★ Alsace Pinot Blanc ♀ unoaked, dry to medium-dry whites

**SPINACH SOUP** ★★ Frascati ♀ medium- to fairly high-acid, unoaked dry whites

**TOMATO SOUP** ★ Vernaccia di San Gimignano ♟ Dolcetto ♀ highish-acid, dry or fairly dry whites

**TUSCAN BEAN SOUP (RIBOLLITA)** ★★ white Côtes du Rhône ♟ a few low-tannin reds ♀ dry, unoaked whites with low to medium acidity

**VICHYSOISSE** ★ Frascati Superiore

**WATERCRESS SOUP** ★★ Bianco di Custoza ♟ mid-weight, savoury and fruity reds ♀ gentle, fairly neutral or fairly fruity dry whites

**ZUPPA DI FAGGIOLI** ★ Valpolicella ★ Frascati Superiore

# FISH, SHELLFISH AND SEAFOOD
*pages 14–40*

## Fish

**ANCHOVY (FRESH)** ★ Aligoté ♀ light, gently flavoured, medium-acid whites

**BASS** ★★ young Tavel rosé ♟ dry rosés ♀ fresh, dry Pinot Blanc

**BREAM (FRESH-WATER)** ★★ Chardonnay VdP d'Oc ♀ unoaked, light whites

**BREAM (SEA)** ★★ Hungarian Sauvignon Blanc ♀ young, medium-acid whites, especially gently flavoured Sauvignon Blanc

**BRILL** ★★ Lugana ♀ bland Italian whites

**CARP** ★★ German Silvaner Trocken ♀ bland whites

**CAVIAR** ★★ simple Chardonnay ★★ Bianco di Custoza ♀ inexpensive, fairly bland still and sparkling wines

**CEVICHE** ★★ dry Vinho Verde ♀ dry, lightly flavoured, high-acid whites

**COD** ★★ gentle, unoaked Chardonnay ♟ dry rosés ♀ soft, unoaked, lightly flavoured whites

**DOVER SOLE** ★★ Bordeaux Blanc ★★ Sauvignon VdP d'Oc ♀ lightly oaked, softly flavoured whites, especially Sauvignon Blanc

**ESCABECHE** ♀ unoaked, crisp,

lightly fruity whites

**FISH AND CHIPS** ♀ dry rosés ♀ lightly fruity whites

**FISH CAKES** ♀ light, unoaked whites

**FISH PÂTÉ** ♀ dry, medium-acid whites

**FISH PIE** ♀ light, unoaked whites

**FISH SOUP** see *Soups*

**FRITTO MISTO DI MARE** ♀ light, unoaked whites

**GRAVADLAX** ★★ Vouvray Demi-sec ★★ Montlouis Demi-sec ♀ medium-dry whites

**GROUPER** ★★ Soave ♀ light, unoaked whites

**HADDOCK** ★★ Bordeaux Blanc ♀ light, crisp, unoaked whites

**HAKE** ★★ Vermentino di Sardegna ♀ light whites

**HALIBUT** ★ Saove ♀ unoaked, light whites

**HERRING** ★★ Soave Classico ♀ unoaked, light whites

**JACK** ★★ oaked Australian Chardonnay ♀ light, fruity Pinot Noir ♀ oaked, fragrant whites

**JANSSENS TEMPTATION** ★★ inexpensive Soave ♀ bland whites

**JOHN DORY** ★★ Pouilly-Fuissé ♀ top Chardonnays; rich, fragrant whites

**KEDGEREE** see *Rice and Grains*

**KIPPER** ♀ bland whites

**LEMON SOLE** ★★ unoaked Victoria Chardonnay ♀ dry rosés ♀ crisp, unoaked whites

**MACKEREL** ★★ inexpensive white Burgundy ♀ unoaked, light whites

**MONKFISH (ANGLER FISH/LOTTE)** ★★ California

Chardonnay ★★ white St-Romain ♀ lightly oaked dry whites, especially Chardonnay

**MULLET (GREY)** ★★ Vernaccia di San Gimignano ★★ southern French Terret ★★ white Penedés ♀ dry rosés ♀ light, crisp, unoaked whites

**MULLET (RED)** ★★ Soave ♀ dry rosés ♀ crisp, dry, unoaked whites

**PIKE** ♀ bland whites

**PLAICE** ★★ Chilean Chardonnay ★★ Trincadeira das Pratas ♀ light, soft whites

**ROLL-MOP HERRING** ♀ medium-dry, acid whites

**SALMON** ★★ Alsace Muscat ★★ Alsace Pinot Noir ♀ light, low-tannin reds ♀ soft, lightly flavoured, unoaked whites

**SALMON FISH CAKES** see **FISH CAKES**

**SALMON TROUT/SEA TROUT** ★★ Chablis Premier Cru ♀ light, fruity reds ♀ oaked, lightly fruity, dry whites

**SARDINES** ★★ Tavel rosé ★★ Trincadeira das Pratas ♀ dry rosés ♀ lightly flavoured, unoaked whites

**SALT COD (BACALHÃO)** ★★ Bianco di Custoza ★★ red Rioja Crianza ♀ young, gently fruity reds ♀ dry rosés ♀ light, unoaked whites

**SALT HERRING** ★★ white Bairrada ♀ unoaked, light whites

**SKATE** ★★ Jurançon Sec ♀ gentle whites, especially Sauvignon Blanc

**SMOKED COD** ★★ oaked Chardonnay ♀ oaked whites

**SMOKED HADDOCK**
★ Bordeaux Blanc ♀ light, crisp, unoaked whites; dry fino sherry
**SMOKED HALIBUT** ★★ oaked white Rioja ♟ Beaujolais ♀ aromatic, and oaked whites
**SMOKED MACKEREL**
★★ dry Vinho Verde ♀ light, highish-acid whites
**SMOKED SALMON** ★★ oaked California Chardonnay ♀ oaked, dry whites
**SMOKED TROUT (HOT)**
★★ Bourgogne Aligoté ♀ dry, bland whites
**SNAPPER** ★ Spanish Tempranillo rosado ♟ light Spanish rosados ♀ soft, unoaked dry whites
**SPRAT** ★★ Soave Classico ★★ Frascati ♀ unoaked, light, fragrant whites
**SWORDFISH** ★ Rioja Rosado ♟ dry rosés ♀ lightly fruity whites
**TARAMASALATA** ★ Retsina ♟ dry rosés ♀ highish-acid, dry whites
**TROUT** ★★ Spanish or southern French Garnacha/Grenache rosés ★ Frascati ★ Lugana ♟ dry rosés ♀ soft, lightly fruity whites
**TROUT WITH ALMONDS (TRUITE AUX AMANDES)**
★★ white Crozes-Hermitage ♀ light, unoaked whites
**TUNA (FRESH)** ★★ inexpensive Australian Semillon-Chardonnay ♀ light, soft whites
**TUNA (TINNED)** ★★ South African Sauvignon Blanc ♀ quite flavoursome whites, especially Chardonnay

**TURBOT** ★★ inexpensive Australian Chardonnay ♀ lightly oaked or unoaked Chardonnay
**VITELLO TONNATO** see *Veal*
**WHITEBAIT** ★★ Spanish rosado ♟ soft rosés ♀ light, crisp whites

## Shellfish

**BOUILLABAISE** see *Soups*
**CLAMS** ★★ Sancerre ★★ South African Sauvignon Blanc ♀ gently flavoured, unoaked, not-too-fruity whites with medium to fairly high acidity, especially Sauvignon Blancs
**Clam Chowder** see *Soups*
**COCKLES** ♀ very bland whites
**COQUILLES ST-JACQUES** see **SCALLOPS**
**CRAB** ★★ Chilean Sauvignon Blanc ★★ South African Sauvignon Blanc ♟ very light, soft reds ♀ unoaked or lightly oaked, dry whites
**Crab Pâté** ★★ Frascati ★★ English dry Seyval Blanc ♀ dry bland whites
**CRAYFISH (ÉCREVISSES)**
★★ Alsace Pinot Blanc ♀ bland to fairly bland, not-too-acid, not-too-fruity dry whites
**LANGOUSTINE** ★ Frascati ♀ gentle, bland, low-acid, unoaked dry whites
**LOBSTER** ★★ Chablis ♀ oaked or unoaked, dry to medium-dry whites, especially Chardonnay and Riesling
**Lobster à l'Américaine** ★★ Arneis ★★ Favorita ♀ dry whites
**Lobster Pâté** ★ Viognier

♀ dry whites with low to medium acidity

**Lobster Thermidor**
★ Vernaccia di San Gimignano ♀ fairly bland, dry whites

**MOULES MARINIÈRES**
★ Muscadet Sur Lie ♀ dry whites with fairly high acidity

**Moules à la Crème**
★ Muscadet Sur Lie ★ Rueda

**OCTOPUS** ♀ a few off-dry whites, especially gentle Sauvignon Blancs

**OYSTERS** ★★ Muscadet ★★ Champagne Blanc de Blancs ♀ dry, highish- to high-acid unoaked whites

**PAELLA** see *Rice and Grains*

**PRAWNS** ★★ dry white Yecla ★★ dry white Valencia ♀ bland, dry whites

**Prawns and Avocado** see *Vegetables: Avocado*

**Prawn Cocktail** ★★ Austrian Pinot Blanc ★★ English Seyval Blanc ♀ medium-weight, fairly high- to high-acid, unoaked dry whites

**SCALLOPS (COQUILLES ST-JACQUES)** ★★ Austrian Grüner Veltliner ♀ bland, not-too-fruity dry whites, especially Sauvignon Blanc

**Scallops Mornay** ★★ white Burgundy ♀ dry, fairly bland, unoaked or subtly oaked whites with medium acidity, especially Chardonnays

**SCAMPI** ♀ bland whites or very gently flavoured Sauvignon Blanc

**SEAFOOD SALAD (INSALATA DI FRUTTI DI MARE)** ★ Soave ★ Valencia dry white ♀ bland

whites with good acidity

**SHRIMPS (PINK)** ★ Aligoté ♀ dry rosés ♀ bland, dry whites

**SQUID** ♀ extremely bland, dry whites

**Squid in Ink (en su Tinta)** ★★ Barolo ▌ medium-bodied, not-too-fruity or tannic oaked reds ♀ dry, not-too-aromatic or fruity whites

**WHELKS** ★★ Muscadet Sur Lie ♀ dry, medium- to highish-acid whites

# POULTRY AND GAME BIRDS *pages 41-55*

## Chicken

**BARBECUED CHICKEN**
★★ Jurançon Sec ▌ not-too-tannic, gently fruity reds ♀ unoaked, lowish-acid, dry whites

**CHICKEN CHASSEUR**
★★ Gewürztraminer ▌ fruity or savoury, not-too-tannic reds ♀ gently fragrant, oaked and unoaked, medium-acid whites

**CHICKEN KIEV** ★★ unoaked Chablis Premier Cru ♀ unoaked, fragrant whites, especially Chardonnay

**CHICKEN LIVER** ★★ Nebbiolo ▌ not-too-tannic, fairly fruity or savoury reds

**Chicken Liver Pâté**
★★ sweet Graves Supérieures ★★ Beaujolais crus ▌ not-too-tannic, fairly fruity or savoury reds ♀ simple, sweet whites

**CHICKEN PIE** ★★ inexpensive Italian Chardonnay ▌ vins de

pays reds ♀ gentle whites
**Chicken and Ham Pie**
★★ Beaujolais-Villages
**COQ AU VIN** ★★ Australian
Shiraz-Cabernet ♥ fruity,
unoaked or very subtly oaked,
not-too-tannic, medium- to
full-bodied reds
**CORONATION CHICKEN**
★★ inexpensive Rheinhessen
Spätlese ♥ off-dry rosés
♀ off-dry, gentle whites
**DEVILLED CHICKEN** ★★ South
African Chenin Blanc
♥ fruity Shiraz ♀ dry to
medium-dry, lightly
flavoured whites
**FRICASSÉE** ★★ unoaked
southern French Chardonnay
♥ medium-bodied Cabernet
♀ light, low-acid whites
**FRIED (AND SOUTHERN FRIED)**
**CHICKEN** ★★ Jurançon Sec
♥ not-too-tannic, gently fruity
reds ♀ unoaked, lowish-acid,
dry whites
**LEMON CHICKEN** ★★ Bourgogne
Aligoté ★★ Hungarian Furmint
♀ highish-acid, bland whites
**ROAST (OR GRILLED) CHICKEN**
★★ Jurançon Sec ♥ unoaked,
low-tannin, light to
medium-bodied, gently fruity
reds ♀ unoaked, lowish-acid, light
to medium-bodied, unaromatic
dry whites
**with Sage and Onion Stuffing**
★★ Chianti Classico
**with Tarragon** ★★ South African
Chenin Blanc
**with Bread Sauce** ★★ red
Minervois
**with Garlic** ★★ California
Chardonnay

**SMOKED CHICKEN** ★★ not-too-
expensive oaked Australian
Chardonnay ♀ gently flavoured,
oaked whites

## Duck
**CONFIT DE CANARD** ★★ Alsace
Tokay-Pinot Gris ★★ not-too-
tannic Barolo ♥ not-too-tannic,
fruity or savoury reds ♀ dry,
gently fragrant whites
**DUCK BREASTS (MAGRETS DE**
**CANARD)** see **ROAST DUCK**
**DUCK PÂTÉ (PÂTÉ DE CANARD)**
★★ Chianti Classico ♥ not-too-
tannic, fruity reds ♀ medium-
acid, dry and sweet whites
**FOIE GRAS DE CANARD**
★★ Sauternes ♀ sweet, medium-
acid whites; fine, dry Australian
Riesling and fine Chablis
**PÂTÉ DE FOIE GRAS**
★★ Sauternes
**PEKING DUCK** see *Chinese*
*Dishes*
**ROAST DUCK** ★★ modern,
low-tannin Nebbiolo ♥ not-too-
tannic, savoury reds ♀ crisp,
medium-acid, unoaked whites
**in Orange Sauce** ★★ Vouvray
Demi-sec
**in Cherry Sauce** ★★ Mosel
Riesling Spätlese
★★ Beaujolais cru
**SMOKED DUCK** ★★ oaked
white Rioja ♀ oaked, crisp
whites

## Goose
**CASSOULET** see *Pork*
**CONFIT D'OIE** see **ROAST**
**GOOSE**
**FOIE GRAS** see *Duck*
**ROAST GOOSE** ★★ mature red

Bordeaux ★★ Barossa Valley Cabernet ★★ Coonawarra Cabernet ★ German Riesling Kabinett ★ Champagne ! not-too-tannic, fruity or savoury reds, especially Cabernet, and especially if mature ♀ off-dry, light whites

**with Prune and Apple Stuffing** ★★ Vouvray Demi-sec

**with Sage and Onion Stuffing** ★★ red Côtes du Rhône

## Guinea Fowl

CASSEROLES AND STEWS see *Chicken*

ROAST GUINEA FOWL ★★ unoaked, inexpensive Chablis ! light, low-tannin Pinot Noir ♀ medium-bodied, unoaked or lightly oaked, not-too-acid, not-too-fruity, gently flavoured whites

## Quail

ROAST QUAIL ★★ Rueda ♀ bland whites

## Turkey

BLANQUETTE OF TURKEY ★★ unoaked Chardonnay VdP d'Oc ! not-too-tannic, light, fruity reds ! Pinot Noir rosés ♀ gentle whites

CASSEROLES AND STEWS see *Chicken*

CURRIED TURKEY ★★ Australian Verdelho ★ red Portuguese Alentejo ! not-too-tannic, full-bodied, fruity reds ♀ fruity, medium-bodied whites

DEVILLED TURKEY see *Chicken*

ROAST TURKEY ★★ Australian Shiraz ! not-too-tannic,

brightly fruity or rich reds ♀ dry, unoaked, gently flavoured whites

## GAME BIRDS *pages 55-59*

### Grouse

ROAST GROUSE ★★ red Crozes-Hermitage ! not-too-tannic, medium- or full-bodied reds

### Partridge

CASSEROLES AND STEWS see *Chicken*

PARTRIDGE WITH CABBAGE (PERDRIX AUX CHOUX) ★★ white Côtes du Rhône ! not-too-tannic, fruity reds ♀ unoaked, gently fruity whites

ROAST PARTRIDGE ★★ Australian Shiraz ! fruity Shiraz or not-too-tannic, mature reds

### Pheasant

CASSEROLES AND STEWS ★★ red Crozes-Hermitage ! elegant, not-too-tannic, fruity or savoury reds

PHEASANT NORMANDE (FAISAN NORMANDE) ★★ Hungarian Pinot Gris ♀ off-dry whites

PHEASANT PÂTÉ (OR TERRINE) ★★ Sangiovese di Toscana ! young, vibrant or mature, savoury reds ♀ dry Chardonnay and/or Pinot Noir sparkling whites

ROAST PHEASANT ★★ Oregon Pinot Noir ★★ red Crozes-Hermitage ! lightly tannic, savoury reds

## Wild Duck

**MALLARD** ★★ red Crozes-Hermitage ❢ fruity, not-too-tannic, rich reds

## Woodcock

**ROAST WOODCOCK** ★★ Cirò Riserva ❢ not-too-tannic, savoury or fruity, medium-bodied reds

## Wood Pigeon

**CASSEROLE (MATELOTE)** ★★ Oregon Pinot Noir ★★ Cirò Riserva ★★ Portuguese Cabernet-Periquita ❢ rich, fruity reds

**ROAST PIGEON** ★ Ribatejo red ❢ not-too-tannic, savoury reds

**WARM PIGEON BREASTS ON SALAD** ★★ Pomerol ❢ fruity, medium-bodied, highish-acid reds ♀ a few off-dry whites

## MEAT *pages 60-92*

### Beef

**BEEF BOURGUIGNONNE** ★★ Australian Cabernet-Merlot ❢ low-tannin, ripe, really fruity, medium-acid reds ♀ dry or dryish whites

**BEEFBURGER** ★★ Dolcetto ★★ Italian Barbera ❢ unoaked, fruity, low-tannin reds ♀ unoaked, crisp whites

**BEEF STROGANOFF** ★★ Brunello di Montalcino ★★ South African Colombard ❢ medium-bodied, low-tannin reds ♀ gently aromatic, low-acid dry whites

**BEEF WELLINGTON** ★★ red Châteauneuf-du-Pape ❢ gently tannic, fruity or savoury reds

**BOILED BEEF AND CARROTS** ★★ Tempranillo rosado ★★ Valpolicella Classico ❢ light, low-tannin fruity reds ♀ dry rosés

**BRESAOLA** ★★ northern Italian sparkling rosé ★★ Valpolicella Classico ❢ soft reds ♀ northern Italian sparkling rosés ♀ unoaked, gentle Chardonnays

**CARBONNADE À LA FLAMANDE** ★★ lager ❢ low-tannin, medium-bodied, gently flavoured reds ♀ bland whites

**CASSEROLES AND STEWS** ❢ low-tannin, light to medium-bodied, fruity reds

**CHILLI CON CARNE** ★★ Coteaux du Tricastin ★★ single-vineyard Valpolicella ★★ Beaujolais crus ❢ unoaked, medium- to full-bodied, fruity reds

**CORNED BEEF HASH** ★★ Beaujolais crus ❢❢ Gamays or Cabernet Sauvignons ♀ unoaked Chardonnays

**COTTAGE PIE** see **SHEPHERD'S PIE**

**DAUBE OF BEEF** ★★ mature red Bordeaux ❢ lightly oaked, full, fruity or savoury reds

**GOULASH** ★★ Meursault ❢ ripe, softly tannic reds ♀ ripe, full-bodied, fruity whites

**HAMBURGER** ★★ California or Oregon Pinot Noir ❢ unoaked, fruity, low-tannin reds
**with Cheese** ★★ Brunello ★★ Zinfandel ★★ young red Rioja

**LASAGNE** see *Pasta*

**MEATBALLS** ★★ Italian Dolcetto ¶ light to medium-bodied, gently tannic, fairly fruity reds ♀ dry, acid whites

**OXTAIL** ★★ Australian Shiraz ★★ Australian Marsanne ¶ rich, unoaked, mature reds ♀ ripely fruity, medium-bodied whites

**ROAST BEEF** see **STEAK**

**SALT BEEF** ★★ Gamay de Touraine ¶ Gamays ♀ light, bland whites

**SHEPHERD'S PIE** ★★ Beaujolais crus ¶ unoaked, soft, fruity reds

**SPAGHETTI BOLOGNESE** see *Pasta*

**STEAK (FRIED OR GRILLED)** ★★ light Beaujolais crus ¶ low-tannin, softly fruity or mature reds

**with Maître d'Hôtel Butter** ★★ Beaujolais crus

**STEAK AND KIDNEY PIE/ PUDDING** ★★ Australian Coonawarra Cabernet ¶ unoaked or gently oaked, savoury or softly fruity reds ♀ dry rosés

**STEAK AU POIVRE** ★★ Chinon ★★ Chianti Classico ★★ Merlots ★★ St-Nicolas-de-Bourgueil ¶ medium-bodied, low-tannin reds

**STEAK TARTARE** ★★ Bourgogne Aligoté ♀ dry, soft, bland, unoaked whites

## Lamb

**CASSEROLES AND STEWS** ¶ medium- to full-bodied, lowish-tannin, ideally mature reds ♀ dry, not-too-fruity whites

**with Flageolet Beans** ★★ red Rioja Reserva ★★ Cirò Riserva

**COUS-COUS** see *Rice and Grains*

**HAGGIS** ★★ full-bodied red Côtes du Roussillon ¶ full-bodied, low- to medium-tannin, not-too-intensely flavoured reds ♀ low- to medium-acid, not-too-fruity, dry whites

**IRISH STEW** ★★ southern French Cabernet vin de pays ★★ Douro red ¶ unoaked or lightly oaked, lowish-tannin, light to medium-bodied reds

**LAMB CHOPS** see **ROAST LAMB**

**LAMBS' KIDNEY** ★★ Barbaresco ¶ medium- to full-bodied reds with low to medium tannin

**LAMBS' LIVER** ★★ Australian Shiraz ¶ low- to medium-tannin, not-too-fruity reds

**with Onions** ★★ Australian Shiraz

**LAMB SHANKS BAKED WITH THYME (KLEFTIKO)** ★★ Greek Nemea ★★ Greek Goumenissa ¶ low- to medium-tannin, medium-bodied reds

**LANCASHIRE HOTPOT** ★★ Soave Classico ★★ Bourgogne Aligoté ¶ light to medium-bodied, fairly fruity, low-tannin reds ♀ dry or nearly dry whites

**MOUSSAKA** ★★ Greek Naoussa ¶ unoaked or subtly oaked reds with medium tannin and acidity ¶ Tavel rosés

**ROAST LAMB** ★★ mature red Bordeaux ¶ low- to medium-acid, low- to medium-tannin, not-too-fruity reds

**with Garlic and Rosemary** ★★ red Rioja Gran Reserva
**with Thyme** ★★ Australian Coonawarra Cabernet
**SWEETBREADS** ★★ unoaked Chardonnay VdP d'Oc ★★ white Corbières ♀ low- to medium-acid, not too fruity whites

## Pork

**BLACK PUDDING** ★★ light red Burgundy ★★ Chablis ♥ very low-tannin reds ♀ dry whites
**BOILED OR ROAST, GRILLED OR FRIED HAM (UNSMOKED)** ★★ Beaujolais-Villages ♥ light-bodied, unoaked, soft, fruity reds ♥ Tempranillo rosados ♀ light to medium-bodied, unoaked, bland or very slightly aromatic whites
**with Pineapple** ★★ Alella Clásico
**BRAISED HAM WITH LENTILS** ★★ Gamay de Touraine ♥ light, low-tannin reds ♀ gentle whites
**CASSOULET** ★★ white Crozes-Hermitage ♥ unoaked, untannic reds ♀ gently flavoured, unoaked whites
**CHORIZO** ★★ Rioja Rosado ★★ Australian Semillon-Chardonnay ♥ reds with very low tannin ♥ dry rosés ♀ unoaked or subtly oaked fruity whites
**CHOUCROUTE** ★★ Alsace Riesling ♀ fairly high- to high-acid, quite fruity whites
**FRANKFURTER** ★★ Fitou ★★ oaked white Rioja ♥ low- to medium-tannin reds, not too strong in flavour ♥ dry rosés ♀ medium- to fairly high-acid, oaked or unoaked whites
**GARLIC SAUSAGE** ★★ basic red Bordeaux ♥ medium-bodied, low-tannin, softly fruity reds ♀ dry, light to medium-bodied, bland whites
**HONEY-ROAST HAM** ★★ northern Italian Pinot Grigio ♥ light to medium-bodied, low-tannin reds ♀ bland, light to medium-bodied, dry or nearly dry whites
**OAK-SMOKED HAM** ★★ Beaujolais-Villages ★★ oaked white Rioja ♥ lowish-tannin, light, softly fruity reds ♀ oaked, gently fruity whites
**PARMA HAM** ★★ Anjou Blanc Demi-sec ♀ unoaked, gently fruity whites, with a touch of sweetness
**with Melon** ★★ Mosel Riesling Kabinett
**PORK CHOPS** see **ROAST PORK**
**PORK PIE** ★★ Dolcetto ★★ Fitou ♥ low- to medium-tannin, medium- to full-bodied, fruity reds ♀ gently flavoured whites
**PORK WITH PRUNES AND CREAM** ★★ Vouvray Demi-sec ♀ fairly high- to high-acid, medium-dry or medium whites
**PORK RILLETTES** ★★ California Cabernet ★★ Chablis Premier Cru ♥ low-tannin, unoaked or subtly oaked reds ♀ medium-weight to full whites, with good but not high acidity
**PORK SAUSAGES** ★★ Chablis Premier Cru ♥ low- to medium-tannin reds ♀ dry, not-too-intensely flavoured whites

**with Sage** ★★ Valpolicella Classico
**ROAST PORK** ★★ Moulin-à-Vent ★★ Chablis Premier Cru ❢ fairly full, low- to medium-tannin reds ♀ dry, fairly bland, medium-acid whites
**with Apple Sauce** ★★ Mosel-Saar-Ruwer Riesling Kabinett
**SALAMI** ❢ a few low-tannin, not-too-intensely flavoured reds ♀ bland whites with low- to medium-acid
**SAUCISSON SEC** ❢ a few low-tannin reds ♀ unoaked, bland lowish-acid whites
**SPARE RIBS WITH BARBECUE SAUCE** ★★ Liebfraumilch ❢ very fruity reds with good acidity ♀ medium or medium-dry, medium- to high-acid whites

## Snails
**SNAILS IN GARLIC BUTTER**
★★ Médoc cru bourgeois
★★ Bourgogne Aligoté
❢ medium-acid, medium to full-bodied reds ♀ light to medium-bodied, bland whites

## Veal
**BLANQUETTE DE VEAU**
★★ Pinot Grigio ♀ bland or very gently flavoured whites
**CALVES' LIVER** ★★ mature Carmignano ★★ mature Chianti Classico ❢ mature or fruity reds with medium to low acidity and tannin ♀ warm-climate Sauvignon Blanc or dry Riesling
**with Onions (Fegato alla Veneziana)** ★★ Dolcetto
**CHOPS IN MARSALA SAUCE**

★ Dolcetto ★ white Côtes du Rhône ★ Alella Clásico
❢ Dolcetto ♀ gentle, slightly aromatic whites
**OSSO BUCO** ★★ Australian Reserve Semillon ♀ full-bodied, fruity whites, with good acidity
**SALTIMBOCCA** ★★ white Côtes du Rhône ♀ unoaked dry whites
**VITELLO TONNATO** ★ Arneis ♀ bland or very gently aromatic whites
**WIENERSCHNITZEL**
★ Vernaccia di San Gimignano ♀ very bland, unoaked, gently flavoured, medium-acid whites

## Venison
**CASSEROLES AND STEWS**
★★ Côtes du Rhône Syrah
★★ Zinfandel ❢ full-bodied, flavourful, fruity reds
**ROAST VENISON** ★ soft red Burgundy ❢ low-tannin, mature reds, especially Pinot Noir

# FURRED GAME
## Hare
**CASSEROLES AND STEWS**
❢ medium- to full-bodied, ripely fruity reds
**JUGGED HARE** ★★ red Côtes du Ventoux ❢ medium- to full-bodied, fruity reds

## Rabbit
**RABBIT IN CIDER** ★ Navarra or Rioja rosado ★ South African Chenin Blanc
❢ low- to medium-tannin, fruity reds ❢ dry Grenache rosés ♀ lightly aromatic, dry or off-dry whites

**RABBIT WITH MUSTARD**
★ German Silvaner Trocken
❢ low-tannin reds ♀ dry, gently fruity, highish-acid, unoaked whites

## ETHNIC DISHES
*pages 93-108*

### Chinese

**BEEF WITH GREEN PEPPERS IN BLACK BEAN SAUCE**
★★ Australian Verdelho
★★ German Riesling Halbtrocken ♀ dry or nearly dry whites

**BEEF AND MANGETOUT IN OYSTER SAUCE** ♀ bland whites

**BEEF WITH ONIONS AND GINGER** ★★ Mosel Riesling or cheaper QbA ❢ Beaujolais
♀ not-quite-dry whites

**CHICKEN WITH BAMBOO SHOOTS AND WATER CHESTNUTS** ♀ bland whites with low to medium acidity

**CHICKEN WITH CASHEW NUTS**
★ Spanish Albariño
★ Valencia dry white ❢ dry rosés ♀ dry or nearly dry whites

**CHICKEN CHOW MEIN** ★ white Châteauneuf-du-Pape ♀ bland, dry or medium-dry, not-too-acid whites

**HOT AND SOUR SOUP**
★★ English Seyval Blanc
♀ medium- to high-acid whites with a touch of sweetness

**PEKING DUCK** ★ Champagne
❢ Cinsault rosés ♀ a few dry whites

**PORK SPARE RIBS** ★ Vouvray Demi-sec ♀ high-acid, sweetish whites

**SPRING ROLLS** ♀ bland whites

**SWEET AND SOUR CHICKEN**
★ Mosel Riesling Auslese
★ Tokay 3 Puttonyos ♀ medium-dry to medium-sweet whites

**SWEETCORN SOUP WITH CHICKEN** ★★ Australian Verdelho ♀ medium-dry whites
**with Crab** ♀ medium-dry whites

**SZECHUAN-STYLE PORK**
★ German Riesling or Silvaner Kabinett Halbtrocken ❢ Syrah rosés ♀ a few whites

**WON TON SOUP** ★ Yecla or Valencia dry white ♀ bland whites

### Thai

**BEEF IN PEANUT CURRY**
★ Alsace Tokay-Pinot Gris
♀ dry, not-too-acid whites

**GREEN CURRY** ♀ a few whites

**LEMON AND CHICKEN SOUP**
★★ VdP des Côtes de Gascogne
★★ German Silvaner Kabinett Trocken ♀ bland, medium- to high-acid whites

**MUSSALMAN CURRY**
★★ Rueda ★★ Hungarian Furmint ♀ fruity, dry or medium-dry whites

**NOODLES AND BEANSPROUTS**
♀ slightly sweet, medium- to high-acid whites

**PRAWN AND LEMON SOUP**
★★ Vernaccia di San Gimignano
★★ Valencia dry white ♀ bland, dry, not-too-acid whites

**RED CURRY** ★ Aligoté
★ Valencia dry white ♀ dry, fairly bland whites

**ROAST DUCK CURRY**
★★ Bordeaux rosé ★★ VdP des Côtes de Gascogne

♥ dry to medium-dry rosés
♀ dry and off-dry, fairly high to high-acid whites

**SATAY** ★ German Riesling Halbtrocken ♀ nearly dry whites

**SPECIAL THAI NOODLES** ★ Mosel Riesling Halbtrocken ♥♀ fruity or slightly sweet rosés and whites

**STIR-FRY PORK** ★ Menetou-Salon ★ Sancerre ♀ dry, bland not-too-acid whites, especially Sauvignon

**STIR-FRY SQUID** ★ Bourgogne Aligoté ♀ fairly bland, gentle whites

## Indian

**CHICKEN MADRAS** ★ Spanish Rueda ♀ a few dry whites

**CHICKEN TIKKA** ★ Pinot Grigio ★ Sancerre ♥♀ Spanish reds or rosados ♀ fairly bland, dry whites

Chicken Tikka Balti
★★ California Pinot Noir
★★ red Rioja Crianza ♥ savoury reds ♥ dry rosés ♀ fairly flavour-ful, dry to medium-dry whites

Chicken Tikka Makhani ★ dry Muscat ★ Sancerre ♥ gentle Shiraz ♀ dry whites

Chicken Tikka Masala ★ VdP des Côtes de Gascogne ♥ light reds ♀ dry whites

**KORMA** ★ Viognier ★ Chilean Sauvignon Blanc ♥ light reds ♀ dry whites

**MAKHANI** see **TIKKA**

**MASALA** see **TIKKA**

**MEAT BALTI** ★★ white Corbières ★★ VdP des Côtes de Gascogne ♥ not-too-fruity, dry

rosés ♀ dry, quite bland, medium- to highish-acid whites

**ROGAN JOSH** ★ Pinot Grigio ★ lightly oaked Chardonnay VdP d'Oc ♀ light, dry, highish-acid whites

**PASANDA** ★★ red Rioja Crianza ♥ light reds ♥ dry rosés ♀ oaked, dry whites

**SAAG ALOO** ♀ bland, low-fruit whites with medium acidity

**TANDOORI** ♥ very light reds, especially Loire Cabernets ♥ dry rosés ♀ unoaked, dry whites

**TARKA DAL** ★ Frascati ★ Sicilian whites ♀ bland, low-acid, unoaked whites

**TUPLI** ♥ light, low-tannin reds ♀ dry, highish-acid whites

**VEGETABLE BALTI** ♥ dry rosés ♀ dry, fairly bland, highish-acid whites

**VINDALOO** ★ New Zealand Sauvignon ♀ dry, fairly to very flavourful whites with medium acidity

## EGGS AND EGG DISHES *pages 109-114*

**ASPARAGUS QUICHE** ★★ Montagny Premier Cru ♀ unoaked or very subtly oaked European Chardonnays

**BAKED EGGS (OEUFS EN COCOTTE)** ★★ simple white Burgundy ♥ Beaujolais ♀ dry, unoaked or subtly oaked, still or sparkling whites, especially Chardonnay

**BROCCOLI QUICHE** ★ Mâcon-Villages Blanc ♀ unoaked or very subtly oaked European Chardonnays

**CHEESE OMELETTE** ♀ fairly low-acid, unoaked dry whites
**CHEESE AND ONION QUICHE** ♀ unoaked Chardonnays
**CHEESE SOUFFLÉ ★** subtle California Chardonnay ♀ unaromatic whites with low to medium acidity
**CHICKEN AND MUSHROOM PANCAKE ★★** unoaked southern French Chardonnay ❢ very soft, light reds ♀ gentle whites
**EGGS BENEDICT ★★** New Zealand Riesling ♀ still and sparkling, unoaked whites with good but not too high acidity
**EGGS FLORENTINE ★★** Chardonnay del Piemonte ❢ unoaked or subtly oaked Zinfandels ♀ unoaked, simple Chardonnays with good acidity
**HAM (OR BACON) OMELETTE** ♀ unoaked dry whites
**MUSHROOM OMELETTE ★** Lugana ★ unoaked Chardonnay VdP d'Oc ❢ Garnacha ♀ bland, dry whites; Chardonnays
**PLAIN OMELETTE** ♀ dry, unoaked, simple whites
**QUICHE LORRAINE (D'ALSACE) ★** Alsace Tokay-Pinot Gris ♀ a few, low- to medium-acid, dry whites.
**SPANISH OMELETTE (TORTILLA) ★** white La Mancha ♀ bland, dry whites
**SCRAMBLED EGG AND SMOKED SALMON ★★** inexpensive Australian Semillon ♀ unoaked or subtly oaked whites, especially Semillon

**SPINACH AND GRUYÈRE QUICHE ★** Bourgogne Aligoté ♀ dry, unoaked or subtly oaked whites
**SPINACH SOUFFLÉ ★** South African Colombard ❢ Beaujolais ♀ subtle, lowish-acid whites
**SPAGHETTI CARBONARA** see *Pasta*
**TOAD-IN-THE-HOLE ★★** white Côtes du Rhône ♀ whites with low to medium acidity, not too strongly flavoured or brightly fruity

## PASTA, PIZZA AND RICE DISHES
*pages 115-124*

### Pasta

**BEEF CANELLONI ★★** Valpolicella Classico ★★ Sangiovese delle Marche ★★ Sangiovese di Romagna ❢ light to medium-bodied, savoury or fruity reds ❢ dry Syrah rosés
**BEEF LASAGNE ★** Barbera d'Alba ❢ medium-weight, fruity, fairly low-tannin reds ♀ a few fairly aromatic, dry whites
**MACARONI CHEESE ★** Australian Semillon ♀ oaked and unoaked dry whites with low to medium acidity
**PASTA:**
**with MUSHROOMS AND GARLIC ★** Frascati ♀ low- to medium-acid, dry whites
**with PESTO ★★** Alsace Tokay-Pinot Gris ★★ Hungarian Furmint ★★ lightly oaked Australian Chardonnay

♥ a few soft reds ♀ dry, not-too-fruity, not-too-acid whites

**with SMOKED SALMON AND CREAM** ★ white Burgundy ♀ dry, lightly oaked or unoaked whites

**with TOMATO SAUCE** see *Sauces: Tomato Sauce*

**PORK AND BEEF RAVIOLI** ♥ dry rosés ♀ dry, low-acid, bland whites

**SPINACH AND RICOTTA CANELLONI** ★ South African Sauvignon Blanc ♀♀ dry and off-dry rosés and whites, with fairly low acidity

**SPINACH AND RICOTTA RAVIOLI** ★ Penedés white ♀ very bland whites with low acidity

**SPAGHETTI BOLOGNESE** ★★ Australian Shiraz ♥ light to medium-bodied, fruity or savoury reds ♥ dry rosés ♀ dry, neutral whites

**with Ragu** ★ Bianco di Custoza

**SPAGHETTI ALLA CARBONARA** ★ Sicilian white ♀ not-too-acid, bland, dry or dryish whites

**SPAGHETTI ALLA VONGOLE (COCKLES)** ★ dry Sicilian white ♀ dry, fairly neutral, highish-acid whites

**VEGETABLE LASAGNE** ★ VdP des Côtes de Gascogne ♥ medium-bodied, savoury or Cabernet-based reds ♀ light, dry or dryish, highish- to high-acid whites

**WILD MUSHROOM, GARLIC, PARMESAN AND RICOTTA RAVIOLI** ★ Sangiovese delle Marche ♥ soft reds ♀ dry, low-acid, bland whites

## Pizza

**CHEESE AND TOMATO PIZZA** ★★ Bianco di Verona ♥ light to medium-bodied, savoury reds ♀ fairly neutral, highish- to high-acid whites

**PIZZA NAPOLETANA** ★ Tuscan Vernaccia-Chardonnay ♥ dry rosés ♀ dry, highish-acid, fairly neutral whites

## Rice and Grains

**COUS-COUS** ★★ Australian Chardonnay ♥ light, not-too-tannic Shiraz ♥ fruity, medium-acid rosés ♀ fruity, hot-climate Chardonnays

**KEDGEREE** ★★ VdP d'Oc Sauvignon Blanc ★★ Bourgogne Aligoté ♀ light, unoaked, dry whites with good acidity, especially Sauvignon Blancs

**MUSHROOM RISOTTO (AL FUNGHI)** ♥ a few very gentle, light reds ♀ dry, low- to medium-acid bland whites

**NUT CUTLETS/NUT ROAST** ★★ Sangiovese delle Marche ♥ very gentle, low-tannin reds ♀ gentle, not-too-acid, not-too-fruity whites

**PAELLA ALLA VALENCIANA** ★ Cava ★ oaked white Rioja ★ Spanish rosado ♥ dry rosés ♀ gentle, fairly neutral to fruity, oaked or lightly oaked whites

**RISOTTO AL BIANCO** ♀ unoaked, bland dry whites

**RISOTTO ALLA MILANESE** ★ Verdicchio ♀ dry, unoaked, low- to medium-acid whites

**SEAFOOD RISOTTO (ALLA MARINARA)** ★★ Frascati ♥ dry rosés ♀ dry, fairly bland, highish-acid whites

**STUFFED VINE LEAVES (DOLMADES)** ★★ English dry white ❢ a few high-acid reds ♀ dry, high-acid whites

**TABBOULEH** ★★ Bordeaux Blanc ♀ dry, fairly high-acid whites

# VEGETABLES, VEGETABLE DISHES AND SALADS

## Vegetables and Vegetable Dishes

**ASPARAGUS (GREEN), PLAIN OR WITH MELTED BUTTER** ★★ mature, oaked white Graves ♀ unoaked or subtly oaked dry whites

**ASPARAGUS (WHITE)** ★★ unoaked Australian Chardonnay ♀ unoaked, ripely fruity Chardonnays, with low to medium acidity

**AUBERGINE DIP (MELIDZANESALATA)** ★★ New Zealand Sauvignon Blanc ❢ Beaujolais ♀ dry whites, especially Sauvignons

**AVOCADO WITH PRAWNS** ★★ Chablis ★★ mature white Burgundy ♀ bland, dry whites with medium to high acidity

**AVOCADO WITH VINAIGRETTE** ★★ Chablis ♀ unoaked or very subtly oaked dry whites

**BAKED AUBERGINE WITH PARMESAN** ★★ Sauvignon de Touraine ❢ Beaujolais ♀ Sauvignon Blanc, New World dry Riesling, a few simple Italian whites

**BEANS IN TOMATO SAUCE (FAGIOLI ALL'UCCELLETTO)** ★★ Chilean Sauvignon Blanc ❢ low-tannin reds with not-too-bright fruit, especially mature ♀ dry whites

**CAULIFLOWER CHEESE** ♀ unoaked, dry to medium whites

**CELERY** ♀ a few dry, unoaked whites

**COUS-COUS** see *Rice and Grains*

**FELAFEL** ★ Verdicchio ♀ a very few whites

**FENNEL** ♀ dry whites with medium acidity

**FRIED/GRILLED AUBERGINES, OR FRITTERED** ★★ Jurançon Sec ♀ dry whites

**FRIED MUSHROOMS** ★ white Burgundy ❢ a few mature reds ♀ unoaked, not-too-acid or brightly fruity dry whites

**GLOBE ARTICHOKES** ★ Australian dry Riesling ❢ Cinsault rosés ♀ dry whites

**GUACAMOLE** ★★ Chilean or New Zealand Sauvignon Blanc ♀ dry whites, especially Sauvignon Blancs

**HUMMUS** ★★ Vinho Verde ♀ high-acid, unoaked bland whites

**LEEKS IN CHEESE SAUCE** ★★ inexpensive Australian Semillon ♀ bland, dry or dryish whites with low to medium acidity

**MUSHROOMS À LA GRÈCQUE** ★ Bordeaux Blanc

**OLIVES (BLACK AND GREEN)** ★ fino or manzanilla sherry ♀ fino and manzanilla sherry; dry, fairly high-acid whites

**ONION TART** ★ Lugana ♀ light, highish-acid, fairly fruity whites
**RATATOUILLE** ★★ New Zealand Sauvignon Blanc ♥ gentle, unoaked, low-tannin southern French reds ♀ unoaked, aromatic dry whites with fairly high acidity
**RED CABBAGE WITH APPLE AND ONION** ♀ medium-dry to medium whites with fairly high to high acidity
**SPINACH** ★★ Frascati.
**STUFFED VINE LEAVES (DOLMADES)** see *Rice and Grains*
**TOMATO** see *Soups, Salads, and Sauces*

## Salads
**AVOCADO, MOZZARELLA AND TOMATO SALAD (INSALATA TRICOLORE)** ★ Chablis ♀ dry whites with good acidity
**BEAN SALAD** ★★ Rueda ★★ Sancerre ♥ soft, unoaked Spanish reds ♥ dry rosés ♀ crisp, fruity, medium- to fairly high-acid dry whites
**BEETROOT SALAD** ★★ white Lambrusco ♀ medium-dry to medium-sweet whites with fairly high acidity
**CAESAR SALAD** ★★ Aligoté ★★ Frascati ♀ dry whites
**CUCUMBER SALAD** ★★ Chablis ★★ California Chardonnay ♀ dry whites with medium to highish acidity, especially Chardonnay
**GREEK SALAD** ★ Retsina ♀ bland whites with fairly high to high acidity
**GREEN SALAD** ★★ Bourgogne

Aligoté ★★ VdP des Côtes de Gascogne ♥ a few very light, low-tannin reds ♀ high-acid dry whites
**SALADE NIÇOISE** ★★ Cheverny ♀ dry whites
**TOMATO SALAD** ★★ Sauvignon de Touraine ♀ dry whites with fairly high to high acidity, especially Sauvignon Blanc
**with Onion** ★ VdP des Côtes de Gascogne
**with Mozzarella and Basil** ★ Verdicchio
**WALDORF SALAD** ♀ medium-dry whites with medium acidity

# HERBS, SPICES AND FLAVOURINGS
*see page 141*

# SAUCES, DRESSINGS AND RELISHES
*see page 155*

# CHEESES *pages 166-181*

**FONDUE** ★★ Chilean Sauvignon Blanc ♀ dry whites, especially Sauvignon Blanc
**RACLETTE** ★ California or Chilean Chardonnay ♀ whites with low to medium acidity

## Hard Cheeses
**CAERPHILLY** ★★ red Rioja Gran Reserva ♥ low-tannin, not-too-fruity, medium- to full-bodied reds
**CANTAL** ★ red Rioja Gran

Reserva ❗ mature, savoury reds with lowish tannin ♀ a few dry whites

**CHEDDAR (MATURE FARMHOUSE)** ★★ Salice Salentino ❗ mature, full-bodied lowish-tannin reds ♀ a few medium-sweet to sweet whites

**Cheddar (Medium)** ★★ Salice Salentino

**Cheddar (Mild)** ★★ Salice Salentino

**CHESHIRE** ★ California Cabernet Sauvignon ❗ full, fairly fruity, lowish-tannin reds

**CHÈVRE** see **GOATS' CHEESE**

**DOUBLE GLOUCESTER** ★★ Cirò Riserva ❗ full, not-too-fruity reds

**EDAM** ★ Greek Nemea ❗ full, not-too-fruity, preferably mature reds

**EMMENTAL (SWISS)** ★ Barbera d'Alba ❗ unoaked reds, preferably mature

**GOATS' CHEESE (HARD)** ★ Alsace Pinot Blanc

**GOUDA (MATURE)** ★★ red Rioja Gran Reserva ★★ mature Vino Nobile di Montepulciano ❗ medium to full-bodied reds ♀ sweet whites

**Gouda (Young)** ★★ Australian Shiraz

**GRUYÈRE** ★★ Dolcetto ★★ Mosel Riesling Kabinett ❗ medium- to full-bodied, not-too-tannic reds ♀ gently aromatic whites

**JARLSBERG** ★★ Chilean dry Riesling ❗ full, low-tannin, unoaked, not-too-fruity reds ♀ dry whites, especially New World Riesling

**LANCASHIRE** ★ Champagne ❗ medium- to full-bodied reds ♀ whites with good acidity

**MANCHEGO** ★ California Sangiovese ❗ medium- to full-bodied, savoury, not-too-fruity or tannic reds

**PARMESAN REGGIANO** ★★ Aglianico del Vulture ❗ full-flavoured, not-too-tannic reds ♀ a few dry whites

**RED LEICESTER** ★★ red Rioja Gran Reserva ❗ medium- to full-bodied, low-tannin, not-too-fruity reds

**SMOKED BAVARIAN CHEESE** ★ Graves Supérieures (sweet) ★ Sauternes

**WENSLEYDALE** ★ Rheingau Spätlese

## Soft Cheeses

**BEL PAESE** ★★ California Barbera ❗ medium-bodied, highish-acid reds ♀ unoaked, dry Chardonnays; other crisp whites

**BOURSIN** ★★ Sancerre ❗❗ light to medium-bodied, Cabernet-based reds or rosés ♀ crisp, dry, unoaked whites

**BRIE (PASTEURISED)** ★ mature Ribera del Duero ❗ gentle, savoury reds ♀ highish-acid, unoaked whites

**Brie (Unpasteurised)** ★ LBV (Late Bottled Vintage) port

**CAMEMBERT (PASTEURISED)** ★ Chianti ❗ medium- to full-bodied, savoury reds ♀ crisp, dry whites

**Camembert (Unpasteurised)** ★★ red Burgundy

**CHAOURCE** ★★ Champagne

medium-bodied, Cabernet-based and savoury reds ♀ highish- to high-acid whites

**CHAUME** ★★ Arneis ♥ medium- to full-bodied, savoury reds ♀ gentle, crisp, lightly aromatic whites

**CHÈVRE** see **GOATS' CHEESE**

**FETA** ★★ Alsace Riesling ♀ highish- to high-acid whites

**GOATS' CHEESE** ★★ Sancerre ♥ medium to full-bodied, not-too-tannic reds, especially Pinot Noir ♥ dry rosés ♀ dry to off-dry, unoaked whites

**MILLEENS** ★ Volnay ♥ savoury, medium-bodied reds ♀ honeyed, slightly aromatic dry whites

**MOZZARELLA** ★ Montagny Premier Cru ♀ delicately flavoured whites

**MUNSTER** ★★ California Syrah ♥ medium- to full-bodied, not-too-oaky reds ♀ dry or nearly dry, aromatic whites

**NEUFCHÂTEL-EN-BRAY** ★★ not-too-tannic red Burgundy ♥ medium to full-bodied reds ♀ not-too-aromatic whites with good acidity

**PONT L'EVÊQUE** ★★ red Rioja Reserva ♥ full-bodied, mature reds ♀ a few dry, gently aromatic whites

**PORT-SALUT** ★★ Valpolicella ♥ low-tannin, low-fruit reds ♀ a very few unoaked, low-acid whites

## Blue Cheeses

**BLUE BRIE** ★ mature red Bordeaux ★ New Zealand Riesling ♥ highish-acid, not-too-tannic reds

**BRESSE BLEU** ★★ Juliénas ♥ light reds

**CAMBOZOLA** ★ California Zinfandel ♥ medium-bodied, highish-acid reds

**DOLCELATTE** ★ red Rioja Gran Reserva ♥ medium-bodied, fruity reds

**GORGONZOLA** ★ mature red Bordeaux

**ROQUEFORT** ★★ Sauternes ★★ Barsac ♥ fruity and savoury reds ♀ sweet whites, especially botrytized; some fortified wines

**STILTON (BLUE)** ★★ 10-year-old tawny port ♥ medium-bodied, highish-acid, fruity reds; aged tawny port and aged Bual Madeira

# DESSERTS, PUDDINGS AND FRUITS *pages 182–203*

## Fruits and Fruit Desserts

**APPLE PIE/CHARLOTTE/ CRUMBLE/TART OR STEWED** ★★ Mosel Riesling Beerenauslese ♀ sweet, medium- to high-acid whites

**APPLE STRUDEL** ★★ Washington State Late Harvest Riesling ♀ very sweet whites, especially Riesling

**APPLE TART WITH CRÈME PATISSIÈRE** ★ Australian botrytized Semillon ★ Barsac ★ Sauternes ♀ sweet, not-too-high-acid whites, especially Semillon

**APRICOT PIE/CRUMBLE/ DRIED/TART OR STEWED** ★★ Australian botrytized

Semillon ★★ Mosel Riesling Beerenauslese ♀ highish-acid botrytized whites

**BAKED APPLE** ♀ sweet, quite high-acid whites

**BANOFFEE PIE** ★★ Australian botrytized Chardonnay ♀ very sweet, botrytized Chardonnay or fortified Muscat, and very sweet Tokay

**BLACKBERRY AND APPLE PIE/CRUMBLE OR STEWED** ★★ Mosel Riesling Beerenauslese ▮ Black Muscat ♀ very sweet, high-acid whites, especially Riesling

**BLACKCURRANT CHEESECAKE** ♀ sweet Muscats

**BLACKCURRANT MOUSSE** ★ Asti ♀ high-acid, fairly sweet to sweet whites

**BLACKCURRANT PIE/ CRUMBLE** ★ Asti ♀ high-acid, sweet whites with not too much botrytis

**BILBERRY/BLUEBERRY/ WIMBERRY PIE** ♀ botrytized Rieslings and Semillons

**CARAMELIZED ORANGES** ★★ Asti ♀ very sweet whites, particularly Muscats

**CRÈPES SUZETTES** ★ Asti ♀ very sweet whites

**FRESH FRUIT SALAD** ★★ Asti ★★ sweet Rieslings ♀ sweet whites with good acidity, especially Rieslings and Asti

**GOOSEBERRY FOOL** ★ Australian botrytized Semillon ♀ very sweet botrytized whites

**GOOSEBERRY PIE/CRUMBLE OR STEWED** ★ Mosel Riesling Auslese ♀ sweet Mosel Rieslings

**LEMON CHEESECAKE** ★ Australian botrytized Semillon ♀ sweet high-acid whites

**LEMON MERINGUE PIE** ★ Asti ★ Moscatel de Valencia ♀ very sweet botrytized whites or lighter Muscats

**LEMON TART** ★★ Austrian Müller-Thurgau Beerenauslese ♀ very sweet, botrytized, high-acid whites

**MANGO** ★ botrytized Riesling ♀ very low-acid, sweet whites

**MELON (GALIA)** ♀ sweet Loire wines, very light, sweet Muscats; 10-year-old tawny port

**NECTARINE** see **PEACH**

**ORANGE BAVAROIS/MOUSSE/ SOUFFLÉ/TART** ★★ Asti ♀ sweet Muscats

**ORANGE CHEESECAKE** ★ Asti ♀ very sweet but gentle, fortified or sparkling Muscats

**PASSION FRUIT FOOL** ♀ high-acid sweet whites

**PEACH/NECTARINE** ★★ Mosel Riesling Auslese ♀ high-acid, fairly sweet whites, especially Riesling

**PEARS IN RED WINE** ♀ sweet and very sweet whites, not Muscat

**PLUM PIE/CRUMBLE OR STEWED** ★★ Australian and South African botrytized Rieslings ♀ sweet and very sweet Rieslings, fortified Muscats

**RASPBERRIES** ★★ California fortified Orange Muscat ♀ fairly sweet to very sweet whites

**with Cream** ★★ New Zealand botrytized Riesling

**RASPBERRY FOOL**
★★ Sauternes ♀ sweet whites with good acidity

**RHUBARB PIE/CRUMBLE/TART OR STEWED** ★ Asti ♀ sweet and very sweet, high-acid whites

**STRAWBERRIES** ★ Clairette de Die ♀ gently flavoured, fairly sweet, not-too-acid whites

**with Cream** see **Strawberry Mousse**

**STRAWBERRY MOUSSE**
★★ botrytized Semillon
★★ Sauternes ★★ southern French unfortified Muscat à Petits Grains ♀ sweet whites, especially botrytized Semillon and fortified Muscats

**SUMMER PUDDING** ★ Mosel Riesling Beerenauslese ♀ high-acid, very sweet whites

**TARTE NORMANDE** ★ Graves Supérieures ★ southern French Muscat à Petits Grains ♀ medium- to high-acid sweet whites

**TARTE TATIN** ★★ Austrian Müller-Thurgau Trockenbeerenauslese ♀ sweet, not-too-high-acid whites

## Other Puddings and Desserts

**ALMOND TART** ★★ Moscatel de Valencia ♀ sweet fortified Muscats, some other sweet whites

**BACLAVA** ★★ 20-year-old Setúbal ♀ very sweet fortified Muscats

**BAKEWELL TART** ★★ Asti ♀ very sweet whites

**BAKEWELL PUDDING**
★ Moscatel de Valencia

★ young Setúbal

**BLACK FOREST GÂTEAU**
★★ Moscatel de Valencia ♀ sweet Muscats with fairly high acidity

**BREAD-AND-BUTTER PUDDING**
★★ German Scheurebe Trockenbeerenauslese ♀ not-too-acid sweet whites

**CHEESECAKE** see **BLACKCURRANT, LEMON, ORANGE AND STICKY TOFFEE CHEESECAKES**

**CHOCOLATE BAVAROIS**
★★ California Orange Muscat ♀ sweet whites, including botrytized whites and especially Muscats

**CHOCOLATE GÂTEAU**
★★ Austrian Müller-Thurgau Trockenbeerenauslese ♀ sweet Muscats

**CHOCOLATE MOUSSE**
★ Moscatel de Valencia ♀ very sweet, not-too-acid Muscat

**with Milk Chocolate** ★★ Asti

**CHOCOLATE PROFITEROLES WITH CREAM** ★ sweet, unfortified Muscat ♀ sweet, unfortified Muscats

**CHOCOLATE ROULADE** see **CHOCOLATE GÂTEAU**

**CHRISTMAS PUDDING**
★★ Asti ♀ very sweet Muscats, botrytized Rieslings

**COFFEE GÂTEAU** ★★ Moscatel de Valencia ♀ sweet whites, especially Muscat

**COFFEE MOUSSE**
★★ Australian Rutherglen Liqueur Muscat ♀ not-too-acid, sweet whites, especially Muscat

**COFFEE PROFITEROLES**
★★ Moscatel de Valencia

★★ Muscat de St-Jean-de-Minervois ♀ sweet, low-acid whites, especially fortified Muscats

CRÈME BRÛLÉE ★★ Australian botrytized Semillon ♀ sweet, not-too-acid Muscats and Semillons

CRÈME CARAMEL ★ sweet, unfortified southern French Muscat à Petits Grains ♀ not-too-acid sweet whites, especially Muscat and Semillon

CUSTARD (BAKED EGG) ♀ whites of similar sweetness

CRÈME ANGLAISE/HOME-MADE POURING CUSTARD ♀ sweet Muscats or Rieslings

FLOATING ISLANDS (ÎLES FLOTTANTES) ★ Muscat de Beaumes-de-Venise ♀ sweet Muscats

MERINGUE AND CREAM ♀ very sweet whites with not-too-high acidity

MINCE PIE ★★ Australian botrytized Semillon ♀ very sweet, highish-acid whites

PANCAKES see CRÊPES SUZETTES

PECAN PIE ♀ low-acid sweet whites

RICE PUDDING ★★ Recioto di Soave ★★ Muscat de St-Jean-de-Minervois ♀ sweet whites, ideally with low acidity

RUM BABA ♀ very sweet, not-too-acid whites

SACHERTORTE ★★ Australian botrytized Semillon ♀ sweet whites, including botrytized, with good acidity

SAVARIN ♀ sweet, not-too-acid Muscats

SHERRY TRIFLE ★ inexpensive medium-sweet sherries ♀ inexpensive medium-dry to sweet sherry

STICKY TOFFEE CHEESECAKE ★★ Recioto di Soave ♀ assorted very sweet whites

TIRAMISU ★★ Moscatel de Valencia ♀ sweet to very sweet, not-too-acid whites

TREACLE TART ★ Asti ★ Tokay 5 Puttonyos ♀ very sweet whites

TRIFLE see SHERRY TRIFLE

## Ice Creams and Sorbets

BLACKCURRANT SORBET ★ South African botrytized Riesling ♀ sweet Rieslings

CHOCOLATE ICE CREAM ★ California fortified Orange Muscat ♀ sweet, not-too-high-acid whites, especially fortified Muscats

with Dark Chocolate ★ fine Marsala ★ Muscat de St-Jean-de-Minervois

LEMON SORBET ★★ Australian botrytized Semillon ♀ sweet whites with good acidity

MANGO SORBET ★★ South African botrytized Riesling ♀ sweet, not-too-acid Riesling, Muscat and Semillon

PEACH SORBET ★ Moscato d'Asti ♀ gently flavoured, sweet whites, especially Muscat

STRAWBERRY ICE CREAM ★ Coteaux du Layon ♀ light, sweet whites

VANILLA ICE CREAM ★★ PX sherry ★★ Australian Rutherglen Liqueur Muscat

# INSTANT MATCHES: WINE TO FOOD

'Instant Matches: Wine to Food' deals very simply in reverse with the business of food and wine matching. If you are poised to open a prized bottle of mature Rioja or fine Sauternes, for example, what food should you choose to show the wine off and enjoy it at its best?

The wines are listed where possible by country and region, and also by major grape variety. You will find New World wines listed under the relevant grape variety. (If you turn to the main grape varieties section, on page 231, you will find further suggestions for good matches, beyond the scope of this 'Instant' directory.)

There is room here only for a selection of the major dishes that go best with these wine styles. Having selected a dish in the 'Instant' directory, it is worth looking it up in the main section (pages 6-230), to delve further. A glance at the following pages will tell you that red Burgundy goes well with salmon trout, or Portuguese reds with chilli con carne. The main section will advise you to choose a *very light fruity* red Burgundy, and a *fruity red Bairrada* from Portugal.

Many of the suggestions may seem geographically misplaced. For instance, what Austrian would ever dream of eating scallops with the local Grüner Veltliner wine? In Europe you can hardly get further from the sea than Austria. In Alsace, on the French/German border, they'd be unlikely to cook up an Italian pesto sauce to partner their Tokay-Pinot Gris. But these combinations taste really good, and the food will flatter the wine.

## FRANCE
### Bordeaux

**WHITE BORDEAUX**
serve chilled with Dover sole, seafood salad and fritto misto di mare, and haddock and smoked haddock dishes, or with fish and chips; also with chicken pie, cassoulet, or with fresh green asparagus served with melted butter.

**SWEET BORDEAUX (SAUTERNES ETC)**
serve with chicken liver pâté, duck pâté, foie gras and pâté de foie gras. The best cheese to serve is Roquefort. Desserts and fruit include strawberries and cream.

**RED BORDEAUX (CLARET)**
serve with roast goose, roast pheasant, roast woodcock; or with beef Bourguignonne,

daube of beef, steak and kidney pie, roast lamb, venison casserole, rabbit in cider or snails in garlic butter.

## Burgundy
### CHABLIS
serve with lobster, salmon trout and cold-smoked trout; or with chicken chasseur, roast chicken with garlic, chicken Kiev, roast turkey or roast guinea fowl. Also with roast pork or pork sausages.

### WHITE BURGUNDY
serve with fresh salmon in a cream sauce, pasta with smoked salmon and cream, scallops Mornay, monkfish, or John Dory. Also serve with roast chicken or roast chicken with garlic, roast pork or ham.

### BEAUJOLAIS
serve with chicken liver pâté, coq au vin, and pheasant casserole. Also with beef casseroles and stews, beef Wellington, roast beef, steak, or roast pork.

### RED BURGUNDY
serve with roast duck; also with venison casserole or roast venison, or snails in garlic butter.

## Champagne
### CHAMPAGNE BLANC DE BLANCS
serve with oysters or cold-smoked trout. Cheeses to serve are Lancashire and Chaource.

## Loire
### MUSCADET
serve with shellfish – especially oysters and moules marinières; also with salade Niçoise.

### SANCERRE
serve with clam chowder, or baked aubergine with Parmesan. Cheeses to serve include goats' cheeses.

### VOUVRAY
serve demi-sec Vouvray with Gravadlax, duck in orange sauce, roast goose with prune and apple stuffing, or pork with prunes and cream.

### LOIRE REDS (CHINON ETC)
serve with roast beef, or with steak.

## Rhône
### WHITE NORTHERN RHÔNE (CROZES-HERMITAGE etc)
serve with trout and almonds and with cassoulet.

### RED NORTHERN RHÔNE (CROZES-HERMITAGE etc)
serve with roast grouse, roast pheasant or pheasant casserole, or wild duck (Mallard), or with roast pork and pork rillettes.

### RED CHÂTEAUNEUF-DU-PAPE
serve with beef Wellington.

### RED CÔTES DU RHÔNE
serve with roast chicken or roast goose or roast turkey with sage and onion stuffing, roast grouse or pheasant casserole. Also with steak and kidney pie, Lancashire hotpot, roast pork, venison casserole or roast venison, or with jugged hare.

# ITALY

### ASTI
serve with a variety of desserts and fruits, including apple pie, apricot pie, blackcurrant pie, caramelized oranges, Christmas pudding, crêpes Suzette, milk chococlate mousse or fresh fruit salad.

### FRASCATI
serve with Vichysoisse or spinach soups, langoustines or trout; also with chicken pie, or roast chicken, vitello tonnato, pasta with mushrooms and garlic, pizza Napoletana, seafood risotto.

### SOAVE
serve with Borscht or Minestrone soups. Also with halibut, red mullet or seafood salad; or with lamb casseroles, Lancashire hotpot, or with salade Niçoise.

### CHIANTI
serve with roast chicken with sage and onion stuffing, duck pâté, calves' liver. Cheeses to serve include Parmesan Reggiano and mature Gouda.

### DOLCETTO
serve with beef Wellington, roast beef, steak, pork pie, or with calves' liver and onions (fegato alla Veneziana) or veal chops in Marsala sauce. Cheeses to serve include Gruyère.

### NEBBIOLO (BAROLO etc)
serve with chicken liver, kidneys, confit de canard, roast duck, roast grouse, or with calves' liver.

### SANGIOVESE (BRUNELLO etc)
serve with pheasant pâté, beef Stroganoff, oxtail, or with cassoulet. Cheeses to serve are mature Cheddar and Parmesan Reggiano.

### VALPOLICELLA (FINE)
serve with Bresaola, liver (lambs') and onions, pork sausages. Cheeses to serve include Port-Salut.

# PORTUGAL

(see individual entries for specific wines)

### VINHO VERDE
serve with ceviche, smoked mackerel, salad Niçoise or vegetable lasagne.

### PORTUGUESE REDS
serve with pigeon, woodcock, Irish stew, venison casserole, or with moussaka.

### MADEIRA
serve with blue Stilton or Roquefort.

### TAWNY PORT
serve with blue Stilton.

# SPAIN

### OAKED WHITE RIOJA
serve with smoked halibut, smoked chicken or Paella alla Valenciana.

### RUEDA WHITES
serve with trout, moules à la crème, and chicken chasseur or roast quail.

### RED RIOJA
serve with chicken chasseur, or roast lamb, roast lamb with garlic and rosemary,

lamb chops, lamb casserole with flageolet beans, or cassoulet. Cheeses to serve include Dolcelatte, Cantal, Pont l'Evêque and mature Gouda.

**SHERRY (FINO OR MANZANILLA)**
serve with olives

**SHERRY (MEDIUM)**
serve with sherry trifle.

## DRY ROSÉS

(See individual entries for specific wines) serve with bass, cod, fresh trout, fresh sardines, swordfish, whitebait, paella alla Valenciana, or with seafood risotto; also with rabbit in cider.

## GRAPE VARIETIES

### Chardonnay

(See also white Burgundy on page 284)

**OAKED EUROPEAN CHARDONNAY**
serve with John Dory, turbot, or with chicken chasseur, or pasta with smoked salmon and cream.

**UNOAKED EUROPEAN CHARDONNAY**
serve with cod, fish pie, fresh-water bream, scallops Mornay, fresh mackerel, lemon sole or turbot; or with fricassée, chicken pie, roast chicken, roast chicken with tarragon, roast guinea fowl, or blanquette of turkey. Also with cassoulet, blanquette of veal, pasta with smoked salmon and cream, risotto alla Milanese, and salade Niçoise.

**OAKED NEW WORLD CHARDONNAY**
serve with various fish, including John Dory, lobster and lobster Thermidor, monkfish, plaice, smoked salmon or turbot. Also with roast chicken with garlic, smoked chicken, pesto or with cheese soufflé.

**UNOAKED NEW WORLD CHARDONNAY**
serve with cod, lemon sole, and scallops Mornay, or with chicken Kiev or blanquette de veau.

### Gewürztraminer

**DRY GEWÜRZTRAMINER**
serve with chicken chasseur, and onion tart 'à l'Alsacienne'.

### Muscat

**DRY MUSCAT**
serve with fresh salmon.

**SWEET MUSCAT**
(see also Asti)
serve with desserts and fruits, including almond tart, Tarte Normande, chocolate gâteau, chocolate mousse, coffee gâteau, Christmas pudding, lemon meringue pie and lemon tart or tiramisu; also with fresh raspberries, strawberry mousse or strawberries and cream.

### Pinot Blanc/ Pinot Bianco

Serve with onion soup and onion tart 'à l'Alsacienne'.

## (Tokay) Pinot Gris/ Pinot Grigio

Serve with foie gras or pâté de foie gras, or confit de canard; also with pheasant Normande, beef Bourguignonne and blanquette de veau. Or with pesto or quiche Lorraine.

## Riesling

**EUROPEAN DRY RIESLING**
serve with beef Stroganoff, and lobster dishes.

**EUROPEAN MEDIUM RIESLING**
serve with lobster or Parma ham and melon; also with Thai satay, roast goose and roast goose with prune and apple stuffing.

**EUROPEAN SWEET RIESLING**
serve with desserts and fruits, including fresh fruit salad, apple pie, apricot pie, blackberry and apple pie or crumble, plum pie, peaches, nectarines or fresh figs; also with tarte Tatin, peach or apricot sorbets, strawberries and cream, or summer pudding.

**NEW WORLD DRY RIESLING**
serve with beef Stroganoff, calves' liver or baked aubergine with Parmesan.

**NEW WORLD SWEET RIESLING**
serve with foie gras de canard, or various desserts and fruits, including almond tart, apple strudel, apricot pie, plum pie, caramelized oranges, Christmas pudding, crèpes Suzettes, fresh fruit salad, raspberries and cream, and strawberry mousse or fool and strawberries and cream.

## Sauvignon Blanc

**EUROPEAN SAUVIGNON BLANC**
serve with various fish dishes, including cod, Dover sole, fish pie, kedgeree, sea bream, and scallops. Also with beef Bourguignonne, or baked aubergine with Parmesan. Cheeses to serve include goats' cheeses.

**NEW WORLD SAUVIGNON BLANC**
serve with asparagus soup, fresh crab, or scallops. Also with baked aubergine with Parmesan or cheese fondue.

## Semillon

**NEW WORLD DRY SEMILLON**
serve with gazpacho, or osso buco.

**NEW WORLD SWEET SEMILLON**
serve with apricot pie, crème brûlée, Sachertorte, strawberry fool or mousse, or strawberries and cream.

## Cabernet Sauvignon

**NEW WORLD CABERNET**
serve with coq au vin, roast goose, or roast turkey; also with beef Bourguignonne, steak and kidney pie, or lamb chops, lamb casserole, roast lamb, roast lamb with thyme, venison casserole and rabbit in cider, or vegetable lasagne. Cheeses to serve include Cheshire.

## Merlot

**NEW WORLD MERLOT**
serve with roast goose, or roast turkey with chestnut stuffing or bread sauce, or with jugged hare or steak au poivre.

## Pinot Noir

**NEW WORLD PINOT NOIR**
serve with coq au vin, pigeon casserole, pheasant casserole, or roast pheasant; also with moussaka, roast pork, or venison casserole; or with rabbit in cider. Cheeses to serve include Cheshire.

## Shiraz

Serve with roast pork, roast chicken with sage and onion stuffing, roast turkey, or roast partridge. Also with liver (lambs') and onions. Cheeses to serve include Cheshire, young Gouda, red Leicester and Manchego.

## Zinfandel

Serve with roast chicken, roast lamb with garlic and rosemary, or with venison casserole, jugged hare or cheeseburgers.

## ACKNOWLEDGEMENTS

Our special thanks go to Winston Moll for keeping us supplied with Wine Savers to preserve our wines, Claire Gordon-Brown of Sainsbury's for constantly replenishing our wines for tasting, Cedric Menuet and Tom Kyme for cooking many of the dishes, Paul Muller of The Salmon Shop, Cowfold and TSJ Woodhouse of London N7 for supplying elusive seafood and game, and to our patient editors Jane Hughes and Claire Harcup.

Also to O Fado restaurant, Taste of the Wild, Bob Campbell, Debbie Collinson, Lenz Moser, Alan Woodward, Didier Keller of Fauchon; and to Florence Fleurie, Natalia Martín Sosa, Gwladys Piton and Eric Merlet for keeping the children so happy while we endlessly tasted and wrote.

**Editoral Director** Claire Harcup; **Editor** Jane Hughes; **Assistant Editor** Pauline Savage; **Design Manager** Jason Vrakas; **Art Editor** Adele Morris; **Desktop Publishing** Jonathan Harley; **Artwork** Michelle Mason; **Cover design** by The Design Revolution